The Lit

# CANNABIS

Printed and bound in the UK by MPG Books, Bodmin

Distributed in the US by Publishers Group West

Published by Sanctuary Publishing Limited, Sanctuary House, 45-53 Sinclair Road, London W14 0NS, United Kingdom

www.sanctuarypublishing.com

ISBN: 1-86074-527-X

The Little Book Of

# CANNABIS

Nick Brownlee

**Sanctuary**

# CONTENTS

# INTRODUCTION

The cannabis debate is very straightforward. You're either an establishment square who wants it outlawed as a menace to society, or a hippie deadbeat who wants it legalized in order to promote love and peace. Trouble is, the argument has never been as simple as that. Where once it was a highly useful source of fibre, food and medicine, at the beginning of the 21st century perceptions and preconceptions about cannabis and its use have never been more blurred.

Leading police officers are prepared to turn a blind eye to users caught in possession but other equally high-ranking officers want it stamped out. Doctors and scientists spend millions investigating its medicinal value yet for every positive piece of research, there is a negative. Hundreds of thousands of tourists take weekend trips to Amsterdam in order to sit in cafés and smoke copious amounts of dope free from molestation, yet they risk prosecution for taking less than 30g (1oz) back through their own country's customs. And, after years of denial, top politicians admit to smoking cannabis in their youth, but, most bizarrely of all, an American president admits smoking a joint but not inhaling.

This book does not aim to preach the benefits or the deficits of cannabis. Instead, it aims to provide an authoritative guide to its history, laws and culture as they stand in the world in the new millennium, as well as its effects on health and the booming commercial business side of producing cannabis.

Over 4,700 years since its first recorded use, modern society's relationship with the cannabis sativa plant, and more importantly its active ingredient delta9-tetrahydrocannabinol, has never been more complex.

In fact, it does your head in, man.

CULTURE

If there is one thing that means more to pot heads than the pot itself, it is the rich culture that surrounds cannabis and those who partake of it. Perhaps because of its ancient mystical and spiritual roots, because of the psychotherapeutic effects of the drug and because it is illegal, even the very act of smoking a joint has deep symbolism. Cannabis has evolved its own language, humour, etiquette, art, literature and music. Its culture is jealously guarded by those who are a part of it and derided, misunderstood – possibly even feared – by those who don't.

'One's condition on marijuana is always existential,' explains the novelist Norman Mailer. 'One can feel the importance of each moment and how it is changing one. One feels one's being, one becomes aware of the enormous apparatus of nothingness – the hum of a hi-fi set, the emptiness of a pointless interruption, one becomes aware of the war between each of us, how the nothingness in each of us seeks to attack the being of others, how our being in turn is attacked by the nothingness in others.'

To those who use cannabis, Mailer's description of the

experience of smoking it probably makes eminent sense. To those that don't, it no doubt sounds like the typical esoteric ramblings of a dope fiend. 'Marijuana inflames the erotic impulses and leads to revolting sex crimes,' claimed the British paper the *Daily Mirror* in 1924, a verdict that still makes more sense than Norman Mailer to a great number of people around the world.

To others, it is not cannabis but the surrounding culture that is hard to take. 'I smoked cannabis a few times with my mates and it was okay,' recalls Colin Byrne, a 28-year-old teacher from Belfast, Northern Ireland. 'But I couldn't get away with all the bollocks that went with it. All the etiquette, all the terminology, everything. It was like my mates, who were just yobs from the backstreets of Belfast, thought they were San Francisco hippies. "Pass the doobie, man," and "Hey, this is great shit." It was pathetic, really. I just wanted to give them a good shake and tell them to stop being a bunch of posers.'

Colin Byrne's experience is neatly summed up by the *New Columbia Encyclopaedia* when it suggests: 'Much of the prevailing public apprehension about marijuana may stem from the drug's effect of inducing introspection and bodily passivity, which are antipathetic to a culture that values aggressiveness, achievement and activity.'

The culture of cannabis is, essentially, the manifestation of this 'introspection and bodily passivity'. The clichéd image of a typical pot smoker is of a slacker who lies around all day listening to The Grateful Dead, gladly evading work and anything that might contribute to a useful existence. It is this image more than any other that has stoked the ire of generations of anti-cannabis campaigners. In America, in particular, cannabis culture has been perceived as an anti-American culture – and, more to the point, the culture of blacks, Indians and Mexicans.

Yet this image is a relatively modern concept. Cannabis has been consumed in various forms for almost 5,000 years – and for most of that time it was prized as a pick-me-up. 'I began to gather the leaves of this plant and to eat them,' wrote the 13th-century Persian monk Heydar, 'and they have produced in me the gaiety that you witness.'

Even as recently as 1895, a correspondent from the *New York Herald* was breathlessly reporting that, 'During the full moon, the Nosairiyeh tribesmen of northern Syria hold a ceremony that involves the consumption of enormous amounts of hashish. The ceremony begins with the ritual sacrifice of a sheep, after which a large earthenware bowl filled with liquid honey-hash is passed around. A bundle of cannabis leaves are attached to the base of the bowl. After drinking this concoction, the eyes of the Nosairiyeh brighten, their pulse quickens, and a restlessness takes possession of their body as they start to dance.'

This account tallies almost exactly with the observations of the Greek historian Herodotus from 2,500 years earlier, when he came across Scythian tribesmen getting high on cannabis fumes: 'They make a booth by fixing in the ground three sticks inclined towards one another, and stretching around them woollen pelts, which they arrange so as to fit as close as possible: inside the booth a dish is placed upon the ground into which they put a number of red hot stones and then add some hemp seed... Immediately it smokes and gives out such a vapour as no Grecian vapour bath can exceed; the Scyths, delighted, shout for joy.'

But it is the widely different modern cannabis culture that is most interesting, because it represents the extraordinary effect of this most ancient drug on societies that pride themselves on their pragmatism and sophistication.

**ARE YOU GOING TO SAN FRANCISCO?**
**HASH AND THE HIPPIES**

If there is one era that sums up the glory years of modern cannabis culture, it is the late 1960s in America. Freed from the austerity of the post-war years, and unwilling to subscribe to the Norman Rockwell idyll of their parents' generation, young Americans discovered a voice of their own through music, sex, travel and dissent – all of it borne along on a cloud of marijuana smoke.

In many ways, cannabis was the obvious accessory for rebellion. Throughout the 20th century, it had been vilified by the authorities as a substance that was the ruin of America's youth. Harry J Anslinger, the government official who was at the forefront of the anti-cannabis movement, had been almost rabid in his attacks on the evil weed, engendering an irrational paranoia of the drug throughout the land. By the 1960s, however, Anslinger's propaganda had run its course and there was a new mood spreading through the USA. Young men were being drafted to fight in Vietnam and were returning in body bags. Those who survived returned to find that their country regarded them as failures. A new generation was growing up disowned, disillusioned and with no compunction to live up to the clean-living all-American ideal that had betrayed them.

More importantly, almost all the draft who went to Vietnam lived through the daily horrors they faced by smoking marijuana. Those who returned introduced it to other young people and its use quickly became widespread. By the late 1960s, a whole counter-culture had emerged whose desire was to drop out of society and the drug of choice was cannabis. The 'hippie' movement had begun.

In the US, the centre of cannabis culture was found in San Francisco. It was there, in the Longshoreman's Hall, that the psychedelic era kicked off in 1966 when a group of hippies staged what they called the Trips Festival. In nearby Golden Gate Park in 1967, an area of the park called the Polo Field played host to a massive outdoor concert/love-in called the Human Be-In. Special guests included Jefferson Airplane and beat poet Allen Ginsberg. In Haight Street, the epicentre of the hippie movement, and on adjacent Ashbury Street, the pot-smoking hordes hung out in head shops – specialist outlets selling hippie paraphernalia – lit incense candles, meditated and bartered for Hindu artwork. One of the main attractions was the Psychedelic Shop, which sold all sorts of hippie items – including dollar bills with Grateful Dead singer Jerry Garcia in the middle. The City Lights Bookstore, founded by Lawrence Ferlinghetti, boasted the cream of hippie intelligentsia. In its basement Allen Ginsberg first recited his poem, 'Howl' – this event supposedly kicked off the whole beat movement and it is chronicled in Jack Kerouac's seminal hippie novel *On The Road*. Fillmore Auditorium became the 'primal venue', where hippie guru Bill Graham hosted such top acts as The Doors and The Byrds.

Meanwhile characters like Ken Kesey were hitting the headlines with their distinctly unorthodox lifestyles. Kesey, author of *One Flew Over The Cuckoo's Nest*, was a former soldier who, in the early 1960s, was the subject of LSD experiments by the CIA. His mind scrambled by his experience, Kesey dropped out of mainstream society, founded a gang called the Merry Pranksters and began touring America in a bus named 'Further', smoking dope and distributing LSD to the nation at a non-stop road party he called the 'acid test'.

The pinnacle of the hippie revolution in the USA, and in many people's opinion the ultimate example of cannabis culture at work, was the Woodstock festival of August 1969.

The festival attracted more than 450,000 young people to a pasture in Sullivan County, 160km (100 miles) from Manhattan. For four days the site became a counter-cultural epicentre where drugs were consumed freely and sex was enjoyed virtually non-stop. The festival closed the New York State Thruway and created one of the nation's worst traffic jams. It also inspired a slew of local and state laws to ensure that nothing like it would ever happen again.

But if the authorities regarded such activities with horror, they were powerless to stop them spreading. San Francisco and then Woodstock became a Mecca for young people from around the world, who were all too eager to return home with the good news. In Britain, cannabis made little impact on society until the 1960s. It was a country where alcohol was king, and where the only concern was stopping young people from drinking too much. If cannabis was used, it was usually by beatniks in London jazz clubs and by members of the West Indian community who had arrived in the country in the 1950s. But soon the authorities had a new problem on their hands. Influenced by bands like The Beatles and The Rolling Stones, who had become fully paid-up members of the hippie revolution, young people turned eagerly to cannabis. A full-page advert calling for the legalization of the drug was placed in *The Times*, the broadsheet of the Establishment. Kids openly smoked dope in Hyde Park during a Rolling Stones concert.

'Everyone was trying it, but to be honest there wasn't a nationwide cannabis revolution,' recalls gallery owner John Lyons, 58, who was one of the thousands present at Hyde Park and who also took place in a pro-legalization march in 1969. 'To be honest I only remember the excitement lasting a few months. After that, it was mainly the die-hards who openly smoked it. I think the rest of us got bored with it.'

Nevertheless, the nation wrung its hands and only began to breathe easier when, in 1971, the government acted by reinforcing cannabis laws in the Misuse of Drugs Act. But by then, London and San Francisco were no longer the places to score and smoke dope if you were a true cannabis connoisseur. People were packing their kaftans and love beads and heading east, to where the karma was ambient and the dope plentiful and strong. So the Hippie Trail was born.

**ON THE TRAIL**
The Hippie Trail evolved out of Europe's beatnik scene, which was always very nomadic. For just a few notes, it had become possible to bunk down in cheap accommodation in ambient, cheap and dope-plentiful cities within Spain, Greece, Turkey and Morocco. By 1967 the scene had pushed beyond Istanbul to India, Nepal, and places further east. They called the journey 'the road to Katmandu'.

First stop was Tangiers, where boats and planes unloaded their cargo of wide-eyed pot heads eager to follow in the footsteps of such earlier hashish explorers as Paul Bowles, Gertrude Stein and William Burroughs. From Morocco they headed to Istanbul – one of the major hash markets – then through the fertile plains of Iran and Afghanistan and finally to nirvana in Goa and Katmandu. To a generation brought up in an atmosphere of repression, this was a whole new world just waiting to be explored. There were few laws governing the use and sale of hash. It was openly sold in coffee shops and bazaars. In Katmandu alone, for example, there were more than 30 hash shops where the dope came in all sorts of shapes and colours.

Of all the venues on the Hippie Trail, however, Istanbul was the fulcrum, the last gateway to all points east for the thousands of wide-eyed hippies who thronged there in the 1960s. Here, for the first time, was the east in all its mystic glory: mosques, bazaars, horns, the non-stop hustle from hawkers and touts, and, of course, the pervading stench of the cheap, plentiful and indigenous hash. And, best of all, the laws were relaxed to the point of non-existence compared to the draconian anti-drugs legislation of Europe and the USA. While it was not advisable to be caught smuggling, and it was officially illegal to be caught in possession of dope, there was an abundance of illicit back-room smoking dens where it was possible to get stoned in peace.

Istanbul was also incredibly cheap. One of the most popular venues for young hippies to stay was 'The Tent', a corrugated iron and canvas shelter on the roof of the

Gulhane Hotel in the centre of town. There, it was possible to pack down for next to nothing on the comfortable straw floor and indulge in all manner of social smoking with the other 'guests' who had washed up on the tide of western visitors. The dope was cheap too – thick slabs of Turkish hash for the same price as they would have paid for a miserly 5g (1/6oz) in the west.

Cities like Istanbul were also important news centres for travellers on the Hippie Trail – particularly when it came to exchanging information about where not to go. One no-go area was the Afghan-Iranian border. During the Shah's reign, if a traveller was caught with over a kilo (2¼lb) of hash, they would be tried by the Iranian Army Council and then shot. There were also stories about unfortunates apprehended in Tashkent doing hard labour in Soviet prison camps, or people who ended up being sent to Greek or Bulgarian prisons and were never seen again.

Yet, for all its dangers, the Hippie Trail was immensely popular. But it was incredibly short-lived. Ironically, it was the very availability of hashish that would spell the end for the Hippie Trail.

Increased demand led to inflated prices and large-scale smuggling, particularly from Nepal into India and abroad. Estimates in the mid-1970s claimed that more hashish was exported than consumed in Nepal. Inevitably, pressure on the Nepalese government to act soon came from the United Nations and the United States and, in 1972, they began to systematically shut down the hash houses. A year later, all hashish dealers' licences were revoked and the last of the hash hops were closed. The Hippie Trail had fizzled out for good – and with it the free and easy cannabis culture of the 1960s.

## I DIDN'T INHALE – THE 1960S GENERATION GETS COY

Surprisingly for a generation who pushed back the boundaries of cannabis consumption, many children of the 1960s are today reticent about admitting they ever smoked – or indeed inhaled. This is especially true of those 1960s kids who went on to become political figures, especially those in the current UK debate about legalization. Jack Straw, the former Home Secretary, was a long-haired radical at Leeds University but claims to have never touched the stuff. The same is true of his successor in the Home Office, David Blunkett. Of the current batch of British MPs, only former Cabinet member Mo Mowlam has ever admitted smoking. Even the Labour MPs Clare Short, Tony Banks, and Paul Flynn, who have campaigned that the legalization of cannabis should be examined, flatly deny they have ever smoked marijuana themselves. Former US President Clinton famously admitted smoking a joint but not inhaling. And George W Bush, Clinton's successor, has denied using cocaine in the past 25 years but refuses to say anything about the years before that, suggesting that he, too, may have smoked marijuana but not inhaled...

When pushed on the subject he admitted that he had 'made mistakes in the past' but would not engage in the 'politics of personal destruction' by talking further about the issue.

It has been left to old lags like Sir Paul McCartney and Sir Richard Branson to keep the 1960s flag flying. 'I think a liberal attitude is not a bad thing,' McCartney said, 'so I favour a decriminalization of it. If my kids ever ask me, "What about it?" I would say, "There is this bunch of drugs. This is probably the least harmful. There is a hit list. You can go up it to heroin but it's not easy, in fact impossible for some people". But I always say to them, "That's the facts of life, but if you ask my advice, don't do any."'

## CANNABIS AND RELIGION

Marijuana is closely connected with the history and development of some of the oldest nations on Earth. It has played a significant role in the religions and cultures of Africa, the Middle East, India and China.

The shamanistic traditions of Asia and the Near East have as one of their most important elements the attempt to find God; getting stoned on cannabis has helped worshippers on their way. And in the days before joints, the quickest and easiest way to inhale the smoke was through cannabis incense.

In the temples of the ancient world, the main sacrifice was the inhalation of incense. In the Judaic world, the vapours from burnt spices and aromatic gums were considered part of the pleasurable act of worship. Stone altars have been unearthed in Babylon and Palestine, which were used for burning incense made of aromatic wood and spices – in many or most cases, a psychoactive drug was being inhaled. In the islands of the Mediterranean 2,500 years ago and in Africa hundreds of years ago, for example, marijuana leaves and flowers were often thrown upon bonfires and the smoke inhaled.

Today, cannabis continues to be the mainstay of the Rastafarian religion, which is discussed in detail later. But the Rastafarians are not alone. One of the most controversial cannabis-based religions in recent years has been the Ethiopian Zion Coptic Church, a religion run by white Americans who claim its roots are in black Jamaica. The Coptics insist that marijuana, which they call by its Jamaican name, ganja, is their sacrament; as valid and as necessary to them as wine is to Catholics during communion. To many, including law enforcement officials, they are frauds – a group of rich dope heads who have been allowed to laugh at the law and get away with it.

Coptic services take place three times a day, but the Coptics partake of cannabis all day. One of their main centres is in Miami, where in the late 1970s they hit the headlines when they bought a house for $270,000 (£185,000), paid for in cash, which they promptly turned into a luxury commune with about 40 members. Trouble soon brewed when it emerged that Coptic women, and even the Coptic children, were encouraged to smoke marijuana. While it was the constant chanting and the smell of marijuana that upset close neighbours, it was scenes of Coptic children smoking marijuana on local television that brought protests from the city as a whole. Then, in November 1978, news broke of the mass deaths of the People's Temple cult in Jonestown, Guyana, and many Miami residents were shocked into wondering if they might not have a potential Jonestown on their doorstep.

**FROM BONGS TO HOT KNIVES: CANNABIS PARAPHERNALIA**
To the casual observer, dope heads appear to spend most of their time on another planet. And indeed most do. But there is more than one way to skin up a joint – and when we consider the various methods of intake that cannabis users have invented, we can only applaud their ingenuity.

Also known as water pipes, bongs are designed to pass the smoke through water in order to cool and filter it. Grass is put in a bowl on the end of a tube, which has its other end in a sealed container partially filled with water. The tube at the end of the bowl is below the level of the water so that as smoke exits the pipe it is bubbled through a layer of water. The air pressure in the chamber is lowered by breathing through another tube that stays above the water level in the chamber. The advantages of the bong method are that the smoke is cooled and carcinogens are removed without affecting the active ingredients. Any liquid can be used to filter the smoke, although beer and other booze is not recommended as marijuana's active ingredients are soluble in alcohol.

A rather ostentatious method of smoking, these pipes are usually made of such heat resistant materials as stone, ivory, metal and glass and are often highly ornate. Grass is inserted in the bowl of the pipe and then lit. An alternative is the stash pipe, a pipe in which a small amount of grass can actually be stored. Some stash pipes are constructed in such a way that the smoke passes through the stash area so the grass inside is bathed in smoke and becomes coated in resin, making it a more potent smoke.

Glass hash pipes are used predominantly for smoking hashish or hashish oil. The material is placed in the bowl as with the other pipes, but instead of heat being applied to the top, it is applied to the bottom. Gas pipes, meanwhile, consist of an open-ended tube with a small bowl mounted near one end, perpendicular to the main axis of the tube. The end near the bowl is covered with the user's hand and the smoke drawn into the tube. When the hand is removed, smoke rushes into the lungs. Tilt pipes are for the connoisseur. These pipes have a heating element built into the pipe at the bowl. The element heats the marijuana to sub-flammable temperatures sufficient to activate and release cannabinoids from the plant material. The pipe is tilted to bring the grass in contact with the heating element.

For those who prefer to smoke on the hoof, one hits, also known as Dug-Outs, are small metal tubes with a cavity at one end and a mouthpiece at the other. The cavity is pressed in a container of grass until it is filled, then it is lit like a cigarette and inhaled steadily until all the grass is gone.

Hot knives are hardly complex, but powerful and efficient. Two wooden-handled knives are heated until glowing red. Small amounts of grass are then burned between the two knives while the smoker sucks up the smoke through a plastic bottle that has had its bottom cut off.

Cannabis can, of course, be cooked and eaten in a brownie. In Amsterdam coffee bars, 'space cake' is available for punters to nibble in between, or in preference to, smoking joints. For the uninitiated, it can often be easy to underestimate the power of these dope-laden snacks. 'I was in Amsterdam with some lads on a stag do, and we ended up in a dope bar,' recalls accountant Gary Miller, 32, of Nottingham, England. 'One of the guys was feeling a bit peckish so he decided to have some chocolate cake. He thought that even if there was cannabis in the mixture it wouldn't be strong enough to have much effect. The silly sod wolfed down about five of these cakes in two minutes flat. Within ten minutes he was absolutely stoned out of his brain and we had to take him back to the hotel.'

Perhaps the most famous 'space cake' recipe is the one dreamed up in 1954 by Alice B Toklas, lover of the writer Gertrude Stein and author of a cult cookbook. In it, she recommends taking 'one teaspoon black peppercorns, one whole nutmeg, four average sticks of cinnamon, one teaspoon of coriander. These should all be pulverized in a mortar. About a handful each of stoned dates, dried figs, shelled almonds, and peanuts: chop these and mix them together. A bunch of cannabis sativa can be pulverized. This along with the spices should be dusted over the mixed fruit and nuts and kneaded together. About a cup of sugar should be dissolved in a big pat of butter. The mixture is then rolled into a cake and cut into balls about the size of a walnut. It should be eaten with care: two pieces are quite sufficient.'

There are also a number of ways to get stoned by drinking cannabis. The easiest is to extract the active ingredients from the grass in alcohol and then use the tincture to make a potent drink. The highest-proof alcohol needs to be used – preferably 190-proof grain alcohol – since the water in alcohol will dissolve other chemicals in the marijuana. Another method is to heat the alcohol to sub-boiling point, then stir in the marijuana. The resulting emerald tincture is called Green Dragon and can be drunk straight, although this is not recommended. A cocktail is usually used, which consists of three parts lemon-lime soda, one part Green Dragon and a dollop of honey served over ice.

## CANNABIS INC: HOW AMSTERDAM'S COFFEE-SHOP CANNABIS CULTURE BECAME BIG BUSINESS

A spectre stalks the cannabis coffee shops of Amsterdam, sending a paranoia rush down the spine of even the most hardened weed smoker. Its name is respectability.

More than 30 years after the city's first café was granted an official licence to sell marijuana on its premises – years in which Amsterdam became synonymous with youthful rebellion, experimentation and personal freedom – so-called 'coffee-shop culture' has slipped inexorably into the pocket of the Establishment.

The air inside the cafés is still heavy with the sweet scent of weed, the background muzak is still the same mix of The Doors and Bob Marley, and the tables are still occupied by glassy-eyed young people who smile seraphically and nod their appreciation of the latest strain of Shiva and Super Polm. But, like an antique watch with a digital mechanism, the whirring of 21st century business can clearly be heard behind the laid-back façade.

Coffee-shop culture, that great free-wheeling creation of the 1970s, has, in 2003, become a Dutch household brand as immediately recognizable as Vincent Van Gogh, windmills and wooden clogs. Today it is a multi-million-pound industry. It is subject to quality control. It is shaped by strict regulation. It is even taxed to fund the Dutch welfare state.

And the greatest irony of all is that these changes have been instigated by the very generation responsible for creating the concept in the first place. The long-haired stoners of the early 1970s are the government officials of today. It is they who have overseen the sea change in Amsterdam's unique relationship with cannabis and its culture; they who have dragged it kicking and screaming into the real world.

Sander Yap, who runs the popular Homegrown Fantasy coffee shop on Nieuwe Zijds Voorburgwal, a busy street just two minutes' walk from Dam Square, pulls on a reefer and remains determinedly stoic about the situation. 'Regulation is something we all have to accept,' he shrugs. 'If we ignored it, there would be no coffee shops.'

Sander is right. Since 1990, when the first tentative regulations came into force, nearly half of Amsterdam's coffee shops have been closed down. Today, there are barely 250 in a city which once boasted well in excess of 500. Those that survive do so in the knowledge that even the slightest breach of the rules will see them put out of business.

In the nearby Wolkewietje coffee shop, owner Melvin Blom points to the neon sign that hangs outside his premises. At first glance, it looks like an abstract starburst in green and white. 'Look at it from a distance and you can see that it is, in fact, a marijuana leaf,' Blom says proudly. 'Like everybody else, we used to have a hand-painted marijuana sign above the shop – but now that is against the rules. We think we have got round it quite well, though.'

The rules are strict and non-negotiable. To run a coffee shop, owners must apply for a licence from the local authority, which is up for regular renewal. They are then limited to sell just 5g of weed and 30g of hemp products per customer, and there is a tax on all sales. Furthermore, they cannot be seen to overtly advertise their products. Dope is usually kept in a drawer under the counter, menus are available only on request, while the marijuana sign – once as identifiable in Amsterdam as McDonald's yellow arches – is now prohibited. Owners must rely on regular customers, word-of-mouth or, like Melvin Blom, go in for a spot of abstract design.

Those who flaunt the regulations face the very real possibility of a raid by Amsterdam's 'hit squad', a team of inspectors made up officials from the tax office, the public health service, the licence registration office, the narcotics squad, and the social welfare office. The punishment they mete out ranges from a first warning, to a fine and temporary closure for a second offence, and finally the permanent withdrawal of the shop's licence.

'Yeah, it is tough and something which none of us want,' says Blom. 'But we have to accept that this is the way things are now. The old days have long gone.' He laughs. 'We are part of the economy now! We have our social responsibilities to uphold!'

Although it may appear that the Dutch authorities are now waging a relentless putsch against the mild-mannered coffee-shop community, such an impression is wholly wrong. Opinion in Holland has not changed: smoking marijuana in moderation is still regarded as the harmless pastime of a small minority. The Dutch government has never subscribed to the theory, most vehemently argued in the UK, that smoking a joint is the first rung on the ladder to heroin addiction. What has changed is that the authorities, praised by smokers for their enlightened liberalism in the 1970s, have introduced a dash of equally imaginative realism to their outlook. It was their legislation which created cannabis culture. They now feel perfectly within their rights to turn it into Cannabis Inc.

Amsterdam's cannabis culture was always a fragile house of cards, built on the uncertain premise that, while the drug is tolerated, it remains officially illegal in Holland. To trace its history, we must return to the heady, hippie days of the mid-1960s and the handful of underground 'speakeasy' establishments which grew up around the city's red-light area to cater for the increased demand for marijuana among young people – and, equally, to cash in on Amsterdam's unique position as a leading European outlet for North African and Middle-Eastern hash. Word soon spread and the underground trade proliferated, boosted by the increasing numbers of foreigners attracted by the quantity and availability of the drug.

At this stage, the Dutch government were no different to any other in their anti-drug stance. Drug offences were actively prosecuted and severely sanctioned, with 12-month sentences for simple cannabis possession being normal.

But, perhaps wary of America's Prohibition disaster in the 1920s in which gangsters grew rich by supplying illegal hooch, the government decided it would be in their own best interests to take some sort of control of the situation.

In 1972, an Amsterdam coffee shop called Mellow Yellow became the first to be granted an official licence. Four years later, the Opium Act was introduced. While maintaining strict penalties for trafficking heroin, cocaine and amphetamines, the Act relented when it came to marijuana use, claiming that limited sale and possession was 'not for prosecution, detection or arrest'.

Bon Kreiser, Head of Drug Care at the Dutch Health Ministry, summarised the government's view when he said: 'We do not believe in punishing young people for using cannabis for a short period of their lives. We think it is irresponsible to give a young person a criminal record for something most will outgrow.'

For the next 15 years, the number of coffee shops grew exponentially. Suddenly, Amsterdam, once famed for its canals and its art, was famous for one thing and one thing alone. It became a marijuana Mecca not only in Europe, but across the world. Foreigners flooded into the city, astonished that here was a place where it was not only possible to buy hash but to smoke it with like-minded stoners and without fear of prosecution.

But what was understandably forgotten amid the frenzy was that while the stoners were free to create Amsterdam's distinctive coffee-shop culture, the whole exercise was underpinned by the government's liberal attitude towards it. All it would take for the scene to change irreversibly would be a subtle shift in that attitude. And, in the 1990s, this is precisely what happened.

Under increasing pressure from the Americans, British, Germans, Scandinavians, and particularly the French (whose President Chirac witheringly described Holland as a 'narco state'), the authorities in Holland were left with a dilemma. With annual sales of hash estimated at around £500 million, of which a substantial percentage is creamed off in tax, they were determined not to drive the thriving market back underground. Equally, they were keen not to be isolated within the European Community. The solution was to target the coffee shops, which had become the high-profile symbol of Dutch drugs culture. 'The coffee shops are strictly controlled by the police,' said Klaas Wilting of the Amsterdam Police Force. 'If there is a disturbance, or selling of hard drugs or stolen goods, we report this to the Mayor and he closes the coffee shop.'

It was the equivalent of a large corporation 'redefining' one of its core businesses. And to prove that it was no mere cosmetic exercise, the government hit teams went to work with a vengeance. Within five years more than 200 coffee shops had been closed down and dozens of others had the threat of closure hanging over them. While it would be easy to imagine the persecuted cannabis community fleeing

Amsterdam like rats from a flooded canal, or at the very least returning to the days of underground speakeasies, the reaction has been surprising. Indeed, the remaining coffee shops have welcomed the crackdowns as an opportunity to put their own house in order. The result is a very different culture to the free-and-easy days of the '70s and '80s.

The Cannabis College is situated in an unprepossessing building on Auchterburgwal in the heart of Amsterdam's red-light district. Among the red neon-framed windows, the sex shops and the porno theatres, it is certainly easy to miss. But it is from here, in this most unlikely of settings, that beleaguered stoners are attempting to breathe new life into cannabis culture.

If you walk through the door expecting to meet characters from an episode of *The Fabulous Furry Freak Brothers*, spouting spaced-out nonsense about the psychotropic benefits of weed, then think again. The five-strong staff who man the Cannabis College are the storm troopers at the front line of the new campaign, and they preach their message with an almost evangelical zeal. Their mission is simple: to show the world that marijuana is a plant it simply cannot do without. The College itself is a mine of information about every possible use of the plant, from medicinal to industrial. In the basement is a vast jungle of hydroponically grown cannabis, lovingly tended 24 hours a day.

Originally from Yorkshire, Lorna Clay came to Amsterdam four years ago and now works full-time at the College. 'Our goal is to provide people with truthful information about traditional, modern and correct uses of the cannabis plant,' she says. 'There is a great deal of misunderstanding and mistrust about it which is due, in no small part, to the culture which has grown up around it. When people think of marijuana, they immediately think of people getting stoned out of their minds. What we want is to show them that the plant should not be demonised. It should be celebrated. If it's used responsibly, then it is neither dangerous nor addictive.'

'Responsibility' is the new buzzword among the latest generation of cannabis enthusiasts – although it can be argued that this has more to do with self-preservation than anything else. Certainly, the remaining coffee-shop owners are keen to stress to the authorities that they are capable of policing themselves. Recently they set up the Cannabis Bond, a self-regulatory collective which monitors the flow of drugs in and out of the coffee shops. Anyone breaking the rules – and thereby bringing the whole collective under unwelcome scrutiny – is kicked out or shopped to the hit teams.

'It's a good thing,' says Sander Yap. 'At the moment the coffee-shop owners are doing their best to exist in difficult times. We are all under pressure. This is not the 1970s and we know that it would not take much for the authorities to close us down. They have shown that they mean business and we have to show that we mean business too.'

In many ways, the changes in Amsterdam's drug culture mirror those of the city's sex industry. From an unwieldy, ungoverned mess in the 1970s, the red-light district is now strictly policed and licensed. As a result, it has become a more streamlined and efficient business. Crucially, it has become safer for both punters and prostitutes alike.

Words like 'streamlined' and 'efficient' may sound alien when referring to coffee shops – but Amsterdam's new-look cannabis culture has won it many friends. Rinus Lieder has been a regular coffee-shop customer for ten years and has experienced the changes at first hand. He says: 'There have always been reputable cafés – places where you can guarantee you won't be ripped off. But in the past, especially if you didn't know the area, there were places that would sell you any old shit. And when you'd smoked that and were off the planet they would try and sell you hard stuff like coke or speed, which was usually drain cleaner or sugar. Now, man, you go into the coffee shops and it's like walking into a shoe shop! They look after you, take your measurements, make sure you're comfortable!'

The new philosophy is underlined by Gerald Smiy, of Creamers Coffee Shop, who believes he is there to offer the public a service. 'Customers come in and ask for some hash or grass and I sit them down and talk to them about their choice,' he says. 'I ask them if they have smoked before and if they say "No" I would usually start them on some not-very-strong stuff to see how they go. If they say "Yes" I ask what they usually smoke and try to find something of about the same strength. I would also give them a leaflet telling them how to use cannabis sensibly.'

Dope-peddlers with a social conscience? It seems unlikely, but this is Amsterdam cannabis culture for a new century.

## WE ARE THE CHAMPIONS – THE CANNABIS CUP

In 1988 the editors of American dope culture bible *High Times* had a brainwave: an annual jamboree of pot culminating in a competition to find the best marijuana and hash. Thus the Cannabis Cup was born, and, as the world's premier showcase for pot there was only one place it could be held: Amsterdam.

Every year more than 1,500 people, ranging from inquisitive amateurs to expert aficionados, make the week-long pilgrimage to the coffee bars of Amsterdam in order to sample the variety of wares on offer. Celebrity judges are asked to present awards including Best Coffee Shop, Best Homegrown Pot, and Best Imported Hash.

Since its inception, the Cannabis Cup has developed into the dope equivalent of a sales convention. Bemused dope heads often find themselves harassed by company reps flogging drug paraphernalia from bongs to vaporizer units. In 1997 the first Hall of Fame award was set up and presented posthumously to Bob Marley. His widow, Rita, flew in from Jamaica to collect the award on his behalf.

## CANNABIS CAFÉS UK STYLE

For British cannabis enthusiasts to set up their own Amsterdam-style cafés seems a logical step – especially as the laws are a great deal more lax than they used to be. But, as a number of hopeful marijuana entrepreneurs have discovered, the law still exists, and there are still police officers happy to apply it to the letter.

In 2001, James Ward from Manchester attended a training course in Amsterdam on how to run a cannabis coffee shop. He returned to England and, with an army of helpers, began to set up his own coffee shop in the English south coast town of Bournemouth. Barely had the doors opened, than 60 members of Dorset police, plus a sniffer dog and its handler, busted the shop. Seven people were arrested for drug-related offences and a quantity of cannabis was recovered.

'Dorset police targets dealers and users in the more harmful Class A drugs like heroin and crack cocaine,' said Detective Chief Inspector Colin Stanger. 'But clearly we will not tolerate the dealing in and use of cannabis because it is an offence and our duty is to enforce the law.' At the same time, police in Rhyl, North Wales and Dundee in Scotland were warning potential café owners that they would not tolerate premises being opened on their patch.

Britain's first cannabis café, the Dutch Experience, opened in Stockport, Cheshire in 2001. It was raided by police on its first day, but supporters immediately reopened it. In the space of seven months, it was raided four times but remained open every day. On one occasion, cannabis campaigners – including two MEPs – marched on Stockport police station carrying cannabis, and demanded to be arrested. After 28 arrests, the police gave up, ignored anyone else possessing the drug and campaigners declared that it had in effect been legalized. The Dutch Experience continues to attract hundreds of people from across the country every day, but in December 2001 its co-founder, Colin Davis, was remanded in Strangeways Prison for breaking bail conditions on drugs charges.

More than a dozen other cannabis cafés are now being planned for Brighton, Liverpool, London, Edinburgh and elsewhere. They will certainly be raided by police and closed down – but all will inevitably open up again just as quickly.

### GOTCHA – CELEBRITY CANNABIS BUSTS

The cannabis-crazy 1960s ushered in a new perspective on the weed. Prohibition was, for the first time, being questioned and the authorities were utterly bamboozled by the sudden and massive upsurge in recreational pot smoking. Anxious to show that they were in control of the situation, narcotics squads around the world sought out high-profile users to prosecute. And the celebrity world did not let them down.

In 1966, English folk singer Donovan was fined £250 ($360) for possession. 'I would like you to bear in mind that you have a great influence on young people,' the magistrate reminded him, 'and it behoves you to behave yourself.' But rock and rollers were far too busy getting stoned to allow such a weight of responsibility to affect their lifestyles. Rolling Stones Mick Jagger and Keith Richards caused a storm when police raided Richards' home in 1967. The police claimed both were high on pot, which they denied. Even so, they were sentenced to one year in prison and a £750 ($1,100) fine. The case went to appeal on the back of a public outcry over the severity of the sentence and was overturned on a technicality – the police hadn't found any pot on the premises. 'Pop stars should be subjected to a system of tests – like horses and greyhounds – before they go on stage,' wrote one affronted member of the public to the *News Of The World* in 1968. In 1976 pop pals David Bowie and Iggy Pop were busted in New York with an alleged 250g (9oz) of marijuana. They were later cleared. Ex-Beatle Paul McCartney famously spent ten days in a Tokyo jail after attempting to import 250g (9oz) of marijuana. He was later deported. In March 2000, singer Whitney Houston was allegedly found with 15g (1/2oz) of marijuana in her luggage at an airport in Hawaii. Officials later decided not to file charges.

Hollywood has also had its run-ins with the cannabis police. Actor Robert Mitchum was arrested for marijuana possession in 1948 and served 60 days in prison. Mitchum said: 'I'm ruined. I've been smoking reefers for years. I knew I would get caught sooner or later.' However, having served his time, he later joked: 'It was the first vacation I've had in seven years, like Palm Springs without the riff-raff.' In 1976 actor Ryan O'Neal fell foul of California's new dope laws when police found 140g (5oz) of cannabis in his Beverly Hills home. He was freed on bail on the understanding that he sought psychiatric help. Woody Harrelson, star of *Cheers*, was arrested but later released after planting four industrial hemp seeds on his property in Kentucky in 1998. 'We're facing a severe worldwide fibre shortage,' he explained. Meanwhile celebrity drugs guru Dr Timothy Leary was sentenced to ten years in jail for transportation of marijuana in 1975. One joint was found in the vagina of his daughter Susan while they were driving from Texas to California. He was released in 1976. In 1999 actor Matthew McConaughey was found naked and playing the bongos with a marijuana bong next to him when police busted his house. After spending a night in jail, the drug paraphernalia charges were swiftly dropped after he agreed to pay a $50 (£35) fine for violating noise ordinances.

Sports stars are not immune to the temptations of a joint either. In 1986 England cricket star Ian Botham admitted he had smoked cannabis. The authorities banned him for eight weeks. Meanwhile teen tennis sensation Jennifer Capriati fell down to earth with a bump when she was busted for possession in 1994. No further action was taken after she agreed to enter a drug treatment centre. It did her good – she bounced back and became the game's number one women's player. And, shortly after the laid-back world of snowboarding hailed a new hero when Ross Rebagliati won the sport's first ever Olympic gold in 1998, he became a cause célèbre among the dope-smoking fraternity when traces of marijuana were found in his blood. Rebagliati was first stripped of his medal, then had it reinstated after he explained that he had not been smoking himself but sitting beside some snowboarding pals who were. 'I'm definitely going to change my lifestyle,' Rebagliati told reporters. 'Unfortunately for you, I'm not going to change my friends. My friends are real. I'm going to stand behind them and support them. I'm not going to deviate from that. I might have to wear a gas mask from now on, but whatever.'

But when it comes to celebrity cannabis smokers, they don't get much more famous than the British Prince Harry. In 2001, the 17-year-old prince was forced to attend a drugs rehabilitation clinic at the request of his father, Prince Charles, after he admitted that he had taken cannabis on several occasions. Harry told his father that he took cannabis at a secret party at Highgrove, Prince Charles's Gloucestershire home, and on other occasions when he was as young as 16. Anxious to be seen to be doing the right thing, Charles swiftly arranged for Harry, who is third in line to the throne, to visit Featherstone Lodge rehabilitation centre, in Peckham, south London. Senior aides to Prince Charles said they hoped that the public and the media would look upon Prince Harry's admission and potential drug problem 'sympathetically'. One official said, 'Unfortunately, this is something that many parents have to go through at one time or another. We acknowledge that on several occasions last summer, Prince Harry experimented with cannabis. It is not that he had or has a serious problem, but he did take the drug.'

A less high-profile but equally embarrassing bust was that of William Straw, the 17-year-old son of the then Home Secretary, Jack Straw. William was nailed by the *Daily Mirror* newspaper in 1997. A reporter, tipped off that Straw was selling cannabis, met him in a pub in Kennington, south London, and bought £10 ($14.50) of dope from him. He was arrested and appeared at the local police station with his father after the Crown Prosecution Service advised that a caution was the most appropriate action. 'William is now learning the lessons of this episode and he has my support in doing so,' Jack Straw said.

## IT'S A GAS – CANNABIS, COMEDY AND COMICS

Every movement needs a standard bearer – and in the case of the pot-head brigade there were two. In the 1970s Cheech and Chong took every nuance of marijuana's laid-back, spaced-out culture and milked it for laughs on record and in the movies. It was funny – but a whole lot funnier if you happened to be smoking a huge joint at the time.

After several unsuccessful years as wannabe folk musicians in Los Angeles and Edmonton, Canada, Richard 'Cheech' Marin and Tommy Chong became a double act in 1970. Identifying that a rich vein of material could be mined out of the booming hippie movement they began performing dope-laced songs and sketches in nightclubs until eventually they were spotted by a record producer. Their 1972 debut album *Cheech And Chong* was a hit and was followed by several others, including *Big Bambu* and *Los Cochinos*. With tracks entitled 'Trippin' In Court' and 'Let's Make A Drug Deal', fans were left in no doubt that here was an act that talked their language – not to mention the fact they often inserted free strips of rolling paper in their album sleeves.

'When I first got turned onto pot, it was almost legal in the sense that no one really knew what it was, so no one really cared about it, especially in Canada,' Chong said. 'I remember smoking it behind this jazz club with the guys that turned me on, and the police came and searched the car for booze. And we were all laughing hysterically. They wanted to know what kind of tobacco that was, and we told them it was Italian tobacco.'

In 1978 the duo made their movie breakthrough in *Up In Smoke*, a frantic caper that proved to be a box-office smash. Several more movies followed but, although the pair retained a strong fan base, their wasted, hippie personas were becoming increasingly outdated in the cocaine-fuelled 1980s. Ironically in the 1990s, the fashion for 1970s retro – with the return of flares, disco and hip movies such as *Dazed And Confused* – sparked a mini-revival in their fortunes. For most aged hippies, however, Cheech and Chong remain a fond memory in the record collection.

While Cheech and Chong undoubtedly cashed in on the dope culture of the 1970s, they would admit a debt of gratitude to the equally popular explosion in underground comic books that began to appear at the same time. Indeed comic books have been described by some as the ideal literature of cannabis culture – easy to read, full of spaced out drawings and often hilariously funny. In particular, *The Fabulous Furry Freak Brothers* provided a blueprint for the kind of character Cheech and Chong would later commit to vinyl and celluloid. Created in 1970 by Gilbert Shelton, the Fabulous Freaks have been described as the stoned equivalent of the Keystone Cops. Their relentless search for narcotic release, usually with all manner of weird and wonderful paraphernalia, swiftly earned them a cult following. Indeed one episode saw the brothers being invited to judge the Third Annual Cannabis Cup. Needless to say, they ended up consuming most of the exhibits.

But the Freaks were not the first cartoon characters to be associated with dope. It is testament to the paranoia of US Federal Bureau of Narcotics chief Harry J Anslinger that in the 1930s he was convinced Popeye the Sailor was in fact a marijuana-munching fiend. Popeye's ability to gain superhuman strength through consuming spinach through his pipe fitted in perfectly with Anslinger's ideas about the cannabis menace. The fact that Popeye was also a sailor didn't help him; sailors were held responsible for the spread of cannabis from the east to 'civilized' countries such as

Britain and the United States. Perhaps as a result of Anslinger's delusions, 'spinach' became a jazz industry code-word for cannabis – and the inspiration for a wicked little number called 'The Spinach Song', performed by Julia Lee And Her Boyfriends in dope-filled jazz clubs in New York in 1938.

A major influence on subsequent cannabis comics was Harvey Kurtzman, the founder of *MAD* magazine in the 1950s and creator of the saucy Little Annie Fannie cartoon series, which appeared in *Playboy* in the 1960s and 1970s. Kurtzman used Annie Fannie as a vehicle for his own beliefs about drugs – and in particular the legalization of cannabis. He frequently allowed his characters to pontificate about the benefits of pot, and then showed them being ruthlessly beaten up by policemen who bore an uncanny resemblance to pigs.

Kurtzman provided the inspiration for Robert Crumb, regarded by most cannabis-culture aficionados as the daddy of dope comics. Crumb, a prolific hash smoker, took Kurtzman's ideas and gave them a psychedelic twist. His series featuring Fritz the Cat and Mr Natural coincided with the hippie revolution of the late 1960s and not only used many of its cultural icons as their inspiration, but helped create many of them as well. It was Crumb's work that opened the door to Gilbert Shelton.

The man who encouraged and published not only Crumb and Shelton but a whole raft of hippie cartoonists was Denis

Kitchen, himself a talented cartoonist who was the founder of the legendary Kitchen Sink Press. Kitchen Sink in turn spawned the likes of Rip Off Press and Last Gasp Press, which gave the world such characters as Harold Hedd, a dope-smoking macho man, and Dr Atomic, who gave readers advice on how to roll the perfect 'doobie'.

'We knew that comics were stultified, largely puerile, and unimaginative, and it was impossible to use the medium with any sense of real freedom and exploration,' Kitchen said. 'Those of us who considered ourselves hippies caught up in the anti-war movement and – yes – smoking pot, just looked at the world in a very different way. And comic books were a part of that world that we questioned. There was an immediate connection between going to buy your rolling papers at a head shop and going to get your comics. That was a natural alliance and I think a lot of people considered getting high and reading underground comics a natural thing to do.'

When the US government decided to clamp down on drug culture in the 1970s, one of their chosen methods was to use comic books. In 1971, the FBI contacted Stan Lee – creator of Marvel Comics and superheroes like Spider-Man – and asked him to create a story telling the dangers of drug addiction. Lee agreed, and later that year Spidey was seen preventing a junked-up black man from attempting to fly from the top of a tall building. Even as recently as 1999, Spidey was still promoting the anti-cannabis message.

In a special four-parter, one of the characters is a pot-head movie star who smokes dope and then goes dancing on steel girders, encouraging his sappy fans to do the same. In 2000, both Marvel's Spider-Man and DC Comics' Batman received White House awards for their continued vigilance against the drug menace.

## WWW.DOPE.COM – HASH ON THE NET

The advent of the Internet has allowed cannabis and its users unprecedented mainstream access. A growing number of dedicated sites now enable cannabis users across the globe the opportunity to discuss anything from medical issues, cooking recipes and different laws to advanced growing techniques and where to buy it. More importantly, the authorities are increasingly aware that the Net has become a major outlet for dealers.

Not only is it possible to purchase different types of seeds and hydroponic devices (see p162), but Internet users can now buy their own grass and have it delivered within a couple of days to their homes. For those frustrated by draconian laws against medical use, or those who simply enjoy the convenience of shopping for their drugs online, the Net is a positive boon.

Finding retail sites is not straightforward. Buying cannabis online is illegal and dealers are well aware of the increased interest of international drug squads. But, by the same token, clamping down on Internet drug sales is almost impossible – especially if the sellers come from countries, like Holland, where the laws are relaxed. Many sites are disguised as the websites of Amsterdam coffee shops. After ordering, customers are sent an email with an address on it and instructions to send cash. One Amsterdam dealer recently admitted to sending out over 1,000 packages a week to online clients across the world, and estimates that 99 per cent of the marijuana he sends out makes it through customs to the addresses intact. Usually it is sent in plastic zipper bags placed inside padded envelopes. While there is always a possibility that customs will intercept your parcel and come round to your house, this is so remote that most people are confident of taking the risk.

Some, however, are not convinced. 'We have run several messages on our website saying that one of the stupidest things you can do is buy pot through the Internet. It's even riskier than going up to somebody in the street,' says John Holmstrom, multimedia director for *High Times* magazine. 'Who knows who's behind the website? What if it's a government agency and they're keeping a list of everyone they're sending pot to?'

The cannabis seed trade is flourishing, both because the tiny, odourless seeds are easy to ship and because selling seeds is far more profitable than actual marijuana. Many seed sites are based in Holland and Canada, where possession of seeds is legal. The sites are places where global cannabis connoisseurs can compare notes or where novices can absorb pages and pages of free advice on cultivation matters.

### RAGE AGAINST THE MACHINE – POT HEADS FIGHT BACK

Increasingly what defines the culture of cannabis today is not so much the self-effacing placidity of the 1960s and 1970s, but a real sense of injustice and anger. It's as if cannabis, sick of being the butt of the joke and the sole territory of spaced-out hippies in flares and kaftans, is determined to be taken seriously.

'When I think of all the skulking around I've done, simply so I can have a nice joint in peace, it seems absolutely ludicrous,' says motor retailer Gareth Burns, 31. 'This is the 21st century, for Christ's sake. It's not as if I'm running around with an Uzi. I've never done anybody any harm in my life.'

In June 2000, charity worker Jerry Ham was busted with 3g of cannabis in his possession. Ham chose to contest the charge in front of a judge and jury. By doing this, he became one of a growing number of cannabis enthusiasts who are no longer prepared to take a slap on the wrist, a probable fine and caution and, more importantly, a criminal record that can be seen by potential employers and be raised in court should offenders face a charge on another occasion.

Two recent developments are behind the new wave of people standing up for their rights to take cannabis. First, the changed public perception towards cannabis has seen a number of high-profile cannabis busts thrown out of court. Second, the legal labyrinth of the Human Rights Act, which was introduced in 2000 to prevent European governments from unduly interfering in the private life of an individual.

Jerry Ham pleaded not guilty, despite admitting possession, on the grounds that it should not be a crime. He argued that the amount of hash he possessed – less than 2g – was so small that prosecution amounted to a 'disproportionate and therefore unlawful response'. Calling for his case to be dismissed because it infringed his human rights, his case was backed by Liberty, the human rights campaign group.

His case mirrored that of 21-year-old labourer Daniel Westlake, who, when caught with a small amount of cannabis, refused to accept a caution and pleaded not guilty under the Human Rights Act. At the time of writing, his case was due to come before the Court of Appeal, which has the power to declare the Misuse of Drugs Act incompatible with the Human Rights Act.

In America, meanwhile, a group called the Oakland Cannabis Buyers' Co-operative took their case for being allowed possession of the weed all the way to the Supreme Court – where, in a landmark ruling in 2001, all eight judges ruled that possession of cannabis was an offence in the United States whatever the circumstances. US Attorney General John Ashcroft hailed the ruling as 'a victory for the enforcement of our nation's drug laws'.

Sadly for Jerry Ham, his bid foundered at the first hurdle, when Judge Rivlin ruled his case should go ahead, saying that courts could only stay trials in exceptional circumstances, where the defendant could not receive a fair trial or where it was integral to the public interest that the trial should not take place. To accept that it should be widened to take into account 'proportionateness' under the Human Rights Act would be 'very wide and dangerously vague'. The judge said: 'The restriction of his right to take drugs in the privacy of his own home is not an intrusion on his personal space or an affront to his personality.' He added: 'No one would wish to stifle debate – nothing could be more healthy. If the defendant and his supporters wish to secure a change in the law, it can be achieved and must be done by normal democratic means. Until there is a change in the law, judges must continue to uphold it.'

Despite a clear direction to convict Ham in the judge's summing up, the jury of seven men and five women took two and a half hours to reach a 10-2 majority verdict of guilty. And Ham was sentenced to just two years conditional discharge.

Cannabis culture has, for over a century in the UK, been a culture of persecution. In 1998, the number of people in the UK given lifetime criminal records for cannabis offences passed the one million mark. The annual number is in excess of 100,000 – more than 90 per cent for personal use. In the USA, the number of convictions tops one million annually.

But, as so often, the statistics mask a number of sad stories – like that of TV cameraman Brian Lace, who was caught in possession of a small amount of cannabis and fined £200 ($290). With a criminal record to his name, Lace suddenly found that he was sacked from his job, evicted from his house and had his car repossessed. Unable to find work after a year of living on benefits in a bedsit, he could take it no longer and hanged himself from the back of a door.

But a more typical scenario is that of the multiple sclerosis sufferer who accepted a police caution for smoking cannabis, not realising that by doing so she was giving herself a criminal record for life. She only discovered this when she applied for a visa to visit the USA and was refused entry on account of her 'criminal' past. Or the bakery manager whose insurance company refused to pay up after a burglary because he had a criminal record from an earlier cannabis caution.

When one former electrician was caught with 43g (1½oz) worth, he was prosecuted for possession and intent to supply, a charge he denies. He spent 11 weeks in jail and 60 days wearing an electronic tag. 'Society has basically written me off,' he says. 'As a cannabis user who has never hurt anyone, I am put in the same category as rapists and robbers.'

## IN THE BEGINNING

Blame the ancient medicine men. If it hadn't been for them and their infernal meddling, cannabis sativa, an otherwise unremarkable species of hemp plant, would have remained just what its name means in Latin: useful hemp. Its tough stalk would have been used for the production of rope and durable textiles such as 'canvas' sails, its edible seeds would have been used for food, its pulp for fuel and paper and its oil as a base for paints and varnishes.

But no. Because cannabis is also a herb, it attracted the attention of shamans, soothsayers, and witch doctors – all of whom were eager to explore the therapeutic properties of its leaves, buds and flowers.

The Chinese medicine men proved to be particularly good pharmacists. As soon as they discovered that various tinctures of cannabis were therapeutic, it was only a matter of time before they realised that, in greater quantities, it was highly narcotic. Around 2600 BC, they began getting stoned on a regular basis and, from that moment, the impact of cannabis on the culture of mankind was to be seismic.

It was Herodotus, the Greek historian, who first recorded the psychedelic effects of cannabis during his travels through northern Europe in 430 BC. Before that, the plant had cropped up in various ancient pharmacopoeia, including that of the Hindus in India in around 1200 BC, in which it was described as 'sacred grass' and recommended as an offering to Shiva – and, some 500 years later, in the *Zend-Avesta*, a sacred Persian text that lists more than 10,000 medicinal plants.

Herodotus came across cannabis for the first time while in Scythia, in what is now northern Asia. He was mightily impressed with what he saw: 'There is in that country kannabis growing both wild and cultivated,' he wrote in his *Histories*. 'Fuller and taller than flax, the Thracians use it to make garments very like linen. The Scythians take kannabis seed...and throw it on the red hot stones. It smoulders and sends up such billows of steam smoke that no Greek vapour bath can surpass it. The Scythians howl with joy in these vapour baths – which serve them instead of bathing, for they never wash their bodies with water.'

By AD 70, cannabis had been appropriated from the heathens of Scythia and was commonplace in the civilized ancient world. Another Greek historian, Dioscorides, observed that tinctures and poultices made from the leaves of the plant were very popular among physicians in Rome who used them for a number of treatments, but primarily as a painkiller. Within 150 years, however, the Roman historian Galen noted another, more familiar use of the plant at social occasions. 'It is customary,' he wrote, 'to give hemp to guests to promote hilarity and enjoyment.'

There can be little doubt that cannabis was taken to Rome by the many eastern merchants and travellers who passed through that most cosmopolitan of ancient cities. Certainly it was the East that provided the most ideal climatic conditions for cultivating the plant, and it was there that the hot-bed of cannabis production and use were consolidated. In AD 800, the prophet Mohammed gave the thumbs up to cannabis use among his disciples, while at the same time prohibiting the consumption of alcohol.

Indeed, right up until the Middle Ages, society's relationship with cannabis was blissfully content. It was used for medicine and for recreation in equal measure, and there was certainly none of the angst that typified later attitudes to the drug. What seems to have driven the first wedge was the fact that cannabis was so firmly associated with the East and, in particular, the religions of the East.

In 1484, Pope Innocent VIII labelled cannabis as 'an unholy sacrament of the Satanic mass' and issued a papal ban on cannabis medicines. This was perhaps one of the first recorded instances of anti-cannabis legislation (although 50 years earlier Ottoman Emir Soudoun Scheikhouni had banned the eating of cannabis).

In the West, the importance of cannabis – or more particularly hemp – was not as a medicine or narcotic. In

16th-century Britain, an island whose might had been largely built upon its navy, hemp was an invaluable source of tough, durable fibre that was used to make sails. Henry VIII went so far as to order every farmer in the land to devote a quarter acre out of every 60 to the cultivation of hemp plants, or face a hefty fine of three shillings and fourpence. To his daughter, Elizabeth I, beleaguered by the Spanish for much of her reign, the hemp plant was even more important. Under an edict issued by her in 1563, farmers were ordered to grow it or face a whopping £5 ($7.25) fine. On mainland Europe, meanwhile, Elizabeth's nemesis Philip of Spain was also aware of the importance of hemp and ordered it to be grown in his colonies as far afield as Argentina and Oregon.

In the 17th century, the popularity of cannabis as a medicine made a comeback among western doctors. In 1653, the English physician Nicholas Culpeper claimed it 'allayeth inflammations, easeth the pain of gout, tumours or knots of joints, pain of hips'. Indeed, in Europe, the idea of smoking the plant for purposes of recreation appears not to have crossed anyone's mind. Tobacco was the drug of choice but even that was frowned upon by the majority.

This was not the case in the Middle East and Asia, where pot smoking had reached epidemic proportions, especially among the poorer classes. Napoleon was reportedly horrified by the scale of cannabis use among the locals when he arrived in Egypt in 1798. He was even more put out when, despite banning his own soldiers from partaking, the pastime arrived back in Paris with them and was enthusiastically adopted by the French lower classes. It was not long before Napoleon's troops were followed by eastern dealers eager to tap into new markets in Europe.

Hash had arrived in the West with a vengeance. No longer was it regarded simply as a medicine or as a source of fibre for making sails. Here was a powerful narcotic, cheaply available to those with hard lives and little money who wanted to get off their heads, and overpoweringly exotic to society dandies and intellectuals who had suddenly acquired a new and exciting way of spending their evenings.

For the next 200 years the humble cannabis plant was to become the centre of a whole new world, one which was embraced by some and despised by others. And, even today, it is a world in which the two sides still refuse to meet.

# WORLD

Across the world, cannabis has inspired such mass outbreaks of judicial schizophrenia, public outcry, religious zeal and general hopeless dithering that even today, 4,700 years since it was first used, it appears that governments still haven't got the foggiest idea of what to do with the humble cannabis sativa plant.

## DAZED AND CONFUSED – CANNABIS IN THE USA

Few countries have had such an angst-ridden relationship with cannabis as the USA. Indeed at one stage, in the 1930s, the country was gripped by such paranoia about the deleterious effects of the weed that it seemed the population as a whole was on a communal bad trip.

Yet, within 30 years, America was responsible for raising the cultural profile of marijuana to iconic status. The peace and free love movement in the 1960s was largely fuelled by cannabis; the Woodstock festival in 1969 was its culmination and the conflict in Vietnam is remembered largely as a war fought under the influence of drugs.

Cannabis – or rather hemp – was originally a godsend to the pioneers of the New World. The likes of George Washington and Thomas Jefferson not only encouraged farmers to grow the plant in order to make durable and versatile hemp fibre, they grew it themselves.

But by the middle part of the 19th century, as the commercial value of cannabis fell, it became clear to the Establishment that the plant's stock as a narcotic was rising. From the hashish houses of cosmopolitan Paris and London, word soon reached the east coast US cultural intelligentsia, who became eager devotees and experimenters. New York began to set up its own fashionable hash houses and attendance there became de rigueur among the well-heeled and open-minded bright young things.

Of these, none was more devoted to 'hasheesh' than Fitz Hugh Ludlow (1837–70), well-to-do son of a respectable New York minister who, in his 34 short years, consumed the drug in heroic quantities and reported its mind-bending effects in a series of first-hand accounts, the most famous being *The Hasheesh Eater* in 1856: 'I had caught a glimpse through the chinks of my earthly prison of the immeasurable sky, which should one day overarch me with unconceived sublimity of view, and resound in my ear with unutterable music,' Ludlow writes. 'A shock, as of some unimagined vital force, shoots without warning through my entire frame, leaping to my fingers' ends, piercing my brain, startling me till I nearly spring from my chair.'

It is worth noting that Ludlow and his fellow hasheesh pioneers were experimenting with cannabis in its purest and strongest form. They were, literally, eating it. And while their accounts of spaced-out hash houses, psychedelic trips and spiritual uncaging fascinated the public, it was little more than titillation, comparable perhaps to the acid-fuelled ramblings of modern American drug experimentalists such as Timothy Leary and Hunter S Thompson.

Cannabis the drug was a middle-class fad and therefore, in the eyes of middle-class American Establishment, it did not present a threat. In the 1870s, however, things began to change. It was around this time that recreational use of cannabis cigarettes began to spread like wildfire in the New World, particularly among impoverished labourers in the Caribbean, Brazil and Central America who sought a hangover-free escape from their backbreaking work in the fields. By the turn of the century, the pastime had spread across the border into the USA, by way of migrant workers and soldiers. Initially it took hold in the Deep South, manifesting itself particularly in New Orleans where it had a clear effect on early jazz musicians who tried to recapture in their music the inhibitions they felt while under the influence of marijuana.

As its use became more widespread across the country, the anxiety of white America became increasingly palpable.

Cannabis became associated with the unspeakable underclasses – the blacks, the poor and the Mexicans. Reports from over the border told of violent ne'er-do-wells like Pancho Villa, the Mexican revolutionary whose army regularly smoked 'marijuana' (Mexican for 'intoxicant') to give them courage for battle. Folk songs like 'La Cucaracha' – written about one of Villa's marijuana-starved 'cockroaches', or foot soldiers – were the first examples of the subject of cannabis entering the mainstream of popular culture.

> *La cucaracha, la cucaracha*
> *Ya no puede caminar*
> *Porque no tiene, porque no tiene*
> *Marihuana que fumar*

In English, the text tranlslates as: 'The cockroach, the cockroach / Can no longer walk / Because he hasn't, because he hasn't / Marijuana to smoke.' (This, incidentally, is also the origin of the word 'roach', a nickname for a marijuana cigarette butt.)

By the 1920s, America had already passed Prohibition laws banning alcohol, so it was no surprise that marijuana was the next to feel the weight of the puritanical Establishment. In 1923 the drug was outlawed in New Orleans and, by the end of the Prohibition era in 1933, 17 states had banned cannabis. But while alcohol made a welcome return to the speakeasies, one man was embarking upon a personal crusade to vilify cannabis. It was a campaign that was, ironically, to raise the profile of what was still a little-known drug into its present status.

Harry J Anslinger was an ambitious bureaucrat who first made his name in the 1920s as a fervent Prohibitionist, chasing rum runners out of the American consulate in the West Indies. When, in 1930, the American government was looking for someone to head up its newly created Federal Bureau of Narcotics, Anslinger was the obvious choice. He set about his new job with a gusto that bordered on the fanatical. As far as he was concerned cannabis was Public Enemy Number One.

More than 70 years after the arrival of the first hash houses, private cannabis establishments were still highly popular in 1930s New York. Known as 'tea pads', they were as secretive and illicit as opium dens and were set up by mutual arrangement in inconspicuous apartment rooms predominantly in the Harlem area. But instead of emaciated addicts, those who regularly frequented tea pads were refined marijuana aficionados, usually of high social standing, who enjoyed sampling different blends of the drug in a manner similar to tea tasters.

Anslinger's response to what he saw as a cancerous cannabis sub-culture eating away at the heart of America was not to clamp down with police raids as he had done during Prohibition. Instead, he issued a series of scabrous anti-cannabis articles in magazines and newspapers. Without doubt the best known is his 1937 diatribe 'Marijuana: Assassin Of Youth':

> *Here indeed is the unknown quantity among narcotics. No one can predict its effect. No one knows, when he places a marijuana cigarette to his lips, whether he will become a joyous reveler in a musical heaven, a mad insensate, a calm philosopher, or a murderer. That youth has been selected by the peddlers of this poison as an especially fertile field makes it a problem of serious concern to every man and woman in America.*
>
> *It would be well for law-enforcement officers everywhere to search for marijuana behind cases of criminal and sex assault. During the last year a young male addict was hanged in Baltimore for criminal assault on a ten-year-old girl. His defence was that he was temporarily insane from smoking marijuana. In Alamosa, Colorado, a degenerate brutally attacked a young girl while under the influence of the drug. In Chicago, two marijuana-smoking boys murdered a policeman. In at least two dozen other comparatively recent cases of murder or degenerate sex attacks, many of them committed by youths, marijuana proved to be a contributing cause.*

Anslinger concluded:

> *Therein lies much of the cruelty of marijuana, especially in its attack upon youth. The young, immature brain is a thing of impulses, upon which the 'unknown quantity' of the drug acts as an almost overpowering stimulant. In New Orleans, of 437 persons of varying ages arrested for a wide range of crimes, 125 were addicts. Of 37 murderers, 17 used marijuana, and of 193 convicted thieves, 34 were 'on the weed'. This means a job of unceasing watchfulness by every police department and by every public-spirited civic organization. It calls for campaigns of education in every school, so that children will not be deceived by the wiles of peddlers, but will know of the insanity, the disgrace, the horror which marijuana can bring to its victim.*

The effect on the American public of Anslinger's vivid propaganda was electrifying. In 1936 a movie was released entitled *Reefer Madness*, inspired almost totally by Anslinger's anti-cannabis tirades. The film depicted how one hit from a cannabis joint led its innocent young cast into insanity and death. Subtitled 'Marijuana: weed from the Devil's garden', and with such tag lines as 'One moment of bliss – a lifetime of regret' and 'Hunting a thrill, they inhaled a drag of concentrated sin', *Reefer Madness* bombed at the box office but remains a vivid example of the national cannabis frenzy Anslinger succeeded in stirring up in 1930s middle America.

Swept along on the mood of the nation, Anslinger succeeded in getting the Marijuana Tax Act passed through Congress in 1937. The law placed prohibitive taxes on cannabis – $1 (69p) per ounce (30g) for industrial or medical use and $100 (£69) per ounce (30g) for people using it for recreational purposes (with prison terms and hefty fines for transgressors) – and effectively outlawed it. The first person tried under the new laws was Samuel Caldwell of Colorado. Charged with selling a small amount of grass, he was sentenced to four years' hard labour at the notorious Leavenworth Prison.

But Anslinger wasn't finished there. Once he had cannabis on the ground he was determined to keep kicking. In the 1940s, he turned his attention back to New Orleans and despatched agents to keep tabs on the thriving jazz scene and reefer-puffing exponents such as Louis Armstrong, Duke Ellington, Cab Calloway, Fats Waller and Jimmy Dorsey. 'At first you was a misdemeanour. But as the years rolled by you lost your "misde" and got meaner and meaner,' Louis Armstrong remarked acidly.

Anslinger continued his one-man crusade until 1961, when the Single Convention on Narcotic Drugs created an international commitment to unilateral war on drugs. Yet the 1960s proved to be the decade in which cannabis truly came of age as America's (and the rest of the world's) recreational drug of choice – and, ironically, responsibility for its popularity has been laid firmly on the shoulders of its arch enemy.

In the 1960s, marijuana use was so commonplace that even the president used it. In an article printed in *High Times* in 1974, an unnamed dealer with links to the White House wrote: 'Early one evening I received a telephone call at my apartment at Georgetown. It was one of JFK's most trusted press liaisons, who informed me the president was planning a short vacation. He was taking his boat out with family and friends, and I was asked if I could provide him with the memos I had drawn up in accordance with our conversation two weeks earlier. Could I have everything ready by ten o'clock that night? I knew exactly what was meant by the call, because the president hadn't asked me to draw up any memos. By ten I had prepared a manila folder full of blank paper. Inside was an ounce [30g] of fresh Panamanian.'

Within a year of the UN Single Convention and the retirement of Harry Anslinger, President John F Kennedy – who was rumoured to smoke marijuana for pleasure as well as a cure for chronic back pain – had ordered a study into the nation's narcotic problem and this produced some startling results. Not only, it concluded, had the hazards of marijuana been 'exaggerated', but the harsh criminal penalties for recreational users (which by 1961 in Georgia included the death penalty for being caught selling twice to a minor), were 'in poor social perspective'. Within a year, Congress was passing laws that made a clear distinction between cannabis and hard drugs.

In his retirement home in Pennsylvania, Harry Anslinger must have been in despair as he watched 30 years of hard work crumble to dust almost overnight. But by oppressing cannabis so vehemently, Anslinger had merely served to make the younger generation insanely curious to try it out. Not only had cannabis proved to be a benign assassin of youth, but that youth had now grown up and taken Anslinger's place. And just as cannabis had provided the early jazz musicians with inspiration, so the drug was enthusiastically embraced by pop musicians in the 1960s. 'We were smoking marijuana for breakfast,' the late John Lennon recalled, while Bob Dylan explained his cannabis philosophy: 'Now these things aren't drugs. They just bend your mind a little. I think everybody's mind should be bent once in a while.'

Dylan first got the taste for marijuana as a student in Minnesota and then set about introducing it to many of the leading musicians of the day, including The Beatles. By the late 1960s, cannabis was as much a part of any self-respecting pop star's accoutrements as their guitar.

Ironically, while musicians urged everyone to make love not war, it was the conflict in Vietnam that cemented marijuana use among millions of young Americans. The battlefields of Southeast Asia were also a source of cheap and plentiful grass and, to the chagrin of the US Army's generals, thousands of conscripts turned to the drug as a means of blotting out the horrors of the war. It is thought that as many as 75 per cent of the soldiers sent to Vietnam smoked cannabis at some point.

Back home, cannabis use exploded. In 1969, *Life* magazine reported that as many as 12 million Americans had tried pot. Even this was a conservative estimate.

The final nail in the coffin of Harry Anslinger's anti-cannabis crusade came in 1970 when the American government declared his Marijuana Tax Act unconstitutional. In truth, Congress was belatedly reacting to the untrammelled rise in the drug's popularity during the 1960s. As the new decade dawned, millions of middle-class Americans were openly flaunting Anslinger's arcane laws and the police were largely turning a blind eye. In the White House, President Richard Nixon declared he was against the legalization of pot, but in 1973 ordered the Shafer Commission to take a fresh look into the subject. Its findings, like those of Kennedy's commission 12 years earlier, were amazing. Not only did it recommend that people should be allowed to possess cannabis for personal use, it argued that selling or giving away small amounts of the weed was totally acceptable.

In the light of the Shafer Commission's report, Congress passed a raft of new cannabis laws. While not legalizing it, the government scrapped many of the punitive minimum sentences and reclassified cannabis as a soft drug.

By the mid-1970s, an estimated 40 million Americans had tried pot. In a speech to Congress, President Jimmy Carter said: 'Penalties against possession of a drug should not be more damaging to an individual than the use of the drug itself. Nowhere is this more clear than in the laws against possession of marijuana in private for personal use.'

The speech, made 40 years after the American government's jack-booted clampdown on cannabis, was a watershed moment in the drug's history. For a brief moment, it seemed that the next logical step was to be the legalization of cannabis. Instead, the rug was about to be pulled from under cannabis's feet.

Less than ten years after the federal government relaxed its anti-cannabis laws and commissions ordered by Presidents Nixon and Ford were advocating legalization, the drugs landscape in America had changed once again. Peace, love and understanding about cannabis had been replaced by guilt, fear and paranoia. The country was gripped by Reefer Madness all over again – only this time, the anti-marijuana backlash made Harry Anslinger's excessive campaign seem tame by comparison.

Where once first-time marijuana offenders could expect nothing more than a fine, they now faced the prospect of anything from probation to life imprisonment and their property was seized indiscriminately. Even people found carrying drug paraphernalia, such as pipes and roach clips, could expect to land behind bars.

The dramatic sea change of opinion began to manifest itself in the late 1970s. In the heartland of America, the conservative majority railed against what they perceived as betrayal by the liberal government in Washington. The medical and legal debate about cannabis had, they believed, clouded the moral issue. What sort of a country were they living in when 1 in 12 high-school students confessed to smoking pot on a daily basis? Soon, concerned parents were setting up anti-pot groups all over the USA. They eventually amalgamated into the National Federation of Parents for Drug-Free Youth.

Conservative politicians were not slow to jump on the bandwagon. Ronald Reagan sailed into the White House on a rabid anti-drugs ticket. In 1982 he created the White House Drug Abuse Policy Office and, over the next six years, set about reinstating all the old marijuana laws. His successor, George Bush, continued the clampdown with equal relish and by the end of the 1980s it was estimated that America had spent an astonishing $3 billion (£2 billion) on its anti-drugs war.

The arrival of Democrat Bill Clinton in the White House was initially viewed with hope by the pro-cannabis lobby. After all, here, for the first time since Kennedy, was a young president. Even better, he was a baby boomer and a draft dodger. Surely Clinton of all people would signal an easier ride for the weed. They were to be sorely disappointed. Although Clinton admitted he had smoked cannabis, he also famously pointed out he did not inhale. It was a blatant cop-out and a bitter blow to those who regarded him as the saviour of marijuana. In 1997, over 700,000 people were arrested for marijuana-related offences. Harry Anslinger couldn't have asked for more.

In 1973, Anslinger's anti-cannabis missionary work was taken over by the newly formed Drug Enforcement Administration (DEA). This is hardly surprising, since the DEA's lineage can be traced back directly to the Prohibition bureaux of the 1920s and 1930s, from which Anslinger first emerged.

Anslinger would have been pleased with his progeny. Far from mellowing in their stance towards cannabis, the DEA hardened it. But instead of the rabid diatribes and scaremongering so beloved by Harry J, the DEA had the weight of some pretty punitive laws behind them. Traffickers, in particular, could expect little or no mercy if caught in the act by agency operatives: the penalty for being caught trafficking 1,000kg (2,200lb) or 1,000 cannabis plants was a jail term of at least ten years. And that was just for a first offence. If caught twice, offenders could look forward to 20 years or more behind bars. Even punters caught dealing amounts of 50kg (110lb) faced a sentence of up to five years for a first offence.

The DEA definitely saw the cannabis scenario in terms of black and white, with no shades of grey in between. Indeed, they showed their colours very early in their existence. In 1973, they were petitioned to reclassify marijuana as a Schedule II drug that could be prescribed by physicians. The matter took no less than 13 years to come to public hearing stage, and even then the hearings lasted two years. Despite the DEA's legal expert recommending rescheduling, and his conclusions that 'cannabis is one of the safest therapeutically active substances known to man', the DEA denied the petition. As far as the DEA are concerned, the marijuana problem among America's youth is rife – and they have extensive research to prove it, as their own literature proclaims: 'According to a survey conducted by Phoenix House, drug abuse treatment and research organization, marijuana was the drug of choice for 87 per cent of teenagers entering treatment programmes in New York during the first quarter of 1999. A national survey conducted in 1996 revealed that 83 per cent of teenagers in treatment perceived, at one time or another, marijuana to be less dangerous than other illicit drugs, and 60 per cent agreed that using marijuana made it easier for them to consume other drugs, including cocaine, methamphetamine, and LSD.

Similar statistics were found by the 1999 Monitoring the Future study, which showed that marijuana is the illegal drug most frequently used by young people. Among high school seniors, 49.7 per cent reported using marijuana at least once in their lives. By comparison, that figure was 41.7 per cent for seniors in 1995 and 32.6 per cent in 1992. The 1999

NHSDA (National Household Survey of Drug Abuse) found that nearly 1 in 13 youths aged 12–17 were current users of marijuana in 1999 and that the prevalence of marijuana use among youth more than doubled from 1992 to 1999. The 1998 National Centre on Addiction and Substance Abuse study indicates that adolescents are first exposed and try marijuana at a very young age. According to the study, '50 per cent of 13 year olds reported that they could find and purchase marijuana, and 49 per cent of teens surveyed said that they first tried marijuana at age 13 or younger.' Armed with such damning research, the DEA's philosophy has been disarmingly simple: kids are taking marijuana, therefore marijuana must be destroyed at all costs.

Recognizing that dope is about the only commonly used narcotic grown within the borders of the USA, in 1979 the DEA initiated the Domestic Cannabis Eradication and Suppression Program aimed at stamping out the cultivation of the cannabis plant. At first, plantations in Hawaii and California were targeted, and the operation saw some initial success. In Hawaii, for example, the DEA claim to have dried up the marijuana supply on the islands and forced traffickers to smuggle from the mainland. By 1985, the operation had spread to all 50 US states and in 2000 the DEA redoubled their efforts by spending $13 million (£9 million) to support the 96 state and local agencies in their aggressive eradication enforcement. In 1999 alone, the DEA claimed to have eradicated over 3.5 million cultivated cannabis plants, securing 12,000 arrests, the seizure of 3,700 weapons and the appropriation of $27 million (£18.5 million) in illegal assets.

In 20 years the operation has, according to the DEA, 'curbed the availability of domestically grown marijuana and...caused the outdoor cultivators to abandon larger outdoor plots for the safety and concealment of smaller, indoor cultivating areas.' But it has also landed the Agency with a new headache. Forced from their fields, dope growers are now turning to sophisticated indoor growing techniques, such as computerized irrigation and hydroponic cultivation – the cultivation of plants in nutrient solution rather than soil. Hydroponic cultivation, incidentally, not only makes it easier for growers to clandestinely cultivate marijuana indoors but it also enables them to produce extremely potent marijuana.

Not to be outdone, the DEA and its co-operating agencies have set about employing equally advanced technology to wage war against the marijuana growers. One such technique is thermal imaging, which identifies indoor cultivation by detecting the signature heat from lighting used to grow the plants.

The DEA are also aware that their efforts to clamp down on home-grown hash have meant that, like the Hawaiians, traffickers in the US are increasingly looking to import the drug from abroad, in particular from South America. Kilos of cannabis chug across the southern US border concealed in false compartments, fuel tanks, seats and tyres of private and commercial vehicles, pickup trucks, vans, mobile homes and horse trailers. Larger shipments (up to multi-thousand kilogram amounts), are smuggled in tractor-trailer trucks in false compartments and among legitimate bulk shipments, such as agricultural products. In 1997, a record 593 tonnes/tons of marijuana was seized along the southwest border in 1997 - approximately 25 per cent more than that seized in 1996 and nearly double that seized in 1995.

As a result, the smugglers, however, have now turned to more traditional routes into the US, using cargo vessels, pleasure boats and fishing boats to sail up the coast of Mexico, either to US ports or drop off sites along the US coast and the Bahamas.

### FIST OF IRON – GENERAL BARRY McCAFFREY
President Bill Clinton famously smoked a joint but never inhaled. Quite what General Barry McCaffrey made of the chief executive's admission remains a mystery - although it isn't hard to guess. During his four year reign as Clinton's director of the White House Office of National Drug Control policy - in other words, the USA's drug tsar - McCaffrey earned himself a reputation as being a man who would quite happily drag anyone who so much as looked at a joint to the electric chair and flick the switch himself.

'There is not a single shred of evidence that shows that smoked marijuana is useful or needed,' he announced upon his appointment in 1996. 'This is not science. This is not medicine. This is a cruel hoax.'

He saved his most potent venom, however, for the Dutch, whose drugs policies are the most liberal in the world. 'The murder rate in Holland is double that in the United States, and the per capita crime rates are much higher than the United States,' he snarled. 'That's drugs.' When the Dutch ambassador to the USA responded that not only did McCaffrey's claims have no basis in fact because he had included attempted murders in his figures, and that in reality America's murder rate was four times as high, McCaffrey was not fazed in the slightest. Far from it. The figures, he argued, proved that 'the Dutch are a much more violent society and more inept at murders – and that's not much to brag about.'

The appointment of someone as hard line as McCaffrey by an administration as supposedly liberal as the Clinton's Democrats may at first seem confusing. But Clinton, acutely aware of his public image, was also very aware that his, 'I smoked but didn't inhale' tag was something of an albatross around his neck. More importantly, he did not wish to be perceived as a president who, after years of Republican zero tolerance towards drugs, let the country go wild by allowing them easier access to pot. In the US, the tide of opinion was increasingly turning in favour of cannabis as a legitimate medicine, largely thanks to organizations like the Lindesmith Center, a drug policy institute funded by billionaire financier George Soros.

To Clinton, Barry McCaffrey must have seemed the perfect antidote to this headache. He was the youngest four-star general in the US Army and a former commander-in-chief of the US armed forces. And, with a massive $17.8 billion (£12.3 billion) federal drug control budget at his fingertips, he soon proved that his vehement anti-drugs pronouncements were not merely hot air. In 1998, less than two years into the job, 60,000 people were jailed for marijuana offences and a further 700,000 arrested for marijuana offences. McCaffrey was also keen to effect changes in the public's perception of the drug menace. Under his reign, around half of all American private companies introduced mandatory drug tests for their employees.

More controversially, he set up a covert arrangement with the TV networks in an effort to steer the nation's youth away from drugs. In exchange for a reduction in the number of mandatory public service announcements they must broadcast, McCaffrey's team were allowed to review scripts and see advance screenings of such popular teen programmes as *ER* and *Beverly Hills 90210* and suggest ways in which characters or plots could be changed to bolster the anti-drugs message.

When the lid was finally blown on the arrangement, there was understandable outrage in the Land of the Free. An editorial in *The New York Times* announced: 'In allowing government to shape or even be consulted on content in return for financial rewards, the networks are crossing a dangerous line they should not cross. On the far side of that line lies the possibility of censorship and state-sponsored propaganda.' Others claimed McCaffrey's arrangement was in direct contravention of the First Amendment, which guarantees the right to free speech.

Predictably, McCaffrey remained bullish in the face of his critics. 'It's been open, public and a wonderful thing because we're very proud that last year [1998] juvenile drug use declined by 13 per cent,' he said.

The storm was duly ridden. But, by the end of 2000, McCaffrey was beginning to realise that the writing was on the wall for him and his hard-line tactics. The Clinton administration was coming to an end, and the Bush campaign were strident in their claims that his war against drugs had failed, pointing out that while marijuana use among young Americans had declined, heroin and crack cocaine use had increased.

Moreover, the call for a radical rethink on drugs policy had expanded beyond the usual suspects that McCaffrey so despised. In June 2000, a number of respected judges from across the country went public in their calls for the restricted sale of cannabis, cocaine and heroin in order to break from what they saw as a vicious circle of violence and imprisonment. In a book entitled *Why Our Drugs Laws Have Failed And What We Can Do About It*, more than 20 judges also suggested allowing individual states to decide on what drugs policy suited them best. Judge James P Gray, of Orange County, California, launched a scathing attack on McCaffrey himself. 'Asking him [McCaffrey] whether the right drugs policy is being pursued, is like asking a barber if one needs a haircut,' he said.

In October 2000, McCaffrey announced he intended to step down from his position. Like the equally tough Harry Anslinger 50 years before, he had made his mark against the drugs menace – but in winning a few battles he came no closer to winning the war.

Barry McCaffrey's replacement, selected by President George W Bush, was former Republican Congressman Asa Hutchinson. But any hopes campaigners might have had that a new head of the DEA would herald new thinking about cannabis legislation – and especially medical use – appeared to be dashed in August 2001. Hutchinson made it clear that he intended to enforce the federal ban on medical marijuana, improve the accountability of paid confidential informants and increase the technology used in the war on drugs.

But spirits were raised somewhat in states like California and Oregon, which already allowed people to grow and dispense the drug on a strictly medicinal basis without fear of prosecution, when Hutchinson said: 'Currently, it's a violation of federal law. The question is how you address that from an enforcement standpoint. You're not going to tolerate a violation of the law, but at the same time there are a lot of different relationships...a lot of different aspects that we have to consider as we develop that enforcement policy.' They were also encouraged by the fact that, as Congressman, Hutchinson had supported local drug courts, which offer alternatives to prison.

The extent of Hutchinson's task – and McCaffrey's failure – was revealed when a survey monitoring drug use by teenagers placed cannabis as the drug of choice among juvenile offenders in the US. In the study, known as the 'Offender Urinalysis Screening Program', marijuana was found in urine samples of 44 per cent of those tested at the state Department of Juvenile Justice facility in Baltimore. Overall, 43 per cent of teenagers tested positive for at least one drug, primarily marijuana. About one per cent tested positive for cocaine, opiates or amphetamine.

The study was based on more than 800 juveniles as they entered state detention centres between May 1999 and June 2000. Inmates told researchers that many of their peers see cannabis 'the same as cigarettes' and that it is easier to obtain than alcohol because you need an ID to purchase beer and liquor.

### 'LEGALIZE IT!' – JAMAICA AND THE RASTAS

While the likes of The Beatles and The Rolling Stones took their cannabis lead from Bob Dylan, reggae star Bob Marley claimed to have an even more authoritative influence: God.

Genesis 1:12 says: '...and the earth brought forth grass, and herb yielding seed after his kind, and the tree yielding fruit, whose seed was in itself, after his kind: and God saw that it was good.' And Psalm 104:14 says: 'He causeth the grass to grow for the cattle, and herb for the service of Man...'

As a Rastafarian, Marley believed the instruction to smoke grass – or ganja as it is known in the Caribbean – came from nothing less than the Bible itself. And if you accept that by 'herb' the Bible is referring to cannabis and not chives, then Rasta logic is difficult to fault.

Rastafarians believe that Ras Tafari, Emperor Haile Selassie I of Ethiopia, who was crowned in 1930, is the living God. Their belief system originated in Jamaica in the 1920s. For believers, true salvation can only come to black people through repatriation to, or spiritual identification with, Africa. The smoking of ganja by Rastafarians is one aspect of the process by which they attempt to gain and develop insight into the central tenets of their beliefs. Bob Marley said that the smoking of ganja was to 'aid dere meditations on de truth'.

Cannabis had been taken to Jamaica by the East Indian labourers who replaced slave labour towards the end of the 19th century. The weed flourished and, happily for the locals, evolved into a particularly potent strain. Although the Rastafarians claim that they were influenced by biblical references, it has been pointed out that the use of ganja as a sacrament and aid to meditation is entirely logical in a country where it grows freely.

As the Rastafarian movement grew, the acceptance of use of 'the holy herb' grew with it. Since the 1960s its use has become an intrinsic part of Rastafarian culture and the religious reasons for its use unquestioned, although West Indian poet Linton Kwesi Johnson has his own, more mundane theory as to the drug's popularity in his homeland. He said: 'It [Rastafarianism] had a great deal which is positive in so far as it brought back to the masses a sense of dignity. It gave them a sense of pride in their African heritage which British colonialism has done a great deal to destroy. There are Rastas who...get high, and for a moment they can find themselves in Ethiopia at the foot of Selassie or sitting on the Golden Throne. But after the weed wears off...then it's back to the harsh and ugly reality of life.'

It may seem surprising that, despite its widespread use among the Rastafarian community, cannabis remains illegal in Jamaica. A main worry for the country's lawmakers is the risk of upsetting influential trade partners such as the USA by green-lighting free use of the drug. In the 1970s Jamaican politicians chose to ignore the findings of its own commission, which recommended no penalty for private use, a $10 (£6.90) fine for public use and that doctors should be able to prescribe marijuana. However, in October 1999, the Jamaican senate unanimously approved a resolution establishing another commission to explore the decriminalization of cannabis.

With the arrival of reggae music in the 1970s, cannabis culture had finally found its backing track. Reggae was predominantly the music of the Rastafarians, its laid-back chugging rhythm a perfect accompaniment to the state of ganja intoxication that the Rastas believed essential to their beliefs. Its emergence as a global phenomenon is largely down to one man: Bob Marley.

Born in St Ann, Jamaica, in 1945, the son of a white sailor and a black Jamaican teenager, Marley cut his teeth as a musician in local bars. And there he might have remained had he not, in 1967, been introduced to Rastafarianism. Marley embraced his new religion totally and, as a result, his own musical career was given a new impetus and direction. His songs of emancipation, spirituality and ganja enlightenment – the basic Rasta tenets – struck a chord not only in Jamaica but also around the world. Hits like 'I Shot The Sheriff', 'Stir It Up', 'Buffalo Soldier' and 'No Woman No Cry' made him an international star. And with albums entitled *African Herbsman* and *Kaya* (another name for ganja) he left people in no doubt about his influences. (Peter Tosh, a member of Marley's band The Wailers, was even more direct when he released an album called simply *Legalize It*.)

But Marley was keen for his message to be heard beyond the confines of the charts. He regarded himself as a Rasta prophet – and arch exponent of cannabis use. 'It's time to let the people get good herbs and smoke,' he said in 1976. 'Government's a joke. All they want is ya to smoke cigarettes and cigars. Some cigars are wickeder than herb. Yeah, man – you can't smoke cigars. Smoke herb.'

By 1975, Marley was clearly a revolutionary standard bearer, the inheritor of the 1960s activist energy and hippie ganja enlightenment. Almost assassinated in 1976 in Kingston, Marley was given the United Nations Peace Medal on behalf of 500 million Africans in 1978 for his humanitarian achievements. He headlined a Peace Concert that same year in Jamaica, uniting the warring factions in the Kingston slums. But his greatest honour came when he was invited to headline the Zimbabwe Independence Celebrations in 1980. A year later Marley was dead, aged 36, of cancer.

In July 2001, British Prime Minister Tony Blair arrived on a flying visit to Jamaica. He was a determined man. Jamaica was in the middle of its commission into the possible legalization of its drugs laws, and Blair – having recently ruled out across-the-board legalization back home (see p102) – was determined to put a spanner in the works of the Jamaican effort. His main concern was the fact that 30 recent murders in Britain had been linked to Caribbean drugs gangs, better known as Yardies. His belief was that legalizing cannabis and other drugs in Jamaica would open up lucrative markets to the Yardies in the UK and lead to yet more gangland violence. 'We really have to strengthen not just our trade and investment, but policing and law enforcement so that we can tackle this evil trade that does so much damage here and in the UK and in the rest of the world,' he said.

## DOPE CITY – AMSTERDAM AND THE 'DUTCH EXPERIMENT'

Amsterdam is the city of sex 'n' drugs 'n' *Van Der Valk*. To the oppressed cannabis smokers from other countries around the world, it may seem that to take a stroll down the Spuistraat, the Waterlooplein or the Nieumakt is akin to being a small child allowed free rein in a sweet shop. On every corner the tell-tale marijuana sign above a coffee house serves notice that here you can indulge in something exotic with your cappuccino. Inside, an aromatic fug assails the nostrils as you peruse the sort of menu you won't find in Betty's Tea Shop. Watch and learn as cannabis aficionados from all over the world sample the dozens of top-quality blends for sale. For just a few guilders you too can indulge in the delights of Black Hawaiian, Cytral Skunk, Thai, White Afghani or Kali Mist.

But even as you slip into a haze of dope-induced transcendence, there is one thing worth remembering. Cannabis, despite its abundance, its availability and its social setting, is actually illegal in the Netherlands. Marijuana has never been decriminalized in the Netherlands and outright legalization is a remote possibility. Instead, the Dutch authorities are the architects of a simple, but wholly unique approach to the drug: within reason, they turn a blind eye.

Up until 1976, however, it was a very different story. Drug offences were actively prosecuted and severely sanctioned, with such draconian punishment as 12 months imprisonment for minor cannabis offences being the norm. However, it soon became clear that despite the stiff sentences, cannabis use was rocketing, especially among Dutch youngsters. The pressure for reform began to bite during the cannabis-crazy 1960s – but whereas governments in the USA and the UK prevaricated and eventually introduced even stiffer penalties, in 1976 the enlightened Dutch acceded to popular demand and introduced the Opium Act.

The Act makes careful distinction between dangerous and less dangerous drugs. Penalties for trafficking heroin, cocaine and amphetamines are harsh and not open to debate. According to the Act, however, a number of activities are designated as 'not for prosecution, detection or arrest'. These include:

- the sale of less than 30g (1oz) of hemp products;
- dealing in, possessing or cultivating up to 5g ($\frac{1}{6}$oz) of marijuana.

And all the sales from coffee shops are taxed – an added bonus for the government.

As an experiment it was pioneering stuff. And so far the results have provided a slap in the face for those who argued that the country would end up staggering around in a pot-induced haze. Indeed, despite its availability, smoking pot remains a minority interest, with less than three per cent of Dutch people admitting to being regular tokers.

However, not everyone is convinced. There are claims that Holland is in the grip of a hard drugs frenzy directly related to the relaxed cannabis laws, with heroin addiction up 50 per cent, the highest rate of cocaine use among 14-16 year olds and increased use of amphetamines and drug-related crime.

Meanwhile recent United Nations figures estimate the global drugs trade to be worth a staggering $567 billion (£391 billion) annually – eight per cent of all global economic activity – and many European politicians see the Netherlands, and in particular Amsterdam, as an open gateway for drugs to pour into their own countries. It is a fact that, as far as many dealers are concerned, all roads lead to Amsterdam, and Liverpool's Curtis 'Cocky' Warren is by no means the first or last foreign drug tycoon to take up temporary residence in tolerant Holland. In 1996 French President Jacques Chirac made Europe's unease clear when he threatened to scrap the Schengen Agreement, which allows unfettered movement across Europe's borders, amid charges that Holland had become a 'narco state'.

## FROM IGNORANCE TO BLISS – CANNABIS IN THE UK

Despite decades of protests from dedicated recreational users – which have included full-page adverts in *The Times*, mass rallies and blatant public smoking – cannabis is illegal in the UK. Indeed, until the recent decision to reclassify cannabis from a Class B to a Class C drug, British law clamped down harder on cannabis than any other western country.

The seeds of cannabis's doom were sown as long ago as 1798. This was the year the British East India Company foundered on a reef of debt, and the British government felt obliged to bale out the Empire's trading flagship. In a bid to recoup its substantial losses, the Crown decided to impose a tax on certain Indian industries, including those involved with the production and refinement of the widely used cannabis-based drugs bhang, ganja and charna. The government defended the punitive Indian Hemp Tax by arguing that it was good for the well-being of the colony: ganja, cheap and potent, was the preferred drug of the downtrodden masses and was blamed by the ruling colonists for the increasing outbursts of social unrest. The colonists were, in fact, all in favour of total prohibition. But the government realised that the natives were quite happy to pay over the odds for their ganja, which resulted in a substantial tax revenue for them.

As in France and the USA, more experimental use of the drug was left to those who frequented illicit hashish houses in London. Perhaps the most famous of these was the Rhymer's Club, which used hash in order to create a sense of the occult. Although not as grand as the Club de Hashishins in Paris, which boasted such luminaries as Beaudelaire and Gaultier among its members, Rhymer's gained a reputation in Britain as being a place of ill-repute, with cannabis at the fore.

Throughout the 20th century, the British Home Office has always had a quaintly alarmist, if not faintly xenophobic, relationship with cannabis. Never sure how to deal with it, never fully convinced of its merits or deleterious effects, and always wary of its foreign origins, bureaucrats have time and again opted for the simple solution: keep it under lock and key in the furthest turret, and never mention its name at the dinner table.

The decision in 1911 by South Africa to ban cannabis – largely because of the effect it was having on its Indian diamond-mine workers – led to a raft of international anti-drug legislation. The Hague Convention of 1912 led to the wholesale banning of opium, heroin and cocaine but, although cannabis was mentioned, it escaped regulation because opium was seen as the greatest threat at that time.

The roots of the drug's prohibition in the UK are suitably bizarre, and begin in 1922 when Home Office analysts were sent a strange substance that had been discovered in the coal shed of an Egyptian coffee-house owner in South Shields on Tyneside. They soon identified the substance as 'hasheesh' – very odd, very suspicious, but not covered by the Dangerous Drugs Act of 1920. The following year, a ship bulging with 10 tonnes/tons of cannabis was detained in UK docks en route from Bombay to Djibouti. Again, the

Home Office was consulted and again, after much chin-stroking, it was decided that as it was not covered by the Dangerous Drugs Act, there was little they could do. But by now, cannabis was beginning to pop up often enough to become irritating. Matters came to a head later that year when two waiters from Italy and Sudan were arrested in Soho, London and accused of offering to supply raw opium. In fact, the substance was the legal hashish, and the men were released. This provoked one irate Home Office official to sound off in the *Daily Mail*, and the resulting media-fuelled controversy led to the police recommending that cannabis be included in the Dangerous Drugs Act, advising that it had 'practically the same effect as cocaine and morphine upon its victims'.

At the Home Office, pragmatism held sway. Officials noted that the result of cannabis prohibition in Egypt had merely been an increase in the price of the drug on the black market. To them, cannabis remained a mainly foreign curse that did not warrant legislation in this country. In the event, however, matters were taken out of their hands.

At the Geneva Conference on Opium in 1924–5, the Egyptians, overrun by hash, threw up their hands in despair and begged the League of Nations to bring in draconian international legislation to prevent its members from dealing or consuming the drug. To stress their point, the Egyptian delegate claimed cannabis was 'a dangerous narcotic, more harmful than opium', and that 'about 70 per cent of insane people in lunatic asylums in Egypt are hashish eaters or smokers'.

The Egyptian pleas were enthusiastically embraced by the Americans, who were keen to enlist their help in their ongoing battle against opium and cocaine. From that moment, it was only a matter of months before the Geneva Conference ratified a ban on the import and export of Indian hemp except for certified medical or scientific purposes. The edict was met with great relief in the UK, where the Home Office immediately rescheduled cannabis as a poison and, in 1925, added it to a revised Dangerous Drugs Act. The Bill was passed by Parliament in double quick time.

Very little changed over the next 30 years. In the 1950s, however, the authorities became aware that the definition of the drug was changing. The arrival of West Indian immigrants had led to a discernible increase in both use and interest in cannabis; and just as in New Orleans in the 1930s, it was the burgeoning jazz movement in London that raised the profile further. A series of raids in 1955 on jazz clubs netted only a handful of arrests, but served notice that the authorities were no longer prepared to turn a blind eye to cannabis use.

The advent of the 1960s, with flower-power influences from the USA and increasingly iconoclastic homegrown pop stars like The Beatles and The Rolling Stones, heralded the first major bust up between the pro-cannabis lobby and those who were against it. The Dangerous Drugs Act of 1964 created the new offence of cannabis cultivation. In 1966, folk singer Donovan was busted for possession fined £300 ($435) and warned ominously that 'it behoves you to behave yourself'. The arrest – and subsequent acquittal – of Mick Jagger and Keith Richards the following year proved that it would take more than the wagging finger of a magistrate to stop the growing tide of cannabis users in Britain.

The same year, 1967, a group called Soma – named after the narcotic in Aldous Huxley's *Brave New World* – published an open letter in *The Times* in which they denounced Britain's 40-year-old marijuana laws as 'immoral in principle and unworkable in practice'. The full-page letter was signed by more than 60 well-known names including David Dimbleby, Jonathan Aitken and all four Beatles. A few weeks later, more than 3,000 people turned up at Hyde Park in London for a Soma-organized 'smoke-in'. Shortly afterwards, the government-commissioned Wootton Report, a review of the current drugs policies, concluded that possession of pot should be legalized. However, the government's response was the Dangerous Drugs Act of 1967, which introduced national powers to stop and search people and vehicles for drugs. And four years later, the 1971 Misuse of Drugs Act put the boot into cannabis even harder.

According to the Act, cannabis plants and resin became Class B drugs, on a par with amphetamines, some barbiturates and tranquillizers and even codeine. Cannabis oil, however, was a Class A drug, alongside heroin, cocaine, crack, LSD, ecstasy and any Class B or C drug that has been prepared for injection.

The maximum penalties under the Misuse of Drugs Act were draconian indeed – although the prospect of serving five years inside for having a tiny amount of Lebanese Black in your pocket was remote, unless it was part of a huge stash you were smuggling in from Amsterdam, of course.

Even before the reclassification of cannabis in October 2001, the law was seen as an ass both by users and police officers. Far from acting as a deterrent against cannabis use or distribution, more and more people were happy to risk the usual punishment of an appearance in a magistrates' court. Why? Although the number of people dealt with for drugs offences involving cannabis rose from 40,194 in 1990 to 86,034 in 1997, less than 1,000 received custodial sentences.

According to one dealer, 'You get in front of the magistrate, you get a slap on the wrist and maybe a fine. It doesn't make any difference. You can get back the money you've had to cough up just by selling some more dope. I quite often end up selling gear to guys I've met in the waiting room in the court.'

Despite this derisory number of sentences, police forces across the country were obliged to devote much-needed manpower and hours to stop and searches. Over 300,000 were carried out for drugs in 1996-7 in England and Wales, bringing the total for four years to over a million. The swoop led to 134,500 arrests where drugs were found – the great majority of which were for cannabis.

Unrest was spreading, however. While the number of stop and searches had grown, the proportion where drugs had been found and arrests made had declined from 18 per cent in 1988 to 12 per cent in 1997–8. According to the Runciman Report of March 2000 (see pp100-2), stop and searches bore disproportionately on young people from minority ethnic communities in inner-city areas.

The police were equally hacked off with what they increasingly saw as a waste of their precious resources. Sir John Stevens, Commissioner of the Metropolitan police, said: 'Cannabis is a soft drug. If it were legalized we'd be fine with it because it's our job. Suppliers are still our emphasis.'

In 1969, a survey asked the British public whether cannabis should be legalized. One in eight agreed. In 1997, one in three agreed. With a new Labour government in power and a new mood of conciliation and debate surrounding the whole cannabis issue, it was clear that it was time for a new look at the cannabis situation in Britain.

'I'd be much more impressed if they criminalized alcohol and cigarettes,' says Fran Healy, lead singer of chart-topping band Travis. 'Nearly everybody in Britain smokes fucking hash, do you know what I mean? So whether or not it's legalized or not legal, you're just going to get a caution if you get done for it. It should be decriminalized but I'd rather people stop drinking. I hate drinking. Personally, I know someone who's a prosecutor for the state in Scotland and she says that all crime that they deal with – and they deal with a lot – at weekends and through the week, is drink-related. And never, ever, ever cannabis related. I think you're letting people get mad drunk and fighting and all that kind of stuff and there's loads and loads of things that are so stupid in law. But that's law. Law is stupid.'

Meanwhile Shaun Ryder, singer with The Happy Mondays, says: 'It's not harmful for you. It's good for you. If it does make you paranoid then you should stop smoking it. It doesn't make you go violent or crazy. You don't see anyone smoking three joints and then going and smashing someone's face in with a pint pot, do ya? That doesn't happen on marijuana. It's not a vicious drug. I don't know why it's illegal.'

These are, of course, viewpoints we might expect from members of the music industry, who have traditionally smoked cannabis on an industrial scale for years. But when it comes to decriminalization, Healy and Ryder have some influential and surprisingly 'Establishment' backers. According to Peregrine Worsthorne, former editor of *The Sunday Telegraph*, criminalizing cannabis is 'a ridiculous thing to do – even more ridiculous than the American Prohibition idea, which, of course, was a terrible flop. You can't pass a law which a significant minority are not going to pay any attention to. You can't get crazier than that. I have smoked it. It wasn't for me. I'm an alcohol addict, so I didn't need anything extra. But so many friends do smoke it. It's now just a common occurrence.'

In 1998, the Police Foundation – the independent charitable research organization of which Prince Charles is a member – set up a committee to look at the drugs problem in Britain. Its brief was similar to that of the Wootton Committee 30 years earlier. And, like the Wootton Report, when the Runciman Report was published in March 2000, its conclusions were political dynamite.

The committee was chaired by Dame Ruth Runciman, a 64-year-old veteran of campaigns and committees, and no stranger to controversy. A founding member of the Prison Reform Trust, which has campaigned for fewer criminals to be jailed and more lenient treatment of those who are imprisoned, Dame Runciman once said she had spent decades in public service on committees concerned with care of 'the sad, the mad and the bad.' In 1974, she was appointed by Labour Home Secretary Roy Jenkins to the Advisory Council on the Misuse of Drugs, serving until 1995. She also chaired an independent inquiry into the Misuse of Drugs Act in 1979, which recommended a relaxation in the laws on illegal substances.

The scope of the committee's investigations was vast, and included evidence from organizations as wide ranging as the Catholic Bishops Conference of England and Wales to the Cardiff Street Drugs Project. A number of surveys were commissioned into public attitudes towards drugs –

and particularly cannabis. The committee also spent a week in Holland, talking to Dutch legislators and law-enforcers. For the most part, they were mightily impressed with what they observed. The committee concluded:

> *We think that the Dutch experience holds two important lessons for the United Kingdom. The first is the potential benefit from treating the possession and personal use of all drugs – not just cannabis – primarily as health problems. This should ensure that young people who experiment with drugs remain integrated into society rather than becoming marginalized. The second is the potential benefit from separating the market for cannabis from that of heroin. By doing so, the Dutch have provided persuasive evidence against the gateway theory of cannabis use, and in favour of the theory that if there is a gateway it is the illegal marketplace.*

But the committee also noted:

> *We recognize that, in the present political and cultural climate, it is difficult to see the introduction of Dutch-style coffee shops in the United Kingdom. The contradictions between domestic and international law and these practices are too great. The Dutch may be able to live with them, but they*

*are likely to cause greater difficulties here. Nevertheless there may be developments that move us towards the Dutch experience, particularly as greater autonomy is devolved to local communities.*

The committee's final conclusions on the cannabis question were unequivocal and scathing about the current state of the laws:

*The present law on cannabis produces more harm than it prevents... It inevitably bears more heavily on young people in the streets of inner cities, who are also more likely to be from ethnic minority communities.*

*Cannabis is the drug most likely to bring people into contact with the criminal justice system. It is, by far, the drug most widely and commonly used. It is the drug most often involved in the main drug offences and is the drug that is most often seized. Because of the frequent use of discretion by the police and customs, it is the drug where there is the widest gap between the law as formulated and the law as practised.*

*Cannabis is also less harmful than the other main illicit drugs, and understood by the public to be so. If our drugs legislation is to be credible, effective and able to support a realistic programme of*

*prevention and education, it has to strike the right*
*balance between cannabis and other drugs.*

The report's main recommendations were that cannabis
should be transferred from Class B to Class C, and that
possession for personal use should no longer be an
imprisonable offence.

The 148-page report took two years to compile and
concluded that implementation of their recommendations
would 'bring the law into line with public opinion and its
most loyal ally, common sense'. However, it took the Labour
government just a few short hours to summarily dismiss
its findings. A government statement said: 'We don't support
the recommendations for a reclassification. The Prime
Minister believes that whilst it is right that the greatest
harm is done by hard drugs, it would send out the worst
possible signal if we were to soften our laws in the way
being suggested.'

If the Runciman Report was rubbished by the
government, its immediate legacy was a major public debate
about the pros and cons of legalizing cannabis for
recreational and medical use, and a furious backlash from
users sick of having their arguments summarily thrown
back in their faces.

Arguments raged in the press as advocates from both
sides took up their cudgels. Indeed the debate at times
assumed an almost surreal edge as traditionally left-wing

and liberal newspapers like the *Guardian* and *The Independent* were joined by staunch right-wing publications *The Times*, the *Sunday Telegraph* and even the arch-conservative *Daily Mail* in calling for a sensible debate over the matter. Although they avoided calling for an all-out decriminalization of recreational cannabis, even the most fervent of right-wing commentators were in favour of it for medical use. And all were infuriated by the government's intransigence and refusal to even entertain a debate.

'Those who have argued for decriminalization in the past have been dope heads,' said *The Daily Telegraph* editor Charles Moore. 'We don't think drugs are a good thing but we want a debate.'

Suddenly, policy makers were being asked awkward questions – especially those who were bright young things in the Swinging '60s. Asked on a television debate whether she had ever tried cannabis, former Northern Ireland Secretary Mo Mowlam said she had, that she had inhaled and that she hadn't enjoyed it. Meanwhile maverick Labour backbencher Clare Short observed that, 'If the press asked every member of the Cabinet if they had ever tried cannabis, most of them would have to lie.'

One of the more controversial comments came from Sir John Stevens, commissioner of the Metropolitan police and Britain's leading policeman. He said: 'Smoking cannabis is not a priority because we have to concentrate on the upsurge in robberies and murders in London. If you go to the Tube in London and don't pay, that also is not a priority for the police, but if we catch someone doing it then we have to enforce the law. Arresting people for cannabis is low on my list of priorities.'

Opponents of cannabis were caught somewhat flat-footed in the face of such Establishment revisionism, but they soon fought back. Home Office minister Charles Clarke – who himself admitted smoking marijuana as a student – laid down the government line, indicating that there were no plans to de-penalize possession of cannabis: 'I believe the most likely impact of a relaxation in the law would be to increase consumption of those drugs. I think that would be bad for the people concerned and bad for society.'

Janet Betts, whose daughter Leah died after taking ecstasy, said: 'We already have decriminalized drugs. If a person found with drugs can convince a police officer they are for their own use, they get nothing more than an instant caution. If cannabis is decriminalized, what is next? Ecstasy?'

Meanwhile Paul Stoker, director of the National Drugs Prevention Alliance pointed out: 'The fact that more people who use cannabis go on to abuse hard drugs is beyond argument. There are now more reasons than ever to keep cannabis illegal.'

The British Medical Association trundled out its usual line on the risks of cannabis smoking: 'Smoking a cannabis cigarette leads to three times greater tar inhalation than smoking a cigarette. Chronic cannabis smoking increases the risk of cardiovascular diseases, bronchitis, emphysema and probably lung cancer.'

But it was left to the then Home Secretary, Jack Straw, to put the final word on the debate:

> *Cannabis is a controlled drug for good scientific reasons. Both the World Health Organization and our own BMA have repeatedly concluded that cannabis is harmful. Were cannabis legalized, it is highly probable that consumption would rise. The price would fall as the premium in the price today for the criminal risk which dealers carry fell away and as dealers piled into the UK from across Europe. The more government tried to choke off demand by taxing cannabis, the greater the incentive for criminals to engage in smuggling. There are many, of course, who are prepared to break the law at present to take cannabis, but the fact that it is illegal does limit its use. I accept that making cannabis legal would not necessarily greatly increase addiction to hard drugs... But what would almost certainly happen is that the UK would take over from the Netherlands as the European drug trade.*

Despite the fact her report had been put on the back burner indefinitely by the government, Lady Ruth Runciman remained defiant. 'My report will have a longer shelf-life than this government,' she said.

Ironically, it was to be a leading member of the main opposition party whose ill-judged opinions of cannabis law were to give the most startling indication of how opinions had changed...

When Shadow Home Secretary Ann Widdecombe stood up to address the Conservative Party at their annual conference in October 2000, she had a bombshell to deliver:

*Today I am able to announce a new policy. Earlier this year I visited New York, where under Mayor Giuliani crime has plummeted. Although we can't replicate exactly what I saw there, we can learn the lessons of tackling crime head on and not conceding a centimetre to the criminals. So today, I can announce a new policy. A policy that means no quarter for those whose trade is dealing in human misery, despair and even death. And so, from, the possession of the most minimal amount of soft drugs right up the chain to the large importer, there will be no hiding place. There will be zero tolerance.*

*Parents want it. Schools need it. Our future demands it. The next Conservative government will do it. What does it mean? It means zero tolerance of possession. No more getting away with just a caution, no more hoping that a blind eye will be turned. If someone possesses drugs, the minimum* *for a first offence will be £100 ($145). But not for a second offence. Then it's into court.*

Almost immediately after her speech, critics were lining up to take a pop at Widdecombe. Leading the way was the Police Superintendents' Association, which pointed out that the manpower and resources needed to lock up every person they found in possession of the smallest amount of cannabis would be astronomical. Not only that, but a hard-line approach to drugs would do much to destroy the fragile co-existence the police force had been trying to build up with an increasingly cynical public.

'They have got completely the wrong end of the stick,' Widdecombe explained hurriedly. 'They thought they would have to do it on present resources, and secondly they thought it would remove all discretion.'

Seeing her grand scheme disintegrating before her eyes, Widdecombe made a desperate attempt to salvage some face. 'The use of the phrase zero tolerance in this area was unfortunate because everybody has their own interpretation of what zero tolerance is,' she said. 'I should have made it clear that zero tolerance does not mean you come down on every single instance of possession. It means you challenge every instance, but the police have got to have the right to decide whether they do go forward. I was trying to ensure that where they did want to go forward, they have more teeth than now.'

Sadly for Ann Widdecombe, it was left to Liberal Democrat leader Charles Kennedy to sum up the true impact of her speech. 'She has performed a public service in the past few days by showing how far public attitudes have changed.'

## A POWERLESS DRUGS TSAR AND A REVOLUTIONARY HOME SECRETARY

We have already encountered ass-kicking General Barry McCaffrey, the man charged by Bill Clinton with ridding the United States of the drugs menace. Following Clinton's lead, in 1998 Tony Blair appointed a drugs tsar of his own in the shape Keith Hellawell, former Chief Constable of both Cleveland and West Yorkshire forces. In many ways, Hellawell was the complete antithesis of McCaffrey: a thoughtful, self-effacing man who believed fervently that the drugs issue was not one that was simply black and white. Two different tsars, two different cultures, two different approaches. Yet by 2001, both had been perceived as having failed dismally in the battle against drugs, and both were looking for new jobs.

As drugs tsar, Hellawell believed there should be drug workers active in every police station and in every school, and listening to those involved in the drug world – especially addicts. Initially, the results were encouraging. After a year in the job, Hellawell's methods were attracting the attention of experts from around the world who were fascinated by this cutting edge approach to the drug conundrum.

One of Hellawell's innovations was the appointment of an anti-drugs chief to every council in the country, a move that was designed to dispense with campaigns run by police, health and educational authorities and other agencies.

But things started to go wrong for Hellawell just as the public perception on cannabis began to change. Those who imagined him as a breath of fresh air in the debate about specific legalization (he had advocated it when Chief Constable) were sorely disappointed when he sided firmly with the government over the rejection of the Runciman Report. They were also dismayed when he failed to stand by his nominal boss, Mo Mowlam, who argued for a clearer demarcation between hard and soft drugs.

But most of all they could not believe that a policeman who had identified and improved social problems in areas like Bradford, could not seem to grasp the damning statistic that although Britain's anti-drugs laws were the harshest in Europe, its population still consumed the most hard and soft drugs.

When David Blunkett took over from Jack Straw in the Home Office in May 2001, Hellawell's days were numbered. By the time Blunkett sidelined him, he was a sad and peripheral Whitehall figure. 'He leaves a strategy which still places far too much emphasis on police and customs and far too little on treatment and education,' said the *Guardian* newspaper.

The appointment of David Blunkett to the job of Home Secretary had an immediate effect on Britain's cannabis laws. Blunkett, it appeared, not only agreed with the thrust of the Runciman Report, but was prepared to act upon it, and quickly. His first move was to take over control of drugs policy from Mo Mowlam. He then began to exercize a series of measures that would have been inconceivable a few short weeks earlier. In July 2001, just two months into the job, Blunkett gave his tacit go-ahead to police in Brixton, South London, who wanted to abandon prosecuting people caught with cannabis. Instead, they would be given a 'stiff telling off', and their stash confiscated. In effect, it was the equivalent of the old-fashioned clip round the ear from the local bobby. According to the area commander, Brian Paddick, there was little point in two officers spending hours charging a suspect only for them to be fined £25 ($36) in the magistrates court.

The Brixton experiment was initially a six-month trial only, and applied to people found with only small amounts of the drug in their possession – but to the legalization lobby, it was a ray of sweet sunshine.

Sir David Ramsbotham, the outgoing chief inspector of prisons, said: 'The more I think about it and the more I look at what's happening, the more I can see the logic of legalizing drugs, because the misery that is caused by the people who are making a criminal profit is so appalling, and the sums are so great that are being made illegally that I think there is merit in legalizing and prescribing, or whatever, so people don't have to go and find an illegal way of doing it.'

In the face of such pro-legalization glee, Blunkett suddenly appeared to turn cagey. A week after the start of the Brixton experiment, he made it clear that he was not opening the door to legalization and insisted there was 'no easy way forward'. He also opposed a Royal Commission on the legalization of drugs, proposed by the Liberal Democrats. But, clearly not wanting to be regarded as another big talking, no-action politician, he did something that no other Home Secretary had done regarding the cannabis issue: he hedged his bets. 'There is room for an adult, intelligent debate,' Blunkett said, 'but it isn't "Are you for or against?" It's "Let's think, let's consider, let's not be pushed by articles in newspapers or hysteria."'

In Brixton, meanwhile, the radical policy was credited with freeing up hundreds of hours of police time and allowing them to concentrate on more serious crime – but many residents claimed it gave the dealers a new-found confidence and made even hard drugs more widely available than before. Many dealers were soon boasting of having received three or four separate warnings since the new scheme began. One shopkeeper said: 'In the last few months, all the dealers have become more confident. They think they're untouchable.'

In the six months before the scheme, 278 arrests for possession were made. In the six months that followed, more than 400 warnings for possession were issued. For many, this is proof that the area is now a magnet for drug buyers across London.

There was still a chink of light but the door had, to all intents and purposes, been shut again. It would not remain that way for long.

What with the Brixton experiment and Blunkett's debate, one of the more extraordinary developments in the serpentine history of cannabis and the UK law went largely unnoticed. A shadowy organization consisting of the heads of MI6, MI5, the Customs and Excise investigation branch, the National Criminal Intelligence Service, the police National Crime Squad and the Association of Chief Police Officers, not to mention the permanent under-secretaries of the Home Office, Foreign Office and Ministry of Defence had all been discussing Britain's on-going battle with drug smugglers. The conclusions of the Cabinet Office Committee, Concerted Inter-Agency Drugs Action (CIDA) amounted to the most radical shift in drugs policy for a generation. Under the new strategy, Britain was to abandon the hunt for cannabis smugglers and dealers. Instead, large-scale cannabis seizures and prosecutions would only take place as a by-product of investigations into Class A drugs like cocaine and heroin.

'It's not that we plan to stop seizing cannabis when we come across it,' one senior Customs source said. 'However, the need to focus on Class A drugs means cannabis seizures will now take place as a by-product, not as an end in themselves.'

What the source was referring to was the government's avowed drugs target of reducing Class A consumption by half by 2008. With shock statistics revealing that Britons were now consuming up to 36,000kg (80,000lb) of heroin and 41,000kg (90,000lb) of cocaine – twice as much as previous official estimates for the whole of western Europe – cannabis users had suddenly paled into insignificance.

On 23 October 2001, Home Secretary David Blunkett finally did what UK pro-cannabis campaigners had clamoured for, but never dared believe would ever happen. On that day Blunkett announced that the UK's laws covering cannabis were to be eased so possession would no longer be an arrestable offence. Although the drug would remain illegal under Blunkett's proposals, it would be re-classified from a Class B to a Class C drug – alongside mild amphetamines, tranquillizers such as temazepam and Valium and anabolic steroids. He said that the aim was to free police to concentrate on harder drugs and improve current legislation so it will 'make more sense' to people on the street.

But he was careful not to suggest this was a complete relaxation of cannabis laws. Possession and supply would remain a criminal offence, attracting maximum sentences of five years for supply and two for possession. But he hinted that police, rather than arresting people caught with cannabis, would be more likely to issue a warning, a caution or a court summons.

Meanwhile, Blunkett announced that the licensing of cannabis derivatives for medical use – such as the relief of multiple sclerosis symptoms – would be given government backing if trials proved to be successful. 'We believe it is right to look at the re-categorization of cannabis,' the Home Secretary told a House of Commons Home Affairs Select Committee. 'I shall therefore be putting to the Advisory Council on the Misuse of Drugs a proposal that we should re-categorize cannabis to 'C' rather than 'B', thereby allowing police to concentrate their resources on Class 'A' drugs – crack cocaine and heroin in particular – and to ensure that whilst they are able to deal with those pushing and dealing in drugs in exactly the same way as they can at the moment, it will both lighten their load and make more sense on the streets than it does at the moment.'

The reclassification of cannabis was seen as the greatest decision ever taken by a Home Secretary, or as the worst, depending on your viewpoint. Within hours of Blunkett's announcement, proponents from both sides of the argument were clashing heads in a battle that promises to rage on and on for years to come.

Veteran journalist and pro-cannabis activist Rosie Boycott said: 'He is too cautious for my taste.'

Meanwhile Susan Greenfield, Professor of Pharmacology at Oxford University argued: '...through decriminalization, we will encourage the development of a society where millions of young people are demotivated, thinking about only their next fix instead of looking at broader horizons, regarding drugs as the solution to all their problems.'

Greenfield's words were backed up by a report that came out around the same time in which England and Wales were dubbed the drug 'capitals' of the European Union, with more cannabis users than any other member state. In the survey, nearly 1 in 10 adults admitted having taken cannabis within the previous 12 months, the highest in the EU. Britain also had the largest number of young users, with 2 in 5 15- and 16-year-olds saying they have experimented.

## SAME OLD STORY – CANNABIS LAWS IN THE REST OF THE WORLD

### AUSTRALIA

Penalties for cannabis offences vary from state to state. Since the '70s several states have lessened penalties for possession, cultivation and use of small amounts of cannabis. In 1987 South Australia, followed in 1992 by the Australian Capital Territories, introduced expiation notice schemes, which required on-the-spot fines for minor cannabis offences; if the fine is paid promptly, no court appearance or criminal record is necessary but, if not, a court appearance will follow. Recently, the Northern Territory, Victoria and Western Australia have followed suit and introduced cautioning. The trend of reducing penalties for possession has been matched by harder penalties for supply.

## AUSTRIA
Use is a criminal offence, resulting in a fine or custodial sentence.

## BELGIUM
On 21 April 1998 Belgium officially decriminalized cannabis, which means, in practice, that those caught in possession for personal consumption will not be prosecuted but industrial production and dealing will not be tolerated. In 2001, it announced that, under radical plans approved by the cabinet, it will soon be legal to grow, import and consume potentially unlimited amounts of pot for personal use in Belgium. 'Any possession of cannabis for personal consumption will no longer provoke a reaction from the justice system unless its use is considered to be problematic or creates a social nuisance,' the Health Minister, Magda Aelvoet, said. Legislation is due to be passed by the end of 2002.

## CANADA
In 2001, Canada became the first country to legalize cannabis for medical use. This effectively undid its 1961 Federal Narcotic Control Act, which made it illegal to possess, traffic, possess for trafficking, cultivate, import or export cannabis.

## CUBA
In February 1999, the Cuban parliament approved a law

that introduced the death penalty for the possession, production, and trafficking of drugs.

## CZECH REPUBLIC

In January 1999, despite the efforts of former President and 1960s hippie Vaclev Havel, the Czech government made 'more than a small amount' of marijuana illegal. Before this law was drafted, marijuana was technically legal for personal consumption.

## DENMARK

Cannabis is allowed to be grown, sold and consumed in an area that is part of Copenhagen. Unfortunately, the people who live there are mostly poor and the area is quite run down, which gives cannabis a bad image in the press.

## EGYPT

In 1868, possession was made a capital offence. In 1874, importation was allowed but not possession. Then in 1879 importation was again made illegal and in 1884 growing also became a criminal offence. These laws were reissued in 1891 and 1894. It is still illegal today, although many locals smoke. Crops in the Sinai are being destroyed and westerners are being given long sentences by the courts.

## FINLAND

Use remains a criminal offence.

## FRANCE

According to Article 630 of the French public health regulations, French citizens are banned from 'portraying in a favourable light and promoting or inciting the consumption of any product classed as a banned substance.'

In theory, the possession and selling of cannabis is banned and anyone caught importing just a few grams can be jailed for up to 30 years. Yet figures indicate that some 7 million of the country's 60 million population have tried the drug at least once, while 2 million are regular users.

## GERMANY

Germany's narcotic laws prohibit the importing, exporting and processing of cannabis, although cultivation of cannabis as a beet-breeding agent is allowed provided the plants do not flower. Smoking a joint is illegal, but a landmark ruling from Germany's constitutional court in 1994 means possession of small amounts for personal use is not usually prosecuted.

## GREECE

The Greek authorities have stopped prosecuting those in possession of small amounts of cannabis. In 1999 stiff prison sentences for possessing recreational drugs such as marijuana were revoked, although smokers caught red-handed are still required to have long periods of counselling. The state has also funded the opening of 36 therapeutic and drug prevention centres in less than a year.

## GREENLAND

In remote Greenland the government authorities are fighting a losing battle against what is a thriving trade in the weed. 'The drug is illegal, but it is impossible to fight the massive cannabis trade in Greenland as it involves the whole of society' said Hans Haahr, chief of Greenland's Drug Squad.

The Drug Squad estimates that the trade in cannabis is worth US $75 million (£52 million), which is equivalent to nearly 10 per cent of the annual gross national product, including the economic assistance from Denmark. This makes the cannabis trade Greenland's third largest industry measured in annual turnover.

## INDIA

Confusion and corruption surrounding the drugs laws abound in India – but the safest policy is not to be caught smoking cannabis. The Indian government has clamped down, making little distinction between soft and hard drugs. Anyone charged with illegal possession risks a mandatory ten-year jail sentence and, under Indian law, you are guilty until proved innocent. In 1997, the *Footprint Guidebook To Goa* warned that in the 18 months following November 1995, 21 foreigners were imprisoned for drug offences. The local police deny that bribery is rife, but many more foreigners who have been caught smoking joints admit they have bought their way out of trouble.

IRELAND
Use is a criminal offence, but first- and second-time offenders are only fined. Thereafter custodial sentences can be awarded.

ITALY
Since April 1998 possession of drugs for personal consumption and small-scale cultivation of cannabis are no longer criminal offences. This move followed a 1992 referendum in which 52 per cent were in favour of decriminalizing possession of cannabis. Possession is now subject to administrative sanctions rather than criminal prosecution, but cultivation, sale and delivery remain illegal. Loopholes in the present law allow personal use but not personal cultivation.

JAPAN
Cannabis was made illegal in Japan by the post-World War II occupying US administration in 1948 – even though it grows abundantly in the wild. Every year in Japan over a million wild cannabis plants are destroyed by narcotics agents. Possession of cannabis can bring prison sentences of up to five years and cultivating or trading in cannabis up to seven years.

LUXEMBOURG
In May 2001, a groundbreaking bill decriminalized cannabis, making its personal use and possession a civil, as opposed to criminal, offence and therefore subject only to fines.

## MALAYSIA

Definitely not the place to be caught with an eighth in your back pocket. Malaysia's drug laws prescribe the mandatory death penalty for people trafficking in more than 15g (½oz) of heroin or 200g (7oz) of cannabis. More than 100 people, around a third of them foreigners, have been hanged in Malaysia for drug offences since the mandatory death sentence for trafficking was introduced two decades ago.

## MOROCCO

African and Asian countries may give the appearance that cannabis is already legal but it remains illegal and many foreigners have to buy their way out of trouble. However, many of the locals smoke it themselves – especially kif, a mixture of leaf cannabis and black (illegal) tobacco. In the Katama area in the north, in the mountains, huge crops of cannabis are grown, providing valuable income through sales to the rest of the world. Possession is not prosecuted in Katama. Elsewhere in Morocco it is usually possible to bribe your way out of a court appearance, which is why police often arrest foreigners.

## NEW ZEALAND

In March 1999, the New Zealand government ruled out the legalization of cannabis. Indeed it went so far as to propose a ban on paraphernalia such as pipes or bongs, with a maximum three-month jail sentence and £1,000 (US$1,500) fine for anyone caught in possession. However east of Auckland, on the rugged Coromandel peninsular, a quiet rebellion is under way. It was here in recent elections that the rest of New Zealand was shocked when seven Green Party MPs were returned to Parliament. By far the most controversial was Nandor Tanczos, a young dreadlock-sporting, dope-smoking Rastafarian. Tanczos and his Green colleagues are dead set on reforming the drug laws and, more specifically, on legalizing cannabis – and they have the support of many young people. According to recent research, more than half of New Zealand's population between the ages of 15 and 45 admit to having used pot, which is the highest per-capita rate in the world.

NORWAY
Use is a criminal offence but authorities are often lenient and only impose a fine for small quantities. In extreme cases, offenders can be locked up for six months.

POLAND
In Poland it is legal to possess small amounts of cannabis for personal use.

PORTUGAL
Despite a reputation for being one of the most socially and religiously conservative countries in Europe, in July 2001 Portugal took everyone by surprise – not least its drug users

– by decriminalizing the use of all narcotics, from cannabis to crack. The reasoning behind the amazing move was summed up by Portugal's drugs tsar Vitalino Canas: 'Why not change the law to recognize that consuming drugs can be an illness or a route to illness? America has spent billions on enforcement but it has got nowhere. We view drug users as people who need help and care.'

## RUSSIA

Up until the 1970s, marijuana was only used in the remote Asian territories of the former Soviet Union. Most of the population preferred vodka. But the hippie revolution in the USA sent ripples as far as Moscow, and in certain bohemian circles it became de rigueur to smoke dope. Today, while alcohol is still the drug of choice among most Russians, almost all young people will admit to having smoked cannabis. They have also developed their own cannabis culture. For a start, instead of rolling the traditional spliff, they prefer to smoke 'papiroses' – short, stubby cigarettes without filters that are infiltrated with weed called 'kosyak'. In the southern regions there is even a popular drink consisting of marijuana boiled with milk fat and butter.

Conviction for buying or selling cannabis can result in imprisonment for between three and seven years. However, the low-paid Russian police are quite happy to accept bribes.

### SINGAPORE
Adults caught trafficking more than 510g (8oz) of cannabis face the death penalty.

### SPAIN
The Spanish authorities prohibit the personal use of cannabis but seldom prosecute for possession of small amounts – whether or not to arrest is left to the discretion of the police. Personal possession is now legally defined as up to 50g (1¾oz), but anything over that is considered to be a public health hazard.

### SWEDEN
Of all of the European countries, Sweden has the harshest anti-cannabis legislation. Indeed, its attitude verges on the paranoid. In 1988 drug use was criminalized and in 1993 the penalty for drug consumption was increased to six months imprisonment. Police have the power to apprehend anyone they even think looks as if they are under the influence of a drug and can take them to a police station and force them to undergo blood and urine tests.

### SWITZERLAND
Concern is growing in Switzerland because a legal loophole allows cannabis to be cultivated openly on farms and sold over the counter or via the Internet as 'hemp'. Unlike most European countries, Switzerland allows cannabis to be

grown legally while prohibiting its use as a drug. In the Alps, cannabis has enjoyed a revival among growers in recent years and is cultivated to produce textiles and cosmetics, to flavour food products and even to brew hemp beer. Dozens of hemp farms have sprung up in Switzerland in the past five years along with 150 hemp shops, where hemp products are sold together with marijuana. To cover themselves legally, the shops pack the dried weed in cellophane and then barcode, price and label it as 'hemp tea', 'dried flowers', 'organic buds' and 'scent sachets'. As a result, Switzerland has become Europe's biggest hemp producer, with 200 tonnes/tons produced every year and a turnover of £200 million ($290 million).

TURKEY
Punitive sentences are issued for anyone caught trafficking drugs.

**CANNABIS – THE NUTS AND BOLTS**

Apart from its distinctive barbed leaves, the cannabis plant is strangely unremarkable and flimsy for one that has so successfully divided the world. In narcotic form, it assumes a totally different form. (This is made from the female plant as the male does not contain the necessary cannabinoids.) There are three distinct types:

- **Herbal** - The dried leaves and flowers of the plant, usually rolled in cigarette paper and smoked. Common street names: marijuana, grass, dope, draw, puff, blow, weed, gear, spliff, ganja, herb, wacky baccy, green, bud, skunk.

- **Resin** - Made by compressing the sap on the leaves and stems into blocks. Usually crumbled into tobacco, rolled and smoked. It can be eaten in cakes and biscuits. Common street names: hash, pot, dope, shit, black, gold, slate, squidgy.

- **Oil** - Formed when the resin is dissolved in a solvent and then allowed to evaporate. The oil can be then mixed with tobacco and smoked or it can be smeared on cigarette paper. Common street names: honey, oil, diesel.

**THE DRUG AND HOW IT WORKS**

The most active chemical in cannabis is delta9-tetrahydrocannabinol (THC). Cannabis creates a 'high' by affecting strategic locations in the brain, including:

- the hippocampus, where linear thinking takes place;

- the cerebellum, which co-ordinates movement and balance;

- the rostral ventromedial medulla, which modifies the intensity of pain sensations.

Recent research has identified natural brain chemicals similar to cannabinoids. Known as anandamides, these chemicals latch onto receptors in the brain to block pain and also help regular sleep patterns. THC latches onto the same receptors. Proponents of cannabis argue that THC is therefore utilizing existing pathways and does not contaminate the brain. Opponents claim that THC 'pirates' the brain's communication network, stealing receptors that should only be used by the brain's chemicals and therefore risking permanent changes to the brain's chemical make-up. The fact that the cannabis debate cannot be resolved at its most basic level is also its most fundamental problem.

## THE EFFECTS OF CANNABIS

When it comes to the effect of cannabis, whether psychological or physical, you can take your pick whose propaganda to believe. During the anti-marijuana purges of 1930s America, the official line was that cannabis was a menace that systematically turned the youth of the day into raving lunatics, mentally, physically and spiritually bankrupt and liable to commit heinous crimes at any time in order to feed their evil habit. Modern opponents are not quite so rabid, preferring instead to include cannabis within the general 'drugs menace' at large and, in particular, as a springboard to hard drugs such as heroin and cocaine.

Equally, cannabis can appear to have absolutely no effect on some people. Those in favour of cannabis argue that not only does it give a mellow, non-addictive high with no proven medical downside, but that 3,000 years' reliance upon its pharmaceutical properties are proof positive of its health benefits.

In the short term, the effect of cannabis depends largely upon the user's mental state before using, the environment and the user's expectations. Cannabis causes perceptual changes that make the user more aware of other people's feelings, enhance the enjoyment of music and give a general feeling of euphoria.

'I think the thing that pisses a lot of anti-cannabis people off is that they think people who smoke are just giggling idiots,' says barman Rudi Dale, 21. 'But they don't get it. I mean, what else can make you split your sides like that? I remember one time me and my buddy were stoned and we laughed for 20 minutes solid 'cos he'd dropped an egg on the floor. It's stupid I know, but I'd rather be laughing than be miserable. People need a laugh 'cos it's a tough life out there. I'm all for it.'

But cannabis can also make the user feel agitated and even paranoid if they are in a situation that is not pleasant – such as if they are with strangers or are trying to hide the fact that they are using it. In extreme moments, the user can feel that everything said around them is directed at them in a malicious and hurtful way.

'I just couldn't be doing with it,' says student Jane Peele. 'It made me on edge like you wouldn't believe. Everybody would be laughing and I'd be thinking they were laughing at me because I was stupid or because I was ugly or something like that. Even hours later the effects would still be there. I'd lie awake in a cold sweat, my heart racing, thinking that I was going to get into trouble because I'd smoked a joint. Now I just don't do it.'

Cannabis causes a number of physical changes including an increased pulse rate, a decrease in blood pressure, the alleviation of excess pressure in the eye, an opening of the airway leading to the lungs and suppression of the vomit reflex. But it can also produce bloodshot eyes, dry mouth, dizziness and an increased appetite – the dreaded 'munchies' in which a fridge full of food can be consumed in seconds. Sometimes short-term memory loss (ie the last couple of minutes) can also occur, although this passes as the effects of the drug wear off. However recent research by the McLean Hospital in Belmont, Massachusetts, found that mental function in heavy users was inhibited for 24 hours after the subjects had smoked pot – long after the high had gone.

Cannabis is also fat soluble, and so someone who regularly uses a large amount of the drug may store some of it in his or her body. It can take up to 30 days for this to be fully cleared by the body.

### 'IT'S NEVER KILLED NO ONE'

Cannabis aficionados boast that no one has ever been recorded as having died of an overdose. This may well be true: to fatally overdose on cannabis it is estimated that you would need to eat about 675g (24oz) of resin in one sitting – which is one big cake. To many experts, the problems with cannabis are less physical and more psychological and social.

However, doctors point out that cannabis smoke contains many of the same toxic chemicals as tobacco smoke, including carcinogens such as tar, carbon monoxide and cyanide. Occasional users do not generally inhale enough smoke to affect the linings of the trachea and bronchial tubes. Heavy users, though, often experience the respiratory problems that 20-a-day cigarette smokers do, such as chronic bronchitis and the exacerbation of asthma. Small-scale studies of chronic cannabis-users' lungs have revealed abnormal changes in bronchial cells, indicating an increased risk of cancer, and many scientists believe that cannabis's lung-cancer risk could prove to be comparable to that of cigarettes.

If a cannabis user does have an unpleasant experience when using the drug it is often the result of a high dose coupled with inexperience – perhaps after eating a large amount (ie more than 2g) and then panicking when the drug takes effect, or when cannabis is used with another drug such as alcohol.

## THE HIGHS AND LOWS OF CANNABIS RESEARCH

In recent years, the call for the legalization of cannabis for medical use has gained substantial voice. In 2000, even British Prime Minister Tony Blair agreed that, in principle, there was a scientific case for decriminalization on medical grounds.

Popular opinion has also rapidly swung in the direction of legalization for medical purposes. In a British poll conducted in April 2000, 48 per cent of people supported the proposition that the Metropolitan police should be persuaded to take no action against the medical use of cannabis. When the same poll was conducted in

December of that same year, 71 per cent supported it.

By the time New Labour swept into its second term of office in May 2001, the perceived swing in political opinion, coupled with the unprecedented openness of public debate on the subject, made legalization of cannabis for medical use seem little more than a formality. All that was required was the rubber stamp of the government's trusted scientists to clear the way.

Unfortunately for the pro-legalizationists, science was providing anything but a united front in their favour. For every research project that concluded cannabis was a good thing, another claimed it was bad. Clinical trials at the James Paget Hospital in Norfolk, England, for instance, revealed that cannabis eased the suffering of 10 out of 13 multiple sclerosis victims.

'Cannabis is my holy grail,' says MS sufferer Claire Hodges. 'It's the only drug that works for me. I function properly when I have a smoke, I can see better, I have more energy, I can move more easily, I enjoy my food more and it even makes my bowels move better.'

At the same time, however, researchers at New Zealand's Asthma and Respiratory Foundation at Otago University, found that smoking cannabis five times a week does as much damage to the lungs as smoking 20 cigarettes a day. After examining the lungs of over 900 people aged 21, they concluded that smoking cannabis 'caused disease, phlegm and coughing fits'.

This problem seemed to be solved by scientists at Aberdeen University, Scotland, who revealed a new process whereby cannabis could be made soluble for the first time. This meant that instead of processing the drug along with other carcinogenic substances commonly found through smoking, cannabis could conceivably be delivered through sprays, injections or aerosols.

No sooner had this revelation raised the hopes of the pro-legalization lobby, then yet more research into the effects of the drug dealt them a double whammy. Scientists from Buffalo University in New York State claimed that cannabis included chemicals that, when smoked by either men or women, overloaded an important signalling system in the brain involved in fertility and reduced the chances of sperm breaking through the surface of an egg.

So not only did cannabis now make you infertile, it also made you a bad driver according to the UK's Transport Research Laboratory. While volunteers drove more slowly and cautiously when under the influence, their steering ability was badly affected – in particular, when trying to follow a figure-of-eight loop.

Meanwhile, researchers linked to the British-government-backed company GW Pharmaceuticals have been investigating 'soapbar', the most common grade of Moroccan hashish, so named because it is pressed into a shape like a bar of Imperial Leather soap. They have discovered that in many cases, 'soapbar' is impregnated with henna, coffee, diesel, boot polish, ghee and liquorice. In some extreme cases, traces of Largactil, a major tranquillizer, have been found.

## CANNABIS – GATEWAY DRUG TO THE HARD STUFF?

In 1939, Dr James C Munch, the US Official Expert on marijuana from 1938–62, testified in court, under oath, that marijuana had turned him into a bat.

Such was the level of the attacks against cannabis during the Anslinger-led persecution of the 1930s. But one area of propaganda that remains an important tenet of the anti-cannabis lobby to this day is the suggestion that cannabis is but the first step on the ladder to addiction to hard drugs like heroin.

Initially, not even Anslinger believed there was a link. Indeed in the 1920s, some US states outlawed marijuana because of the belief that heroin addiction would lead to the use of marijuana. In 1937, Anslinger testified before Congress that there was no connection at all between marijuana and heroin. In 1951, however, Anslinger suddenly, and apparently on the spot, changed his mind when, testifying once again for a stepping up of the anti-cannabis laws, he asserted that marijuana was the certain stepping stone to heroin addiction. It has been the basis of US marijuana policy ever since, despite statistical evidence to the contrary.

In 1970, the Canadian government did their largest study ever of the subject and found no connection between marijuana and heroin. In 1972, the US government did their own study and again found no connection between marijuana and heroin. This was also the conclusion of the largest study ever carried out by the American Consumers Union, published in the same year.

Subsequent studies in both America and the UK have failed to find any solid evidence of a link, although in the last few years, as the laws on the use of cannabis have been loosened in the UK, fears have inevitably been articulated that it will result in more young people moving onto heroin. Former drugs tsar Keith Hellawell was one of those who warned of the dangers, claiming that research from New Zealand proved that youngsters who smoked cannabis were 60 times more likely to move onto the hard stuff.

By far the most interesting comment, however, has come from literary drugs guru Irvine Welsh, author of *Trainspotting*. 'I'd always done a lot of sniffing glue as a kid,' he said. 'And then I went onto lager and speed. I drifted into heroin because as a kid growing up everybody told me, "Don't smoke marijuana, it will kill you". '

RECENT UK HASH HISTORY

As we have seen, although it had been available for over a century, and its therapeutic use promoted by luminaries such as Queen Victoria's private physician, prescription cannabis was withdrawn as part of the 1971 Misuse of Drugs Act. But in the late 1990s, medical research and increased lobbying by multiple sclerosis sufferers in particular, led to a reappraisal of the official line.

In 1997, the British Medical Association (BMA) acknowledged the therapeutic benefits of cannabis, but expressed concern that joints containing tobacco cause more lung damage than cigarettes. In the same year Home Secretary Jack Straw gave GW Pharmaceuticals a licence to grow cannabis, acknowledging that an extract could become available on prescription. And in 1998 the House of Lords called for the government to allow doctors to prescribe cannabis for medical use.

In 1999, after testing different strains of hash, GW Pharmaceuticals claimed cannabis sativa, normally grown for its flowers rather than its resin, was the most effective pain-relieving strain.

By 2000, the first study proving that cannabis eases the symptoms of MS had been published in the science journal *Nature*. Scientists in London, Aberdeen and South Carolina reported that they had direct proof that a cannabinoid compound used on mice with an MS-like condition helped ameliorate symptoms within minutes.

When newly appointed Home Secretary David Blunkett reclassified cannabis to a Class C drug in 2001, he refused to legalize it for medical use until tests were complete. Meanwhile, the first clinical trials pronounced cannabis to be a 'wonder drug' capable of radically transforming the lives of very sick people. Preliminary results of the UK government trial suggested that 80 per cent of those taking part derived more benefit from cannabis than from any other drug, with many describing it as 'miraculous'.

In 2002, scientists discovered a natural brain molecule that mimics the effects of cannabis. The find should help researchers to develop pharmaceuticals with the therapeutic effects of the drug but without the 'high' and unwanted side effects.

THE US MEDICAL DEBATE
In the United States, the movement to legalize cannabis for medicinal purposes has been gradually cranked up from state to state. According to a poll taken in 1999, 73 per cent of Americans support the use of marijuana as a physician-prescribed pain reliever. In 1990, a survey revealed that 44 per cent of American oncologists had suggested that a patient smoke marijuana for relief of the nausea caused by chemotherapy. In 1997, the American Medical Association recommended controlled clinical trials on the medical uses of smoked marijuana. Meanwhile products using synthetic cannabinoids are selling well in the United States. The annual sales of dronabil - a synthetic cannabinoid sold under the trade name of Marinol - are estimated to be worth $20 million (£13.8 million) in the US. Around 80 per cent of the prescriptions are as appetite stimulants for people with AIDS or HIV, 10 per cent to counteract the nausea associated with chemotherapy and 10 per cent for other purposes.

Meanwhile, the Eli Lilly Company has developed nabilone. Under the trade name Cesamet, it too is used to counter nausea brought on by chemotherapy as well as treating patients with anxiety problems.

But, as in the UK, American campaigners have found the authorities – both at state and federal level – unwilling to commit themselves to a relaxation of the current laws. In many cases, the laws of the individual states differ to a confusing degree, and there is always the spectre of the ultra-conservative Drug Enforcement Administration on hand to clamp down on anything it perceives as illegal.

This, however, has not stopped dozens of so-called 'cannabis clubs' from springing up. These are places where sufferers of everything from multiple sclerosis to AIDS regularly turn up to smoke cannabis. A typical example is the Los Angeles Cannabis Resource Center. The centre boasts its own indoor plantation where over 400 plants are grown under lights. Upstairs is a comfortable lounge where 833 patients with a range of illnesses are invited to smoke the drug to alleviate the nausea and pain associated with their treatment. A patient needs a recommendation from a physician to become a member of the centre, and before the centre gives the patient marijuana it requires the doctor's certification that there is a legitimate need and also checks that the physician is licensed by the state.

Democrat Congressman Barney Frank has called on Congress to reclassify cannabis so that it can be distributed on prescription. 'Marijuana and the people who use it are treated far more harshly than the actual substance justifies,' he said. 'We allow doctors to prescribe substances that are far more damaging.' But even Frank is pessimistic after the Supreme Court's ruling. 'With that ruling in their pocket, they could bring injunctive actions against every club they could find.'

Not only that, but the DEA are taking a typically hard line on the issue. 'Marijuana is illegal, and any place that distributes marijuana, that grows marijuana, is illegal under federal law,' said a spokesman.

## THE CANADIAN ENLIGHTENMENT

As campaigners around the world fight what they see as intransigent governments to get marijuana legalized for medical use, many cast an envious glance at unfashionable Canada. For, in July 2001, Canada became the first country in the world to do just that.

Indeed, the sweeping nature of their legislation means that use of the drug is not solely restricted to sprays or pills containing cannabinoids extracts. In Canada - as long as you've got a doctor's certificate and testaments from two legal witnesses that you have either a terminal illness, AIDS, arthritis, cancer, multiple sclerosis, epilepsy or degenerative muscle and bone disease - you can grow it, smoke it, eat it or put it in pies. It's entirely up to you. You can even get someone to grow your hash for you.

Such is the progressive nature of Canada's cannabis legislation, the country's Supreme Court has agreed to hear arguments that criminalization of the weed is unconstitutional on the grounds that it poses no significant health risk. Meanwhile, in the depths of a disused mineshaft in Manitoba, the government have funded an enormous cannabis plantation designed to produce 185kg (400lb) a week for use in medical experiments.

## THE MYSTERIOUS WORLD OF GW PHARMACEUTICALS

They are described as a 'cross between a spaceship and an operating theatre' and, unless you have the required strict clearance, that description is the nearest you will ever get to the greenhouses of GW Pharmaceuticals. For it is in these hi-tech greenhouses, situated in a heavily guarded, secret location in the south of England, that more than 40,000 man-sized cannabis plants are being grown under computer-controlled conditions. And despite the cloak-and-dagger approach, the cannabis here is being grown with the blessing of the British government.

GW Pharmaceuticals is the country's largest licensed grower of cannabis, and its on-going mission is to develop prescription drugs using the medical properties of cannabinoids, the molecules unique to the cannabis plant which have been shown to have analgesic, anti-convulsant, anti-tremor, anti-psychotic, anti-inflammatory, anti-emetic and appetite-stimulant properties.

For the last five years, GW's scientists have been working at developing a range of products targeted at multiple sclerosis, spinal cord injury, neurogenic pain, spasticity and other neurological dysfunction, arthritis, migraine, head injury, schizophrenia, weight loss associated with cancer and AIDS and chemotherapy-induced nausea and vomiting. The company's founder, former hospital doctor Geoffrey Guy, has lobbied the government to permit prescriptions of cannabis-based drugs, and claims that the Home Office has pledged that if GW's clinical trials are successful, it will reschedule cannabis to permit its use in pharmaceuticals.

Patients in the trials programme take different formulations of cannabis-based medicines by means of a sub-lingual spray device – it is sprayed under the tongue and absorbed, rather than swallowed. The patients also take an inactive 'placebo'. Neither the researchers nor the patients know whether they are using the active substance or the placebo at any given time. According to Dr Guy, results from his clinical trials to date have been encouraging, with patients showing 'significant reduction in pain, muscle spasm and bladder dysfunction as well as improved neurological function'.

'Data from our studies in approximately 70 subjects is positive and encouraging,' he said. 'Patients are clearly gaining benefit. These results provide enough confidence for us to increase the number of trial centres and the number of patients taking part. We are seeing a significant improvement in quality of life for sufferers of a range of medical conditions and look forward to extending the trials programme.'

In 2001, GW began clinical trials at Ottawa Hospital in Canada. This is because the change in legislation now means that Canada allows sufferers from chronic conditions such as multiple sclerosis and arthritis to apply, to possess and to cultivate cannabis legally for medical purposes.

## THE 'BENEFICIAL HERB' – THE SO-CALLED ETHICAL DRUGS TRADE

By the turn of the century, a void had been created by the general public's growing confidence in cannabis as a beneficial herb and the increasingly laissez-faire attitude of the authorities towards prosecution. It was not long before entrepreneurial spirit filled the gap in the market, in the shape of 'ethical' drugs traders.

A typical example is Tony Taylor, a health food shop owner based in King's Cross, London. Taylor openly imports cannabis from farmers in Switzerland – both buds and hashish – and sells it to more than 200 medical patients at cost price in the form of hemp cream, a tincture that can be dropped into water for MS patients and even a preparation made during a full moon for women with PMT.

'We have a protocol,' he says. 'We fill in a form, you get interviewed by me. I don't charge anything for consultation.' Under the 1971 Misuse of Drugs Act, Taylor could be imprisoned for up to 14 years. Yet the local police turn a blind eye. Taylor believes the reason for this is because of his 'ethical' stance towards the sale of the drug.

The reason Taylor makes regular trips to Switzerland for his supplies is that Alpine cannabis farmers can grow it in their fields with impunity. Although it is currently sold in Swiss hemp shops, a government advisory committee there has recommended that it should be sold in pharmacies on a non-profit basis – a situation that Tony Taylor and others would like to see in the UK.

Unfortunately, while the police in King's Cross are prepared to allow Taylor to sell his illegal wares without interference, other forces have proved somewhat more intransigent. In April 2000, Lancashire police were criticized for their treatment of great-grandmother Jean Jackson. In the six months since she had been smoking cannabis to ease her arthritis, Miss Jackson's antiques shop in Lancaster had been raided six times. On the last occasion, she gave officers a key to let themselves in after ten detectives proceeded to take apart the sewage pipes in her home.

'A number of officers go to carry out searches of this kind and when searching for drugs it is common practice to make a rapid entry,' explained Chief Superintendent John Thompson. 'Possession of cannabis is an offence and if people are in possession they can expect to be prosecuted.'

Colin Davies, who set up the Medical Marijuana Co-operative, slammed police tactics. 'The police have been a bit heavy-handed by turning up in this jack-booted fashion to tread on ill people,' he said. 'It is bizarre the way they pick out people who are ill, who are like sitting ducks, and they do not actually check whether these people have reasons in the first place.'

During a visit to a day care centre in Cheltenham, Gloucestershire, in December 1998, Prince Charles met MS sufferer Karen Drake. Asking about her health, he inquired whether she had experimented with alternative remedies to deal with her crippling pain.

Ms Drake, 36, said: 'He asked me if I had tried taking cannabis, saying he understood that, under strict medical supervision, it was one of the best things for it. I was surprised that he asked me, but it was nice of him to be so considerate. It showed that he had thought about the condition and knew what was helpful.'

Prince Charles' comments were gleefully seized upon by campaigners for legalization such as Labour MP Paul Flynn, who said: 'It is splendid advice from a most unexpected source. I am encouraged to learn that the high level of popular support for the use of cannabis for medicinal purposes has reached Buckingham Palace.'

A Royal spokesman was more circumspect when asked about the Prince's comments. 'Prince Charles is aware of the issue of the use of cannabis for MS sufferers. Health is one of his major portfolios, and I think people would be surprised if he wasn't aware of the debate on the treatment of MS sufferers.'

MONEY

For such a little plant, cannabis is truly big business. But then, for all the talk of the history and culture of the drug, it remains just that: a drug. A soft one in some eyes perhaps, but a drug nonetheless and as lucrative to manufacturers and dealers as any other. Before it reaches the rolling papers of millions of smokers, cannabis is still subjected to a complex and secretive smuggling process that takes it from the growing fields of the Middle East and South America across the borders of dozens of countries in which the penalties for trafficking are severe. It might not have the kudos of cocaine and heroin in the eyes of the drugs authorities, but every year they still crack down with all their resources on those responsible for its production and distribution. And as long as 'cannabusiness' remains highly profitable to the criminal underworld, the battle will continue.

In March 2000 detectives arrested four people following a raid on one of Britain's best-organized cannabis production factories. Several hundred high-strength skunk cannabis plants – with a crop worth £500,000 ($725,000) – were found growing in the old aircraft hangar at an industrial estate at Breighton, near York. The plants were almost ready for harvest but some had already been picked and were being dried.

In June 2000, police in Rotterdam arrested 16 people after a crop worth almost £1 million ($1.5 million) was discovered in a series of plastic greenhouses in the city.

## ALL ROADS LEAD TO AMSTERDAM

The Dutch authorities turn a deliberately blind eye to cannabis. But while this largely unique attitude of tolerance makes the cannabis cafés of Amsterdam a magnet for pot heads from all over the world, it leaves Europe's drug squads with an enduring headache. Amsterdam and Dutch ports like Rotterdam and Europort have become a gateway for the drugs trade, and Holland is the major distribution centre for the international trafficking of narcotics including cannabis throughout western Europe and, in particular, Britain.

In 1998, the UK accounted for more than a fifth of cannabis seizures within the 15 member states of the European Union. It's a short hop across the North Sea for British dealers to meet up with like-minded gangs of smugglers from all of the major European capitals, and there is no way the thin blue line of customs officials and drug squad officers can keep tabs on the thousands of consignments of cannabis, ranging from a few grams to several hundred kilos, that arrive in Britain every week.

'It's like trying to keep back the tide,' said one British customs official. 'You think you've done well stopping one consignment coming in from the continent, then it quickly dawns on you that while you've been patting yourself on the back another six have come in under your nose.'

Cannabis resin, the form most widely used in the UK, traditionally comes from the so-called Golden Crescent of countries, which includes Morocco, Afghanistan and Pakistan. It is also highly prevalent in Asia, especially in Cambodia, where the Khmer Rouge sanctioned huge production sites for drug cartels from Sweden, China and Thailand. Consignments from South American countries such as Venezuela and Colombia are regularly shipped into the European ports.

According to the International Narcotics Control Strategy Report of 2000: 'While Cambodia is not a major producer of opiates or coca-based drugs, marijuana is cultivated in significant quantities for export, mainly to Europe... Poorly paid and ill-trained police and judicial officials frequently look the other way in narcotics and other criminal cases.'

Commercial cannabis is grown and processed on an industrial scale. In Afghanistan, the narcotics industry was the primary source of income for the ruling Taliban government and, intelligence sources believe, the al-Qaeda terrorist organization of Osama bin Laden that was based there. Following the destruction of the World Trade Centre on 11 September 2001, many of the subsequent US and British attacks on Afghanistan were aimed at disrupting and destroying this link.

Cannabis shipments follow a route up through Turkey and eastern Europe to the main trafficking centres of Germany and Holland. Generally the crops are cultivated and processed by peasants who, depending on the demand, either turn the cannabis into resin or grass. Of the billions of pounds their labours will eventually realize, most will get peanuts. It is, however, their living – and while hard-hitting government clampdowns on cannabis production in some countries have disrupted the trafficker, the real effect has been felt by the farmers who are left penniless.

When Lebanon wiped out the Bekaa Valley's $500 million (£345 million)-a-year cannabis industry in the 1990s, it was a catastrophe for the impoverished area. But farmers in this remote area have decided that there is nothing for it but to crank up production of the drug once again, believing that risking the wrath of the authorities is better than starving to death. In 2001, according to reliable estimates, 6,000ha (15,000 acres) of cannabis were planted – by far the largest amount since the Lebanese government began its eradication programme ten years ago at the end of the civil war. The rewards are great: a single hectare can reap £14,000 ($20,000) for the farmer – which is why Dr Mohammed Ferjani, the Tunisian head of the Bekaa's UN-sponsored integrated rural development programme, predicts a full-scale rebellion if the illicit crops are destroyed. 'The people are obliged to search for a cash crop to ensure a respectable income,' he says. 'This year, I'm sure they will fight.'

## BLACK IN THE USSR – THE DRUGS EXPLOSION IN THE FORMER COMMUNIST STATES

The fall of the Soviet Union and the disintegration of its empire into separate states known as the Central Independent States (CIS) was greeted with unbridled joy in the West. But less than ten years after the death of communism, western governments are discovering that its legacy has a bitter taste. For no one celebrated the new freedoms in the eastern bloc more than the drugs cartels, who gleefully turned parts of the former USSR into a drugs production and trafficking centre that has now superseded the traditional heartlands of Asia and the Middle East.

In 1999, police in Primoriye discovered more than 120 cannabis fields covering close to 100ha (250 acres). This followed hot on the heels of the discovery of 200ha (500 acres) of cannabis in the Khabarovsk region. Although arrests were made, drug enforcement agencies acknowledge that this is merely the tip of the iceberg.

Communist leaders in the Soviet Union and eastern Europe formerly believed that illegal drugs trafficking was a problem that belonged to the decadent western capitalists.

As a result, when the Soviet Bloc collapsed, the authorities in former communist states found themselves woefully lacking in the training and expertise to deal both with drug users and traffickers.

Drug use is not a crime in the Czech Republic, Kazakhstan, Poland, the Russian Federation, Slovakia or Turkmenistan. In Poland, existing penalties for trafficking are rarely imposed, while in the Czech Republic and Slovakia it is completely legal to cultivate cannabis, and seeds are sold openly in local shops.

The sheer scale of cannabis availability in the East compounds the problem. It is estimated that more than 1 million ha (2½ million acres) of mostly wild cannabis grows throughout the CIS. A report by a visiting UN team in 1992 revealed that in Kazakhstan and Krygyzstan alone there were more than 200,000ha (500,000 acres) of cannabis plantations – more than five times the recorded marijuana cultivation in the rest of the world.

Drug syndicates have been quick to exploit both the natural abundance of cannabis and the incompetence of the local authorities. They are able to set up harvesting and processing plants largely with impunity. And, once the cannabis has been processed, the absence of any centralized or cohesive drug enforcement in eastern and central Europe makes it easy to traffick the finished product to the greedy markets of the West. Where once the primary conduit for cannabis trafficking used to be Turkey, the authorities are beginning to realise that the drug is now flooding into France, Holland and Germany from Poland. With largely non-existent trafficking laws, Polish gangs have flourished. It is thought that much of the drugs currently reaching western markets come through the so-called Polish Pipeline – a broad network of Polish gangsters who serve as links in the wholesale trade of Central Asian hashish, Afghan heroin or even Colombian cocaine, receiving the drugs from Poland and selling them to local dealers.

While busts are an inconvenience, traffickers are more than happy to endure the occasional setback as long as the trade remains so lucrative. It has been estimated that for every £10 ($14.50) of hash bought on the street, around £6 ($8.70) of that goes to the trafficker, compared to £1 ($1.45) to the grower, £1 ($1.45) to the dealer and £2 ($2.90) in 'administration' incurred by the various stages of its transport.

And it is not only crime syndicates who recognize the money-spinning opportunities of the drugs trade. Almost all the major terrorist groups in the world rely on trafficking in some form as a means of fund raising. While initially it was South American insurgents such as the Revolutionary Armed Forces of Colombia who exploited drug money, their lead has been followed by other groups across the world such as Peru's Shining Path, the IRA and the Kurdish Workers Party in Turkey. Even religious fundamentalists like Osama Bin Laden's al-Qaeda, Hizbullah in Lebanon and the Tamil

Tigers of Sri Lanka are not averse to pocketing substantial amounts of money from the cannabis trail in their country.

## THE SMUGGLERS

One morning in 1992 a woman walking her dog near Sea Palling, between Great Yarmouth and Cromer in Norfolk, England, came across ten kitbags containing plastic containers of what was apparently sauerkraut. She alerted the police, who opened the containers and discovered 140kg (300lb) of Lebanese Gold cannabis. 'We believe the drugs had been landed by boat and left for collection,' said Assistant Chief Constable Colin Sheppard. 'We would ask other dog walkers to keep their eyes open for strange pieces of flotsam.'

This incident was typical of the drug-smuggling business from the continent into Britain. While cannabis can be moved between the borders of landlocked European countries with relative ease, Britain, because it is an island, presents something of a problem to the smuggler. Ports and airports are scrupulously manned by customs officials, making the illegal import of drugs highly risky. Consequently, traffickers are obliged to be increasingly ingenious in their efforts to get their haul ashore, resulting in surreptitious midnight boat drops reminiscent of something from *Treasure Island*. Norfolk, with its 160km (100 miles) of largely exposed coastline, is a favoured drug-running route. Every year, Norfolk police arrest over 1,000 people on drugs charges.

In even more remote Scotland, one of the biggest hauls ever found occurred in the 1970s when several tonnes/tons of cannabis were found washed up on the Mull of Kintyre.

The advent of the Channel Tunnel has provided another popular route. Between 1996 and 1997, seizures of cannabis from vehicles passing under the sea from France leapt threefold to 1,400kg (3,000lb), while the total haul of drugs seized – including cocaine and heroin – had a street value that had doubled to £17 million ($25 million). Drugs were found in caravans, in the front seat passenger's emergency airbag and even in a false plaster cast on one woman's arm. A total of 600kg (1,300lb) of cannabis resin was found in a fuel tanker's false compartment, while at Felixstowe 500kg (1,100lb) of resin was discovered in sealed tins of vegetables. Among the advantages of the undersea network to the smuggler is the fact that it hides the origin of the courier, as everyone goes through France.

Numbers of smugglers on the Eurostar rail link are also increasing, as they realise how easy it is to lose their identity. Traffickers from South American countries can disguise where they have come from by travelling through several countries. A typical route, according to Customs officials at Waterloo International, London (a station that deals with Eurostar passengers), is from Brazil to Portugal, Spain, France and then the UK.

According to customs officials, cross-Channel day trippers are increasingly being used as a cover for international drug traffickers smuggling cannabis into Britain. Couriers posing as day trippers on ferries collect consignments in France, Belgium and Holland and attempt to re-enter the UK through customs, hoping to slip unnoticed among millions of legitimate travellers. Pensioners and young mothers with children are lured into smuggling by big cash payments. In one such incident, a minibus carrying a party of senior citizens on a day trip was used to smuggle 156kg (344lb) of cannabis from Belgium. The large numbers of British people who enjoy a day trip to shop at French supermarkets make it increasingly difficult for customs officers, who have found cannabis and other drugs concealed among cases of beer, bags of wine, cheese and salami.

In recent months, US officials have been surprised by the ingenuity of South American, Mexican and European drug-smuggling rings, whose operations virtually shut down in the days after the 11 September terrorist attacks in 2001 because of dramatically increased security at US borders. At key crossings in California and South Texas, seizures of cannabis doubled from the same period the previous year. From 1 October to 31 December 2001, customs agents seized 19,176kg (42,283lb) of marijuana, worth about $17 million (£11.7 million) to the distributors who sell to the street dealers. Arrests in the past few months indicate that smugglers are using creative new tricks, such as traffickers in the Caribbean Sea and the Pacific Ocean who chain drug-filled metal containers to the undersides of luxury cruise ships and send divers to retrieve the booty after the ships dock in US ports. Others use drug-carrying speedboats to cross deep ocean routes in the Caribbean, where Coast Guard cutters have abandoned some anti-drug patrols since 11 September. 'Our adversary is greed and the human imagination,' said Joseph Webber, special agent in charge of the US Customs investigations office for the New York City area.

One of Britain's leading drugs traffickers was Curtis 'Cocky' Warren, who grew up in Liverpool's Toxteth estate and rose from abject poverty to be ranked in the top 500 of *The Sunday Times*' 'Rich List', with a fortune estimated conservatively at around £40 million ($58 million) and privately at over £180 million ($260 million). Warren's money was purely a result of the drugs trade. When police raided his Dutch hideout in 1996, they found – along with vast quantities of heroin, ecstasy and cocaine – over 1,500kg (3,300lb) of cannabis resin with a street value of millions.

Warren is now serving 12 years in a Dutch jail and, while customs officers regard this as a success, they also know that his place will already have been filled by opportunist traffickers eager to earn a highly lucrative living importing drugs into Britain from the continent. The number of drug traffickers currently operating the cannabis trail can only be a matter for speculation. Suffice to say, the number still operating far outweighs the number behind bars. For every high-profile syndicate bust, dozens more continue to operate their global business. Indeed the power struggle for the distribution of cannabis and other drugs often only comes to light when it erupts into brutal violence.

An indication of the way the cannabis trail has shifted to eastern Europe is the recent spate of gangland murders involving crime bosses from the former communist states. In December 1999, Andrzej K, a leading drug trafficker from Warsaw, Poland, was enjoying a skiing holiday in the winter resort of Zakopane when two men pulled up beside him in a saloon car and shot him twice in the head. Andrzej's murder was just the latest in a spate of drug-related killings across eastern Europe as a vicious turf war over the distribution rights to the CIS's burgeoning cannabis supply spilled into bloodshed. A week earlier, a rival gang member was killed in a car bomb attack in the Slovak capital Bratislava, while in the Croatian capital Zagreb a passerby was killed by a rocket-propelled grenade that bounced off the car it had been fired at.

In many ways, it is astonishing that the same fate never befell the man widely regarded as being the number one cannabis trafficker in the 1970s and 1980s. Oxford educated Howard Marks built up a worldwide smuggling network that was allegedly responsible for supplying the majority of marijuana smoked in the western world in that period. By the mid-1980s, he owned 25 companies and possessed 43 aliases – among them Mr Nice, which was also the title of his bestselling autobiography. Accused of importing 15 tonnes/tons of cannabis into Scotland in 1981, Marks persuaded the jury that he was in actuality an agent for MI6 and that his drug-smuggling activities were nothing but a front to disguise his attempts to infiltrate the IRA. His acquittal left British Customs and Excise, in the words of one of its senior officials, 'astonished, disbelieving and incredulous'.

When he was finally caught in 1990, he admitted two counts of racketeering in a federal court in Florida and was sentenced to 25 years. He served seven, and now works for magazines and newspapers as well as touring Britain with his one-man show. In May 2000, he even stood for election for London Mayor, representing the Legalize Cannabis Campaign.

'I'm an outlaw, in the true sense of word,' Marks said in an interview in 1998. 'I'm not a petty criminal, I'm someone who refuses to accept that this [cannabis prohibition] law is unworkable. But you can be a gentleman criminal no matter what the crime, and that wasn't me. I was a purist, I smuggled only dope. I would have never smuggled guns. Or cigarettes. Why? Because they're bad for you.'

Marks is estimated to have made more than £48 million ($70 million) from his trafficking activities.

## THE DEALERS

Like all profitable businesses, cannabis relies heavily on strong distribution chains to get it from the supplier into the hands of the customer. And, like warring supermarkets, suppliers will try any innovation in order to give them an edge over their rivals. The advent of the Internet, in particular, has been exploited by dealers who have been able to expand from back-street transactions to global deals and virtual home delivery at the click of a mouse. However, the illegality of cannabis means that those distribution chains are largely shrouded in secrecy. The casual user will purchase his or her supply from a dealer in a pub or during a house call, but from there the trail gets less easy to follow.

What is clear is that cannabis suppliers on the continent rely upon a network of middlemen and sales operatives to distribute the drugs on the ground. The network has to be secure, which means that various levels of operatives are often kept in the dark.

As one London-based dealer explained: 'As far as I am concerned, I get the dope from somebody higher up the chain. I don't know who he is, or who he works for. To be honest, my view is the less I know about it, the better. I'd guess there are probably another two or three above him before you get to the main man, and I bet nobody knows who that is unless they are his best mates. I know there are gangs in London involved, but I reckon most of them are just in the distribution business. They'll all be getting their shit from someone higher up the chain.

'The usual format is that we meet at a pre-ordained location, usually his flat, and he will hand over the resin or the weed. The amount depends, as does the price, on the quality of the shit. I'll usually buy around a grand's worth off him. It's like going to the wholesalers, I suppose. Then, basically, it's up to me. I've got a fairly steady client base, quite reliable, and I reckon on making a three or four hundred quid [about $500] profit on that initial outlay. There are dealers who rip people off, giving them crap and charging over the odds. But my view is that people are only naïve once, and after that they won't touch you with a bargepole. It just isn't good business. The only people who make a fortune out of this are the traffickers and smugglers. I'm just a minion, the lowest of the low – but that's all right with me. I make enough to get by.'

In the US, the Mafia frowned upon drug dealing for many years. But since the 1970s, the earning potential has proved hard to resist. Hard drugs tend to be the currency used more often than not, but the ready supply of South American marijuana is equally a cash cow for the bosses. Dealing on the streets is rife, and the supply plentiful.

'You think that it's just poor black folks who smoke shit,' said one Harlem dealer. 'You'd be wrong. I've had rich white guys in flash cars pulling up to score on the way home, and high school kids you wouldn't never normally see in this area. In fact, if you ever see a white face in Harlem, most times they are looking to score some shit for their weekend parties.'

In Holland, the acceptable face of dealing is in cannabis cafés – but the government restrictions on the amount it is permissible to buy has seen an upsurge in backstreet dealers. In Italy, meanwhile, the government has been keen to remove dealers from the streets with the same broom they are currently using to remove lay-by prostitutes – not out of any great legal clampdown, but because they believe such people give the country a bad name among visitors.

Such is the wild west nature of the eastern European drugs trade since the end of communism, the selling of dope is strictly controlled by rival gangs. 'I made a big mistake trying to buy some hash in Moscow when I was there on a visit,' says student Ricky Hunt. 'I found one guy who looked promising – I even saw him dealing to some other people. But when he clocked I was American he ran for the hills. Turns out you got to work for a specific gang to sell to American tourists, because American tourists pay more money. This guy was just selling to the locals. He was small time.'

## HOME-GROWN HASH

Not surprisingly, growing your own cannabis is increasing in popularity, given the relative ease with which a crop can be grown. The favoured method is via a hydroponic growing system, in which plants are grown without soil but are fed on nutrients dissolved in a piped water supply and given artificial sunlight with powerful lighting rigs. The technique is much favoured by cannabis growers as it requires very little maintenance. Most systems can be fixed up to timers, avoiding suspicious numbers of journeys to the location. The chemistry behind a hydroponic systems is complex, but getting your hands on one is anything but. A starter kit is available on the Internet for less than £400 ($580). A top-of-the-range kit can cost up to £2,000 ($2,900).

Plant seizures in the UK were up from 11,839 in 1992 to 116,119 in 1996, and these ranged from small garden plots to large, almost industrial-sized factories. One seizure in Exeter uncovered hydroponic equipment worth £6,000 ($8,700) and cannabis with a street value of almost £70,000 ($100,000). It's a similar story across Europe: in Germany, a group of neighbours from Munich were discovered to be growing communal hydroponic hash worth in excess of £200,000 ($290,000), while in 1999 alone similar busts in France, Belgium and The Netherlands have netted home-grown cannabis worth over £2 million ($2.9 million). In the United States, the DEA will occasionally make an example of someone caught growing their own, but privately admit it is an impossible task keeping tabs on the estimated nine million hydroponic farmers.

Richard Tamlyn, of the Exeter Drugs Project, is well aware of the huge profits cannabis growers can now make. He says: 'Some of these operations are on a large scale. Run on the lines of a business they involve significant setting-up costs, but can bring a considerable return. With all the elements of water, light and heat under artificial control, the plants can be grown for up to 18 hours a day. And, learning from continental cannabis farms, growers will choose to produce the most potent varieties, which in turn fetch the highest prices. It's a long way from the classic image of one man with a couple of plants sat beneath a lightbulb in his bedroom.'

Of course, only a tiny percentage of home-grown hash is destined to be sold on the wider market. The majority is for the personal use of the grower and their friends, thus cutting out the middleman. Indeed, such is the popularity of home-grown hash, that research in 2002 suggested that half of the cannabis smoked in Britain was being grown at people's homes rather than being imported by drugs barons, a figure consistent with the rest of Europe. The average cannabis smoker also uses almost twice as much of the drug – 44.5g (1½oz) a year – than they did in 1994, when the figure was 24.8g (⁷/₈oz).

This has led critics to reason that the relaxation of the laws on cannabis possession proposed by some European governments will lead to a steep rise in the number of smokers growing their own supplies without fear of arrest, and believe that a message is being sent out that the drug is safe. However, one leading UK government adviser on drugs believes that cannabis users should be allowed to grow dope plants in their own homes without any fear of being prosecuted. Roger Howard, a member of the Home Office Advisory Group on Drugs, said that as David Blunkett, the Home Secretary, has announced that cannabis possession is to be downgraded from a Class B to a Class C offence, it made sense to allow people to grow it. He said:

'As the government moves towards making small-scale cannabis possession a non-arrestable offence, I hope it will resolve this contradiction by differentiating in law between small-scale cultivation for personal use and large-scale production controlled by organized crime.'

## MARIJUANA MONEYSPINNER – WHAT IF IT WERE LEGAL?

'Cannabusiness' is big business – and one person following the legalization debate with interest is the taxman. Hardly surprising, when figures in the billions are routinely quoted as the income from the illegal cannabis market. Governments, who already cream off substantial amounts in excise duty from drink and tobacco, are all too aware that if the cannabis consumed illegally was produced and taxed exactly like booze and cigarettes, it would raise vast amounts. It's estimated that the US government could swell its coffers by upwards of $400 billion (£276 billion) were it to nationalize its cannabis industry, while most European countries would be looking at an annual windfall of around £16 billion ($23.2 billion). As we have seen, the Dutch taxman already makes a healthy income from cannabis café licences – the amount he could potentially realize if the entire market were taxed would be astronomical.

But how would it work in practice? Where would you buy your legal, government-approved cannabis, and in what form? According to veteran campaigner Steve Abrams, who organized and composed the famous 1967 full-page advertisement in *The Times* demanding decriminalization of the drug, a nationalized cannabis industry, with profits going to the British National Health Service, would boost NHS funds by £2 billion ($2.9 billion) a year 'on conservative estimates'. Abrams believes good-quality cannabis could be grown in sufficient quantity to satisfy domestic demand without the need for imports that would breach Britain's obligations under international treaties. Users would register with their GPs and obtain supplies from chemists.

But if that sounds like too much hassle, don't worry: the tobacco industry have had the whole thing mapped out for years. As early as 1993, anticipating the eventual legalization of the drug, US tobacco giant Philip Morris filed a trademark application for a brand of cannabis cigarette called 'Marley'. Other firms registered names like Acapulco Gold and Red Leb. In 1998, it was revealed that British-American Tobacco had laid down secret plans for cigarettes laced with 'subliminal' levels of marijuana in case the drug was ever legalized.

It may soon be possible to pop down to the off-licence and purchase a pack of 20 Acapulco Gold cannabis-laced cigarettes for the price of a normal pack, with between £2 ($2.90) and £3 ($4.35) going to the Treasury in tax. Now that's something for the taxman to put in his pipe and smoke.

### ADVERTISING DOPE

The policy of almost all governments is that cannabis advertising of any sort is prohibited. The Internet, however, has provided a regulation-free billboard for anyone wanting to sell, buy or promote cannabis to a worldwide audience. A world of online cannabis commercials are available 24 hours a day on hundreds of cannabis-related sites available at the click of a mouse. Indeed, traditional methods of advertising have been left behind, leaving governments and drug agencies chasing their tails. And, ironically, for all the millions spent on anti-drug campaigns aimed at highlighting the dangers of narcotics, in some quarters this has proved far more successful for the pro-cannabis lobby than for the government. A survey in the US actually charted an increase in drug use among some teenagers who saw the government's multi-million dollar anti-drug warnings on television.

### HEMP – THE CANNABIS CASH CROP

Back in the 16th century, marijuana was known as hemp and that substance, in a world where sea power was all important, was crucial in the production of sails. So, as stated before, in 1533 a royal decree was issued in England, forcing farmers to sow part of their land with hemp. The penalty for disobedience was three shillings and fourpence. Thirty years later, under Elizabeth I, the fine had rocketed to £5 (£7.25), underlining the importance naval Britain placed on the cultivation of the tough, fibrous cannabis plant.

The versatility of hemp was not lost on the American pioneers either. Both George Washington and Thomas Jefferson urged colonists to grow the plant, and took the lead by growing it themselves. The fathers of the American nation would therefore have some sympathy with US farming folk today, who are currently fighting a lengthy battle to be allowed to grow hemp on their land without being punitively fined.

In May 2000, Maryland became the fourth US state to authorize the production of hemp. To struggling farmers, the decision was a godsend since the bottom had fallen out of the market for tobacco, which was their traditional crop. But the battle had been a long one – because hemp is marijuana, and under federal law, growing marijuana is still illegal.

In the face of sagging farm economies, even the hard-line DEA has reviewed its stance against hemp production. But its involvement in the Maryland project reveals the innate suspicion it still has about marijuana being grown on US soil. Interested farmers face an extensive criminal background check and must be licensed by the DEA. State police are also authorized to search the site at any time. And the law requires agriculture officials to closely control the supply of hemp seeds, which are classified as a controlled substance. The seeds are imported from Canada or further abroad with DEA approval. If, at the end of the four-year pilot scheme, the federal authorities are not convinced, Maryland's farmers will have to dig up their crop and go back to tobacco.

Other than Maryland, only Hawaii, North Dakota and Minnesota have laws allowing hemp production. All were passed in 1999. In Virginia, lawmakers passed a resolution in 2001 urging federal officials to 'revise the necessary regulations' to permit experimental hemp production there. Hawaii, where the DEA claimed most success in its efforts to kick out illegal marijuana cultivation, is ironically the only state so far to receive DEA approval to plant hemp. The site is guarded by a 24-hour alarm system and a 2m- (6½ft) high fence topped with razor wire.

As a mark of solidarity, in the summer of 2001, pro-cannabis campaigner Grayson Sigler and his wife, Kellie, along with their companions Scott Fur and Charles Ruchalski, spent three months travelling across the US in a hemp-powered Mercedes station wagon, hoping to promote the use of hemp oil as alternative fuel. They used hemp 'biodiesel', which is a thin, oily, bright green liquid made from hemp seed oil through a process called trans-esterification.

## ADDITIONAL INFO

**SUMMARY**

Cannabis has been described as 'the world's most extraordinary plant' and there can be little argument with that claim. Even without the obvious psychotropic effects of smoking cannabis, this surprisingly flimsy, fork-leafed plant has had a fundamental impact on human civilization from its very earliest days because of its sheer versatility – it can be used as a source of building materials and food and medicine.

But of course, it is as a drug that cannabis has found fame and infamy for most of recorded history. When we think of it in terms of pot, hash or any of the multifarious terms dreamed up to describe the plant in its narcotic state, we think of spaced-out hippies protesting against the Vietnam War, dancing like shamans to Jefferson Airplane at Woodstock or marching defiantly behind banners demanding its immediate legalization. We think of Amsterdam cafés filled with pungent fug, laid-back Haight-Ashbury in 1967 and the chaos and culture of Marrakesh in 1970. We think of dope icons like Bob Marley, Bob Dylan, The Beatles and

The Fabulous Furry Freak Brothers. In short, we think of a youthful generation finding its voice against the smothering social and legal constraints of the 'square' Establishment.

But it must be remembered that all this is merely a snapshot of the last 40 years. In cannabis terms, that is a blink of an eye. Indeed, it demeans the impact of cannabis to think only in terms of its recent history. Even when the Greek historian Herodotus first stumbled upon what must have been to his eyes mind-blowing Scythian cannabis rituals in 450 BC, the plant had been regarded as sacred for over 2,000 years. While it's understandable that Herodotus should wish to record the graphic details of the stoned Scythians for his audience back home, it is a shame that he did so because this is the one aspect that has influenced our perception of cannabis ever since. The paranoid fear about the effects of cannabis on people's minds, personified by Harry J Anslinger in the USA in the 1930s, not to mention the worldwide ban on growing the plant, would have been unfathomable to the ancient Chinese, Indians and Persians. To them, the current wrangling about whether to legalize the drug for medical use would have been laughable. Cannabis was a drug for medical use. Its hallucinogenic side effects were pleasant, but they were by no means the be-all and end-all.

The last 2,000 years of the cannabis story have been a lot more fraught than the first 2,000. In AD 70, Dioscorides talked of the widespread use of cannabis as a medicine in

Rome, but that is one of the last times it was referred to in purely medicinal terms – up until the 16th century that is. The writing was on the wall 130 years later when Galen described dinner parties in the same city being enlivened by the consumption of weed. But, by then, medical science had progressed; cannabis was just one substance in a growing global pharmacopoeia and people were beginning to use it more as a social drug. The anti-cannabis edicts of the next 1,000 years reflected the fear among spiritual leaders like Ottoman Emir Soudoun Scheikhouni and Pope Innocent VIII that the drug is ruinous to society – and more particularly to their control over it. This is a common refrain that can be found right up to the present day.

The roots of western society's paranoia about cannabis are to be found in its equal paranoia about the East. Wars and geography had kept weird and ungodly eastern culture at arm's length for centuries – but when cannabis, the drug of the heathen, began sweeping across Europe and into the USA there was nothing anyone could do to stop it. And what made matters worse for God-fearing folk was the enthusiasm with which the drug was taken up by their own people. To them, to read excitable reports of bohemians experimenting with hash in New York, London and Paris must have seemed like the end of the world was nigh.

In the 20th century, nowhere was this better illustrated than in the USA. To waspish North Americans, cannabis equated to everything bad that threatened their largely delusionary existence: namely blacks, Mexicans and jazz music. They claimed to fear for the health and well-being of their children, but in reality they were panicking about themselves and their future as the dominant race on the continent. It was the Americans who petitioned the world for a ban on cannabis – not out of some sort of global philanthropy, but because they wanted to stop it flooding into their own country. The fear spread like wildfire; the British couldn't give two hoots about cannabis in 1901, and the Royal Commission concluded that it wasn't harmful enough to bother prohibiting. Within 30 years, however, they had followed the lead of the Geneva Conference on Opium and issued a draconian set of laws banning this 'dangerous drug'.

Again we must turn to the role played by Harry J Anslinger in all this, for he is the pivotal figure in the modern cannabis story. It has been suggested that Anslinger was just a regular guy doing his job. But what was Anslinger's job? As an arch-propagandist of the evils of cannabis, there is no doubt that he was without equal. His Reefer Madness diatribe was a masterpiece of hyperbole, paranoia and racist rabble-rousing. But ultimately, Anslinger failed abjectly in his true aim, which was to rid American society of the spectre of cannabis. Indeed, it's arguable that Anslinger switched more all-American kids onto cannabis out of sheer curiosity than he prevented from trying it. The young people at the heart of the 1960s drug-taking scene in America were the same generation Anslinger had been trying to save from 'reefer madness'.

The 1960s are held up as cannabis's golden era but, to all but a few die-hard pot heads, a joint was little more than a symbol of the turbulent times. People changed the world, not cannabis, despite what some may think, and today the kaftaned tokers preaching love and peace in San Francisco and Woodstock look horribly dated and more than a little ludicrous. Many of them, now middle aged and respectable, look back on those days with embarrassment. Similarly, choreographed legalization marches and full page ads in *The Times* signed by celebrities may have seemed like big news at the time, but their effect was negligible; if anything, the 1970s and 1980s marked a period of sustained governmental oppression on drug taking that Harry J Anslinger could only have dreamed about. The 1960s were 'Cannabis – the cabaret years'. There was glamour, tinsel and lots of noise, but there was little substance.

Since then, Holland has been held up as a model for modern cannabis use. The laid-back cafés of Amsterdam are the perfect example of how soft drug taking, properly regulated, can have a place in modern society. Again, the jury is out on this one. Holland's relaxed laws have made it not only a Mecca for cannabis enthusiasts, but a centre for global drug trafficking. In a world where drugs are banned, a country that lowers its guard is one that is ripe for exploitation. It is all very well sitting in a café enjoying a civilized spliff, but if traffickers from Azerbaijan are scoring deals in the adjacent alleyway then it rather sours the experience.

Experts have yet to make a definitive link between cannabis and the numbers of heroin junkies littering Dam Square – but it would stand to reason that even if cannabis is not a 'gateway' drug to the hard stuff, the very culture of the country is conducive to substance abuse of one sort or another. Until the rest of the world follows Holland's lead – which simply will not happen in the foreseeable future – then cannabis cafés pose more danger than they are worth.

It is only since the mid-1990s that we have entered a rational debate about cannabis. Ironically, the catalyst for the current move towards decriminalization has not been protest but a renewed appreciation of the drug's medicinal qualities – the same qualities that first attracted ancient man to the plant in the first place. Progress has, as ever, been painfully slow. In the UK, successive Home Secretaries have been too scared of the political fall-out to sanction any definite action. Even Jack Straw, who at one stage filled the pro-cannabis lobby with hope, bailed out hopelessly at the crucial moment. It has taken a Home Secretary with the courage of David Blunkett to actually make the first move. He has, of course, been cunning: there are still years of clinical trials to be completed before legislation is rubber-stamped, and by then David Blunkett will be long gone. But he has done enough. When even Cabinet ministers feel confident enough to admit that – shock horror! – they smoked dope like the rest of the population, the momentum, one feels, is nigh-on unstoppable.

It is a movement that is gathering pace across the more enlightened EU countries and one that will result in a decriminalization of cannabis for medicinal use sooner rather than later. Whether this will lead to full legalization is another matter, and for most politicians this is as yet a step too far. The most likely scenario is that strictly regulated personal use of cannabis will eventually be sanctioned, with the respective governments raking in revenue from licensed outlets and the products themselves being made by multinational tobacco companies. But if it happens, it must happen across the board: there is no point in German off-licences selling 20 Aruba Golds if Austria's don't. The only people who benefit from a scenario like this are the drug traffickers.

Even then, it is likely that the USA will be left out in the cold. Bill Clinton's laughable admission that he smoked but didn't inhale says much about the American Establishment's on-going cannabis guilt. When a supposedly liberal-minded US president would rather admit to screwing an intern in the Oval Office than to smoking a joint, it seems inconceivable that any future administration would even dream of relaxing the laws on cannabis. The election of ultra-conservative Republican George W Bush to the White House would appear to be the final nail in the coffin – for the time being, at least.

Whatever the outcome, one thing is for certain: the 'world's most extraordinary plant' will continue to weave its extraordinary influence on us for as long as it finds soil to grow in. Four thousand years is a long time to walk hand-in-hand with something we still can't fully understand – but it is, I suspect, only the beginning of the story.

## GLOSSARY

Anslinger, Harry J – legendary US anti-drugs enforcer, author of *Reefer Madness*

Bale – compressed block of marijuana, usually between 4.5–18kg (10–40lb)

Bhang – an Indian and Middle Eastern smoking mixture consisting of pollen from marijuana flowers and ghee, an oily butter

Bifta – a cone-shaped joint

Blazed – term used to describe a feeling of being totally high

Block-up – a feeling of cannabis intoxication, ie 'I'm totally block-up'

Blunt – a joint rolled in the tobacco-leaf wrapper of a Phillies Blunt cigar

Bogart – to hog the joint

Bong – a water-cooled pipe for one smoker, usually made of bamboo or glass

Brick – a cube of compressed cannabis weighing 1kg (2¼lb)

Bucket – unusual smoking device made from a bucket filled with water, a bottle with its base removed and a pipe in the top

Bud – the fresh or dried flowers of the female marijuana plant

Bhudda stick – another name for *Thai stick*

*Cannabis indica* – scientific name for a species of marijuana plant, the Indian hemp

*Cannabis sativa* – strain of cannabis most popularly used for smoking

Cheech and Chong – Cult 1970s *pot heads* responsible for comedy records and films

Chiba-Chiba – a Brazilian form of pot, usually compressed into *bricks*

Chillum/chalice – a small cone-shaped pipe made of clay, or sometimes fruit and vegetable rinds

Chronic – high-quality or potent joint

Cocktail – a joint of combined tobacco and marijuana

Colombian – the most common type of grass

Doobie – joint. The term originated in the 1960s and 1970s on the cult
US TV show *Romper Room*, where the good children were called
'Good Do-Bes'. It was later popularized by *Cheech and Chong* and
the *Fabulous Furry Freak Brothers*

Donovan – 1960s UK folk singer who became the first celebrity to be
busted for cannabis possession in 1965

Dope – any controlled substance, although usually refers to marijuana

Durban Brown – Marijuana from the Natal Province of South Africa

Dylan, Bob – US folk singer who advocated marijuana and is thought to
have introduced the drug to The Beatles

Elbow – 0.45kg (1lb) of pot

Fabulous Furry Freak Brothers – Cult cartoon characters created by
Gilbert Shelton in 1970

Fresh – great, good, grand. 'That's fresh!'

Froggy – refers to a dry mouth after smoking

Gage – 1940s slang for pot

Ganja – Jamaican/Indian term for pot

Gold – yellow pot from Acapulco, Mexico

Grass – cannabis, marijuana, weed

Hash(ish) – smoking mixture that varies by region. It is primarily
associated with resin obtained from Middle Eastern marijuana

Hemp – stalk and stem of the cannabis plant, traditionally used to make
rope and fabric

Herb – Jamaican term for marijuana. Derived from biblical references

Hippie Trail – popular route taken by 1960s pot heads, which went from Morocco to India and incorporated many hash shops

Hogleg – large, overfilled joint that looks like a hog's leg

Hookah – hashish water pipe with four stems that enables four people to smoke at the same time. Used by the caterpillar in *Alice In Wonderland*

Jefferson airplane – 1930s US term used for a *roach* holder fashioned from a matchbook cover. Later the name of a hippie band fronted by Grace Slick

Jive – slang word for the marijuana-influenced music and dancing of 1930s and 1940s America

Johnson – 1960s US term for a joint, as in 'Gimme a toke on that johnson, man'

Joint – marijuana cigarette, also known as a jay

Kief/kif/kaff/khayf – golden pollen hash from Morocco, Lebanon and other Middle East nations

Lambsbread – large *buds* from Jamaica, shaped like a lamb's tail, that can be carved like a loaf of bread

Marijuana – term popularized in Mexico (translation means intoxicated) for the smokable flowers and leaves of the female cannabis plant

Marley, Bob – Jamaican musician who promoted the use of *herb* through Rastafarianism

Maryjane/MJ – female cannabis plant. Male plants have almost no active *tetrahydrocannabinol*

Mezz – another name for marijuana. Derived from Mezz Mezzrow, 1930s jazzman and dope dealer who supplied the New Orleans jazz greats such as Louis Armstrong

Monged - describes the tiredness smokers feel when they come down from a high - 'I'm monged'

Muggles - US term for marijuana, which originated in the 1930s

Munchies - insatiable appetite following marijuana smoking

Nickel bag - US term for $5 (£3.45) worth of marijuana

Oil - purified and concentrated resin from hashish or marijuana

Oz - 1oz (28g) of pot

Paraquat - weedkiller that has been used by the American government to destroy cannabis plantations since the 1970s. It led to the great Paraquat Scare of 1976, where *pot heads* believed they were smoking contaminated marijuana

Panama Red - potent strain of marijuana from Panama

Pot - cannabis, marijuana, grass

Pot-head - devotee of marijuana

Reefer - turn-of-the-century term for marijuana that is still in popular use today

Rizla - brand of cigarette papers used for rolling joints

Roach - cardboard filter used in joints

Rope dope - low-quality pot from a leafy hemp

Shit - another name for cannabis

Sinsemilla - flowering tops of seedless plants

Skunk - aromatic sinsemilla, usually cultivated from Afghani marijuana

Smoke - another term for pot, marijuana, reefer, grass etc

Soma - British protest group (named after the drug in Aldous Huxley's *Brave New World*) who sent a full-page letter to *The Times* demanding the legalization of cannabis in 1967

Spliff - Jamaican term for a joint, now popular worldwide

Stash – supply of dope, usually hidden

Stoned – intoxicated by marijuana

Tea – Slang for marijuana

Tea pad – Illicit marijuana den popular in 1930s New York

THC/tetrahydrocannabinol – psychoactive cannabinoid in marijuana that is responsible for the high

Thai stick – variety of marijuana usually wrapped around thin bamboo splints

Thyme – spice commonly used by dealers to defraud customers because it looks like marijuana

Toke – to inhale/puff from a joint

Toklas, Alice B – creator of a cult hashish fudge

Twigs and seeds – unsmokable leftovers from screening marijuana before sale, or the detritus in the bottom of the bag after purchase

Viper – name given to people who frequented *tea pads* and smoked *jive* – derives from the hissing noise they made when inhaling smoke

Wasted – term meaning 'out of your brain' on weed

Weed – another term for marijuana, grass, reefer, etc

Zonked – wasted

Zig-zag – popular brand of US rolling papers famous for the silhouette of a bearded smoker on the label

## TIMELINE

2700 BC: First recorded use of cannabis as a medicine, in China

1200 BC: Cannabis mentioned in the sacred Hindu text *Atharvaveda* as 'sacred grass', one of the five sacred plants of India. It is used as an offering to Shiva

550 BC: The Persian prophet Zoroaster writes the *Zend-Avesta*, a sacred text that lists more than 10,000 medicinal plants. Hemp is at the top of the list

500 BC: Hemp is introduced into the countries of northern Europe for the first time by the Scythians of Asia

430 BC: Greek historian Herodotus observes the ritual and recreational use of cannabis by the Scythians

AD 70: Dioscorides mentions the widespread use of cannabis as a medicine in Rome

AD 200: Roman historian Galen observes that it is sometimes 'customary to give Hemp to guests to promote hilarity and enjoyment'

AD 800: Islamic prophet Mohammed permits cannabis use – but forbids alcohol

1100: Cannabis smoking is, by now, commonplace in the Middle East

1150: Moslems use cannabis to start Europe's first paper mill, mashing the hemp leaves into pulp and rolling them into tough parchment

1200: Arab traders take cannabis to the Mozambique coast of Africa

1378: One of the first dissenting voices is heard when Ottoman Emir Soudoun Scheikhouni issues an edict against eating cannabis

1430: Joan of Arc is accused of using herbal 'witch drugs' such as cannabis to hear voices

1484: Pope Innocent VIII labels cannabis as an unholy sacrament of the Satanic mass and issues a papal ban on cannabis medicines

1533: The use of hemp for fabric assumes vital importance in naval Britain, where it is used to make sails. Henry VIII issues a decree in 1533 that for every 60 acres (24ha) of arable land a farmer owned, a quarter acre (0.1ha) was to be sown with hemp. The penalty for not doing so was to be three shillings and four pence

1563: Queen Elizabeth I orders landowners with 60 acres (24ha) or more to grow cannabis or face a £5 ($7.25) fine

1564: King Philip of Spain orders cannabis to be grown throughout his empire, from Argentina to Oregon

1597: English physician John Gerard recommends cannabis as it 'consumeth wind and dryeth up seed [semen]'

1650: Cannabis becomes a major trade item between central and southern Asia. Its recreational use spreads across the Middle East and Asia

1653: English physician Nicholas Culpeper claims cannabis 'allayeth inflamations, easeth the pain of gout, tumours or knots of joints, pain of hips'

1798: While in Egypt, Napoleon is stunned by the use of cannabis among the lower classes. He bans it – but his soldiers take the pastime of cannabis smoking back to France with them

1840: Cannabis-based medicines become available in the USA, while cannabis is sold in Persian pharmacies. Le Club Hachichins, or Hashish Eater's Club, is established in Paris

1842: Cannabis becomes a popular medicine in Victorian England, used to treat ailments such as muscle cramps, menstrual cramps, rheumatism and the convulsions of tetanus, rabies and epilepsy

1883: Hashish houses become commonplace in America

1890: Queen Victoria is prescribed cannabis for period pains. Her personal doctor, Sir Robert Russell, claims: 'It is one of the most valuable medicines we possess.' In the same year, it is made illegal in Greece and Turkey

1901: The British Royal Commission concludes that cannabis is relatively harmless and not worth prohibiting

1915-27: Cannabis is prevented for non-medical use in California (1915), Texas (1919), Louisiana (1924) and New York (1927)

1924: Cannabis is outlawed by the Geneva Conference on Opium

1928: The Dangerous Drugs Act makes cannabis illegal in Britain

1937: The US Federal government outlaws cannabis. The Federal Bureau of Narcotics prosecutes 3,000 doctors for 'illegally' prescribing cannabis-derived medicines. Its chief, Harry Anslinger, writes the polemic *Marijuana: Assassin Of Youth*

1967: Mick Jagger and Keith Richards of the Rolling Stones are sentenced to prison for smoking cannabis. A 'Legalize Pot' rally is held in Hyde Park, London. An advert in *The Times*, paid for by Beatle Paul McCartney, states: 'The law against marijuana is immoral in principle and unworkable in practice.' Signatories include The Beatles, author Graham Greene, Jonathan Aitken and eccentric psychiatrist RD Laing

1969: The Rolling Stones hold a free concert in Hyde Park, London, during which an organization called the Bong Parade pass a foot-long joint among the crowd

There is mass use of the drug at Woodstock

1971: The UK reinforces its anti-cannabis stand with the Misuse Drugs

Act. The plant and its resin are classified as Class B drugs, cannabis oil Class A, while cannabis itself is defined as Schedule 1 - of no therapeutic use

1973: The Drug Enforcement Administration (DEA) is set up in the United States and vows to destroy all marijuana cultivated on its own soil

1976: The Dutch authorities legalize the sale of cannabis in dedicated cannabis cafés

1980: Paul McCartney is busted for cannabis possession at Tokyo airport and spends ten days in jail

1981: Direct action group Smokey Bear sends cannabis plants to 60 English MPs

1990: Los Angeles police chief Darryl Gates testifies before the US Senate Judiciary Committee that 'casual drug users should be taken out and shot'

1992: President Bill Clinton admits to having smoked cannabis - but claims he never inhaled

1996: Clinton employs General Barry McCaffrey as his new, hard-hitting drugs tsar. Transform, the campaign to liberalize drug policy and legislation, is launched. Several US states allow medicinal cannabis to be distributed in special 'cannabis clubs'

1997: William Straw, son of British Home Secretary Jack Straw, is arrested for dealing cannabis, following a *Daily Mirror* sting. He is cautioned by police. The new Labour government appoints Keith Hellawell, former Chief Constable, as the new drugs tsar. *The Independent On Sunday* launches a campaign to decriminalize cannabis. Editor Rosie Boycott keeps a cannabis plant in her office

The Alliance for Cannabis Therapeutics launches a major advertising campaign in the national press for the legalization of marijuana for medical use

1998: *The Independent On Sunday*'s campaign culminates in a march on Trafalgar Square, which attracts thousands of supporters

2000: English Prime Minister Tony Blair agrees that cannabis should be legalized for medical purposes. His Home Secretary Jack Straw refuses to do so

The Police Foundation Report suggests that certain drugs be reclassified and penalties reduced. The government rejects the recommendations

Staunch right-wing newspaper the *Daily Mail* calls for a 'mature and rational' debate on the drugs issue. The *Daily Telegraph* suggests an 'experiment with legalization'

General Barry McCaffrey loses his job as US drugs tsar

2001: Canada becomes the first country in the world to legalize cannabis for medical use. Portugal, Belgium and Switzerland all make the first moves towards decriminalizing the drug

David Blunkett, the new British Home Secretary, sacks Keith Hellawell. He gives tacit support to a scheme in Brixton, South London where police will not arrest people using cannabis. He also announces that cannabis is to be reclassified from a Class B drug to a Class C drug, putting it on a par with amphetamines.

## SOURCES AND RECOMMENDED READING

Boyd, Neil: *High Society* (Key Porter Books, 1991)

British Medical Association: *Therapeutic Uses Of Cannabis* (Taylor & Francis, 1997)

D'Oudney, JR and D'Oudney, KEA: *Cannabis: The Facts, Human Rights And The Law* (Scorpio, 2000)

Estren, Mark J: *A History Of Underground Comics* (Straight Arrow Books, 1974)

Frank, Mel: *The Marijuana Grower's Guide* (Publishers Group West, 1997)

Gold, D: *Cannabis Alchemy: The Art Of Modern Hashmaking: Methods For Preparation Of Extremely Potent Cannabis Products* (Ronin Publishing, 1990)

Gottlieb, Adam: *Ancient And Modern Methods Of Growing Extraordinary Marijuana* (Ronin Publishing, 1998)

Grossman, Andre: *Greetings From Cannabis Country* (Green Candy Press, 2001)

Grotenherman, Franjo and Russo, Ethan (editors): *Cannabis And Cannabinoids: Pharmacology, Toxicology, And Therapeutic Potential* (Integrative Healing Press, 2001)

Health and Safety Executive: *Pilot Study: Effects Of Cannabis* (HSE, 2000)

Herer, Jack: *The Emperor Wears No Clothes: The Authoritative Historical Record Of The Cannabis Plant, Marijuana Prohibition And How Hemp Can Still Save The World* (Green Planet Co, 1998)

*High Times Greatest Hits* (Trans-High Corp, 1994)

Iverson, Lesley: *The Science Of Marijuana* (Oxford University Press, 2000)

King, Jason: *The Cannabible* (Ten Speed Press, 2001)

Matthews, Patrick: *Cannabis Culture* (Bloomsbury, 2000)

McAllister, William: *Drug Diplomacy In The 20th Century: An International History* (Routledge, 1999)

Morgan, John P and Zimmer, Lynn: *Marijuana Myths, Marijuana Facts* (Lindesmith Center, 1997)

Nelson, Robert A and Robinson, Rowan: *The Great Book Of Hemp: The Complete Guide To The Commercial, Medicinal And Psychotropic Uses Of The World's Most Extraordinary Plant* (Park Street Press, 1995)

Police Foundation: *Drugs And The Law: Report Of The Independent Inquiry Into The Misuse Of Drugs Act 1971*

Potter, Beverly and Joy, Dan: *The Healing Magic Of Cannabis* (Ronin Publishing, 1998)

Ratsch, Christian: *Marijuana Medicine: A World Tour Of The Healing And Visionary Powers Of Cannabis* (Healing Art Press, 2001)

Select Committee on Science and Technology: *Therapeutic Uses Of Cannabis: Government Response To The Report* (HMSO Books, 2001)

Sherman, Carol and Smith, Andrew: *Highlights: An Illustrated History Of Cannabis* (Ten Speed Press, 1999)

Solman, Larry: *Reefer Madness* (Grove Press, 1979)

Storm, Daniel: *Marijuana Hydroponics* (And/Or Books, 1986)

*Therapeutic Uses Of Cannabis With Evidence: House Of Lords Papers* (HMSO Books, 2001)

Witton, John: *Cannabis: The Facts* (Avebury Technical, 2002)

The Little Book Of
# HEROIN

Printed and bound in the UK by MPG Books, Bodmin

Distributed in the US by Publishers Group West

Published by Sanctuary Publishing Limited, Sanctuary House, 45-53 Sinclair
Road, London W14 0NS, United Kingdom

www.sanctuarypublishing.com

ISBN: 1-86074-525-3

The Little Book Of

# HEROIN

Robert Ashton

**Sanctuary**

# CONTENTS

# INTRODUCTION

The world is in the grip of a frightening drug: heroin. Crime, poverty, dependency, death and destruction trail in its wake. Over a century's experience of fighting the drug has failed to kill or tame it and heroin's stranglehold remains as tight in the 21st century as it was in the 20th. The drug has been outlawed for most of its life and abused almost since the day it was discovered in the late 19th century.

In every western country its use has grown considerably in the past few decades and the production of opium, the raw material used to manufacture heroin, has increased exponentially to meet demand. There's no question, heroin is here to stay.

...and it presents a massive problem. Heroin is made dangerous because it is traded by criminals and almost always misused. It is illegally supplied, cut with myriad – and sometimes noxious – adulterants, and often used in harmful and unhygienic environments, causing problems for both user, society and governments. The latter, picking up the bill for everything from soaring crime rates to spiralling healthcare costs.

The challenge facing the world's governments is how to deal with it. For most of its life, more and more prohibitive laws have been introduced to deal with heroin. But, as Prohibition in 1920s and 1930s America demonstrated, a total ban has largely served to entrench global drug cartels and create billions in funds for the criminal organizations that run them.

Society's obligations to provide education about heroin, prevent life-threatening temptation and treat chronic addiction became more sophisticated in the second half of the last century, with methadone programmes and advertising campaigns. Any successes have rarely been clear-cut, however, because heroin spins a complex web of issues and problems, and the pace of change around its orbit often outstripped the legislators and doctors; the moral climate shifted, new research revealed new problems, heroin supply increased, heroin prices dropped and purity levels improved.

This means that methods and tools for tackling the problem need to be continually adapted and reviewed. That's the difficult part – changing minds and policies that deal with heroin always poses tricky trade-offs and judgements about their impact, essentially because it is the young who are most at risk.

But, by the 1990s, that radical sea change had begun to take place. A more enlightened, better-managed and better-financed approach to the problem was adopted by several countries. Some European governments and a number of other western-model countries, notably Australia, began to take harm-reduction issues more seriously. Treatment, not punishment, became the new watchword.

The speed of this change was clearly demonstrated by the UK's experience. In 1998 its first 'drugs tsar', Keith Hellawell, unveiled a ten-year drugs strategy based around young people, communities, treatment and availability, setting major long-term targets: to cut heroin use by 25 per cent in 2003 and, by 2008, halve its use, reduce its availability by 50 per cent and double the number of heroin abusers in treatment.

By 2001 some of these targets were believed to be unachievable; Hellawell's role as anti-drugs co-ordinator had been sidelined; and, although his strategy template was still being applied, it was under review. It appeared that the problem of heroin was beginning to be seen more as a public health issue than a criminal one.

In 2002 UK police chiefs broke new ground by recommending that heroin users be sent for treatment rather than prosecuted, and the reintroduction of widespread prescription of heroin was being examined by a Home Affairs Select Committee and the UK's National Treatment Agency.

Further, a former UK cabinet minister and a serving police chief added their voices to the pro-legalization of heroin lobby, which seeks to break the drug's link with crime and to hand governments a sizeable income from taxing its legal sale. It is argued that these funds, potentially worth millions, can then be used for addiction treatment or prevention.

However, after more than a century of living with heroin and its associated problems, it is clear that there are no easy solutions. Complete prohibition hasn't worked, yet legalization of heroin or even decriminalization remain distant, and bring with them their own problems of control and increased demand.

As countries, their governments and their populations become more mature and sophisticated with regard to their perceptions of the drug and its use, politicians and experts will continue to weigh the evidence for an overhaul of drug laws, and examine and test new techniques for dealing with heroin. In the meantime, the drug's hold remains firm.

01 CULTURE

## HEROIN IS HEADLINE NEWS

The impact of drugs on modern media and culture has been enormous. Arguably, though, heroin has had more success than any other at imprinting its bewitching power on to the cultural consciousness. The media is fascinated by heroin. The public fear it. And politicians make capital from it.

As the 20th century turned into the 21st, there was no let-up. In fact, heroin was filling increased acres of newsprint and giving anxious leader writers more opportunities to warn of the drug's perils.

In 1997, for example. when the leafy Texas town of Plano was haunted by a string of heroin overdoses, the drug was rarely off the front page of US tabloids and the leader position in radio broadcasts.

In Britain another banner headline, 'This Is How Heroin Killed Our Girl', in March 2002, reminded everyone that the drug doesn't discriminate. Beneath the headline were two pictures of the same girl, Rachel Whitear. One showed her dressed in her school uniform; the other was a harrowing colour shot of Rachel dead. The 21-year-old university dropout had been found on her knees, slumped on the floor of a bedsit, a hypodermic syringe still clasped in her hand. She had been dead three days.

The 11 September terrorist attacks on New York also had the effect of reinforcing heroin's media profile as the ultimate evil. US President George W Bush didn't hesitate to link heroin with the 21st century's first big battle: the war against terror. The drug was perceived as an ally of Osama bin Laden's al-Qaeda terrorists and the Taliban regime, which ruled Afghanistan until its overthrow in late 2001.

## HEROIN CHIC

Although ubiquitous, heroin's success has been bolstered by its ability to reinvent itself and add new layers to its myth. This was most notable in the early 1990s. Before then, it was perceived by most as a drug for losers – Wall Street winners used cocaine.

Images of junkie losers with dirty needles in filthy squats were replaced with scenes of bone thin, sexy models in filthy squats. Heroin wasn't just dangerous, it was cool. And once it made it on to glossy double-page fashion spreads it soon passed from the underground to the mainstream. Wall Street brokers traded their coke spoons for smack spikes.

Dubbed 'heroin chic', photographers like Corinne Day, David Sims and Juergen Teller shot fashion spreads against seedy backdrops with models who appeared strung out, their dark-rimmed, sunken eyes reflecting an elegantly wasted look.

The dangers of a heroin epidemic being unleashed were recognized by former US President Bill Clinton when he attacked the fashion industry for popularizing heroin chic in May 1997. He said, 'They [fashion leaders] are admitting flat out that images projected in fashion shoots in the last few years have made heroin addiction seem glamorous and sexy and cool. And as some of those people in those images start to die now, it has become obvious that that is not true. You do not need to glamorize addiction to sell clothes.'

But the fact that the rich and the famous were using heroin gave editors the opportunity – and excuse – to fill their pages with pouting photographs of models and actors, which compounded the link between heroin and fame. Heroin had acquired a new image, far from dirty needles and hookers in dark alleys.

Heroin use has escalated and its cultural influence is more prevalent than it has ever been. It's possible to put together a whole heroin-themed jukebox, starting out by slipping Alice In Chains' 'Junkhead' or The Velvet Underground's 'Heroin' out of the CD collection.

Even the local cinema could mount a smack retrospective, kicking off with the double bill *Requiem For A Dream* followed by *French Connection II*. And for a heroin read, library shelves are literally groaning under the weight of all the literature – Irvine Welsh's *Trainspotting*, Luke Davies' *Candy* or practically anything from William Burroughs – celebrating the drug.

## HEROIN MOVIES

A 1997 study of movie rentals in the USA found that 22 per cent of the 200 most popular films depicted illicit drugs and about a quarter of those (26 per cent) contained graphic portrayals of their preparation and use. Also, surprisingly, very few (15 per cent) contained an anti-drug message.

In the very early years of cinema, drug use and the possession of narcotics were not legislated upon and an opium user or heroin addict didn't carry the moral stigma they do today. This meant a crop of US and European movies set in opium dens – such the 1906 French film *Rèves D'Un Fumeur D'Opium* ('The Opium Smoker's Dreams') – played in theatres before legislation and changing social attitudes dictated a new agenda in Hollywood.

The first attempt to curb the proliferation of heroin and morphine in film came in October 1927. In an attempt to stave off rigorous censorship, the Motion Picture Association agreed to endorse and boycott a list of 36 controversial subjects drawn up by Will Hays. The use of drugs and drug trafficking were listed near the top of this list. This was reinforced by the 1930 Motion Picture Production Code, which prohibited any mention of addiction or trafficking on screen. This gave the Production Code Administration

(PCA) a licence to deny a seal of approval to any film that broke the code, effectively dooming its release.

For the next two decades sex not drugs occupied the moral guardians. Then, in 1955, Otto Preminger's *The Man With The Golden Arm* blasted apart the taboo surrounding narcotics abuse, with Frank Sinatra portraying heroin addict jazz drummer, Frankie Machine. The film was in violation of the PCA, which refused to grant it a certificate; however Preminger released the film himself. Its success helped convince the PCA to amend its code a year later to allow treatments of drug addiction. Although the audience never gets to see the needle in Sinatra's arm he is seen preparing to tie off a tourniquet and the camera lingers on his face as the rush hits. Heroin had become a major movie star.

Since the early 1970s, smack movies have been packing them in. In 1970 Paul Morrissey's *Trash* featured the first shot of needle puncturing skin. But it was 1971 that was to herald a turning point for the drug: in that year no fewer than four mainstream heroin movies were screened. *Jennifer On My Mind* was released alongside *Born To Win* (aka *Addict*), starring George Segal, T*he Panic In Needle Park*, which made Al Pacino's reputation as an actor, and Floyd Mutrux's *Dusty And Sweets McGee*. The latter featured a character getting a fix under his tongue and, like many early heroin movies, did not stack the screen with authority figures expressing their moral outrage about the drug.

The 1980s saw a shift of emphasis to concentrate on real-life casualties: Sid Vicious, Charlie Parker and Chet Baker were all featured in biopics. In 1989, Gus Van Sant established the cinematic vocabulary and visual template of the contemporary heroin movie with *Drugstore Cowboy*.

Film-makers began to realise that an injection of smack into a movie script will always fill seats. Visually, what gives heroin the drop on other drugs is that it isn't simply snorted, smoked or swallowed. There is the whole shocking paraphernalia of the junkie: the syringes, the belts for tying off, the cotton wool and spoon are all perfect props for the cinematographer to shoot in close-up. The act of injecting is much more visually shocking than popping an E. The syringe will break skin and then fill with blood as it hits a vein. It'll also leave the film's character with lasting physical effects and they will wear these track marks and scabs like battle scars as the movie draws to its climax.

Moreover, heroin wasn't just appearing in films. Real-life Hollywood stars had come to embrace the drug. River Phoenix, who played a junkie hustler in Van Sant's *My Own Private Idaho*, died in 1993, aged 23. Blood tests verified the presence in the actor's blood of alcohol, Valium, heroin, and cocaine, the last two being the vital ingredients of a speedball.

A few years later, Robert Downey Jr, an Oscar nominee, fought a public battle against heroin and other drug addictions, culminating in rehab and a prison sentence on the back of narcotic and weapons charges.

## HEROIN MUSIC

It's an old story. Heroin and music. Since the turn of the last century musicians have enjoyed an uneasy – and often devastating – association with heroin. It has spawned songs, even movements. Progressive rock was an unfortunate side effect of LSD; the nihilism of punk's blank generation and grunge ran on heroin.

Musicians have been singing about it or dying from it since Charlie Parker, Miles Davis, Art Pepper, and Chet Baker defined 'cool' in the 1950s. They used heroin to ease the days between the long sweaty nights blowing their horns or mashing the piano keys. Then heroin was cool. In his frank memoir about heroin, *The Trumpet And The Spike*, Baker admits that most of the musicians he played with were on junk and that 'spiking myself became a gesture as automatic as lighting a cigarette is with you'.

The British mod scene in the early 1960s fuelled itself on purple hearts, and the hippies saw out that decade by opening their minds with LSD and magic mushrooms. But of course, heroin never really went away. Iggy Pop, Keith Richards, and Lou Reed were all users. But their influence on lifestyle didn't spread much beyond New York's East Village or those who bought The Velvet Underground's *White Light/White Heat*.

Punk's arrival in 1976 was ostensibly about blowing away anything that had gone before. Two drugs it didn't dispense with were speed and heroin. Johnny Rotten was scornful of heroin and – for the most part – the British punks at the Roxy contented themselves with amphetamines. His fellow Sex Pistol Sid Vicious was to become dope's heroin ambassador. Vicious was soon a smack casualty. Out on bail on a charge of stabbing his junkie girlfriend Nancy Spungen at the Chelsea Hotel, Sid died of an accidental overdose in New York.

However, by the early 1990s heroin wasn't playing second fiddle to any other drugs. It was *the* drug. In the USA, street heroin was becoming increasingly pure, although the price remained resolutely stable. Snorting and smoking became popular. Seattle was gaining a reputation as the heroin capital of America and one of the city's bands, Nirvana, were providing the bleak soundtrack for a new youth movement: grunge. Heroin was the drug to play when they dropped the needle on *Nevermind*. Suddenly every band had a junkie, detoxing, getting busted, or passing out in photo shoots.

## HEROIN-RELATED DEATHS IN ROCK

- In 1959 Billie Holiday finally succumbed to the twin ravages of heart disease and heroin under police arrest on a hospital bed.
- Frankie Lymon's career came to an abrupt stop in 1968 when the singing sensation (he was the frontman in Frankie Lymon And The Teenagers) was discovered on the bathroom floor of a New York apartment with a syringe by his side.

- In 1970 the hit of the Monterey Pop Festival, Janis Joplin, died of an accidental heroin overdose in the bedroom of her suite at the Hollywood Landmark Hotel. At 27, she was at the peak of her short career.
- Jimi Hendrix died of a barbiturate overdose within weeks of Joplin, but the 27-year-old guitarist had been a known user of heroin.
- Aged 27, Jim Morrison was found dead of heart failure in the bath at his Paris apartment in 1971. The full facts surrounding the premature death of The Doors' vocalist in the early hours of the morning are still unclear, although it is thought he acquired a fix earlier that night and, if that didn't cause the fatal heart attack, many blame his death on the cumulative effects of his heavy drug use.
- The 24-year-old Scottish drummer of The Average White Band, Robbie McIntosh, was killed at a Hollywood party in 1974 after he was spiked with a lethal dose of heroin.
- Tim Buckley died in his sleep in 1975 after snorting prodigious amounts of heroin supplied by a friend.
- Just months after his girlfriend Nancy Spungen was found stabbed to death in New York's Chelsea Hotel, punk rocker Sid Vicious scored a lethal dose of heroin and suffered a fatal overdose in his sleep. He was 21.
- Darby Crash of the Los Angeles punk band The Germs died of an overdose at the end of 1980, just a week after reforming the group.

- After years of heroin addiction and a career that remained resolutely underrated, singer/songwriter Tim Hardin died at the end of 1980.
- Malcolm Owen of UK punk group The Ruts, who dealt with his heroin addiction in many of the band's lyrics, lost his battle with the drug in 1980.
- Heroin split The Pretenders, literally. Guitarist James Honeyman-Scott and bass player Pete Farndon both met their ends after taking speedballs in 1982 and 1983 respectively.
- Red Hot Chili Peppers lost their 26-year-old lead guitarist when Hillel Slovak's drug lifestyle caught up with him and he died of an overdose in 1988.
- Chet Baker was hooked most of his adult life. Before his death in 1988 – falling from a hotel room in Amsterdam – the drug ravaged his film-idol looks, drew him beatings from connections, earned him dozens of busts on narcotic violations, and landed him a spell in Riker's Island jail.
- After more than a decade of heavy drug abuse, the former New York Dolls, and Heartbreakers, guitarist Johnny Thunders died of a heroin overdose in New Orleans in 1991. The proto-punk, who was 38 at the time of his death, recorded The Ramones' classic 'Chinese Rocks' and often played it at gigs.
- In 1994, Nirvana's Kurt Cobain was found dead. The guitarist/vocalist with the Seattle-based grunge band,

had struggled with years of smack abuse. Although Cobain shot himself, he delivered the self-inflicted fatal injury just a week after almost succumbing to a heroin overdose.

- Kristen Pfaff, the 27-year-old bassist in Courtney Love's female grunge band Hole, died of an overdose in a bathroom in 1994.
- The drug-related lifestyle of Grateful Dead's Jerry Garcia finally caught up with him in 1995 when he died from health complications during withdrawal from heroin addiction.
- While preparing for a Blind Melon concert in New Orleans in 1995, the group's 23-year-old singer, Shannon Hoon, died of an overdose.
- Jonathan Melvoin, keyboardist with Smashing Pumpkins, died of an overdose in a Manhattan hotel in 1996.
- In 2002, Alice In Chains' lead singer Layne Staley was found dead in his Seattle home. Staley's long-time battle with drug dependency was a central component of the band's sound, which included the song 'Junkhead'.

## HEROIN LITERATURE

Books about smack are a writer's dream. All that hollow-cheeked desperation and grubby hopelessness sends authors scurrying to their word processors, clutching their thesauruses tightly. Junkie lit offers opportunities for some unremittingly bleak prose, dark, dark characters – everyone loves a loser and you can't get a better loser than a junkie – and a dramatic final chapter in which someone overdoses in a grubby council flat.

As a plot device, heroin can take off in any direction the author wants to go – from introspective angst, as in Alexander Trocchi's *Cain's Book*, to crazy road odyssey in *Go Now* by Richard Hell. The rituals connected with heroin use, from the cooking to the injecting, are excellent vehicles to show off literary dexterity. The vocabulary for jacking up can easily up a writer's word count if the plot is running out of steam, and those similes and adjectives just can't be reined in when it comes to writing about veins, needles and blood.

## THOMAS DE QUINCEY

There's no doubt that heroin has inspired a wealth of ground-breaking and searing work, all the more so when written by an author with first-hand experience of addiction. This applies to one of the earliest memoirs on the subject, *Thomas De Quincey's Confessions Of An English Opium Eater*, published in 1822.

This autobiographical account of his opium addiction is De Quincey's most famous work. The writer took opium to ease physical pain but became addicted to it. The book charts the psychological effects of the drug, from the euphoria of his initial experiences to the darkness and nightmares arising from long-term usage. Richly written, it is a seminal tale of the effects of addiction on a brilliant mind.

## COLLINS, KIPLING, AND CROWLEY

In the days when books about drug addiction were frowned upon, it was a very daring author who would break the taboo and shine a light on such behaviour. In Wilkie Collins' 1868 novel *The Moonstone*, opium is used as a plot device for both its medicinal properties and its exotic and deviant connotations.

Rudyard Kipling's 1901 novel *Kim* also makes a pointed comment about the ready availability of opium in India, and its power to addict and corrupt.

In 1922 Aleister Crowley shocked British Victorian society with his book *Diary Of A Drug Fiend*. Crowley called himself Beast 666, totally rejected the Victorian hypocrisy of his day and was a constant user of heroin, cocaine, opium, hash and peyote. *Diary Of A Drug Fiend* was an eye-opener to those who knew little of drugs, but Crowley wanted to show the true nature of drug addiction, that there were moments of joy and elation, not just despair.

## WILLIAM S BURROUGHS

Burroughs is the classic junkie lit author who lived it, and *Junky* is generally regarded as a classic of its type. *Junky* starkly recounts Burroughs' decades-long addiction to heroin. Written when the USA was in the grip of anti-drug hysteria, the first edition contained a number of disclaimers by the publisher whenever Burroughs made some unorthodox claims about the nature of addiction. The disclaimers were outlined at the beginning: 'For the protection of the reader, we have inserted occasional parenthetical notes to indicate where the author clearly departs from accepted medical fact or makes unsubstantiated statements in an effort to justify his actions.'

### ALEXANDER TROCCHI

Yet there are others who believe the contrary, that heroin destroys brains and creativity. In 1960, *Cain's Book* by cult Scottish writer Alexander Trocchi was published. Known as the 'Scottish Beat', Trocchi was a heroin addict who turned his young wife to prostitution to pay for drugs.

### JIM CARROLL

In 1978 the role of author who lived it was passed on to the poet, playwright, musician and author Jim Carroll whose memoirs, *The Basketball Diaries*, were based on his own heroin addiction. The book covers the period 1962–6 when the teenage Carroll, growing up on the mean streets of New York. He tells of his posh private schooling and his years playing basketball, stealing and hustling gay men to support his growing heroin addiction.

In the 1980s heroin seemed to have been overtaken by other drugs as a literary muse. Writers like Brett Easton Ellis and Jay McInerney favoured cocaine and tranquillizers as plot drivers, and bright young things snorting Charlie from toilet seats occupied young fashionable novelists. Heroin all but disappeared from the bookshelves and it wasn't until the 1990s that it made a comeback – in spectacular fashion.

The protagonists of books like Linda Yablonsky's semi-autobiographical novel *The Story Of Junk* and Peter Trachtenberg's memoir *7 Tattoos* are swamped by the mechanics of drug use, which the authors clearly find more fascinating than characterization and plot.

It probably took the work of Will Self in the 1990s and Irvine Welsh's *Trainspotting* to revitalize the genre. Self, journalist and writer, first injected heroin at 17 and was a full-time junkie for almost 20 years. Many of his short stories and articles deal with heroin and addiction, but he is strongest when writing about the drug as an incidental element within a story.

Welsh could never be accused of taking his subject too seriously and although he doesn't stint on the despair of addiction, he manages to wring a lot of humour from his subject. The protagonists have no future, but Welsh doesn't moralize.

The appeal of heroin to this latest generation of writers goes beyond its illegal status. Heroin doesn't give up. It has a definite hold on a writer like no other drug – especially a writer who is an ex-user. Luke Davies is a poet and writer whose novel *Candy* didn't follow the usual drug novel path. It's a love story first and a heroin novel second and, although the presence of heroin is powerful and all-pervading, the relationship between two people and the nature of obsession is the central theme.

## HEROIN STREET SLANG

Heroin's long history, cultural impact and prevalence among literary figures – with a poetic bent for adding to the argot – has ensured that it probably has more slang words associated with it than any other drug.

There are hundreds of different names for heroin. The death of John Belushi in 1982 gave some heroin users the inspiration for another name to describe the speedball cocktail of heroin and cocaine, which led to the comic's demise. And, following the death of River Phoenix in 1993, some culturally aware addicts in north Hollywood and Santa Monica would, for as long as the actor's name continued to appear in newspapers, talk about 'falling' or 'swimming in the river' when they jacked up. Bart Simpson, the character from the TV show *The Simpsons*, has also been added to the slang list, as has TV host Jerry Springer.

With the drug's capacity to suddenly end life neither is it any coincidence that, more than any other drug, the slang draws on words associated with death ('heaven dust', 'dead on arrival', 'hell dust') or its methods ('bombs away').

There is a definite geographical bias to the slang, which operates at a countrywide or even citywide level. Thus, 'chieva' or 'black tar', a type of cheap heroin smuggled up from Mexico, and which has flooded west coast US cities, is popular around Haight-Ashbury in San Francisco, but will never be used in the estates around Moss Side in Manchester, where 'skag' has entered the vernacular. However, a London junkie in a Brixton squat may often prefer to use the more widespread 'smack'.

Even illegal drugs have brand names and heroin is no exception. In New York and many other US cities, dealers often branded the heroin they were supplying, even accompanying this with a distinctive logo on the $10 (£7) bags it was sold in. Some well-known 'brands' include names that are designed to appeal to the target consumer group by drumming home the dangerous outlaw status of the product: Homicide, Poison, Kill City, Last Payday, Body Bag, Lethal Injection, Silver Bullet.

By picking ever more outrageous names the dealers demonstrated they had learned a lesson from the media and advertising: shock sells and an established brand can lead to customer loyalty. These brands were traditionally sold from one spot and were recognizable because they would consistently have similar levels of purity and be cut with the same – non-narcotic – additives. In short, the addict knew what they were getting.

# HISTORY

## POPPY'S PROGRESS

Heroin is made from morphine, a naturally occurring substance found in the seed of the opium poppy. The history of heroin, therefore, starts with the opium. And this begins with the cultivation of the poppy, *Papaver somniferum*. The milky fluid extracted from the plant's ovary is highly narcotic after drying. This is opium, the name derived from the Greek word for 'juice of a plant'.

Around 3400 BC the first poppy was cultivated in lower Mesopotamia. Some archaeologists also claim to have found evidence of fossilized poppy seeds, which suggests that Neanderthal man may have used opium over 30,000 years ago. Excavations of the remains of Neolithic settlements in Switzerland have unearthed evidence that the poppy may have been cultivated then: perhaps for the food value in the poppy seeds.

The first reference to the poppy appears in a Sumerian text, which refers to it as Hul Gil, the 'joy plant', and the Sumerians soon passed on the art of poppy culling – and its euphoric effects – to the Assyrians. Some 2,000 years later, the Babylonians introduced opium to the Egyptians, who began to cultivate fields around Thebes.

Priests encouraged the use of opium preparations for remedies, sometimes called thedacium after the potent Thebes poppy fields. A trade in opium soon flourished, throughout the reigns of Thutmose IV, Akhenaton and King Tutankhamen, with the Minoans and Phoenicians operating profitable routes across the Mediterranean into Greece and Europe. It also became common practice to entomb pharaohs with opium artefacts.

In 460 BC the father of medicine, Hippocrates, acknowledged opium's use as a narcotic and styptic in treating internal diseases and, by AD 400, Alexander the Great had introduced opium to Persia and India, and Arabic traders were shipping the poppy to China.

Opium became a taboo subject during the Inquisition and it largely disappeared in Europe during the 14th and 15th centuries. However, by around 1500 the Portuguese had discovered that smoked opium produced instantaneous effects, and smoking the narcotic began to be the accepted method of taking the drug.

In 1527 opium was reintroduced into Europe through laudanum, a mix of alcohol and the drug, which was discovered by the Swiss physician Bombastus von Hohenheim. This gave successive generations, who added various spices to produce their own versions, access to mass sedation.

By the mid-17th century, opium had become the main commodity of British trade with China, its use thus taking root in the Far East. By 1839 it had also caused a war between the British and Chinese. The East India Company had enjoyed a monopoly on shipping opium from Bengal into China, and had ridden roughshod over Chinese licences imposed to restrict imports of the drug by selling it to Indian merchants who smuggled it for them.

Despite the instigation of a House of Commons Committee of Enquiry in 1830, set up to investigate the company's opium dealings, the £2 million ($2.9 million) trade continued unabated, causing an epidemic of addicts among the Chinese population. At its highest point it was believed that there were around 15 million opium users.

In 1839 the Chinese government finally acted and confiscated some 20,000 chests of opium from British warehouses in Canton. In 1840 the British Foreign Secretary, Lord Palmerston, sent out a force of 16 British warships, which besieged Guangzhou and threatened communications with the capital.

This first Opium War was settled in 1841 with the Treaty of Nanking and China ceding Hong Kong to the British. The opium trade with China continued, with new trading partners – the French and Americans – becoming involved in shipping the drug.

Some 15 years later Britain and China fought a second war when, in 1856, Chinese officials boarded and searched a British-flagged ship, the *Arrow*. The French joined the British in launching a military attack in 1857, at the end of which they demanded that the Chinese agree to the Treaty of Tianjin in 1858. This opened further ports to western trade and provided freedom of travel to European merchants inland. Trade in opium nearly doubled over the following two decades, but by this time China had also begun to grow its own poppy, which it traded in over the next century.

Many literary figures were also being seduced by opium, including John Keats, Shelley, Byron and Thomas De Quincey, who, in 1821, published his autobiographical account of opium addiction, *Confessions Of An English Opium Eater*. And, in 1860, the English doctor Thomas Sydenham was moved to write, 'Among the remedies which it has pleased Almighty God to give to man to relieve his sufferings, none is so universal and so efficacious as opium.'

Opium is a complex chemical cocktail including sugars, proteins, fats, gums, ammonia and myriad alkaloids, notably morphine, codeine, noscapine, papaverine and thebaine. Apart from thebaine, these alkaloids are used as analgesics and can reduce or abolish pain without loss of consciousness. However, it wasn't until 1805 that German scientist Friedrich Wilhelm Sertürner isolated the first alkaloid in its pure form from opium. Sertürner named the substance morphium (morphine) after Morpheus, the Greek god of dreams and sleep. It wasn't until a decade later that the powerful effects of morphine – the drug had at least ten times the potency of opium – were recognized and in 1821 a London pharmacist began producing it. Six years later German manufacturers E Merck & Company began the commercial production of morphine and in 1836 morphine entered the London Pharmacopoeia.

A new technique for administering the drug – and a crucial tool for today's junkie – arrived in 1843 when an Edinburgh-based physician, Dr Alexander Wood, discovered the process of injection using a syringe. Injected morphine is up to 300 per cent more potent and, because the effect is almost instantaneous, it rapidly led to the intravenous use of the drug as a painkiller and for recreational use.

Opiate abuse in Europe and the USA had increased significantly by the mid-1800s. Opium dens, often run by Chinese immigrants, were opening in most American cities and even in Old West towns where cowboys sat out herding duties laid up in dimly lit rooms smoking opium with prostitutes.

Opiate consumption in the USA also received a boost following the American Civil War in 1866. The wounded had been treated with morphine intravenously on the battlefield and, consequently, tens of thousands of soldiers became addicts. The medical establishment began to raise concerns about a new epidemic: morphine was being used by European and American doctors as a remedy to combat opium dependency and the addict would simply switch his addiction to morphine. Also, many patent medicines around at this time, such as laudanum and paregoric, contained opium extract. By the end of the 1890s the United States was desperate to curb the non-medical use of opium.

Then a new drug was discovered, diacetylmorphine, or heroin. It was first synthesized from morphine by the English researcher CR Alder Wright in 1874, by boiling morphine with acetic anhydride over a stove. He was trying to isolate a powerful but non-addictive alternative to morphine. He failed. The white crystalline powder he discovered is between three and eight times more potent than morphine...and easily as addictive.

However, this wasn't realised at the time. In 1895 Heinrich Dreser, who was in charge of drug development at German drug manufacturers Bayer, began production of diacetylmorphine and coined the name 'heroin' after the German word for hero, *heroisch*.

Dreser tested the new synthetic drug on animals, human volunteers and himself, and declared it was an effective treatment for a range of respiratory ailments, including tuberculosis, asthma, coughs, emphysema, and bronchitis. He also declared that the drug was not habit-forming. In 1898, *The Lancet* introduced it to British physicians. It advised, 'Heroin is said to be free from other disagreeable secondary effects of morphine.'

Commercial production of heroin began in 1898 and it was advertised by Bayer as a sedative for coughs rather than an analgesic. It was prescribed for a wider range of respiratory problems, such as whooping cough and hay fever. Doctors were also assured that its effects on motor skills and intellect were minimal.

Some dissenting voices warned of the dangers of addiction but, despite this, free samples of heroin were handed out to physicians. They often treated their patients' complaints with small doses of heroin administered orally via pills or pastilles, and drug companies manufactured over-the-counter drug kits containing a glass-barrelled hypodermic needle and vials of heroin. Bayer was soon selling heroin to dozens of countries, including the USA. The sales pitch was that it was a cure for morphine addiction: the modern heroin addict was born.

However, by the early 1900s doctors began to notice that patients were consuming inordinate amounts of heroin-based cough remedies, and that heroin addiction in the UK and USA was out of control. Users – and the medical profession – soon realised that an addiction to heroin was more problematic than an addiction to morphine.

Heroin addiction in the USA became linked to legislative measures directed against illegal drugs and recreational usage, such as the introduction of the Smoking Opium Exclusion Act 1909, which meant that American opium smokers found it difficult to find affordable opium. They switched almost exclusively to heroin, with heroin snorting soon becoming the popular method of administration.

During World War I, politicians and the media also whipped up a climate of hysteria against dope fiends enslaved by heroin. However, the arrival of the Harrison Act only managed to spread heroin use. Before 1914 most drug users remained loyal to one narcotic, but when new laws meant that their supplies of cocaine and other drugs were cut, they turned instead to cheap heroin. And once they had tried heroin, they stuck with it.

Heroin was finally outlawed in the USA in 1924. By that time, though, the market was already well established. There were too many addicts – some estimates put the figure at 200,000 by the mid-1920s – for the health authorities to deal with. These addicts had already found ways to pay for their drugs and support their habit. They were turning to crime, principally stealing scrap or junk metal. Consequently, they became known as junkies – the name stuck.

## HEROIN MANUFACTURING, PURITY AND TYPE

Heroin is a semi-synthetic opiate produced from morphine. But its journey to New York's East Village or London's Soho starts as the milky sap of the opium poppy – Papaver somniferum – probably grown in a field somewhere in Afghanistan, Pakistan or Myanmar.

Growers often use a technique called slash-and-burn farming to prepare the poppy fields for planting. After all the trees have been cut down and the vegetation has been cleared and burned, the farmers sow the poppy seeds.

Poppies can take about three months to mature, but harvesting will take place at different times of year depending on the part of the world they are being grown in. Just before reaching maturity, the poppy plant produces a flower, which indicates it is ready for harvest. After about a week, the flower petals fall off, leaving a capsule.

Raw opium gum is harvested from this capsule. The surface of the capsule is cut or scored with a knife containing three or four small blades and the opium gum oozes out. The following day, the gum is scraped off the capsules with a flat tool. Each capsule is usually scored in this manner three to five times, or until no more gum exudes out.

After the harvesting process is complete, the capsules are cut from the stem, allowed to dry, and broken open so that the seeds inside the capsule can be used for next year's crop. Once the gum is collected, the farmer sets it out to dry for several days and then wraps it in plastic, or sometimes banana leaf if it has been harvested in Asia. Opium gum is dried, washed, boiled and reboiled to form the gumlike opium, which is ready for smoking. This also has a very long shelf life and can gain value over time.

Opium is used as a substitute for modern medicines in some remote areas, such as Southeast Asia, because few medical supplies are available. There are dozens of alkaloids in opium, but the principal ones of interest to recreational drug users are codeine and morphine. Codeine is often used in cough medicine or mild painkillers, but is not nearly as powerful as morphine and will usually only be of interest to drug abusers if their regular supply is cut.

Morphine is up to 1,000 per cent stronger than opium and is used medically as an analgesic in its pharmaceutical form, as a suppository, pill or an injectable ampoule. Often the supply found on the streets is from medical stock following a burglary at a pharmacy and legally produced morphine pills are also smuggled from countries such as India.

Refining raw opium into heroin is a long, multi-step process. The opium gum is transported to a refinery and converted into morphine, which is dried and made into bricks ready for the chemical process to convert them into heroin. The morphine and acetic anhydride, used in the manufacture of film and synthetics, are then heated together at temperatures of 85°C (185°F) for six hours, which forms impure diacetylmorphine (heroin).

Water and chloroform are added to precipitate impurities before draining and the addition of sodium carbonate to solidify the heroin. Activated charcoal is used to filter the heroin out of the sodium carbonate solution and then it is purified with alcohol before being heated to evaporate off the alcohol.

**PURITY**

The refining process has been perfected to the point where heroin purity levels above 90 per cent can be achieved by the time the product leaves the refinery. Heroin's appearance can vary quite considerably depending on the manufacturing process and how much it is refined. Pure heroin is a white, odourless powder with a bitter taste.

However, because most heroin is illegally manufactured, levels of purity and colour can vary considerably depending on the production process involved and the sub-stances with which the drug has been cut in order to maximize bulk and profit. The commonest non-narcotic adulterants include baking powder, chalk, glucose powder, caffeine, quinine, flour, talcum powder, powdered milk or sugar. The colour can, therefore, vary dramatically from dark brown, through beige to pink and white.

Pure heroin is rarely sold on the street. A bag – slang for a single dosage – may contain 100mg of powder, but only a fraction of that will be heroin; the remainder could be anything. In the 1970s the purity of heroin in a bag ranged from 1 to 10 per cent. However, in the mid-1990s drug enforcement agencies found that it was ranging between 15 and 99 per cent, and was routinely 50 per cent or more pure.

This was because dealers on the street, realising that higher levels of purity meant users could inhale or smoke the drug without the fear of HIV associated with intravenous needles, attempted to expand their market beyond the injecting junkies. The higher levels of purity also reflected the greater amounts of heroin available. In 2000, the US national average of heroin purity was 35 per cent, and in the UK in 2002 it was running at around 47 per cent across a purity range of 2 to 90 per cent.

Analysis of the US Drug Enforcement Administration (DEA) drug buys and seizures between 1981 and 1997 shows that purity increased from 7 per cent in 1981 for purchases of 0.5g or less, to 36 per cent in 1988 and rising to 56 per cent in 1997.

**TYPE**

Crude morphine is sometimes called heroin number one and the white to off-white, pale grey or dark brown, powdered or solid heroin base, prior to its conversion to hydrochloric salt, is called heroin number two. A hard granular material, light brown, dark grey, red or pink in colour, and containing between 25 and 45 per cent heroin hydrochloride and cut with other (sometimes non-narcotic) substances, is called heroin number three. This is also a smokable form of the drug.

The most highly refined heroin, with a purity level of 98 per cent heroin hydrochloride, no additives and white in colour, is heroin number four. Similarly, the medium-brown hard chunks of crude heroin produced without a purification process and between 40 and 60 per cent pure with a vinegary odour, are often referred to as 'brown heroin'.

One of the most crudely processed types of heroin is black tar, which is illicitly manufactured in Mexico and has become popular in the USA in recent years. This has a purity level of between 30 and 60 per cent heroin hydrochloride, is very dark brown or black coloured, and either sticky like roofing tar or hard and brittle like coal. Again there is a strong vinegary smell and it appears to melt when heated.

## SYNTHETIC DRUGS

Heroin is manufactured, but its roots are clearly from the opium poppy. However, many other drugs exhibit similar effects but don't rely on the poppy for their source material. These are called synthetics and are mostly produced legally for medical use, but are illegally traded on the streets.

Many users of these clinical opioids, which often have recognizable brand names, believe they are safer than heroin simply because they are manufactured in licensed laboratories. Sometimes, however, these 'designer drugs' are produced in illegal laboratories and are often more dangerous and potent than heroin if misused.

## FENTANYL

Known on the street as 'china white' and one of the most commonly known opioid analogues, fentanyl was introduced in 1968 by a Belgian pharmaceutical company as a synthetic narcotic to be used as an analgesic in surgical procedures because of its minimal effects on the heart. Fentanyl is particularly dangerous because it is 50 times more potent than heroin and can stop respiration rapidly, although the euphoria is less than morphine. This is not a problem during surgical procedures because machines are used to help patients breathe; however, on-the-street users have been found dead with the needle used to inject the drug still in their arms.

## DEXTROMORAMIDE

An opioid analgesic used for the treatment of severe pain. It is short-acting and causes less sedation than morphine. Dextromoramide is available in tablet form or as a suppository and may cause depression of breathing.

## ACETAMINOPHEN-OXYCODONE

This is a combination of two different types of pain medicine used to treat moderate to severe pain. Generic acetaminophen-oxycodone tablets and capsules are available, but the powerful painkiller is only available on prescription and normally dispensed only to the terminally ill. Oxycodone, known as 'percs' on the street, has been dubbed 'hillbilly heroin' and has been responsible for hundreds of deaths in the USA. Essentially a synthetic form of morphine, the tablets are crushed together to provide a hit, and experts say it is more potent and more addictive than heroin. The small white tablets can be swallowed whole, crushed and snorted or mixed with water and injected. Each tablet costs £5-20 ($7-30) depending on its strength.

## PETHIDINE

Pethidine is an analgesic and an anti-spasmodic, which is a drug that helps people relax. It's a similar drug to morphine, which midwives often prescribe and administer during childbirth. It is given as an injection and often combined with another drug - an anti-emetic - to control sickness. For drug abusers it can produce a short buzz.

## DIHYDROCODEINE

The opioid dihydrocodeine (DHC) is frequently used as an analgesic and is one of the most commonly prescribed painkillers in the UK, but can cause severe constipation.

## BUPRENORPHINE

Buprenorphine is available by prescription (under the brand name Subutex) as a treatment for heroin. It has been found to be effective in preventing the need to use heroin and also in helping people to withdraw. But buprenorphine, which is also prescribed to treat severe pain, became a real problem in the 1980s when it was used illegally as a heroin substitute on the streets.

## PENTAZOCINE

The effort to find an effective analgesic that is less dependence-producing led to the development of pentazocine. Introduced as an analgesic in 1967, it has frequently been encountered in the illicit trade, usually in combination with tripelennamine. It can give users morphine-like effects if the tablets are dissolved and injected; some users have also reported that it can cause hallucinations.

## DIPIPANONE

Dipipanone hydrochloride is medically used as a painkiller and can be taken orally or injected after it has been crushed and dissolved in warm water. It is a very strong painkiller (often prescribed to cancer patients) with definite physical dependent-forming potential, as it causes strong withdrawal symptoms and signs similar to heroin and morphine use. However, the high silicon content of the drug means that veins can quickly silt up, causing circulation problems.

## METHADONE

Synthetic methadone was devised by German chemists during World War II at the German group IG Farbenindustrie. Also called 'dollies' by abusers, methadone works well taken orally and can be effective for over 20 hours. Prescribed as a substitute for heroin, it comes in several different formats: tablets, 10mg ampoules, a linctus, and a liquid green, yellow or brown mixture, which usually contains glucose and chloroform water to dissuade injectors.

## HEROIN COCKTAILS

Drug users don't usually confine their choice of narcotic to just one. Heroin dependants are no different. Most are poly-drug or multiple-substance abusers.

Some heroin addicts use a multitude of different narcotics, but alcohol, tranquillizers, barbiturates, amphetamines and cocaine are the most popular. The junkie will use them when their regular supply of dope is cut or their dealer is out of town, to heighten the effect of heroin and, sometimes, to help them cope during withdrawal.

Mixing heroin with other drugs can have two effects: it can increase the buzz and the danger. Pairing dope with barbiturates, tranquillizers or alcohol can cause severe depression of the central nervous system and lead to coma and death.

Also, the combination of heroin and alcohol often causes vomiting, which is particularly dangerous if the mix of the drugs has caused unconsciousness. Cocaine and heroin are the best-known double act: the speedball. The ultimate stimulant paired with the number one soporific.

## HEROIN PRODUCTION

The global supply of illicit opium, the raw material for heroin, has varied enormously in the last century. But the real growth in supply – to meet the demand for the drug – kicked off in the 1980s when production levels tripled from around 1,000 tonnes/tons in 1981 to 3,000 tonnes/tons less than a decade later.

By the 1990s production levels hit the 5,000 tonne mark and remained relatively stable until 2000, although a bumper Afghan harvest of 4,600 tonnes/tons in 1999 helped boost worldwide production to 5,800 tonnes/tons. Despite this increase in production, the global area under opium poppy cultivation in 1999 was almost 20 per cent less than in 1990, when over 250,000ha (617,500 acres) was under cultivation. This suggests that cultivation techniques had improved over the decade and producers were able to gain better yields per hectare.

In terms of the global heroin market, Afghanistan and Myanmar (formerly Burma) are in a league of their own. They are by far the biggest producers of opium, accounting for over 90 per cent of the opium produced in 2000. Figures for 1999 suggest that Afghanistan alone had a total area under cultivation of 91,583ha (226,210 acres) and, by the late 1990s, Afghanistan was estimated to be the source of 75 per cent of the world's heroin and 90 per cent of the supply that found its way to the UK.

With such a monopoly on the global market, natural disasters such as droughts, improving law enforcement, a new government regime and – in the case of Afghanistan – a war, could have a massive effect on the world's supply.

## AFGHANISTAN

Opium has flourished in Afghanistan's southern desert region and northern provinces since the time of Alexander the Great. The poppies are well suited to the rugged terrain and arid climate, requiring little water or attention, and making them easier and cheaper to cultivate than wheat and other crops.

The poppy crop and trade in heroin has thrived through countless regimes, from the 1933–73 reign of King Zahir Shah, through the Soviet occupation during the 1980s, the bloody years of the Mojahedin and the rise of the fundamentalist Taliban in the 1990s.

The Taliban surprised illegal producers and traffickers in 2000 when the government's leader, Mullah Mohammed Omar, issued an edict outlawing opium production in Afghanistan. As the world's largest producer of heroin throughout the 1990s, the Taliban, which had seized control of the country in 1996, had earned millions from the heroin trade because drug traffickers were required to pay the

Taliban's commerce ministry a 10 per cent tax on cultivation profits and 20 per cent on smuggling profits.

Afghan farmers were forced to turn to planting other, less profitable, crops or vineyards in place of their poppy fields and only areas under the control of the opposition Northern Alliance continued to produce opium. The result was that poppy cultivation fell to just 7,706ha (19,034 acres) in 2001 from 82,515ha (203,812 acres) the year before.

Some experts believed the Taliban may have been attempting to strangle supply and drive up the price of opium on the international market. This would have had the effect of significantly increasing the cost of a bag of heroin on a New York or London street. The economics supported this theory: in September 2001, when there was no prospect of a fresh crop under the Taliban, 1kg (2¼lb) of opium cost between $570 (£390) and $655 (£450).

The 11 September 2001 attacks on the twin towers of New York's World Trade Center changed that. The USA traced the terrorists' network to Osama bin Laden's al-Qaeda network, which was being harboured by the Taliban in Afghanistan. The war against terrorism that followed, and the subsequent fall of the Taliban regime at the end of 2001, meant the Afghan farmers reverted to their more lucrative crop: opium. The motivation wasn't hard to find. In the 1990s the opium trade was estimated to be worth around $98 million (£68 million) to Afghan growers and a farmer, fresh from the crippling conflict with the defeated Taliban, could have expected to make thousands trading with Pakistani and Iranian buyers if he replanted his wheatfields with opium at the end of 2001.

One radical solution proposed was for European governments to buy the poppy crop, but this would have been highly controversial as well as costly. There was also recognition that providing aid and substitute crops to poor farmers would not necessarily solve the problem because any attempt to control the trade would be resisted by local warlords.

EU External Affairs Commissioner Chris Patten blamed Afghan-sourced heroin for 'devastating' lives and funding organized crime. He added, 'Beating drugs helps beat terrorism and will help Afghans have a brighter future.'

## MYANMAR

Myanmar, formerly Burma, is part of Southeast Asia's infamous 'Golden Triangle', which also comprises parts of Laos and Thailand. It is also the world's second largest producer of illicit opium and in 1999 had 89,500ha (221,000 acres) under cultivation.

Illegal drugs have had a long history of supply and manufacture in the country, although it was only in the last decade of the 20th century that Myanmar became a global capital for opium growing and heroin production, helping to fuel the number of addicts worldwide.

The manufacture and supply of heroin in the country boomed following the bloody takeover of the country by the Law and Order Restoration Council (renamed the State Peace And Development Council [SPDC] in November 1997) in 1988. Drug lords, who had close links with Burma's army dictators, were able to act almost with impunity, and there was a lack of commitment from the government towards stamping out narcotic trafficking and the money laundering that followed it.

There were some successes, such as the surrender of drug warlord Khun Sa. He was the leader of the southern Shan state and on America's 'Most Wanted' list following an indictment on narcotics racketeering charges in a New York court. But some commentators argued that his arrest was largely a public relations exercise and that the government was practically a trade partner in the cultivation, supply and manufacture of illicit drugs.

This was largely confirmed when a ceasefire was called in the late 1990s. This essentially gave the opposition parties free rein, leading to massive increases in the opium harvest and purer forms of heroin on the street. Between 1988 and 1997 the average purity of heroin shot up from 34 per cent to 62.5 per cent. The US State Department stated in its 2000 International Narcotics Control Strategy Report: '...the ceasefire agreements have permitted former insurgents to continue their involvement in narcotics cultivation and trafficking activities.'

## OTHER MAJOR HEROIN PRODUCERS

After Afghanistan and Myanmar, the Lao PDR, Colombia and Mexico produced the largest quantities of illegal opium in 1999. They had 22,550ha (55,700 acres), 7,500ha (18,500 acres) and 3,600ha (8,900 acres) of poppies under cultivation, respectively.

Opium production in Mexico and Latin and Central American countries such as Peru and Venezuela, was mainly destined for the US heroin market at the beginning of 2002, with Colombia replacing Southeast Asia as a prime source of the drug in the late 1990s: 65 per cent of the heroin seized in the USA during this period was sourced from Colombia.

Other major opium producers in 2002 included Pakistan, Thailand and Vietnam. However, production of opium and heroin fell in Southeast Asia in the late 1990s, and Thailand and Pakistan also drastically cut cultivation, with the latter reducing the number of hectares under the poppy from 7,500ha (18,500 acres) in 1990 to just 3,000ha (7,400 acres) in 1999.

China, the largest producer of opium in the inter-war period, Guatemala in Central America, Lebanon, Iran and Egypt, which all had fairly sizeable fields under cultivation, had also reduced production to practically zero by 2000.

## HEROIN SUPPLY AND TRAFFICKING ROUTES

Once the opium crop has been harvested, raw opium or heroin is trafficked across the globe to the main drug centres. Sometimes this can involve long and complex routes, facilitating the use of every imaginable mode of transport – from donkey to aircraft.

Trafficking of heroin and the main routes via which it is shipped can be traced by the number and pattern of seizures. Generally seizures of illicit drugs have increased, with 170 countries around the world reporting drug seizures in 1997/98 compared to 120 in 1980/81.

However, heroin is not the world's most widely trafficked drug. Of those countries that successfully seized drugs in 1997/98, only 91 per cent reported finding opiate substances, including heroin, compared with 98 per cent of the countries that reported finding cannabis products in their hauls.

However, along with the increase in the number of countries reporting seizures, heroin trafficking has shown an upward trend over the last 30 years. Less than five tonnes/tons of the drug was seized each year between 1975 and 1980, but by 1998 this had increased to nearly 35 tonnes/tons.

Of seizures of heroin and morphine in 1987/88, 72 per cent were made in Asia, with some 42 per cent discovered in Iran, reflecting its proximity to the trade routes coming out of Afghanistan. As befits its status as the world's largest opium producer, Afghanistan is the main supplier of heroin to a wide range of countries, from neighbours such as Iran and Pakistan to western European markets, including France and the UK.

The UN warned in early 2002 that unless measures were successful to stop the harvest of that year's Afghan opium crop, then the 'best ever opportunity' to suffocate the illegal trade would be lost. The Taliban ban on poppy growing in Afghanistan, introduced in July 2000 and coupled with severe droughts in 2001, reduced Afghanistan's opium yield by 91 per cent in 2001. It was thought, however, to have had little effect on trafficking throughout Europe because traders had stockpiled significant amounts of heroin along their supply routes.

Between 1987 and 1988 Europe accounted for about 23 per cent of worldwide seizures, at over 10,000kg (22,000lb), with most taking place in western countries including Turkey. The Americas accounted for about 3.7 per cent of heroin and morphine seizures in 1997/98.

In 1999, over seven tonnes/tons of heroin were seized in the EU, of which one-third was accountable to the United Kingdom. Heroin seized in the EU comes mainly from the so-called 'Golden Crescent' – a mountainous area including Iran, Afghanistan and Pakistan – followed by the 'Golden Triangle' routed via Turkey, the Balkans and The Netherlands. However, after 2000 smugglers moved their routes north and US drug enforcement agencies reported that the number of heroin shipments from Afghanistan through the central Asian states to Russia had increased; Tajikistan was a favourite destination. In 2002 one heroin trade expert estimated that only 20–30 per cent of heroin was shipped to Europe via the usual Iranian-Turkish route.

At EU level, heroin seizures increased up until 1991/92 and then stabilized. The number of heroin seizures has grown steadily in Luxembourg, Portugal and Sweden since 1985, while marked decreases have been reported since 1996/97 in Austria, Belgium, Denmark, France, Germany and Spain. In every member state, the quantities seized fluctuated over the period. In 1999, marked decreases in the quantities of heroin seized were reported in Austria, France, Greece, Ireland and The Netherlands, while in Italy and Spain there were large increases in the amount of heroin seized.

Seizures in the UK increased by more than 80 per cent in 1999, which is significant because the UK already accounted for around 30 per cent of all heroin and morphine seizures in the EU during 1997/98, more than The Netherlands (about 20 per cent) and Germany (12 per cent). In 2001 it was reported that Afghanistan and the Golden Crescent were the source of 90 per cent of the heroin reaching Britain's streets.

The impact of the drug trade from Myanmar has been felt by its neighbours, Bangladesh, China, India, Singapore, and Thailand. They all experienced increased incidents of heroin seizures, a rapidly expanding community of addicts and a rise in HIV in the 1990s. In a 1998 survey throughout the northern state of Kachin, over 90 per cent of heroin users tested HIV positive.

Turkey has always been an important part of the heroin map and, between 1990/91 and 1997/98, heroin and morphine seizures in the country have increased by more than 10 per cent to over 3,000kg (6,600lb). In the late 1990s Turkey, midway between the producer countries Afghanistan and Pakistan and the European market, also emerged as a final destination and transit territory for acetic anhydride, one of heroin's major precursor chemicals, which is manufactured throughout Europe and shipped to Asia.

The majority of heroin crossing Turkey is shipped along the Balkan route to its final destination, although some new developing markets emerged in eastern Europe in the late 1990s and many countries along the main trafficking routes – such as Iran, Pakistan and Central Asian countries – became bigger buyers.

Pakistan, which shares a border with Afghanistan, remains an important player in the global heroin market despite a decline in seizures during the 1990s because of a reduction in domestic production and large scale re-routing of heroin traffic via Iran. However, Pakistan still accounted for 9 per cent of all worldwide heroin and morphine seizures in 1997/98 and its geographical importance was demonstrated in 1999 when large amounts of Afghanistans's bumper opium poppy harvest of 4,600 tonnes/tons were shipped across the country, leading to an increase in seizures.

India, the world's largest legal opium producer, has improved controls over manufacturing and cut seizures of heroin and morphine by more than 60 per cent between 1990/91 and 1997/98, with seizures in 1997/98 between 1,000kg and 3,000kg (2,200lb and 6,600lb).

Around 16 per cent of global seizures in 1997/98 were made in Southeast Asia, an area incorporating the notorious Golden Triangle, traditionally one of the main outlets for heroin. However, there were some radical changes in trafficking patterns in the 1990s with Thailand's importance as a main route in the area diminishing. By 1997/98 Thailand only accounted for around 5 per cent of all seizures of opiates in Southeast Asia, compared to almost 60 per cent in the late 1980s.

The Asia-based criminal networks supplying the USA have virtually been squeezed out of the market, although there is evidence that Southeast Asian heroin is being smuggled into the United States in smaller multigram or multikilogram amounts by couriers or mail and package delivery services.

Its place in the league of suppliers has been taken by China, where heroin was smuggled directly from Myanmar for export to the USA, usually via Hong Kong. However, poor weather conditions in 1999 reduced production, and seizures in China were down 30 per cent that year.

The US heroin market is supplied entirely from foreign sources of opium produced in four distinct geographical areas: South America, Mexico, Southeast Asia and Southwest Asia. In 2000, 1,415kg (3,119lb) of heroin was seized in the USA under the Federal-wide Drug Seizure System, which includes the DEA, FBI and US Customs. This was significantly up on the 1,239kg (2,732lb) seized in the previous year.

Trafficking patterns have changed significantly since the mid-1990s when Southeast Asia was the main supplier for the North American markets and accounted for around 3 per cent of global heroin and morphine seizures in 1997/98. By 1999, however, Southeast Asia accounted for only around 10 per cent of heroin seized in the USA, and Southeast Asia accounted for just 6 per cent.

The flow of South American heroin began to increase dramatically around 1993 when Colombia-based gangs, already in control of the cocaine trade, expanded into heroin. They quickly saturated the USA heroin markets using Dominican distribution rings and by providing low-cost, high-purity heroin. They also employed surefire marketing tactics such as providing free samples of heroin in cocaine shipments, and using brand names to build their client base and customer loyalty.

The South American and Latin American countries supplied 75 per cent of US heroin in 1997, 65 per cent in 1998 and around 60 per cent in 1999. Virtually all of the six tonnes/tons of heroin produced in Colombia during 1998 was believed to have been shipped to the US market, and Colombian heroin began to dominate the streets of east coast cities such as New York and Washington in 1999. The heroin trade in Colombia was in the hands of many independent trafficking groups and the drug is smuggled mainly in quantities of 1kg (2¼lb) or 2kg (4½lb) by couriers on commercial airlines.

Criminal organizations based in Nigeria and West Africa, with drug connections in Southeast and Southwest Asia, also distributed heroin to some major cities in the United States, particularly the Chicago area. Similarly, nearly all heroin produced in Mexico between 1999 and 2001 was destined for US distribution. Mexican heroin, which accounted for 24 per cent of US seizures in 1999, became more popular in southwestern US cities such as San Diego and Los Angeles.

Evidence suggests that trafficking organizations from Mexico were attempting to produce higher-purity heroin in the late 1990s. A 1997 analysis of Mexican heroin distributed in the USA revealed purity levels of 30 to 60 per cent, with some samples reaching levels of more than 70 per cent.

## HEROIN INJECTING, SMOKING AND SNORTING

Heroin is a very adaptable drug. Many narcotics can only be popped as pills or snorted. Heroin, however, can be administered in a variety of ways with different effects. It can be sniffed, smoked, swallowed or injected. These methods can involve different techniques. Heroin can be smoked though a water pipe or normal pipe (often glass), mixed with a marijuana joint, inhaled as smoke through a straw (chasing the dragon), snorted as a powder (commonly through a straw), or dissolved in water and injected under the skin, into muscles or intravenously (into a vein).

Sniffing or snorting is done in the same way as cocaine users do Charlie. The heroin is chopped with a blade, razor or credit card, drawn into lines and then snorted up one nostril with the aid of a rolled-up banknote or tube. The bitter flavour of heroin can put users off this method, and sniffing largely remains the preserve of the cocaine addict.

Swallowing heroin is pretty rare because it is an inefficient way of delivering a rush. The stomach converts heroin into morphine and the liver does a good job of breaking down the morphine before it can have an effect.

With smoking, a small amount of H is placed on a piece of aluminium foil and a flame held beneath it. As the drug is heated it turns black and wriggles like a snake. The resulting fumes are sucked up into the nose with the help of a tube.

### INJECTING

Injection can be done in three ways:

- **Skin Popping** – The common name given to subcutaneous injection, which targets the fatty tissue lying just beneath the skin (usually in the buttocks, stomach or thighs);

- **Intramuscular Injection** – When the user targets their large muscle groups, normally in the thigh, buttocks or the top of the arms;
- **Intravenous Injection** – Also called mainlining, which targets veins.

Typically, a heroin abuser will inject up to four times in a day. Mainlining directly into veins provides the greatest intensity and most rapid onset of euphoria (between seven and eight seconds), while intramuscular injection or skin popping produces a slower high, sometimes taking as long as eight minutes before the onset of euphoria.

When heroin is snorted or smoked, peak effects are usually much longer – taking between 10 and 15 minutes – and, in addition to a slower 'rush', these methods don't create the intensity of intravenous injection. All forms of heroin administration are addictive.

Intramuscular or subcutaneous injection was used almost exclusively in Britain in the early part of the 20th century. But intravenous use, which was more common in the USA, eventually spread to the UK and Europe around the 1950s, possibly because injection is the most practical and efficient way of administering low-purity heroin.

Intravenous use carries with it all the primary health risks facing heroin users. Mainlining means that any toxic substances cut with the drug are shot directly into the blood, leading to abscesses, blood poisoning or worse.

In the process of injecting heroin users will usually place a small amount of the drug (anything up to the size of a pea, although it varies enormously depending on the addict) on to a spoon. If they are fixing with brown they will add a drop of citric or ascorbic acid and water to help dissolve the heroin. Sometimes vinegar and lemon juice are more easily available for the junkie, but can cause infection.

The mix is heated over a naked flame from a lighter until it dissolves. Once the heroin has melted and cooled it can be drawn up into a syringe and injected. Often a small swab of cotton wool or a filter from a cigarette will also be used to screen some of the toxins in the heroin, but bacteria can still be drawn into the hypodermic.

At the start of a habit, the needle user will inject in the most accessible veins, which are the main arteries located in the inner portion of the arm near the elbow joint. Usually, a right-handed person will inject in the left arm and a left-handed person into the right arm. Sometimes injectors will also pump their arms or use a tourniquet such as a belt or tie to make a bigger target of the vein.

**FIRST PERSON**
LISA S, HEROIN ADDICT
'I started with a needle in the 1970s. I was 17 at the time and didn't know there was anything but mainlining. Also, I never smoked, never have, which is pretty unusual I guess with heroin users. My boyfriend at the time was a user and

he showed me what to do. He fixed me up with my first shot and I thought it was wonderful.

'You hear all these stories about people feeling bad and puking up. But that was not my experience. I thought it was really wonderful. I suppose I'd been around drugs quite a lot then and had tried most of everything, especially acid. I had the best two or three years of my life. Fantastic music, great gigs, and smack.

'There'd be some bad times where we couldn't get hold of any dope for a few days and then I couldn't cope. That was dreadful. I was working on the tills in a market, just a small corner convenience store really, but I just couldn't face it without a fix. I'd ring in at least once a week and tell them I was ill. I don't know if they suspected anything. I kept myself pretty presentable and it wasn't like there were many heroin addicts around then. I could fix myself and did sometimes, but mostly my boyfriend did it.

'What happened then was he had a terrible motorbike accident and was in hospital for nearly a year. The doctors got him off heroin while he was there and I started to visit him less and less because I was still doing it. Although, by this time my health was really shot. I'd miss veins and get bruising all over my arm. Then I met someone else who was also dealing a bit. He moved in and, although I knew he was ripping me off, we stuck together because of the dope I knew he could always get.

'By this time my veins were pretty fucked up. I was spilling loads of blood all over the place and the hits seemed to be becoming less and less. I just didn't get that feeling back. I don't know if it was the quality of the dope or something. So we both started doing cocaine as well. Around this time I realised I couldn't keep a lid on everything. I'd lost the supermarket job and was just doing odd shifts in a local bar.

'Then my first boyfriend came out of hospital and I saw him one night in another pub. Even though his leg was a bit fucked, he looked really good. He was completely clean and he'd been away on holiday somewhere and was suntanned, and that's what I noticed most, his skin and hair. Also, the idea of going away had never been something we would have done. In fact, I hardly recognized him because he'd been a user ever since I'd met him.

'He didn't give me any lecture, in fact I can't remember if we even spoke, but something clicked then and I knew I had to move out of the flat with the dealer. It probably took another two years to get off the gear altogether, but I've been clean since.'

## SNIFFING AND SMOKING

In the 1980s and 1990s there was a shift in heroin-use patterns in some US cities and the UK: from injection to sniffing and smoking. Evidence suggests that heroin snorting is widespread in cities and countries where high-purity heroin is available. Snorting heroin is now the most widely reported means of taking heroin among users admitted for drug treatment in Newark, Chicago and New York.

Along with the shift in abuse patterns to new, young users lured by inexpensive, high-purity heroin that can be snorted or smoked, heroin has also been appearing in more affluent communities. In the past, groups such as students and business executives have traditionally avoided the drug because of negative images of needles and the stigma associated with track marks. However, smoking and snorting bypass this.

Snorting and smoking are also more appealing to a new group of users because these methods eliminate the fear of acquiring syringe-borne diseases such as HIV and hepatitis B and C.

When smoked, heroin is heated on a small piece of baking foil and the fumes inhaled through a tube. Chasing the dragon – so called because the smoke spiralling off the aluminium foil looks like a dragon's tail – became popular in 1980s Britain when fairly large supplies of heroin were flooding council estates in cities such as Liverpool, Manchester and London.

There is certainly less equipment necessary for chasing the dragon. The mainliner will have his 'works'. He needs to be able to cook up the dope, often using something like a rubber hose to tie off his arm and, most importantly, a working sterile syringe with a sharp needle.

The smoker only needs to rip off a piece of kitchen roll or buy some chocolate wrapped in silver foil – both easily available, cheap and reusable. However, there is some skill necessary with chasing. The user needs to be quick with their tube because if the heroin is heated too quickly smoke will be lost.

Chasing the dragon has one final, but important, advantage over mainlining: smokers can test the quality of the dope they are using. Mainliners will dissolve the dope, fix a shot and inject it. Only then will they know how pure the heroin is. Smokers have the chance to gradually discover the quality of the heroin they're taking by only lightly inhaling the first puff.

## HEROIN SYRINGES

Syringes, needles. The works. Next to heroin itself, they are the most important part of the junkie's kit. Some junkies sleep with them. However, they can also be the weapon that finally kills them. Needles deliver the OD. They can also serve up HIV.

The threat of HIV in the early 1980s prompted action from governments and led to the introduction of pilot needle-exchange schemes in the UK in 1986. These, which have been followed by similar schemes in many other countries, allowed users to swap their old works for a new, clean syringe. By 1987, 15 needle-swap schemes were operating in UK cities such as Liverpool and Sheffield and, by 1991, some four million syringes were being distributed from around 200 swap agencies in the UK.

Needle exchanges are criticized by some politicians and pressure groups, who argue that they legitimize heroin consumption and encourage the most dangerous method of administration. There are also complaints from the local population, worried that needle exchanges will draw heroin addicts to their neighbourhood, resulting in it being littered with their dirty needles.

## HEROIN ABUSE LEVELS

Heroin use is a global phenomenon – and problem. Of the 180 million people the United Nations estimates use an illegal drug, some 9.18 million around the world – or 0.22 per cent of the global population – were estimated to be heroin users in the late 1990s.

There are very few countries that heroin doesn't touch and infect with its attendant problems. This is demonstrated by the UN Office for Drug Control and Crime Prevention (ODCCP) World Drug Report 2000, which showed that of the 134 countries and territories surveyed, plant-based drugs such as the opiates, including heroin, were the most commonly abused. Some 76 per cent of those reported an abuse of heroin during the 1990s, significantly more than the 64 per cent and 24 per cent who reported cocaine and ecstasy abuse respectively.

The main regions of consumption are traditionally close

to the areas of production and the large markets. Thus the highest rates of abuse of heroin are mostly concentrated in Asia (the highest levels of abuse are in Iran, Pakistan, India, and the Lao PDR) and Europe, where 5.74 million and 1.5 million addicts respectively are believed to live.

## PROFILE OF A HEROIN USER

Who takes heroin? Junkies, sure. But how does one brother in a stable middle-class family take up the needle, while the other becomes a journalist on a national newspaper?

It's more complicated than sociology, genetics and psychology can explain on their own, and clearly there are myriad reasons and influences that will persuade someone to use heroin. Environment, education, peer pressure, personality type and ease of availability of heroin all play a part.

Studies show that certain people are more susceptible to using drugs – and subsequently becoming dependent on them – than others. There is no standard heroin-using profile. Users come from all socio-economic groups and from a wide range of personality types and family backgrounds.

However, studies have identified a series of risk and protective factors which can work at various levels on the psychological development of an individual, including the local or family environment, the personality of the user and education. Generally the greater potential for drug misuse

71

and escalation to dependence and addiction depends on the balance of risk and protective factors.

For example, risk factors in the environment will include a high prevalence of drug taking among peer groups and easy availability of drugs such as heroin in the user's area. Again, a depressed, sensation-seeking personality will also predict a risk that could lead the individual to seek out a drug like heroin. Against this, someone with high self-esteem and an easy temperament is perceived as having in-built protection against turning to heroin or other drugs.

Some attempt has also been made to create a picture of a typical heroin user, and a glimpse is provided by the 2001 study, Drug Misuse Declared In 2000: Results From The British Crime Survey (BCS). This outlined drug-use patterns among the population of England and Wales, and demonstrated that a young white man from Manchester with no academic qualifications is much more likely to become a junkie than a middle-class Pakistani woman from a rural background, who went to university.

Some experts believe this UK study can be extrapolated to provide a profile of the features of drug and heroin users in Europe and many other western countries. Drug Misuse Declared In 2000 showed that drug use was more prevalent among young people, with 50 per cent of 16- to 29-year-olds reporting that they have tried drugs in their lifetime.

The study also found that people tend to restrict their drug use to a single drug. In the last year, 15 per cent of

16- to 29-year-olds used one drug, compared to 4 per cent who had used two drugs.

Use of opiates, including heroin, crack and methadone, was relatively low compared to drugs like cannabis, ecstasy, LSD, and magic mushrooms. Only 5 per cent of 16- to 59-year-olds had tried opiates in their lifetime and, in the last year, only around 1 per cent of 16- to 29-year-olds had taken heroin and crack.

The survey also suggested that drug use is not spread evenly around the UK and that certain drugs are more popular in different regions. London tends to have the highest rates of drug use, with over 30 per cent of 16- to 29-year-olds reporting Class A drug use in the last year (of the study). That compared with about 20 per cent in Wales. However, in the same age group, use of heroin was highest in the north of England, the south and the Midlands with less than 0.5 per cent taking the drug in London and negligible usage in Wales.

The study also found that socio-economic factors – income level, education, type of neighbourhood – can contribute to drug usage and also influence the type of drug favoured. For instance, whereas cocaine use is relatively widespread across the whole population, heroin tends to be associated with less affluent groups. Very few 16- to 29-year-olds from affluent urban, suburban, rura, or family areas reported using heroin in 2001.

This relationship between heroin and the less affluent was reinforced by measuring use of heroin with factors such as income, qualifications and employment status. The proportion who used heroin in the last year was found to be highest in the poorest households – those earning less than £5,000 ($7,300) – among those with zero academic qualifications, the unskilled and the unemployed.

Heroin use in the UK has increased slightly since 1994 and the BCS 2000 survey showed that it is in the 16- to 29-year-old age group where the main increase has taken place. In 2000, 0.7 per cent of those surveyed in that age group said they had used heroin in the last year, compared to just 0.5 per cent in 1994 and 0.3 per cent in 1996.

The report shows that usage of the drug between genders has not shifted significantly over the years between 1994 and 2000, but rates of use of the drug in the last year for the unemployed were noticeably higher in 1998 and 2000 than for those in work.

Ethnic comparisons of drug use are also possible and the BCS 2000 survey found that, irrespective of age, white people were more likely to have taken drugs than black people, Indians or Pakistanis. Heroin, in particular, is almost unused in the UK among the latter two ethnic groups.

## HEROIN PHYSIOLOGY

Heroin mimics the action of natural chemicals, called endorphins (endogenous morphines), which are produced in response to pain. They will act on specific opiate receptor sites in the brain and spinal cord to dampen the flow of nerve impulses in nerve tracts that carry pain information to the brain.

The opiate receptors – proteins embedded in the cell membrane – are not designed to recognize heroin, but are part of the human body's defence against pain and are normally activated by the endorphins. These chemicals are released in conditions of great stress and anxiety to 'cut off' pain, and explain why a soldier shot in battle may not immediately feel a wound or even realise that he has been hurt.

There are three different types of opiate receptor located in various parts of the human body and these will be activated by heroin entering the user's system. Those located in the brainstem are responsible for alerting the user to pain and one opiate receptor in particular – the mu-opioid receptor – is responsible for the pain-relieving and pleasurable effect of heroin. For example, if someone burns their finger on a hot saucepan, messages will be sent from the fingertips to the spinal cord, which telegraphs another message to the arm muscles to remove the hand – quickly. These are messages aimed at putting a direct stop to the painful stimuli.

However, to prevent the person from burning their fingers again, another signal is simultaneously sent from the spinal cord to the part of the opiate receptors in the brainstem, that will 'alarm' pain. However, the presence of opiates or heroin will remedy this through their analgesic effect. The feeling does not entirely disappear, but it loses its threatening character.

The critical aspect of heroin and other opiates is that this painkilling effect has little or no effect on other sensory perceptions such as motor functions and consciousness. This is very different from other non-opiate drugs, such as barbiturates, or substances like alcohol, which also have painkilling qualities, but will have a very significant effect on motor co-ordination, consciousness and intellectual capability. Although, at very high dosage levels, heroin can cause drowsiness.

Heroin does, however, have some major physical effects on other areas of the body. It can also have an effect on breathing because opiate receptors are also located in the respiratory centre. These are designed to regulate the frequency and beat of breathing, and allow steady inhalation depending on the level of exertion a person is experiencing. However, heroin will also have an inhibiting effect on these cells, often reducing the depth and frequency of someone's breathing. In the event of a heroin overdose, respiration will shut down completely. This will cause a shortage of oxygen to the brain and muscles and stop the heart.

Similarly, by influencing the hypothalmus, the area of the brain responsible for the hypophysis, controlling the body's hormonal balance, heroin can effect the levels of cortisol and testosterone in the blood and body temperature. This will decrease or increase slightly, depending on the dosage, but the affect may diminish through use and tolerance.

Opiate receptors can also cause vomiting. Normally stimulated by contaminated food, these cells are also pushed into activity by heroin, which explains why many first-time users throw up after a fix. Tolerance to this quickly builds, however, and it is unusual for regular users to vomit.

Heroin will also cause constipation because of the effect of opiates on the digestive system where many opiate receptors are also located. This is why opiates, which inhibit intestinal functioning, have been used as painkillers and for diarrhoea.

Another side effect of opiate use is that veins in the skin will be widened by the release of histamine. This has the result of giving the user a flushed and sweaty appearance, and it can also lead to constant itching.

The most visible and sometimes shocking side effect of heroin abuse is the effect on the pupils of the eye. They become like pinpoints, due to miosis (where the pupils contract), and this can happen almost immediately. This occurs even if the heroin user is fixing up in a darkened room, when the pupils are normally expected to become enlarged or dilated (mydriasis).

At the same time as creating euphoria by dampening distress, pain and other negative stimuli, heroin use can also lead to mood change. The opiate receptors in the limbic system can severely reduce the heroin user's appetite for sex. The signals to opiate receptors are not cut, but any cognitive link leads to total emotional indifference.

Heroin is the fastest-acting of all opiates. Its increased liquid solubility allows it to cross the blood-brain barrier rapidly and the drug is reconverted back to morphine before it binds to the opiate receptors.

The effect of the drug is essentially the same regardless of the method of administration. However, when injected intravenously it reaches the brain in seven to eight seconds. This is the 'rush', an intense sensation following injection. Intramuscular injections, or skin popping, produce a relatively slow onset of this euphoric feeling, taking between five and eight minutes. The peak experience through smoking or snorting can take up to 15 minutes.

Users will offer a variety of responses to heroin, but there will always tend to be three effects associated with heroin use: those that are sought-after, such as euphoria and the removal of tension, and then the short-term and long-term side effects of taking the drug. These can range from nausea to malnutrition.

The surge of pleasure – the rush or buzz – seems to start in the abdomen. A warmth then spreads throughout the body and with this a dissipation of pain, fear, hunger, aggression, frustration, tension and anxiety. The user will feel calm. Time may seem to slow down, users may feel that they have a dry mouth and their limbs become heavy.

> I heard all this stuff about being in your mom's womb,
> you know like being in a warm place. Somewhere safe.
> Wrapped up in cotton wool, inside a big air bag. And
> they were right. That's exactly what heroin is.
>                                        – Kerry James, heroin user

The euphoria produced by heroin does not lead to a happy, smiling person. But it does remove the weight of the world from the user's shoulders. After the intense euphoria passes, users experience a period of tranquillity, sometimes referred to as 'being on the nod'. They will feel alternately drowsy and wakeful, warm and content, and may fall in and out of a sleeping state, often burning themselves or furniture if they are smoking a cigarette at the time. The narcotic power of the drug will diminish any feeling of pain if a user does injure themself. Mental functioning can become clouded because of the depression of the central nervous system. This feeling can last for up to an hour or more.

Experienced heroin users will inject between two and four times each day. After taking heroin, some people feel cocooned and emotionally self-contained. Others feel stimulated and sociable. Either way, there is a profound sense of control, and heroin also detaches the user from any feelings of pain or worry. They will also have slowed and slurred speech, a slow gait, constricted pupils, droopy eyelids and impaired night vision.

The euphoria gradually subsides into a dreamy and relaxed state of contentment. Higher doses of heroin normally make users very sleepy and very high doses will cause the user to slip into a semi-conscious state. The effects will wear off in three to five hours, again depending on the dosage.

## HEROIN HEALTH

Heroin is not associated with good health. It's perceived as dirty and dangerous. Evil in a needle. In an ICM Research poll conducted for the UK's *Observer* newspaper in February and March 2002, 27 per cent believed that heroin was the drug likely to cause the greatest risk to health. Crack came in second at 19 per cent.

However, heroin has had a bad press. Unlike many narcotics, the drug is actually benign and there is little evidence to suggest that a lifetime of using pure dope would lead to anything more than a strong tolerance to the drug. This could lead to serious problems of dependency and withdrawal, but the real medical concerns that arise from chronic heroin use are due to other factors. These include adulterants in the dope, infected hypodermic syringes, the environment and habits of the addict, and methods of administration. Because the heroin abuser is always on the lookout for their next fix, they often neglects the normal necessary functions that people take for granted, such as eating and sleeping, and health problems set in through their general run-down condition. Spending any spare cash on drugs also means that their living conditions and diet are likely to be poor.

Initially, a new user will be recognized by their pale or jaundiced complexion and dramatic weight loss. The myriad complications associated with longer-term use include septicaemia, pulmonary abscesses and skin abscesses, and a long-term user may also find that the veins they use to inject become scarred or collapse, and they will have to find new veins to inject.

Chronic users may also develop bacterial infection of the blood vessels, infection of the heart lining and valves, cellulitis and liver disease. Pulmonary complications, including a number of different types of pneumonia, may result from the poor health condition of the abuser as well as from heroin's depressing effects on respiration. Long-term physical effects can also result in respiratory system problems – breathlessness is a common complaint, as is coughing up phlegm – and chronic sedation.

Pure, unadulterated heroin does no damage to the body's organs. However, street heroin may have additives that do not really dissolve, resulting in clogging of the blood vessels that lead to the lungs, liver, kidneys or brain. This can cause infection or even the death of small patches of cells in vital organs. Immune reactions to contaminants can also cause arthritis and other rheumatological problems.

Users also risk overdosing (ODing) because heroin is generally obtained from illegal suppliers and, therefore, the dose is unpredictable and may be dangerously adulterated by the dealer. An overdose (OD) will cause rapid heartbeat, heart failure, shortness of breath, ringing in the ears or head, pin-point pupils, clammy skin, convulsions, unconsciousness and coma. When unconscious, users also risk the danger of choking on their own vomit.

Protracted use also causes extreme constipation and a loss of appetite. This can lead to malnutrition in addicts because they are never hungry and because the constipation can become so painful that they do not want to eat food.

Mental health problems can also result. Addiction and the psychological symptoms of withdrawal include depression, mood swings, and hypersensitivity to pain. The user will also lose their appetite for sex.

Abuse can also cause additional complications for women, whose livers are smaller than men's and will therefore be placed under more strain. Menstrual irregularity is likely and some women will cease ovulation. Pregnant drug users also risk miscarriage, stillbirth, or giving birth to smaller babies as a result of retarded growth in the womb or premature delivery. Congenital abnormalities are also common; they often exhibit a number of developmental problems and are at greater risk of cot death or SIDS (Sudden Infant Death Syndrome).

Pregnant abusers can also cause irreparable damage if they suddenly withdraw from heroin, although it is very common that the baby will experience withdrawal symptoms after birth. Symptoms can vary enormously, but usually the baby will be hyperactive and restless. Sometimes the infant may even go into seizure, but often these effects can be minimized by a programme of tranquillizers such as chlorpromazine or benzodiazepine.

**PHARMACOLOGICAL EFFECTS**
DESIRED
- Warmth
- Sense of well-being and contentment
- Detachment from physical and emotion distress
- Relief from pain
- Reduced levels of tension and anxiety

SHORT TERM
- Nausea
- Vomiting

- Drowsiness
- Apathy and inability to concentrate
- Constricted pupils
- Death if respiratory depression caused by overdose

LONG TERM
- Diminished appetite leading to weight loss and malnutrition
- Constipation
- Abscesses, if injected
- HIV
- Irregular periods
- Physical and psychological dependence
- Increased tolerance
- Chronic sedation
- Withdrawal symptoms, including sweating, chills, cramps, and diarrhoea

Potentially the most serious health risk to heroin addicts is that of contracting human immunodeficiency virus (HIV), hepatitis C and other infectious diseases through sharing and re-use of infected needles and injection paraphernalia. Drug abusers may also become infected through unprotected sexual contact with an infected person.

HIV is responsible for AIDS, and takes hold by attacking the immune system – the T-cells – of its host, which are normally responsible for fighting infection. HIV gradually destroys the ability of the immune system to mount a defence against other viruses or infections. Reported HIV incidence among those using heroin, and other injecting drug users (IDUs), is now a worldwide problem affecting countries from Australia to Argentina.

The UN Office for Drug Control and Crime Prevention report Global Illicit Drug Trends 2000 stated that the practice of injecting heroin and other drugs was also spreading to developing countries and taking the HIV virus with it. It blamed injection drug use (IDU) as the major, if not the main, mode of transmission for HIV infection in North Africa, the Middle East, East Asia, Latin America, eastern Europe, Central Asia, western Europe and North America. In the USA, it is thought that IDU has been a factor in an estimated one-third of all HIV and more than half of all hepatitis C cases.

In 1999 the steepest HIV curve was found in the former states of the Soviet Union. The virus is understood to have spread from the Ukraine in the mid-1990s to the Baltic states, the Caucasus and Central Asia, where IDU is perceived as the primary cause of HIV. In Moscow alone, in 1999, 2,700 new HIV cases were reported, three times as many as in all previous years combined; a high proportion of these were blamed on heroin users fixing up.

Other central and eastern European countries believed by the report to be at risk from the HIV epidemic spread by IDUs are the Czech Republic, and Serbia and Montenegro.

Drug injection – and HIV – was also believed to be on the increase in China and Myanmar, where it was understood to be diffusing from urban to rural areas. Heroin injection, already established in Hong Kong and Thailand, was also reported to be spreading to Vietnam and Lao PDR. In 1995 it was estimated that 77 per cent of HIV infections in Malaysia were among IDUs.

In Australia, heroin is the most commonly injected drug and HIV prevalence among IDUs is less than 5 per cent. The number of people with HIV in Austria is thought to be between 12,000 and 14,000, nearly half of whom are drug users. HIV infection in Austria among drug users varies from around 12–30 per cent in Vienna to 50 per cent in western parts of the country.

In the UK, the spread of HIV among heroin users and other IDUs has been largely stopped because of the success of the mid-1980s decision to implement a policy of clean needles. By March 1999 almost 3,500 drug injectors had tested positive for HIV, and more than 1,000 had been diagnosed with AIDS. However, drug researchers believe this has abated.

Research has also discovered that drug abusers can change their risk-taking behaviour – sharing syringes, unsafe sexual practices and so on – through drug-abuse treatment, prevention, and community-based outreach programmes.

Sharing needles also puts the heroin user at risk of hepatitis, a viral infection that attacks the liver and has affected the drug-injecting community for longer than HIV. There are three strains of hepatitis:

- **Hepatitis A** - Associated with poor hygiene, and spread through water and food contamination
- **Hepatitis B** and **C** - Most relevant to injectors.

Hepatitis B is transmitted through blood, but can also be passed though saliva and semen. It incubates for around three months before exhibiting a range of flu-like symptoms. The virus will clear up and a full recovery is normally expected in around six months.

Hepatitis C (HCV) is probably the most serious form of hepatitis and, unlike hepatitis A, can lead to chronic liver damage in 70 per cent of sufferers, and sometimes death. It is estimated to have infected around 35,000 people in the UK alone and although it is impossible to put a figure on the number of those infected through heroin use, it is likely to be in the low thousands. The disease kills about 8,000 people annually in the USA, and about 3.9 million Americans are believed to be infected with the virus. By 2010 it is estimated that up to 39,000 people in the USA will die from the disease each year.

However, it is not necessary for the heroin addict to have shared a needle with a hepatitis C sufferer. The National Center for Infectious Diseases warns that the sharing of any drug equipment, such as razors or mirrors, can potentially be harmful.

What makes the virus particularly difficult to diagnose is that around 80 per cent of those with hepatitis C do not display any symptoms. Those that do will experience flu-like aches, fatigue, jaundice, diarrhoea, abdominal pain and loss of appetite. Around one-fifth of sufferers will clear the virus from their systems in up to 12 months, but in others the disease can remain dormant for anything up to 30 years and by that time irreversible liver damage may have been done.

> I think I got it [hepatitis C] from dirty needles in the 1980s and it means I've had to give up any hard drinking. I can just about manage a pint of cider every so often, but that's against doctor's advice. Hepatitis has really fucked me up physically.
> – Lee M, heroin addict with hepatitis C

It is estimated that some 40 per cent of hepatitis C patients can be successfully treated with recent advances in medication administered for the disease. Alpha interferon (IFN-alpha) alone, or in combination with oral ribavirin, is commonly used and combination therapy (interferon plus ribavirin) is rapidly superseding interferon monotherapy because this dual therapy is significantly more effective.

The standard interferon regimen for patients with chronic hepatitis C consists of three IFN-alpha injections per week for up to 18 months. Some 40 per cent of patients treated with IFN-alpha alone can retain normalized liver function.

Treatment with interferon leads to a variety of side effects, which can significantly impair quality of life. Some clinical trials suggest that over 60 per cent of patients treated with IFN have influenza-like symptoms. Other common and disabling side effects are chronic fatigue and depression.

Treatment with IFN and ribavirin is effective in clearing HCV in almost 40 per cent of treated patients. However, combination therapy is expensive and carries significant side effects, particularly anaemia, depression and weight loss.

The ultimate price to pay for using heroin is death. Many heroin deaths are through suffocation, usually if the user's air passages are blocked by vomit and they have fallen asleep or slipped into unconsciousness.

## OD

Overdose of heroin – OD, or dropping – when the body hasn't built enough tolerance to cope with the quantity of heroin taken, is another frequent danger. Overdose is very common and even small amounts of heroin may cause some people to OD after a period of non-use. This often happens if an addict has been in prison or hospital: when they return to heroin and pump their normal dose into a vein, the body can't cope. Sometimes junkies can simply take too much, perhaps because they have a supply from a new source, or the heroin they score could be significantly purer than the cut dope they regularly inject.

## PHYSICAL SYMPTOMS OF HEROIN OD

- Abnormal or very slow breathing
- Cold skin and low body temperature
- Slow heartbeat
- Muscle twitching
- Slow working of the central nervous system
- Gurgling sound in the throat from vomit or saliva
- Blue tips of fingernails and toenails because of low oxygen
- Small pupils
- Drowsiness
- Unconsciousness
- Coma

An OD victim may go into a coma or die. OD death - or in junkie argot, pulling a blue one or bluey - can take the form of heart failure, liver failure or respiratory failure. The physical symptoms of a fatal heroin dose will start with slow, shallow breathing and the pupils will turn to pinpoints. Blood pressure will drop alarmingly, the skin will turn blue and the OD victim will slip into unconsciousness and coma. Death can be almost immediate or the whole process can take up to ten hours.

The best way of preventing overdose is not to use heroin alone, and many users have buddies to fix up with. Neither should heroin be used in tandem with alcohol, tranquillizers or other drugs, and if the drug has been bought from a new dealer, a small amount should be tried first to test how pure the heroin is. Antagonists, which block the action of opioids such as naloxone, can also sometimes reverse the effects of OD.

## OD DOS AND DON'TS
DO
- Phone an ambulance immediately and tell the operator that the person has overdosed
- Stay with the OD victim
- Keep the OD victim awake by walking them around and talking to them
- If the OD victim is unconscious, put them in the recovery position
- Check their breathing and clear their airway
- Administer mouth-to-mouth resuscitation if they stop breathing

DON'T
- Inject the person with any other drug

- Put them under the shower
- Put anything in their mouth

Real problems can also result if the injector hits an artery (arteries take blood away from the heart, whereas veins return the blood to the heart). Sometimes the plunger in the syringe will be forced back by the high pressure of the blood and rapid bleeding will result; this will need urgent attention, otherwise it can result in the loss of limbs and sometimes death.

It is almost impossible to get accurate statistics on heroin-related deaths, because the definition of heroin-related deaths is potentially very wide. It could, for example, include accidental overdose, suicides through overdose, poisoned heroin, accidental death while under the influence of heroin, death from AIDS after contracting the HIV virus through injecting heroin, and murder or manslaughter while under the influence of heroin.

Often, doctors will record the cause of death without making any mention of the drug in the system. However, the UK's Office for National Statistics (ONS) has estimated the number of drug-related deaths for England and Wales (see table opposite), which includes accidental and deliberate narcotic overdose (excluding paracetamol). In 1993 there were about 900 deaths caused through drug abuse, rising to just over 1,700 in 1997. Of these, 255 were directly related to heroin and another 421 were linked with methadone, commonly used by heroin addicts to break their dependence. There were 38 deaths caused by cocaine and 12 through ecstasy use.

Further research implicated heroin and morphine in 43 per cent of the 1,296 drug-related deaths during 2000 in England and Wales, which suggested that the number of heroin deaths had risen by one-third to 551. Many of the heroin-related deaths were caused because users had taken a cocktail of drugs, and the statistics appear to show that 'most at risk' is the heroin addict.

| DRUG-RELATED DEATHS | |
|---|---|
| DRUG TYPE | NUMBER OF DEATHS |
| Methadone | 421 |
| Heroin | 255 |
| Temazepam | 104 |
| Amphetamines | 40 |
| Cocaine | 38 |
| Ecstasy | 12 |

Source: Office for National Statistics, 1997

Heroin deaths also appear to be on the increase, around the world. In Australia there were just six in 1964 compared to 600 in 1997. Austria reported 86 drug-related deaths in 1988 and Belgium had 91 drug deaths in 1990, most through heroin abuse.

## HEROIN ADDICTION

Addiction or dependence means that a large part of a

person's life is governed by drugs. Buying them and taking them. It is a chronic, relapsing disease, characterized by compulsive drug seeking and use, and by neurochemical and molecular changes in the brain.

And it's a growing problem. Dependence – a strong compulsion to keep taking drugs – is an insidious aspect of any recreational abuse. UK charity group Action on Addiction estimates that around one in three adults in the UK suffers from some form of addiction, costing the tax-payer around £5 billion ($7.25 billion) in 2002.

Not all drugs are as addictive as others. Many drugs users can drink alcohol and then not touch a drop of the hard stuff for months. And US research, available through the American National Comorbidity Survey, demonstrates that cannabis has a very low potential for dependence.

Heroin is a different matter. Heroin produces profound degrees of tolerance and physical dependence, which are also powerful motivating factors for compulsive use and abuse. As with abusers of any addictive drug, heroin abusers gradually spend more and more time and energy obtaining and using the drug. Once they are addicted, the heroin abuser's brain becomes wired to that drug and their primary purpose in life is to seek out and use more and more heroin. (Physical dependence is not inevitable, however, and some heroin users are able to take it on an occasional basis.)

Although heroin is not used as widely as many other drugs, such as tobacco or alcohol, once tried, a very high proportion of users will go on to use it regularly: they will become totally dependent on it. They will be addicted, and dependence is one of the main characteristics that pervades heroin use and informs treatment for the drug.

One symptom of heroin use is physical dependence, which does not occur with ecstasy, LSD or softer drugs like cannabis. This results from repeated, heavy use of the drug and can alter the body chemistry, building up tolerance to the drug. The body adapts to the presence of the drug and withdrawal symptoms occur if use is reduced abruptly. Withdrawal may occur within a few hours after the last time the drug is taken. With regular heroin use, tolerance develops. This means the user must use more and more heroin to achieve the same intensity or effect.

Withdrawal symptoms will occur if use is reduced or stopped. Withdrawal begins between 8 and 24 hours after the last fix and the symptoms are muscle aches, diarrhoea, cold flushes, goose bumps (cold turkey) and tremors, sweating, chills, runny nose, nausea, insomnia, muscular spasms, kicking movements ('kicking the habit'), yawning and sneezing. Elevation in blood pressure, pulse, respiratory rate and temperature occurs as withdrawal progresses. These effects will fade after a week to ten days, but a feeling of weakness may persist for several months after quitting the drug.

Major withdrawal symptoms peak between 24 and 48 hours after the last dose of heroin and subside after about a week. However, some people have shown persistent withdrawal signs for many months. Heroin withdrawal is never fatal to otherwise healthy adults, but it can cause death to the foetus of a pregnant addict.

Tolerance develops to the respiratory depressant, sedative, analgesic, emetic and euphoric effect through heroin use, so addicts will need to inject increased dosages to achieve the same effect they did weeks, months or years before, and if they terminate use they will suffer withdrawal effects. Sometimes addicted individuals will endure many of the withdrawal symptoms to reduce their tolerance for the drug so that they can again experience the initial rush.

Craving and relapse can occur weeks and months after withdrawal symptoms are long gone. However, patients with chronic pain who need opiates to function (sometimes over extended periods) have few if any problems leaving opiates after their pain is resolved by other means. This may be because the patient is simply seeking relief of pain and not the rush sought by the addict.

At the same time, the heroin addict will also evolve a psychological dependency, which is more common with users of other drugs. Essentially, this means the person using the drug feels they are unable to cope with the world unless they are under the influence of heroin, and friends, family and activities such as work take a secondary role.

Heroin dependency will often include both physical and psychological factors, and this has helped to produce more accurate definitions of drug dependence. Historically they have been framed in pejorative terms because early thinking tended to perceive addiction as simply a physical concept – a vice. More recently, psychological dependence has played a greater role. An expert committee working for the UN Commission on Narcotics in the early 1950s stated that addiction characteristics included an 'overpowering desire or need to continue taking the drug and to obtain it by any means; a tendency to increase the dose; a psychological and sometimes a physical dependence on the effects'. This differs markedly from a description of a habit-forming drug, which is generally understood to mean a narcotic that can be taken repeatedly without creating the bonds evident in addiction and that doesn't adversely affect the user.

In her 1999 account of her own experiences with the drug, *How To Stop Time: Heroin From A To Z*, Ann Marlowe attempts to explain her dependence to addicts as being similar to the satisfaction they will experience with their first coffee of the day. Subsequent coffees will never be the same. Marlowe wrote, 'The chemistry of the drug is ruthless: it is designed to disappoint you. Yes, once in a while there's a night when you get exactly where you're trying to go. Magic. Then you chase that memory for a month', adding that her definition of heroin addiction would be 'a form of mourning for the irrecoverable glories of the first time'.

The intensity of the intravenous high created through heroin means it is very likely that recreational use of the drug will lead to physical addiction and dependence. Heroin's ability to create dependence is neatly summed up in the table below, which shows the use of five drugs by a US sample group and the proportion of those who developed a dependence. Alcohol was the most commonly used, with 91.5 per cent of the US Household Survey admitting its use. However, transition from use to dependence for alcohol was relatively low with only 14.1 per cent developing an addiction.

At the other end of the scale, only 1.5 per cent of those surveyed had tried heroin, but of those 0.4 per cent developed an addiction. Thus, almost a quarter of those who do try the drug will end up with an addiction. That compares with less than 1 in 10 of people who develop an addiction to cannabis, despite it having been tried by approximately 30 times more people.

**DEPENDENCE**

| Drug | Proportion of population who have used | Proportion who have developed dependence | Proportion of dependence |
|------|------|------|------|
| Tobacco | 75.6% | 24.1% | 31.9% |
| Heroin | 1.5% | 0.4% | 23.1% |
| Cocaine | 16.2% | 2.7% | 16.7% |
| Alcohol | 91.5% | 14.1% | 15.4% |
| Cannabis | 46.3% | 4.2% | 9.1% |

Source: US Household Survey

## HEROIN PREVENTION

Preventing people from becoming heroin addicts in the first place is an objective of all governments attempting to contain their drug problems. If they are successful at stopping new users adopting heroin, their countries' injecting and smoking population will gradually reduce to zero.

Unfortunately, most drug experts concede that until prevention models become more complex to match the social factors being brought to bear on a heroin user, they will have only moderate success. History seems to support this view because prevention methods have had little or no effect on stopping the growth of the world's heroin problem.

## DRUG PREVENTION AND EDUCATION

- Drug education has limited effect on behaviour and is unlikely to prevent teenagers from experimenting with drugs
- Education can increase knowledge, but strategies need to be based on a range of consistent approaches
- Education can contribute towards increased safety
- Shock tactics are generally believed to be counter-productive
- Measuring the effectiveness of drug prevention programmes is very difficult
- Prevention is neither a cheap nor easy option

Drug prevention is about raising knowledge and awareness which, given enough resources, are achievable objectives. However, in tandem with increasing information about heroin, is the objective to change behaviour. Harry Shapiro, communications director at UK drug resource DrugScope, says this is the hard part, 'It is very difficult to do. How can you get people to change their habits? There is a very rapid decay factor with information campaigns, a couple of weeks later people forget all about it.' However, Shapiro believes that the messages can sometimes sink in over time in the way that 'it has now become a lot less fashionable to drink and drive'.

What is clear is that the most effective prevention messages are those that have clear, well-defined aims, are relevant to the audience, and are sustained and consistent. Prevention strategy can encompass a wide range of tools to help deliver this. In the UK the Drug Prevention Advisory Service (DPAS) was established as an interface between the government and offices that can deliver prevention. It ensures that all prevention material and information conform to the four strands of the UK's anti-drugs strategy, which includes education and prevention.

**EFFECTIVE HEROIN PREVENTION**
- Should have a well-defined purpose
- Needs to be relevant to the audience
- Should include the most accurate and the most up-to-

the-minute information

- The messages need to be credible and delivered through credible sources such as youth services
- They should also challenge stereotypes
- Delivery needs to be through a well-thought-out plan, repeated often, but in a variety of imaginative ways
- Should be built on existing values and should reinforce existing anti-drug beliefs

At one end of the scale, prevention may also include harm-reduction approaches, which are particularly appropriate for needle-using heroin users. These might include prevention strategies to reduce the likelihood of succumbing to a drug overdose by offering resuscitation and awareness training to addicts or providing more access to methadone treatment, the established medication of choice for treating heroin addiction.

Prevention could also involve reducing the risk of HIV or hepatitis and will include the provision of information on sterilizing injecting equipment and making clean syringes more widely available.

An August 2001 consultation document addressing drug-prevention approaches suggested that the routes leading users towards heroin and addiction are so complex that several prevention strategies need to be developed.

Written by David Best and John Witton of the UK's National Addiction Centre, *Guidelines For Drug Prevention* suggested that prevention programmes can fall into two distinct groups: universal and targeted programmes. The former approach aims to reach the general population or a wide cross-section of society, and will include awareness campaigns and anti-drug education programmes, possibly at school.

The elements of school prevention are essentially the same throughout the world and will include a mix of drug-education classes and school visits by drug experts, social workers, former users or law enforcement. Results from the USA show that because two-thirds of all initiation to drug use in 1998 took place mostly during the school years – 12 to 17 years old – substance-prevention programmes in the classroom are vital.

However, Shapiro admits that the quality of drug information in schools varies enormously 'from the local police officer coming in for a chat, to the school putting on a play about the issues'. The level that messages should be pitched at is also hard to gauge because, within a class of 30 children, some will know nothing about drugs, some may be using drugs and others will think they know everything, but probably don't. Drug information in schools also flies in the face of how kids are normally taught. They are presented with drug information and asked to make up their own minds, but throughout the rest of the school curriculum they are told exactly what to do and how to behave.

There is a school of thought that prevention strategy in classrooms should accept drug experimentation as a given and concentrate mostly on how children can protect themselves and be safe if they use drugs. Shapiro accepts this is an option, but says the moral climate and opposition from some politicians, parents and teachers means that is unlikely to be accepted in the short term. 'I'm not sure teachers are going to be comfortable teaching kids how to inject,' he says.

Presenting a credible message to media-savvy children is also a problem faced by teachers. Gary Sutton, heroin project adviser at Release, doesn't believe enough is made of former drug addicts going into schools. Sutton argues that at the very least they can provide a credible message because they have been through heroin addiction, but believes the problem for schools asking outsiders to come in is that this may be seen as a tacit admission that the school has a drug problem. Sutton adds, 'Unless there is a borough-wide policy, then certain headmasters will be nervous because the implication of having a drug addict visit is that heroin or other drugs are used at that school and that has obvious implications for parents and school governors.'

Media campaigns also fall within the universal programme, and their role in drug prevention is to inform people about the services on offer, influence opinion formers and also create a climate where drugs are discussed.

However, there has been extensive debate about the use and effectiveness of campaigns, especially in the UK.

The UK's first national drug campaign came about in the mid-1980s. It featured heroin. Prior to that, heroin wasn't seen as being near the top of the political agenda because until the late 1970s there was a fairly stable and older injecting community. However, in the early 1980s there was an influx of smokable heroin.

The response of the Conservative government, in 1984, was to create a ministerial group chaired by the then Home Office minister David Mellor to create a strategy to stamp out heroin. This sparked one of the most high-profile and controversial episodes of Prime Minister Margaret Thatcher's political reign. The Department of Health and Social Security (DHSS) and the Central Office of Information (COI) approached Yellowhammer, an ambitious advertising agency based in London's West End, to produce a high-profile poster and press campaign aimed specifically at heroin users.

The images the agency produced were designed to shock. Under the white-on-black strapline 'Heroin Screws You Up', one showed a teenager in jeans and sweat-soaked shirt hunched up, his mouth pressed against his filthy hands and fingernails. 'Your Mind Isn't The Only Thing Heroin Damages' it warned, alongside seven well-documented by-products of heavy heroin use, including skin infections, wasted muscles and liver complaints. The copy was equally hard-hitting: 'You'll begin to take heroin not to get high any more, but just to feel normal. And, as you lose control of your body's health, you could lose control of your mind too. Until one day you'll wake up knowing that, instead of you controlling heroin, it now controls you.'

The same image accompanied by the same side effects – mental problems, skin infections, blood diseases, constipation – associated with long-term heroin addicts was given another eye-catching strapline – 'How Low Can You Get On Heroin?' – followed by the no-holds-barred copy 'Take heroin and before long you'll start looking ill, losing weight and feeling like death. So, if you're offered heroin, you know what to say.'

Another teenager, with dark rings under his eyes, spotty skin and a lank fringe, peered from another bleak ad. This strapline read 'Skin Care By Heroin'. Other ads used another withdrawn-looking male model and the line 'All He Wanted Was A Few Laughs'; one of the few ads using a female model had the copyline 'How You React Could Decide Whether She Rejects Drugs Or You'. Later the campaign was used in women's magazines to target mothers, whom the agency had identified in its research as the most important figure in the family for dealing with drug-related problems.

The campaign appeared at the same time as the street price of heroin had fallen, making heroin cheaper than some soft drugs and bringing in a new market of kids willing to smoke the drug. Few campaigns have attracted as much public attention as the £2 million ($2.9 million)

Yellowhammer campaign, which appealed to adolescent vanity. At the time Sammy Harari, the board account director at the ad agency, said, 'All this campaign is trying to do is to begin to shift people's attitudes.'

### THE 'HEROIN SCREWS YOU UP' ADVERTISING CAMPAIGN
ARGUMENTS FOR
- Used as effective part of overall drug strategy, advertising is a persuasive instrument
- Helps increase information provision
- Is high profile

ARGUMENTS AGAINST
- Advertising has no effect on behaviour
- Unable to reach target groups
- Seems to be 'marketing' drugs
- Simplistic
- Glamorizes heroin and encourages anti-establishment teenagers to try it

The advantages of advertising and other universal programmes are that they don't label or stigmatize individuals and they may provide the groundwork for targeted programmes. However, it is often difficult to measure the effectiveness of broad prevention strategies and there doesn't appear to be any robust scientific evidence to show they work or have any lasting impact.

Drug experts suggested that the 'Heroin Screws You Up' campaign, for example, would only put off people who wouldn't try the drug anyway and wouldn't necessarily impact that much on those people who are already using. In other words, it may have the greatest effect on those at lowest risk.

The advertising also drew criticism from drug-charity workers and other experts, who thought that it may actually be counter-productive because young people would be drawn to the grunge images. They argued that the ad campaign was too simplistic because the posters gave the impression that people end up a mess if they take heroin, whereas the reality is that heroin is just one part of a combination of factors including drink and social circumstance. Therefore, they argued that it is better to spend the money on education in schools and throughout communities because then subtleties can be raised and understood.

The campaign also caused some problems for health workers. It scared many parents who thought that the onset of spots on their teenager's face meant they were on heroin. Heroin was being blamed for every problem in a family, even if no member of that family was actually taking it.

Significantly, this kind of campaign may also have the opposite effect to that it sets out to achieve. Teenagers are predominantly anti-Establishment, and there was anecdotal evidence that many found the emaciated models accompanied by the tough copylines attractive because they were seen as a product of the Establishment machine. The poster featuring the adolescent boy was a favourite of students, who hung it in their bedrooms next to posters of Nick Cave and David Bowie.

### DEAD RINGERS

More recently, a UK media campaign featuring a young victim of heroin put the drug on the political agenda again. It showed the corpse of Rachel Whitear, which had lain slumped in a bedsit for several days after she had suffered an overdose. The image was undeniably powerful and garnered extensive national coverage on television and in newspapers.

However, there were many dissenting voices. Opponents of this and similar shock tactics argue it is scattergun scaremongering, rarely targeting users or potential users or communicating hard information about minimizing the effects of the drug or treatment. Also, because several similar campaigns have targeted heroin, some drug experts believe they give the impression that other Class A drugs, such as cocaine, are less harmful.

Thinking about prevention tactics in the early 2000s began to swing towards more targeted programmes, which aim to reduce the influence of the risk factors that lead people to heroin and build on creating coping strategies or other skills. Shapiro says, 'This one-size-fits-all campaign improves the profile of things, but it doesn't have that much impact. People don't change until they see they are at immediate risk.'

Best and Witton also believe targeted prevention programmes will single out the individuals who are most susceptible to drug misuse and suggest they have the potential to catch misuse early and are an efficient tool for directing resources to tackle the problem.

However, the biggest headaches arising from these methods are the difficulties associated with accurate targeting, cost and increasing the risk of stigmatization. They also ignore the wider social context that has led a user to drugs.

Targeted approaches can again encompass a wide variety of projects and drug support groups. For some heroin users they may involve the family or peer group. For example, if it is discovered that the addict is taking heroin because of pressure from friends, then a project could be developed to remove or reduce peer-group influence.

Sutton adds that both universal and targeted approaches always need to be used in conjunction with one another. 'We need to offer alternatives,' he says. 'Not just for preventing heroin use, because people drift into drug use because they don't have anything else in their lives. The alternative is to provide a different path, but of course it is very expensive to provide youth clubs and activities, which give young people a direction.'

Evidence from the US does seem to suggest that mass-media prevention campaigns are having some success. Following the United Nations Drug Control Program's (UNDCP) 1997 $200 million (£138 million) National Youth Anti-Drug Campaign, which used more targeted approaches, drug use in US schools fell away from an alarming upward swing. The Monitoring the Future studies group, which collects data on US school students, found that drug use among 14-year-old eighth-grade students fell in the USA between 1996 and 1999 by 12 per cent.

**FIRST PERSON**
MARK MCLEAN: UK NATIONAL DRUGS HELPLINE MANAGER
'We receive between 250,000 and 300,000 calls each year. It's a free and confidential service and then the National Drugs Helpline (NDH) refers one in five callers to drug agencies.

'We take more calls about heroin than any other drug. I'd say a quarter of our calls relate to heroin. After the death of Rachel Whitear we had lots of calls from parents. Parents respond more to stories like this than young people. Our remit is not to lobby the government or influence policy. We're like an older brother or sister to the young people who contact us. We're not judgmental, we don't tell them to get off drugs. We point out the legal risks and health risks associated with heroin or any other drug. People are going to take heroin anyway and our job is to advise them how to inject, to use clean needles, to avoid contaminated heroin, and also how to minimize harm.

'Campaigns like the "Heroin Screws You Up" advertising have the government stamped all over them, and for that reason are less credible among young people. The face of the person on the poster doesn't match the face of their mate who uses heroin so they aren't likely to trust the campaign.

'"Heroin Screws You Up" had an impact because people still remember it, but whether it has an impact on behaviour is debatable. The key for the campaigns we're involved in is to promote the services we offer and for that reason campaigns have to be credible and constructive, and direct people to information and support.'

## HEROIN TREATMENT

When governments construct their drug budgets there is always a trade-off between how much they will spend on treatment and the resources put into tackling drug crime. For most of the last century, law and order has been the priority and so in the UK in 1998 only 13 per cent of the £1.4 billion ($2 billion) spent on drug-related activity went towards treatment.

However, the amount spent on treatment in most countries is generally increasing, boosted by the growing conviction that there is a better chance of winning the war on drugs if addicts are given treatment instead of punishment. Results from the USA also back up those who favour treatment over legislation. The US SAMHSA National Treatment Improvement Study 1996, which investigated the effectiveness of publicly funded drug treatment, discovered that there was a 47 per cent decline in heroin use one year after treatment ended.

Another US report, the Drug Abuse Treatment Outcome Studies conducted on behalf of the USA National Institute on Drug Abuse (NIDA) in the 1990s, also confirmed that treatment could significantly curb hardcore heroin use. One year after the end of treatment the study found that consumption levels of heroin had fallen by about two-thirds. In May 2002, the UK's Association of Chief Police Officers (ACPO) issued new proposals suggesting that, in some circumstances, treatment for heroin addiction should be considered as an alternative to prosecution. The ACPO report said it looked forward to the time when those who appear in court for misuse of Class A drugs, such as heroin, have immediate access to treatment.

Spending on drugs misuse in the UK was £700 million ($1 billion) in 2000/01 and expected to rise to £1 billion ($1.5 billion) in 2003/04. Of this, £234 million ($340 million) was spent on treatment in 2001/02, rising to over £400 million ($580 million) in 2003/04. Of this, the UK's National Treatment Agency (NTA), which is a joint initiative between the Home Office and the National Health Service to improve the quality and quantity of drug treatment, had a £234 million ($340 million) annual budget. By 2003 the NTA was expecting to have £400 million ($580 million) to spend on treatment, with funds significantly increasing until 2008.

In addition to this, £32 million ($46.5 million) was spent on young people and prevention work in 2001/02, due to rise to £71 million ($103 million) in 2003/04.

Any intervention – from providing better housing to creating jobs – that makes someone less likely to use heroin can be defined as treatment. However, health organizations normally focus on a much narrower definition of treatment, which is essentially providing healthcare and counselling. There are many different care pathways for kicking a heroin habit. Some are more successful than others, and they can be delivered in a variety of ways. Many are also used in tandem. The NTA boils the main methods down to five:

- counselling
- day centre
- detoxification
- prescribing
- residential

These can be delivered by and through a bewildering array of different services and agencies, which may vary slightly throughout the world depending on factors that include the policies of national and local government and the health authorities.

**HEROIN TREATMENT**

|  | NO OF ADMISSIONS | YEAR |
|---|---|---|
| Italy | 121,000 | 1997 |
| France | 94,400 | 1997 |
| Switzerland | 19,000 | 1998 |
| The Netherlands | 19,000 | 1999 |
| USA | 216,900 | 1998 |

However, the first port of call for an addict wanting to quit a habit will probably be a call to their country's national drugs helpline, such as Narcotics Anonymous. This is likely to give confidential free advice 24 hours a day, and can put the heroin user in touch with other local agencies or groups. When someone is arrested they can also be routed towards drug agencies if they need treatment.

The family doctor or local hospital will also offer help to addicts trying to kick smack. In the UK, doctors make more referrals to specialist drug services than any other point of contact. The doctor can usually provide advice, sometimes prescribe substitute drugs, sometimes – although very rarely – prescribe heroin, often in tandem with a wide network of other specialist agencies and services.

There will also be a huge variety of different drug agencies, volunteer services, street agencies and community drug teams (which are multidisciplinary teams including counsellors, psychiatrists, social workers and advice services via the phone, drop-in centres or home visits). These confidential services will probably not simply confine themselves to the user, but will also involve the user's partner and friends.

Some may also have their own doctors, who may be able to prescribe drugs for detox or maintenance programmes and, if necessary, will steer the heroin user to other more appropriate services.

The quality of counselling and the qualifications of those providing it can vary, but these services are essentially designed to determine how serious users are about ridding themselves of their habit and to point them in the right direction to facilitate this. The street agencies and drug teams will also probably provide aftercare treatment, possibly combined with home visits or group therapy.

Syringe- and needle-exchange facilities are also available in many countries, including the UK, which pioneered their introduction in the 1980s. They provide clean works to heroin and other drug injectors, and are designed to stop the spread of HIV and other blood-borne viruses such as hepatitis C. Many are sited near drug-advice projects or hospitals, and some have their own confidential advice services and counsellors. Gary Sutton, heroin project adviser at Release, says he believes there is no proof that needle exchanges will increase the number of addicts on the streets, and that they have been 'absolutely central' in halting the spread of HIV in the UK. Outreach services will also attempt to bring the service to the user and may include a needle exchange and counselling service going into a heroin user's home.

The services of drug-dependency units are normally available for people who are heavy, long-term heroin users. Drug-dependency units are usually based within a hospital and provide another level of services on top of counselling, advice and information. These may include psychiatric treatment, advice on better syringe practice, needle exchange and home visits. Some may also offer a prescribing service and a detox service. Most can prescribe substitute drugs, such as methadone, in reducing script or maintenance programmes to stabilize the addict. Treatments can vary in different countries or even in different regions of a country, but will usually require a referral from a doctor or social worker. There is normally a waiting list.

Residential rehabilitation centres are also sometimes available for longer-term heroin users. Some offer detoxification on the premises, but most are only open to those who have already been through detox and are drug free. The addict will live in these rehabs for several months or more in a bid to kick their habit, although length of stay is often determined by costs, which are often very high. There are several types of programme available, but for heroin use the main ones tend to be based on the 'Minnesota model', which sees addicts work through a stepped programme, or a therapeutic approach, which includes intense therapy sessions.

**FIRST PERSON**

EDDIE COWLEY: DRUGS ARREST REFERRAL WORKER

'A lot of young drug users are in a terrible mess and it's very disheartening. Sometimes I want to pack it all in and become a dustman, but I carry on because I'd like to think I can do some good. It's a result when anyone gets off heroin but it's also a result to see someone clean and healthy even if they're still using.

'When someone is arrested they are asked if they want to see a drugs worker, irrespective of the offence. This is a Home Office initiative aimed at tackling criminal behaviour that is motivated by drugs. If the person in the cells says "yes", I go into the police station to see them and assess the problem, and refer them to drug agencies if they need further treatment. Drug users' problems vary: they could be jobless, homeless or maybe they have family problems. The referral process can take six to eight months, which is far too long.

'There are various options open to us within the criminal justice system. The Drug Treatment and Testing Orders (DTTOs) are mostly targeted at heroin users. People committing crimes to feed their habit are put on a DTTO and assigned a worker. They are put on a methadone programme and tested regularly. The programme is designed to keep them out of prison. The problem is that you have to be arrested before you can get on to this type of programme. Unless you've broken the law you can't get help.

'Methadone is prescribed in different ways. First, there is maintenance prescribing script in which users sign a contract and go on to a methadone programme. These tend to be long-term users. The problem with methadone is that it's very addictive. Drug users generally don't like it because it zonks them out completely. But at the moment methadone is all that's available for drug agencies.

'Second, there is the reduction prescribing script for people who want to come off heroin and methadone. The methadone dose is gradually reduced. Finally, there is the maintenance prescribing script with a view to detoxing. This is a residential detoxing programme and tends to be aimed at older people in their late twenties and thirties. Young people normally haven't finished their drugs career and aren't receptive to this particular remedy.

'I think the government genuinely does want to do something, but the money gets distributed in the wrong way. Services for people with drug problems are incredibly limited. The government concentrates too much on punitive measures and not rehabilitation and it isn't addressing the social causes of why people take heroin. Votes have a lot to do with it. The government wants to tackle crime figures rather than dealing with the underlying problems of heroin abuse.'

## TYPES OF TREATMENT
Once a heroin addict has approached one of the main agencies or services for help, it will point them towards

one or more of a whole range of treatment types and delivery models that are available. Again, different care and treatment types exist around the world, but the NTA's experience in the UK is typical.

In 2002, there were 120,000 people in drug treatment in the UK, approximately 100,000 of whom were heroin and opiate users. The NTA had set a target to have 200,000 entering treatment in 2008. However, treatments are really only successful when the heroin user wants to give up the drug and is not simply succumbing to pressure from a husband, wife or other family member or has been forced to reassess use because they are facing a prison term. There is no simple cure for heroin addiction and the user must decide for themselves that the drug is taking over – often ruining – their lives and they need help.

Treatment is also more effective if abuse is identified early. But in the early months and years of abuse many heroin users may not have been sucked into the debilitating side effects of the drug. It is only when their health suffers, they lose their jobs, homes and family or contract HIV that they look for help. Accessing people earlier also aids the efficacy of the resources ranged against drug addiction because younger people are more able to detox, whereas heroin users in their later twenties or early thirties often need methadone maintenance to first stabilize them, and that clogs the system.

Some evidence suggests that the method of administration may dictate how long a user waits before they ask for help. According to the US Substance Abuse and Mental Health Services Administration (SAMHSA) Treatment Episode Data Set 2001 those who inhaled heroin in 1998 sought treatment sooner than heroin injectors. On average, those snorting or smoking heroin sought treatment after six years. Injectors waited until they had been using a needle for about 11 years before seeking treatment.

More success is likely to result when agencies and services are combined or co-operate to offer the addict a multidisciplinary treatment. Thus, if a heroin user is trying to kick the drug with methadone at a residential clinic, then specialist drug workers should offer support when they returns home. Perhaps a support network of other past users will also operate in their area and they should be encouraged to attend.

In 2002 the NTA was seeking to introduce a Models of Care system, which would provide an integrated system for the heroin addict and highlight clearer care pathways. Someone would be responsible for determining the optimal route of treatment for an individual and also appointed to manage the whole 'journey' of an addict, through counselling, to detox or prescription.

According to Best and Witton, evidence also shows that the greatest gains are likely to result from longer stays in treatment. Other factors that could impact on the success of heroin treatment are whether the patient is allowed to take methadone home and the type of regime offered. They suggest that the treatment is likely to be more successful the more control the addict has.

## METHADONE REDUCTION AND MAINTENANCE PROGRAMMES

Methadone, a synthetic opiate usually taken orally, is used in heroin replacement treatments. It induces less euphoria and blocks opioid receptors in the brain, avoiding withdrawal. It stabilizes the patient and reduces risks to their health in preparation for counselling, group work and reintegration into the community.

The effectiveness of treatment is largely dependent on the quality of the treatment and the commitment of the addict taking part. Properly prescribed methadone is not intoxicating or sedating, and its effects do not interfere with ordinary activities such as driving a car.

The medication can suppress narcotic withdrawal for 24 to 36 hours, and patients are able to perceive pain and have emotional reactions. Most important, methadone relieves the craving associated with heroin addiction; craving is a major reason for relapse. Methadone's effects last for about 24 hours – four to six times as long as those of heroin – so people in treatment need take it only once a day.

Methadone is used as a replacement for heroin in treatments aimed at either maintenance or gradual withdrawal. The reduction method is not particularly new and was suggested to help wean opium addicts off the drug in Thailand in the early 1800s. The modern treatment model was devised by the American physicians Professor Vincent Dole and Marie Nyswander in 1964. Methadone reduction treatment usually takes place in community settings and is designed to help the user withdraw or detoxify completely from opioid use. The aim is to gradually reduce the quantity prescribed until the user experiences no withdrawal symptoms and is drug free. The degree of reduction and length of time used to achieve abstinence can vary from a few weeks to many months, and motivation is the key to the success of these programmes.

Methadone maintenance treatment is a form of respite care, maintaining users by prescribing the drug to stabilize them. Methadone is medically safe even when used continuously for ten years or more. The theory behind the treatment is that methadone maintenance reduces some of the criminality associated with heroin and, because it is usually delivered in community settings, removes the risk of infection and enables those on the programme to live a normal life. In 2000 about 150,000 people were on methadone maintenance programmes in the USA. However, methadone does not automatically convert a heroin addict into a law-abiding citizen and must be backed up with aftercare, which can plug the abuser into a new, more fulfilling way of life.

Those opposed to methadone replacement argue that there is little evidence to suggest that criminal behaviour has been reduced or that those on programmes have been successful at finding work. Also, because it replaces one drug with another, it is not perceived as being a cure and, often, some methadone will find its way on to the black market.

Many heroin users approach methadone treatments, which have no aftercare or back-up, as simply another drug supply – a pharmacological stop-gap – and when they can't find a ready supply of smack they will take the next available drug – methadone.

The US Substance Abuse and Mental Health Services Administration (SAMHSA) Treatment Episode Data Set 2001 also found that heroin inhalers were less likely than heroin injectors to receive methadone treatment. The use of methadone as part of treatment generally declined for both heroin injectors and inhalers from 1993 to 1998. The number of injectors on methadone fell from just over 60 per cent to less than 50 per cent and, for inhalers, from less than 50 per cent to 25 per cent in 1997.

Methadone remains the most widely used narcotic in treatment, but in recent years other synthetic drugs have been tested and in some countries, such as Australia and France, have been introduced into narcotic detoxification and maintenance therapy programmes as an alternative to methadone.

Buprenorphine was previously available for treating severe pain and its use in narcotic addiction is now spreading rapidly. A man-made narcotic, it is the least addictive powerful narcotic, and both an agonist and a blocker of the opioid nerve receptors. This means that it provides a moderate narcotic effect and blocks the craving for and effects of other narcotics.

Buprenorphine also produces a lower level of physical dependence, which means that patients who discontinue medication generally have fewer withdrawal symptoms than those who stop taking methadone. Because of these advantages, buprenorphine is also more appropriate for use in a wider variety of treatment settings.

Naloxone and naltrexone are medications that also block the effects of morphine, heroin and other opiates. As antagonists, they are especially useful as antidotes. Naltrexone has long-lasting effects, ranging from one to three days, depending on the dose. It blocks the pleasurable effects of heroin and is useful in treating some highly motivated individuals.

Naltrexone has also been found to be successful in preventing relapse by former opiate addicts released from prison.

**OPIATE DETOXIFICATION**

The primary objective of detoxification is to relieve withdrawal symptoms while patients adjust to a drug-free state. Not in itself a treatment for addiction, detoxification is a useful step only when it leads into long-term treatment that is either drug free (residential or out-patient) or uses medications as part of the treatment. The best-documented drug-free treatments are the therapeutic community residential programmes lasting at least three to six months.

However, it has also been known for some users to detox at home where the addict simply stops taking dope and goes through four or five days of painful withdrawal symptoms. The heroin user should cut down their dose to the minimum just prior to detox and make themselves comfortable, usually in bed. They should eat well and take cool showers and plenty of liquids. A family member or friend should also be enlisted to help out. However, even in a special detox unit there may be some suffering and often a high failure rate. There is also a high risk of OD if the detox fails and the heroin user returns to the streets for another score.

**HEROIN PRESCRIBING**

Heroin prescribing is available in several countries with more liberal attitudes towards heroin treatment, including the UK, The Netherlands, Australia, Switzerland and Spain. Before May 2002 there were only about 30 doctors in the UK who were still prescribing heroin to around 300 heroin users under licence (the government had stopped wholesale prescribing in 1968).

However, in early 2002 the NTA announced that it would examine the efficacy of reintroducing a wider system of prescribing heroin. Chief executive Paul Hayes said there were around 5 to 10 per cent of heroin users who didn't respond well to methadone and would probably do better on prescribed diamorphine. However, he conceded that the 'willingness of doctors is not great' and there were a number of issues that the treatment agency needed to address. 'There are cost implications because it is much more expensive. People have to use three times a day for the rest of their lives. And we've got to make sure it doesn't leak on to the market like it did in the 1960s and make sure we are not entrenching people in injecting behaviour. It is not an easy solution, but I'm pretty sure it's got a role to play,' he said.

Support for heroin prescribing also came from the UK police. In 2001 the Association of Chief Police Officers (ACPO) called for the mass prescription of heroin to addicts through specialist units in police stations, GPs' surgeries and hospitals. This would ensure that addicts had clean needles and health advice, and would keep contaminated needles off the street. ACPO president Sir David Phillips said at the time, 'The system has failed. We have an out-of-control drugs industry and it is time to try a new approach.' However, an ACPO spokesman said, 'It's not about legalizing heroin, but just the possibility of having heroin monitored and regulated from police stations.'

The Royal College of General Practitioners, however, voiced concerns about heroin prescribing in the UK in 2002. The college claimed it had a low therapeutic index and for a user who has lost their tolerance may be fatal. It also suggested it was too expensive, claiming that one year of methadone treatment cost £2,000 ($3,000) compared to around £10,000-15,000 ($14,500-22,000) for heroin.

Despite this, the UK drugs inquiry by the House of Commons Home Affairs Select Committee, chaired by Chris Mullin, recommended in May 2002 that a nationwide network of 'safe injecting areas' should be set up, with medical heroin prescribed by the National Health Service. Models of how heroin prescribing could be achieved were also being examined by the NTA.

Supervised consumption needs to be open at times that users can access it - usually late at night - and should also be secure so that drugs cannot be supplied to the illegal market. Often called 'shooting galleries', clinics where addicts can go for a health check, with provision for injecting and resuscitation equipment, have been piloted and used in Australia, Switzerland, Germany and other parts of Europe.

Switzerland's large-scale, long-term heroin maintenance experiment, in which a number of addicts were given regular doses of heroin under controlled conditions, has resulted in some dramatic results. Ueli

Minder of the Swiss Federal Office of Public Health said it has been accompanied by a fall in homelessness, a major reduction in illicit heroin and cocaine use, an improvement in the employment rate (in the treatment group) from 14 per cent to 32 per cent, and an eventual significant switch to other, more conventional treatments such as methadone maintenance and abstinence therapy.

Encouraged by five-year trials, the Dutch government also asked its parliament in March 2002 to endorse proposals to hand out heroin in combination with methadone to addicts who were 'beyond help'.

Sutton is in favour of shooting galleries because he says they reduce the visibility of addicts hanging around street corners and also the prevalence of discarded syringes. However, there are associated problems, he says. 'There are always people who don't want these things in their backyard. Also, how many addicts will go to a shooting gallery three times each day? But the alternative to shooting galleries is people's homes and you have to weigh the social consequences. What is the most damaging?'

Hayes said it would be unlikely that heroin prescribing would become the main form of medical treatment for heroin addiction. 'Methadone is likely to remain the most appropriate form of treatment for the majority of cases. There are, however, users who are not accessing treatment either because they have not responded well to the use of methadone, or because they refuse this form of treatment.'

He proposed that heroin prescribing could be used as a 'gateway treatment' to encourage users to enter other forms of treatment.

He also conceded that politics and the media play an important part in these treatments being made available. 'If there was a political move that this wasn't on, then it would be more difficult to achieve it,' he said. 'Certainly from our point of view we are being told to follow evidence. And if the evidence shows X works, then we want more X, whatever it is.'

## BEHAVIOURAL THERAPIES

Although behavioural and pharmacological treatments can be extremely useful when employed alone, integrating both types of treatment will ultimately produce the most effective results. There are many effective behavioural treatments available for heroin addiction, which can include residential and out-patient approaches. An important task is to match the best treatment approach to the particular needs of the patient.

Several new behavioural therapies, such as contingency management therapy and cognitive-behavioural interventions, have been developed with some success for heroin addiction. Contingency management therapy uses a voucher-based system, where patients earn 'points' based on negative drug tests, which they can exchange for items that encourage healthy living.

The cognitive behavioural interventions are designed to help modify the patient's thinking, expectancies and behaviour and to increase skills in coping with various stress factors they encounter in the real world.

MONEY

## HEROIN MONEY

Like all commodities, heroin's market value goes up or down depending on a series of factors, such as the supply of opium, the size of the user market and its demand, the cost of smuggling and the scale of the profits taken by the crime organizations handling the drug. The National Criminal Intelligence Service estimated in 2002 that the mark-up on a kilo [2¼lb] of heroin was between £130,000 and £250,000 [$190,000 and $360,000], depending on the size of the drug-trafficking organization.

US research by the Office of National Drug Control Policy shows that heroin is getting cheaper. The 2001 study, 'The Price Of Illicit Drugs', shows that in the early 1980s users were spending up to $5 (£3.45) per milligram, but by the 2000s they were spending closer to $0.40 (28p) per milligram.

Heroin prices have fluctuated enormously since the beginning of the 1990s, partly due to law enforcement and the influence of governments in the main opium poppy regions. But one of the main catalysts has been the wars fought in Afghanistan. In the early 1990s, when the civil war in the country was at its height and opium production went unfettered, 1kg (2¼lb) of raw opium fetched around $40 (£28) on the open market.

With the Taliban gaining power, the price of Afghan opium – and therefore heroin – remained relatively stable. However, the regime's ban on poppy growing in 2000 sent the price of opium up to about $800 (£552) per kilo (2¼lb). The price crashed back to around $500 (£345) and stabilized in 2002 when the USA led attacks against the Taliban and Osama bin Laden in Afghanistan because opium farmers began planting again.

However, despite the massive fall in the production of opium it had little effect on prices in the UK and other European countries that are serviced by Afghan heroin. This was because producers had stockpiled supplies following a bumper crop in 1999 to keep supplies – and prices – level, although Luxembourg, Portugal, Sweden and the UK reported a slight decrease in 1999.

By 2002 there were signs that this was changing, with reports from users that the quality of heroin was dropping and the cost expected to increase. According to Addiction, the UK's biggest treatment charity, the cost of a gram in London, traditionally the most expensive market, was £60 ($87) in 2002. In other major UK cities, such as Birmingham, a gram could be bought for around £40 to £50 ($58 to $72).

Finding out how much the heroin market is actually worth in different countries is a difficult proposition, but in 2001 the UK Home Office attempted to put a value on it. The 'Sizing The UK Market For Illicit Drugs' report (see table overleaf), by the National Economic Research Associates for the Home Office, estimated that there were 270,000 regular heroin users in England and Wales, some 25,329 occasional users and several thousand in the prison population.

Assuming a regular heroin user, who on average used the drug on 24.6 days in the last 30, and spends about £28.80 ($42) per day on heroin, this equates to an annual drugs bill of £8,516 ($12,340). However, heroin users are often poly-drug users: the report cited that 53 per cent of regular heroin users also used crack cocaine and 24 per cent were regular cocaine users; almost 20 per cent of regular heroin users were regular users of both crack and cocaine; and the vast majority of regular crack users – 83 per cent – were also regular heroin users. The report therefore suggested they would spend a total of around £16,500 ($24,000) per year. It was, therefore, able to estimate that the total market for illicit drugs was £6.6 billion ($9.6 billion), with the heroin market easily the biggest part of that at £2.31 billion ($3.35 billion).

**ILLICIT DRUG MARKET**

| TYPE OF HEROIN USER | NUMBER | SPEND |
|---|---|---|
| Regular | 270,097 | £2,299.9m |
| Occasional | 25,329 | £1.4m |
| Prison | 3,331 | £11.7m |

| TYPE OF DRUG | TOTAL VALUE OF MARKET |
|---|---|
| Heroin | £2,313m |
| Amphetamines | £257.7m |
| Cannabis | £1,577.9m |
| Cocaine | £352.8m |
| Crack | £1,817.4m |
| Ecstasy | £294.6m |
| Total value of illicit drug market | £6,613.5m |

Note: £1 = $1.45 (approx)
Source: 'Sizing The UK Market For Illicit Drugs'

## HEROIN LEGISLATION

Almost as quickly as drugs were introduced into society, laws were passed to limit their supply or – in more recent years – outlaw them totally. As long ago as 1729 the Chinese emperor Yung Cheng issued an edict prohibiting the smoking of opium and its sale, and in 1799 Kia King decreed poppy cultivation and its trade illegal.

In the West, the possession or supply of illicit drugs was largely not subject to prosecution until the middle of the 19th century, when the 1868 Pharmacy and Poisons Act was introduced following a spate of fatal opium overdoses in Britain. But it wasn't particularly effective as it was based on self-regulation and users could still get opiates over the counter at pharmacies.

In the USA, controls were also lax and inconsistent until 1875, when San Francisco passed a law to prohibit opium smoking. In 1890, in its earliest law enforcement legislation on narcotics, the US Congress imposed a tax on opium and morphine and, in 1906, followed up with the Pure Food and Drug Act. This required contents, labelling on medicines and other products containing opiates, and immediately cut the availability of opiates in drugstore powders and pills.

In 1909, the US Congress passed the first federal drug prohibition law – the Smoking Opium Exclusion Act – outlawing the importation and use of opium. Then, in 1910, the Chinese, who had fought two Opium Wars – in 1839 and 1856 – with Britain in a bid to stop opium trafficking, finally persuaded the British government to dismantle the India-China opium trade and strictly enforce laws to restrict opium.

All modern global heroin legislation can essentially be traced back to 1909, when the first international Opium Commission was hosted by Shanghai. It focused primarily on opiate use in the Far East and countries with interests in that region and Persia were represented at the convention, which was chaired by Charles Henry Brent, the American Bishop of the Philippines, who became one of the most influential figures in combating drugs in the early part of the 20th century.

This conference laid the foundations for the International Opium Conference, held in The Hague in 1911. The British contingent, alarmed at the increased levels of smuggling in the Far East, proposed that the treaty should extend to the preparation and trade in morphine and cocaine. However, some countries – notably Germany – resisted this because they had huge pharmaceutical industries producing morphine-based drugs.

However, the conference did produce a treaty, the Opium Convention of 23 January 1912, which committed its 12 signatories to reducing opium and morphine abuse, and the drugs prepared from them, which included heroin. However, in reality, the Convention went no further than obliging the countries to take measures to control the trade in opium within their own legal systems.

A second conference, held in The Hague in 1913, was equally unsuccessful at ratifying the Convention and halting the production of heroin. Although the German pharmaceutical company Bayer ceased production of the drug in the same year, heroin supply was out of control, with many cocaine addicts switching to the cheaper alternative. It was only at a third conference in The Hague in 1914 that a protocol was signed allowing the Convention to take effect.

The USA gave substance to this Convention in 1914 with the Harrison Narcotics Act. This was the first comprehensive control of opiates, which curbed heroin and cocaine abuse and addiction by requiring doctors, physicians and chemists to register and pay a tax. Illegal possession of substances named in the Convention also led to a maximum fine of

$2000 (£1,380), five years' imprisonment or both. This also formalized the basis for the criminalization of the use of drugs in the USA for the next century.

The outbreak of World War I in 1914 interrupted further international law-making, though several European powers did move to tighten their border controls and domestic drug laws. For example, under a 1916 Spanish regulation, the sale of medicines was confined to prescriptions supplied at pharmacies, with stricter controls covering morphine.

The Netherlands also introduced an Opium Act in 1919 to outlaw opium-based drugs. However, by 1928, when possession was criminalized, the Dutch police often turned a blind eye and did not strictly enforce the country's drug laws.

In the UK, the government was worried about the uncontrolled supply of morphine and heroin throughout the armed forces and, in 1916, enacted Article 40(b) of the Defence of the Realm Act (DORA). This prohibited the supply of drugs, although not morphine, to army personnel and was later extended to encompass the whole country.

Following the end of the war and the signing of the Versailles peace treaty in 1919, the implementation of the 1912 international Opium Convention was made one of the conditions – Article 295 – of the peace deal. Responsibility for international narcotics legislation was put in the hands of the League of Nations and, in Britain, Article 295 became the Dangerous Drugs Act 1920.

This stipulated that only authorized bodies were allowed to manufacture or supply cocaine and opiates, such as morphine and heroin. Sales of drugs were logged and the Home Office began to regulate the import of opiates. Further legislation followed in 1923 with the Dangerous Drugs and Poisons Act, which amended the earlier Pharmacy Act.

In 1919, the League of Nations established the Social Questions and Opium Traffic Section and, by 1920, an Advisory Committee on Opium and other Dangerous Drugs was appointed. Britain, France (who in 1922 introduced a new law threatening ten years in prison for supply), The Netherlands, Japan, India, Portugal and China all had permanent representation on this committee.

The climate for opium and heroin legislation was also influencing a wider world. In 1925 a new narcotics law in Egypt outlawed trafficking in drugs and the growing of opium poppies, and a few years later introduced the Central Narcotics Intelligence Bureau, following a sharp rise in the number of heroin addicts in Cairo's slums.

Despite opposition from some prominent physicians, who believed that heroin offered relief to patients, drug supplies in the USA were further controlled in 1922 with the Jones-Miller Narcotic Drugs Import and Export Act. Heroin was eventually outlawed completely in 1924, with the introduction of the Porter Act. This made the manufacture and use of the drug in medicine illegal.

This set a pattern for much of the resulting prohibitionist

legislation governing heroin and opium supply over the next few decades, and demonstrated that the USA had not learned any lessons from the prohibition of alcohol: stamping out supply did not result in a downturn in demand. US narcotics agents, or narcs as they became known, from the Narcotics Division of the Prohibition Unit, were sent out to raid clinics and strangle the supply of legitimately produced medical supplies to addicts.

By 1923 the USA, which had not joined the League, began to attend Advisory Committee sessions and a further Opium Conference was opened in Geneva in November 1924. The first phase was directed at the issue of opium smoking, with a second phase, two months later, aimed at curbing opium derivatives, especially heroin.

The US was represented at the conference by chairman of the House Foreign Affairs Committee Stephen Porter, who proposed the world prohibition of heroin. However, most participants believed that, while illicit supplies remained uncontrolled, complete suppression was impossible, and rejected his blanket ban. The US delegation walked out.

Despite the walk-out, the Opium Conference, it passed a Convention that, in 1928, effectively put the control, manufacture, supply and sale of drugs in the hands of governments. Records on the levels of stocks of heroin and other drugs were ordered to be kept, and government departments took responsibility over their import and export.

The move had the effect of bringing into line the demand for legal morphine and heroin, required by legitimate hospitals and chemists, and the levels produced by licensed pharmaceutical companies. In the four years between 1928 and 1932, the global supply of 'legal' heroin fell by nearly 600 per cent.

In 1931, further conferences, which took place in Geneva and Bangkok, made efforts to suppress the illicit trade in narcotics and went further towards criminalizing the use of drugs by requiring all the Convention partners to introduce imprisonment for drug offenders. Restrictions were also placed on heroin, which at this point was being widely trafficked. However, with opium still being cultivated legally in the Far East, heroin use was not made a punishable offence at this stage.

A League of Nations convention for the Suppression of the Illicit Traffic in Dangerous Drugs followed in 1936, which made drug offences a crime punishable by extradition. A central office to supervise the prosecution of heroin and other drug traffickers was also established. Ironically, the USA refused to put its signature to the Convention because it did not include the trade in opium.

World War II also had the effect of mobilizing the legislators. Concerned that its troops would become junkies, the USA forced through an agreement to outlaw opium smoking in the Dutch East Indies in 1943, and the British also agreed to stop selling opium in its territories. This meant that just a few years after the war, opium smoking had been outlawed everywhere in the world apart from Thailand, which eventually got around to banning it in 1959.

The United Nations took over responsibility for heroin and other dangerous drugs from the League Advisory Committee on Opium and Dangerous Drugs in 1946. The UN established the Commission on Narcotic Drugs, made up of 40 member states, and this began preparations for a worldwide drugs policy.

In 1948, the World Health Organization (WHO) was drawn into helping to formulate this policy and, in 1949, attempted to instigate a worldwide ban on the manufacture and use of heroin. That view got a good hearing in the USA, where the Federal Bureau of Narcotics pushed for the compulsory imprisonment of drug users. The 1951 Boggs Bill also called for mandatory minimum sentences for opiate use and supply, ranging from between 2 and 5 years for a first offence and up to 20 years for third-time offenders.

The bill continued the momentum for more punitive overseas drug policies. The WHO recommended further drastic measures in 1953, when it called for all heroin production and imports to be wiped out. Then, in 1954, the UN pressed for the prohibition of the manufacture and trade in heroin unless it was destined for research or medical use. The British government, fearing that a blanket ban on legally produced heroin would create a massive market of illicitly produced heroin, did not seek to ban heroin manufacture.

However, it continued to restrict and control imports and exports of the drug. Also, in 1955, it did not renew licences for heroin production used in many cough remedies. Some other European countries, notably France and The Netherlands, followed suit.

The Boggs Bill was superseded by the 1956 Narcotic Control Act, which continued to pursue the USA's prohibitionist policies. Meanwhile, on the international stage, the UN introduced a single Convention on Narcotic Drugs in 1961. This replaced all previous Conventions and required participating governments to restrict the trade, production and possession of narcotics to scientific purposes. Any other activity was subject to punishment.

The Convention had four lists of substances, which were governed by a different regime of supervision. Also, on recommendations from the WHO, it could add new drugs to the lists if it could be shown that they presented a serious threat to public health or were part of illicit trafficking. Depending on the degree of misuse, substances could be transferred between lists and national legislation would then be adapted to reflect the changes.

A series of laws was also introduced in the UK during the 1960s to act on drug-abuse problems. These included the Drugs (Prevention of Misuse) Act 1964 and the Dangerous Drugs Act 1964, which ratified the 1961 New York convention, and imposed the requirement for safe keeping and recording of heroin and other drugs.

In 1967 the Misuse of Drugs Act made it necessary for a UK doctor to be issued with a Home Office licence to prescribe heroin to a patient, and also gave the authorities powers to rescind that right. The act also introduced stop-and-search powers on a national level, giving police more tools to investigate misuse and dealing if they suspected someone was in possession of a controlled drug.

In response to America's growing drug problem, Congress passed the Controlled Substances Act of the Comprehensive Drug Abuse Prevention and Control Act 1970. It replaced more than 50 pieces of drug legislation and came into effect on 1 May 1971.

This law established a single system of control for both narcotic and psychotropic drugs for the first time in US history. It also established five schedules to classify controlled substances according to how dangerous they are, their potential for abuse and addiction, and whether they possess legitimate medical value.

The Misuse of Drugs Bill 1971 became the template for the UK's modern drug laws, which aim to balance legislation to stop abuse without restricting the correct use of drugs to help manage disease and pain. The bill consolidated various pieces of legislation dating back to the early part of the 20th century and provided heavier sentences for trafficking and lighter ones for possession.

## DRUG CATEGORIES

This bill outlined three categories (classes) of drugs according to their seriousness and awarded tariffs to punish offenders accordingly. Until 1985 it excluded barbiturates and still does not include other recreational drugs such as caffeine or amyl nitrate.

- Class A includes heroin, morphine and opium.
- Class B includes codeine and dihydrocodeine; Class B drugs can be classed as Class A if injected.
- The least severe, Class C, includes benzodiazepine, mild amphetamines and anabolic steroids.

Further efforts by the UK government to stop heroin traffickers from profiting from assets gained in the illegal supply of the drug came about with the Drug Trafficking Act of 1994. This holds that, if a defendant cannot provide a reasonable explanation as to the source of their assets, they can be seized.

Governments worldwide have not always followed logical and productive drug policies, primarily because drug use has been perceived as a criminal activity and not a treatable problem. However, as the new millennium dawned and it became clear that purely prohibitionist policies had failed to cut the supply of heroin or the number of addicts, the voices - and arguments - calling for the legalization of heroin became more powerful.

**DECRIMINALIZATION**

Governments have now started to examine policies that allow some decriminalization or legalization and would minimize the harm caused by drug abuse. The case for legalizing heroin begins with economists, who argue that any success in reducing the supply will raise the price of illegal drugs and cause more crime as addicts commit more burglaries or thefts to feed their habit. The resulting increase in profit margins earned by drug gangs will also spur them to greater efforts. The history of the drug trade is that supply always increases to meet demand.

In his respected 1994 book, *Winning The War On Drugs: To Legalize Or Not?*, Richard Stevenson, an economist at Liverpool University, wrote that all drugs should be legalized, marketed and regulated so that they can be controlled. He described a scenario where large companies produce, distribute and market heroin, and invest heavily in research to make drugs safer: 'I am prepared to argue that drugs should be as legal as beer. They could be available from chemists clearly labelled and unquestionably with a government health warning.'

Stevenson and others suggest that the benefits of legalization would be avoiding the criminal acts attributed to the cost of maintaining the supply of the drug. Policing and legal costs would fall, as would the size of the criminal sector and the attendant strain on the legal system, saving the country millions. Legalization would pass heroin production, supply and profits from criminals to respectable tax-paying businessmen, and the government could earn millions. It is also likely that the price of heroin would fall by removing the legislation controlling it, which would leave the addict more money for food, clothing and to look after their health needs.

This view has drawn wide – and sometimes surprising – support from a number of quarters, which argue that governments cannot control the supply and quality of drugs until they are in charge of things, and that treatment, rather than jail sentences, should be available for drug abusers.

Fulton Gillespie, parent of a heroin victim and a witness to the 2002 UK drugs inquiry by Chris Mullin's Home Affairs Select Committee argues that it is futile to try and stop young people taking drugs. He suggests that society has a greater responsibility to make drug taking safe. 'Those who believe legalization will make more hard drugs available to more young people overlook the fact that drugs of all kinds are more available to more young people now than ever, even with prohibition in force. There is not a whit of evidence to support the idea that there is some massive reservoir of disaffected youth about to rush out and die. There are more pushers out there than chemists' shops, so those who want to use hard drugs are using them now and will continue to use them, come what may,' he said.

In 2001, a call for a debate about legalization also came from certain sectors of the police. North Wales chief constable Richard Brunstrom published *The Drugs Debate: Time For Change?* in which he conceded that the war against the illegal drugs trade has failed, and also said that the attempt to control drugs' availability and supply had not worked. 'Proscription is not working,' he wrote. 'Drugs are ever more freely available... There is no logic to the proscription list – alcohol and tobacco are our biggest killers.' His views were supported by former Gwent police chief constable Francis Wilkinson, who called for heroin to be legalized. He added, 'The current drug laws make the situation worse and any form of legalization would be preferable.'

In 2002 former UK government cabinet minister Mo Mowlam also argued that strict prohibition had not worked and called for the legalization of all drugs, including heroin. Mowlam said that the money raised from taxing drugs could be used for treatment. 'If the kids get hold of it because it's a high, they will get hold of it. Why not regulate it, take the tax from it, and deal with addiction?' she asked.

## UK HEROIN OFFENCES
### POSSESSION
A person has heroin under their control; but supplying a person who is legally entitled to have the drug is not an offence. Possession of heroin in the UK will result in six months' imprisonment, a £5,000 ($7,570) fine, or both, in

a magistrates' court. In a crown court, penalties are more serious, at seven years, an unlimited fine or both.

## POSSESSION WITH INTENT TO SUPPLY

The amount of heroin is not always relevant and even giving a small bag to a friend for safe keeping falls under this charge. If the friend returns the bag, they will also be found guilty of supply. If the amount seized in a person's possession appears to be more than for personal use that might also be used as evidence of intent. Evidence of scales, cutting equipment and bags, used in the wholesale supply of heroin, will also be used by the prosecution. In a magistrates' court, possession of heroin with intent to supply could earn six months' jail, a £5,000 ($7,550) fine or both. In the crown court, the person could be sentenced to life or be required to pay an unlimited fine.

## USE OF PREMISES

If a householder allows their premises to be used for the consumption of heroin, then they are liable to between six months' and 14 years' imprisonment and a fine of £5,000 ($7,550) or more.

The Misuse of Drugs Act regulations divide controlled drugs into five schedules, which list drugs according to who may lawfully produce, trade and handle them:

- drugs in Schedule 1 include heroin and are the most stringently controlled because they can only be supplied or possessed with a Home Office licence;

- drugs in Schedules 2 to 4 are available for medical use, but are normally controlled by a prescription: temazepam, for example, is listed under Schedule 4 and can be possessed if it has been prescribed for medical use;
- at the other end of the scale, Schedule 5 drugs can be sold over the counter at chemists.

## LEGISLATION AROUND THE WORLD
### AUSTRALIA
Heroin production and importation were prohibited in 1953 by Commonwealth legislation.

### AUSTRIA
The Narcotics Law 1951 originally allowed consumption of narcotics. But in 1985 tighter legislation was introduced and the Methadone Act 1987 now regulates methadone substitution.

### BELGIUM
The Ministry of Interior, Ministry of Justice and Ministry of Health divide up crime prevention, legal and criminal areas, and drug-prescription monitoring. Providing syringes for the illegal consumption of drugs is a crime.

### BULGARIA
Several laws were passed in the early 1970s to restrict and

prohibit drug trafficking and consumption. Anyone testing HIV positive is obliged to report for a medical.

## CZECH REPUBLIC
Restrictive drug laws were introduced after the Velvet Revolution in 1989, although heroin is still cheaper here than in western Europe.

## DENMARK
Danish law makes no distinction between hard and soft drugs, and needles are sold from vending machines in Copenhagen and other cities.

## FINLAND
The Care of Substance Abusers Act 1985 enforces the use of compulsory treatment where applicable. Possession and use of drugs is illegal.

## FRANCE
No distinction between hard and soft drugs. Severe penalties for trafficking and most prosecutions are for possession, not use.

## GERMANY
Germany's Drug Act has three levels of categories for narcotics: completely forbidden (which includes heroin); strictly regulated and not acceptable to prescribe; and

strictly regulated, but can be prescribed medically.

## IRELAND
Possession for personal use is punishable with up to seven years for hard drugs, and a fine and up to three years for soft drugs.

## ITALY
An action plan to consolidate the country's fight against drugs came into force in 1990 with a law on drug dependence.

## LATVIA
No distinction between hard and soft drugs.

## LITHUANIA
No distinction between hard and soft drugs. Drug use could result in a prison sentence of between 15 days and 24 months, depending on number of convictions. Trafficking punishable with prison terms of between 6 and 15 years.

## LUXEMBOURG
Heroin users can be compelled to undergo compulsory treatment.

## THE NETHERLANDS
No police action to detect offences involving the possession

of drugs for personal use. No legal restrictions on the distribution of methadone or the sale of syringes.

NORWAY
Crimes against the country's Drugs Act are liable to heavy fines, with a maximum prison sentence of 21 years. A tip-off telephone line was introduced in 1990 to enable the public to inform on heroin or other drug dealers.

POLAND
Poland's Drug Abuse Prevention Act 1985 includes obligatory treatment for users under the age of 18.

PORTUGAL
Heroin traffickers and users face prison sentences. Syringes are available free under a needle-exchange programme.

ROMANIA
Drug laws were passed in 1969 and 1979 to regulate the production, possession and circulation of narcotics.

RUSSIA
In 1998, the liberal Federal Law on Drugs and Psychotropic Substances, which made a distinction between the dealer and consumer of heroin, was replaced by a new Federal Law. An amount of heroin exceeding 0.005g is now punishable by a prison sentence of up to 15 years.

## SPAIN
Distinguishes between hard drugs and soft drugs. The sale of syringes is permitted.

## SWEDEN
Generally, drug policy is repressive and restrictive, and the maximum sentence for a drugs-related offence is 14 years.

## UK
The principal legislation is the Misuse of Drugs Act 1971, which divided drugs into three categories (Class A, Class B and Class C) according to their degree of harmfulness. Heroin is a Class A drug.

## UKRAINE
Still governed by tough laws from the Soviet regime. Syringes are not widely available.

## HEROIN CRIME
As soon as drug laws were introduced, handling heroin became a crime, and criminal gangs grew to profit from it. Like the alcohol-banning Volstead Act 1919 in the USA, which heralded a decade of Prohibition and created criminal gangs willing to supply bootlegged booze, the introduction of tougher drug legislation in the USA and Europe ledinexorably to control of the heroin business by organized crime.

DRUG RUNNING

The American smugglers John Cushing and John Jacob Astor had already made vast profits from shipping Turkish opium to Canton in the 18th century after poppy cultivation in China had been banned. But the new drug laws of the early 1920s were seen as a new opportunity for a new breed of gangster: the drug runner.

One of the first and biggest American drug traffickers was Arnold Rothstein, who had made a fortune from gambling, illegal liquor and Prohibition dens such as the notorious Cotton Club. Almost as soon as the Jones-Miller Narcotic Drugs Import and Export Act 1922 and the Porter Acts were in place, Rothstein's and gangs run by others were shipping opiates and cocaine back to the USA from Europe.

The drugs were cut and distributed stateside and the criminals' success was illustrated by a sixfold increase in the amount of narcotics seized by US Customs in just one year, from 1925 to 1926. Organized crime and the smuggling of heroin exploded alongside the new prohibitionist policies, sponsored by the USA and followed by Europe, during the 1920s.

The earliest drug racketeers included the Frenchman Henry de Monfreid in Europe and Africa and, in the USA, the Jewish gangster Meyer Lansky, the mobster Lucky Luciano, a hired hand of Rothstein who had been arrested in 1916 for dealing in heroin, and Jack 'Legs' Diamond, another Rothstein employee suspected of killing a New York heroin courier in 1928.

They set the rules, ruthlessly enforced them and became the prototypes for the cold-blooded, but hugely profitable Turkish, French and Corsican heroin drug gangs that emerged in the 1970s and were followed by the Colombians and Mexicans a decade later.

The injured of World War I increased the number of morphine – and later heroin – addicts and as demand for drugs rose, illegal supplies also increased. Initially illicit heroin found its way on to the illegal drug market following break-ins at pharmaceutical manufacturers. However, opiates were also supplied from legitimate drug companies with the Allied occupying forces in Germany and across Europe, providing well-trained traffickers of heroin and morphine.

The British banned Hoffmann-La Roche's products throughout its empire in 1925, although lifted the control a year later after the Swiss group introduced a system of controls on exports. But leaks of heroin, which found their way on to the illicit market, came from other European drug companies, and secret illicit laboratories were also set up to take over the supply of opiates and heroin.

In Britain, Assistant Under Secretary of State, Sir Malcolm Delevingne, urged the elimination of traffickers as the only way to cut out heroin and other drug users. Similarly, the USA was taking steps to stop the international traffickers. An international network was set up in 1930 to catch the gangs, with US agents spread through Europe and working with British and French drug-enforcement units.

The problem with breaking the gangs was that the supply and production of opium had increased. India had always been an important producer of opium, but Persia became an increasingly important exporter of poppies to the Far East, Russia and Europe in the 1920s. The opium was turned into heroin in illegal labs set up in Japan and throughout Asia.

Opium was also available in China and opium gangs quickly sprang up to supply illicit heroin in this region and Hong Kong, which became a magnet for organized crime gangs in the 1930s. In the early years of heroin manufacture and trafficking, the Balkans also became an important crime centre. Bulgaria, Serbia and Turkey all produced opium poppies, and European and Japanese traffickers set up heroin factories in cities such as Constantinople.

By 1930 poppy growing was being phased out in India, and Turkey had assumed the mantle of the world's major heroin producer. Istanbul became a magnet for French and Japanese illegal producers and traffickers, and by the mid-1930s it was estimated that over 72,000kg (65 tonnes/tons) of heroin was being manufactured in the city.

France also had its problem with illicit heroin manufacturers, who bought opium in Turkey, processed it into heroin and supplied the drug to the USA and the Far East. And in Bulgaria, which was party to the Geneva limitation agreements, opium-poppy cultivation multiplied in the early part of the 19th century, with illicit heroin factories established in Sofia.

In Japan, mercenaries were used throughout the 1920s and 1930s to help traffic the illicit heroin that Japanese pharmaceutical companies were manufacturing, for supply mainly to China. By the mid-1930s the Japanese army gave protection to drug traffickers in China, and the government actually encouraged opium growing and the supply of narcotics like heroin to overseas countries as part of its foreign policy to help colonize parts of the Far East. By the start of World War II, Japan was the world's biggest supplier of heroin.

Opium and heroin traffickers also emerged in Russia, where Manchuria became an important centre for shipping illicit drugs. In Germany and Austria, pharmaceutical companies were also manufacturing more morphine-based drugs than domestic supply warranted and much of it found its way into criminal hands. US trafficker Arnold Rothstein often bought directly from Berlin factories, although the rise of Hitler and the Nazi Party clamped down on leakages.

In the same way as the Opium Exclusion Act 1909 had caused an increase in the illegal trade in heroin, a 1925 crackdown on opiates in Egypt also helped increase the use and supply of heroin. Switzerland was also a notorious supplier of morphine and heroin, which was sometimes smuggled inside clocks or boxes of chocolates, or disguised as less harmful drugs.

Tough drug laws also encouraged drug trafficking in Latin America in the mid-1920s. Chile, Argentina, Peru and Honduras all became major centres for gangsters dealing in opium, morphine and heroin. Some couriers employed fake certificates to get around the limitations imposed by the League of Nations and also used the practice of diplomatic immunity to bypass customs.

Illegal heroin labs had first been discovered near Marseille in 1937. These labs were run by the legendary Corsican gang leader Paul Carbone. For years the French underworld had been involved in the manufacturing and trafficking of illegal heroin abroad, primarily to the USA. Marseille's convenience and the frequent arrival of ships from opium-producing countries made it easy to smuggle the morphine base, but the port's prominence as a major centre for heroin export was sealed in the late 1940s when the US Central Intelligence Agency (CIA) armed and funded Corsican gangs in their opposition to French communists.

**THE FRENCH CONNECTION**

Corsican gangs took control of the French port's illegal trade in opium and heroin and, by the early 1950s, it was a major link between the Sicilian Mafia and US heroin users: this was the 'French Connection'. This new phase in the development of heroin crime came when the USA unwittingly helped traffickers by linking them to the Mafia in Sicily.

In 1946, America deported hundreds of gangsters, including Lucky Luciano, whose experience and expertise in the heroin trade interested Mafia bosses in Palermo. The Mafia began buying opium. They mostly bought from Turkey, whose farmers were licensed to grow opium poppies for sale to legal drug companies, but sold their excess to the underworld market. The Mafia also opened heroin labs in Marseilles and Sicily to process the heroin and then smuggle the drug to US and Canadian cities.

The first significant post-World War II seizure was made in New York in 1947, when 3kg (7lb) of heroin were seized from a Corsican seaman disembarking from a vessel that had just arrived from France. In 1949, more than 23kg (50lb) of opium and heroin were seized on the French ship *Batista*, but the first major French Connection case occurred in 1960 when an informant told a drug agent in Lebanon that Mauricio Rosal, the Guatemalan Ambassador to Belgium, The Netherlands and Luxembourg, was smuggling morphine base from Beirut to Marseilles. In one year alone, Rosal had used his diplomatic status to smuggle about 200kg (440lb) of smack.

The French traffickers continued to exploit the demand for their product and by 1969 were shipping to the US between 80 to 90 per cent - around ten tonnes of heroin - of all its heroin supply. The heroin they supplied was also very good, approximately 85 per cent pure. The French Connection continued into the 1970s, but was finally cut following a 1971 political coup in Turkey, which saw a new regime willing to ban opium growing in return for US aid.

**NEW ROUTES**

With the fall of the French Connection new supplies were needed to satisfy the USA market, and Mexico helped fill the gap, with the rise of Latin smugglers shipping across the Texan and Californian borders. At about the same time the Mafia was being joined by Cuban gangs in importing heroin into the USA. Cubans had begun settling in Florida following the disastrous 1961 Bay of Pigs invasion, but further criminal immigrants arrived over the next two decades, including thousands of criminals deported by Fidel Castro.

Further illegal heroin supplies followed another disastrous US foreign policy intervention. The CIA began to give assistance to the Chinese Nationalists in the 1950s. Unfortunately, they trafficked in opium. In the following decade, the CIA pumped arms into Laos near the border with Vietnam to support Hmong tribesmen in resisting communism. Again, the anti-communists' main source of funding was the opium poppy and these heroin warlords expanded opium production by pledging that the money raised would help fight communism. The CIA was even complicit in helping move the opium to labs in the Golden Triangle (Myanmar, Laos and Thailand), and heroin was shipped to Vietnam and other countries in the region.

During the Vietnam War, some 10 per cent of US soldiers

were thought to be heroin users and until the US withdrawal from Vietnam in 1973, it is thought that about one-third of the illicit heroin that washed up on the streets of US cities came from the Golden Triangle labs the CIA had helped set up.

In 1979, US President Jimmy Carter began helping the Mojaheddin guerrillas in resisting the Soviet occupation of Afghanistan. However, like the tribesmen in Laos, the Afghan fighters grew and sold opium poppies to help finance their war. By 1980, over half of the heroin flooding into the USA was from Afghanistan and the country remains the world's largest illicit opium producer, with a proliferation of heroin factories in Pakistan.

The war in Kosovo in 1999 also inadvertently led to Europe being flooded with smack. Following the NATO bombing campaign, which forced Serbian forces out of the ethnic Albanian province, the region became a centre for smugglers unfettered by law enforcement. Agencies estimated that some 40 per cent of the heroin sold in Europe and North America was flowing through the province in 2000, with the traffickers handling up to five tonnes of heroin each month compared to around two tonnes before the conflict.

The links between heroin and crime were made startlingly clear in 2001 when UK Home Office research showed that 29 per cent of all arrestees tested positive for opiates or cocaine, and that about one-third of the proceeds of acquisitive crime went back towards buying heroin or crack.

Partly as a result of these findings, the UK shifted its emphasis on tackling criminals to targeting the profits they make through heroin. Marking the introduction into Parliament of the Proceeds of Crime Bill, which was designed to dismantle and disrupt criminal gangs, Home Office minister Bob Ainsworth said, 'Criminals should not be allowed to profit from their crime. Crime barons make their money off the back of local communities' misery. They cash in on the illegal drug markets, burglary and muggings that plague innocent people's lives.'

By 2002 the UK's law-enforcement agencies also admitted that they had adopted the wrong strategy – of focusing resources on individuals and seizing heroin shipments – for drug crimes. It was also reported that they had accepted they did not know about 60 per cent of the drug trade.

In a radical shift, UK police and customs accepted that their future approach would concentrate on choking off the profits of traffickers: chasing profits, not powder. One tactic was to mount covert surveillance on suspected bureau de change outlets, which are used by drug gangs to launder money.

## HEROIN TRAFFICKING METHODS
### THE SEEDS OF SMUGGLING
Heroin's journey to the streets of New York, London or Paris begins with the planting of the opium poppy. Around three

months after the poppy seeds have been planted, the milky opium sap is harvested, and the dark brown gum shaped into bricks or cakes and wrapped in plastic.

These are sold by the farmer to a dealer, who will probably have a morphine-refining plant – nothing more elaborate than a few drums and a stove in a rudimentary lab – close by. The opium brick will be mixed with lime in boiling water until a band of morphine forms on the surface and can be drawn off; it is then reheated with ammonia, filtered, and boiled again until reduced to a brown paste.

The morphine base, with the consistency of modelling clay, will be poured into moulds and dried in the sun ready for further processing into heroin. This may take place in another illicit lab, albeit a more sophisticated one.

When the heroin emerges from these labs it enters a complex chain of distribution. Large dealers will usually deal in shipments of anything up to several hundred kilos, which will then be divided into smaller packages of between 1kg (2¼lb) and 10kg (22lb) for sale to street gangs. These will be split further into bags of a gram or less for sale to users. The number of street dealers in a given area can vary enormously and will depend on the number of heroin users present, police activity and even the area's historical status as a drug-dealing centre. King's Cross in London and the East Village in New York, for example, have reputations as places to cop.

## SUPPLYING DEMAND

The more the law-enforcement measures are upgraded, the more complicated the drug traffickers' modus operandi becomes. In the course of the struggle against drug trafficking, anti-drug control forces have been faced with a wide spectrum of concealment methods.

Typically, different drug gangs will control cultivation and production levels, and regulate prices. At the wholesale level, however, the trafficking process becomes more diversified and can involve a number of different smuggling groups and brokers. Brokers will often have close connections with several rival producers, and heroin traffickers form limited partnerships with different groups to ensure business flexibility, continual supply and a measure of protection from the law.

## CONCEALMENT METHODS

Heroin moves from the region of source and production to the consuming markets by a variety of methods, usually involving either air, sea or land, or a combination of these. Heroin smugglers have been forced to be more creative because trafficking laws are increasingly stringent, and police and customs officials are devising new ways to detect drugs.

It is a challenge traffickers are rising to. New techniques are seemingly limited only by a trafficker's imagination and are being helped by new technology. However, invariably the most effective methods are the simplest. Air and sea remain the principal methods of transporting large amounts of Southeast Asian, Afghan and South American heroin to markets such as the USA and Europe. The high volume of commercial air and maritime traffic provides a natural camouflage for heroin concealed in containers, and multiple port transfers help obscure the origin of the illicit cargo.

## COURIERS AND MULES

Trafficking groups also use couriers, or 'mules', to smuggle small amounts of heroin, usually up to 2kg (4½lb), on commercial flights or through border crossings in private cars or on foot. The mules conceal the heroin in their luggage, body cavities or stomachs by drug swallowing. This is one of the commonest and most dangerous methods of concealment; the narcotics are packed in small multilayered plastic bags. Despite the danger of these being torn up in the stomach, the mules are paid very little.

Other, more imaginative and bizarre ways of smuggling heroin through customs are always being tested and, in February 2002, one mule flying into a Florida airport was stopped after it was discovered that a Colombian laundry had starched all his shirts and jeans using over two pounds of heroin. Customs inspectors stopped the mule after noticing the unusually stiff clothes that smelled of vinegar and left a trail of white powder. Another border patrol in

Texas uncovered $5 million (£3.5 million) worth of narcotics stuffed inside the body parts – legs, arms and intestines – of a stolen corpse. The traffickers used the body to disguise the scent of the drugs from sniffer dogs.

Criminal groups supplying the USA from South America or from Mexico often use the land route through the southwest border with Texas. Illegal immigrants and migrant workers smuggle between 1kg (2½lb) and 3kg (6½lb) loads, but larger amounts are delivered by truck.

Mexican heroin-distribution networks in the United States are managed almost entirely by criminal organizations operating from Mexico and by Mexican-American criminal gangs that are in charge of the street-level distribution of heroin. Groups from the Dominican Republic have also played a significant role in retail-level heroin distribution using bases in east-coast cities, including New York, Boston, and Philadelphia.

In Afghanistan and neighbouring countries like Pakistan and Iran, less sophisticated, but by no means less successful, modes of heroin transportation are used. These can include jeep, motorbike or even camel caravans, which can carry up to seven tonnes (tons) of narcotics. The advantage of these methods is that there is no need for smugglers to accompany the caravan, which can be controlled by traffickers operating from remote mountainous areas.

Trafficking organizations employ drug distribution network and creative marketing techniques to expand the heroin market in the country they are supplying. There have been instances of some gangs providing free samples of heroin to traditional cocaine or other drug buyers in order to attract new custom.

During the smuggling process the weight and the bulk of the drug is kept to a minimum and heroin is handled in as highly concentrated a state as possible, often with a purity exceeding 90 per cent. Before sale, it is diluted several times. The substances used for adulteration vary considerably, but include fenacetine and methaqualone, which have intoxicating properties themselves.

Southeast Asian heroin traffickers typically deal in 700g (25oz) units, in contrast with South American, Mexican and Southwest Asian heroin traffickers, who traffic in kilogram quantities. When produced in refineries in Southeast Asia, heroin is usually packaged in half-unit blocks (350g [12oz] per block) of compressed powder. These rectangular blocks are 2.5cm (1in) thick and measure 13 by 10cm (5 by 4in).

## CONTAINERIZED CARGO

Because of the huge volume of worldwide commercial trade and the necessity of containerized cargo, heroin traffickers continue to employ commercial containerized cargo on aircraft and merchant ships as a successful smuggling method.

For example, heroin processed in the Golden Triangle (Myanmar, Laos and Thailand) is smuggled overland to Myanmar, China, Thailand, Malaysia and Vietnam for transhipment by air or sea within containerized cargo through Taiwan, Hong Kong, Singapore, Japan and Korea. From these transit countries, the heroin is shipped to consumer markets in Europe, Australia, Canada and the USA.

Many characteristics are common among containerized-smuggling heroin trafficking gangs. They include renting or buying import/export companies or warehouses within the source and transit countries, such as Thailand and the USA, for the sole purpose of smuggling and storing drugs. Heroin traffickers will frequently change the names of these 'front companies', but they sometimes maintain the same addresses and will remain as long as the companies have not themselves been compromised.

Typically, one entire 8m (20ft) or 16m (40ft) container is leased and filled with a cheap range of goods. Popular lines for heroin smugglers are plastic bags, soy sauce, T-shirts and chopsticks; however, gangs often use seafood and other perishables as a way of discouraging customs inspection.

Usually the commodity is packed in cardboard cartons of uniform size and weight, and stacked on pallets. The cartons containing the heroin are placed deep within the container. There may be only one pallet that contains all the cartons of heroin, or single cartons of heroin may be placed among the individual cartons of the commodity, but as a rule fewer than ten cartons of heroin will be concealed within around 1,000 cartons of the commercial cargo.

Concealment methods in the cartons also vary. For example, the heroin may be placed in cans that are weighted the same as the canned commodities or it may be formed into the shape of the items in the cartons. Traffickers will also add weights in an attempt to minimize differences between those packs containing heroin and those not.

Drug-laden cartons will also be marked or numbered to distinguish them from the legitimate commercial cargo cartons. For example, a woman's image was stamped on one shipment, and the boxes containing the heroin were identified by shading in one of the woman's eyes.

Containers will also be insured for up to ten times more than the actual value of the commercial cargo and, in many cases, heroin shipments will transit a secondary port prior to shipment to the final destination to put officials off the trail. For example, heroin produced within the Golden Triangle may be shipped to secondary ports in Taiwan, China, Hong Kong, Malaysia, Singapore, Tokyo or South Korea. A new bill of lading will be issued to indicate that the cargo originated somewhere other than the Golden Triangle.

## HI-TECH SMUGGLING

New technologies are also increasingly being used by the heroin smuggler. In its 2001 Annual Report, the International Narcotics Control Board (INCB) highlighted its concerns about the misuse of new technologies in international drug control. The board said that drug-trafficking groups utilize new technologies, such as the Internet and electronic pocket organizers that can store contact- and bank-account details, sales records and coordinates for landing strips, to improve the efficiency of heroin's delivery and distribution. Drug traffickers were also using encrypted messages in computers to conceal information about drug shipments, and to protect themselves and their illicit operations from investigation by drug law enforcement agencies.

## WHAT HEROIN CRIME COSTS

It costs money to fight, but there are a number of other links between heroin and crime. Addicts often resort to burglary, shoplifting, fraud or other theft to support their habit. This contributes a large share of costs to a country through the damage or loss of property, the cost of replacing it and insurance.

Some people will be caught in possession of, or supplying, illegal heroin. This will add to law enforcement, police and court time and costs.

Further crimes, ranging from manslaughter to driving offences, may also be committed while under the influence of heroin. Violence between rival gangs of heroin dealers, or between a dealer and a dependent user, will also count towards the crime figures and costs.

Finding out how much heroin crime costs is a very complex process, however, and little or no consensus has been reached. In the USA, annual economic costs related to drug abuse were estimated to be $110 billion (£76 billion) a year, or 1.5 per cent of GDP in the mid-1990s (UN drug report, 2000), but the many estimates that have attempted to find out the 'cost-of-crime' element have pitched figures anywhere between $1 and $3 billion (£0.7 billion and £2 billion).

Similarly, in the UK, attempts have been made to accurately assess the size of the illegal market in heroin and the cost of drug-related crime, specifically, how much heroin contributes to the bottom line of the UK bill.

UK researchers have suggested that there are between 130,000 and 200,000 problematic drug users in the UK, committing theft and other crimes to support habits costing each of them up to £30,000 ($43,500) annually. However, since stolen goods only fetch about one-third of their value, the total cost of stolen goods could be up to £2.5 billion ($3.6 billion) each year.

Further research about the cost of heroin abuse on society was revealed in 2002 when research by the University of York was presented by Bob Ainsworth, Parliamentary Under Secretary of State at the UK's Home Office with responsibility for anti-drugs co-ordination and organized crime. It showed that drug abuse in England and Wales costs society up to £18.8 billion ($27.2 billion) a year, with hardcore heroin and crack cocaine addicts responsible for some 99 per cent of that bill (it estimated that there were 281,125 heroin or cocaine users whose 'habits were no longer under control' and that they are each costing the state around £30,000 [$43,500] a year, or £600 [$870] each week).

Furthermore, the research stated that the UK's National Health Service spent £235 million ($341 million) on doctor services, accident and emergency admissions, and other treatment linked to drug abuse. When these health-service costs are added to the criminal justice system and the welfare state, costs rise to between £3.7 billion and £6.8 billion ($5.4 billion and $9.9 billion). However, with the addition of social costs the bill rises to between £10.9 billion and £18.8 billion ($15.8 billion and $27.2 billion).

## SUMMARY

For the past few decades, the world has been fighting a war
on heroin, but with many countries using only the limited
weapons of legislation and punishment, few have managed
to isolate the enemy, let alone slay it. Most have tried to
reduce the user population, only to see it rise. They have
tried to strangle the supply, only to see it increase and
heroin prices fall. And they have tried to inflict casualties
on crime gangs that profit from heroin, only to see them
proliferate and get richer.

It seems that almost every effort to wipe heroin from
the face of the planet has failed. The policy makers in many
countries are now at an important crossroads and face a
tough question: will they persist in fighting a principled
but ultimately ineffectual campaign against heroin, or do
they accept that the war cannot be won and opt for living
with the drug while putting in place systems and treatment
to minimise its effects on users and society?

It appears that most westernized countries are now
acknowledging the fact that, if there is one single lesson

to be learned from the experience of the last 30 years, it is that policies based on enforcement are destined not to succeed. The best that the world's lawmakers can claim to have done is to partly stem heroin's spread. At worst, they have simply created new problems of organised crime. Therefore, the reduction of harm rather than retribution seems to offer a more effective way of dealing with the problem.

As Chris Mullin, chairman of the UK's Home Affairs Select Committee, which in May 2002 published one of the most far-reaching reports on drugs in Britain, said, 'We have to face the fact that, whether we like it or not, large numbers of young people take drugs. As far as users are concerned, our priorities should be realistic education, readily available treatment, and harm reduction. Above all, we have to focus on that relatively small minority of drug users who are making a misery of their own lives and those of others.'

With this in mind, it appears that more countries are now willing to pick up and use new tools to combat heroin and its abuse, and some have signalled their intention to follow the lead set by countries such as Australia, The Netherlands and Switzerland, who have adopted progressive drug measures and taken a more enlightened approach to the ways in which they tackle the problem of heroin. In due course, these new ways of reaching and treating the heroin addicts who cause most damage to themselves and others will include looking at the efficacy of prescribing heroin – which would undercut the illegal heroin market and drug-related crime – and the provision of 'shooting galleries' – safe-injecting rooms – which would take the most chronic addicts off the street.

These and other new methods will also be tried and tested – and, in some instances, discarded – over the next decade as evidence is gathered to back up their use. However, in the long term, as costs are met and political and social resistance is overcome, it is likely that more harm-reduction treatments will move automatically from the pilot stage to being nationally or universally adopted. In some countries, use of these methods may even require changes in law to allow pharmacists to supply drug users with relevant paraphernalia, such as swabs, citric acid and needles, in order to reduce the risks of heroin use.

At the same time, the future success of moves to deal with heroin lies in better education, with a view to stopping users from taking up heroin in the first place. Drugs are increasingly part of most young people's lives and it's essential that the world's governments get balanced, accurate information about them across to their young. However, the area is under-resourced and there is still a huge and unresolved debate over the effectiveness of many of the drug campaigns that have been used to reach teenagers and educate them. Few have moved on radically from the rhetoric of the 'just say no' tactics, where education was based on fear rather than knowledge. Indeed, there is evidence that these warnings may actually stimulate drug experimentation. And there have been fewer still campaigns still aimed solely at heroin.

Today's youth knows that one puff on a joint doesn't lead inexorably to a full-blown heroin addiction, so drug-education messages need to accept that reality and ensure that messages are credible if kids are to listen to them in the first place. This means that, if the war against heroin is not winnable in absolute terms, then at least it will claim fewer casualties.

## GLOSSARY

Agonist – A compound that will bind to a receptor and create a pharmacological response.

Analgesic – A drug that reduces pain. Analgesics act on the brain; opium derivatives such as morphine are powerful, but easily produce addiction. Non-narcotic analgesics, of which paracetamol and anti-inflammatories (such as aspirin) are the most common, act peripherally by preventing the formation of pain-producing substances, and are effective for headaches and minor pains.

Antagonist – A compound that will bind to a receptor to form a complex that does not give any response.

Codeine – Found in opium, but this mild to moderate painkiller is usually synthesized from morphine in medical products. Known on the streets as T-Three, cough syrup and schoolboy.

Drug – Any chemical substance that alters the physiological state of a living organism. Drugs are widely used in medicine for the prevention, diagnosis and treatment of diseases; they include analgesics, anaesthetics, antihistamines and anticoagulants.

Endomorphin – Two endogenous peptides that function as mu-agonists.

Endorphins – A peptide that functions as a selective agonist for the mu-opioid receptors.

Heroin – Heroin, or diacetylmorphine, is a narcotic compound that is a synthetic derivative of morphine. The compound is easily absorbed by the brain, and is used as a sedative and powerful analgesic. Very addictive.

Morphine – Naturally occurring substance in the opium poppy. Called

M, morph and Miss Emma on the streets, it is a potent narcotic analgesic.

Narcotic – A drug that induces drowsiness, stupor or insensibility. Narcotics include the opioid and synthesized compounds with morphine-like properties. They are powerful analgesics, used in medicine.

Opiate – One of a group of drugs derived from opium, an extract of the poppy plant that depresses brain function (a narcotic action). Opiates include morphine and its synthetic derivatives, such as heroin and codeine.

Opioid – Any one of a group of substances that produces pharmacological and physiological effects similar to those of morphine. Opioids are not necessarily structurally similar to morphine, and include fentanyl and methadone.

Papaver – A widely distributed, summer-flowering annual somniferum plant: *Papaver somniferum*, of the poppy family, Papaveraceae. It is grown in hot, dry climates for the drug opium, which is extracted from its sap. The raw material is refined to produce heroin.

Partial agonist – A compound that possesses affinity for a receptor, but will produce only a small pharmacological response.

Semi-synthetic – A compound with some opioid receptor similarities, synthesized by modification of product extracted from opium and including heroin.

Synthetic opiate – A compound with some opioid receptor similarities but using no material extracted from opium. Includes methadone.

## TIMELINE

c3400 BC: The opium poppy is cultivated in lower Mesopotamia by the Sumerians, who would later pass on their poppy culling art to the Assyrians

c1300 BC: Egyptians begin cultivation of poppies in Thebes, and the opium trade flourishes under Thutmose IV

c1100 BC: Opium harvested on Cyprus

c460 BC: Hippocrates recognizes opium's use as a narcotic and for treating diseases

330 BC: Persia and India are introduced to opium by Alexander the Great

300 BC: Arabs, Greeks and Romans begin to use opium as a sedative

AD 400: Arab traders introduce opium to China

1300–1500: Opium becomes taboo and disappears from Europe for 200 years

1500: Portuguese traders begin the practice of smoking opium

1527: Laudanum painkillers, which contained opium, introduced to Europe

1606: Elizabeth I orders ships to transport Indian opium back to England

1680: Thomas Sydenham combines opium, sherry and herbs to produce Sydenham's Laudanum, which becomes a popular remedy for various ailments

1689: Tobacco is mixed with opium in East Indies opium dens

1700: Indian opium exported to China and Southeast Asia by the Dutch, who introduce the practice of smoking opium with a tobacco pipe

1729: Chinese emperor Yung Cheng prohibits opium smoking

1750: The British East India Company (BEIC) takes control of the Indian opium growing districts of Bihar and Bengal; Britain dominates the trade in opium between Calcutta and China

1767: The BEIC imports 2,000 chests of opium to China, most for medicinal use

1780: British traders establish an opium depot at Macao

1793: Indian poppy growers are only allowed to sell opium to the BEIC, which gains total monopoly over its trade

1796: China bans the import of opium, but illegal trade continues

1799: Opium poppy cultivation in China is banned

1803: Friedrich Sertürner discovers morphine, the active ingredient of opium, after dissolving it in acid and neutralizing it with ammonia

1804: Opium trading resumes at Canton, despite 1799 edict

1805: American smuggler Charles Cabot attempts to smuggle opium into China

1812-16: Opium smuggling becomes big business with trade between Turkey and Canton

1819: Writer John Keats and other literary figures, such as Byron and Coleridge, indulge in recreational use of opium

1821: Thomas De Quincey publishes *Confessions Of An English Opium Eater*

1827: The German pharmaceutical company, E Merck & Co, starts to manufacture morphine in commercial quantities

1832: Codeine extracted from opium

1839: The start of the first Opium War between Britain and China

1841: Britain defeats China, which cedes Hong Kong

1843: Dr Alexander Wood uses syringe to administer morphine

1852: British introduce Indian opium to Burma

1856: Second Opium War with China

1874: English researcher CR Alder Wright first synthesizes heroin; smoking
opium banned in San Francisco

1878: Opium Act passed in Britain, which restricts the sale of opium to
registered Chinese opium smokers

1890: US Congress imposes a tax on opium and morphine

1895: Working with morphine at the German company Bayer, Heinrich
Dreser produces diacetylmorphine (heroin) and Bayer begins
commercial production

1905: US bans opium

1906: Britain and China move to restrict the Sino-Indian opium trade;
the US Pure Food and Drug Act requires medicines to label contents

1909: International Opium Commission in Shanghai

1910: Britain dismantles the opium trade between India and China

1914: Harrison Narcotics Act in USA, which requires pharmacists and
doctors who prescribe heroin and other narcotics to register and
pay tax

1923: US Treasury Department's Narcotics Division bans all narcotic
sales, leading addicts to turn to illegal sources

1945: Burma gains independence, and opium cultivation and trade
flourishes

1948: Corsican gangsters begin their illegal assault on the US market
with heroin refined from Turkish opium in Marseille labs

1950s: US foreign policy aimed at containing the spread of communism
in Asia (by financing and arming drug warlords in the 'Golden Triangle'
– Myanmar, Laos, and Thailand) unwittingly increases production and
flow of heroin

1962: Burma outlaws opium

1965-70: The number of heroin addicts in the USA estimated at around 750,000

1970: Controlled Substances Act passed in USA, divides drugs into groups and establishes penalties; the USA creates the Drug Enforcement Administration (DEA)

Mid-1970s: A new source of raw opium found in Mexico's Sierra Madre, which introduces 'Mexican mud' to US cities

1978: Opium fields in Mexico are sprayed with Agent Orange in a massive joint anti-drug initiative by the US and Mexican governments; drug smugglers turn to new supplies of opium from the 'Golden Crescent' – Iran, Afghanistan, Pakistan

1988: Opium production increases in Burma under the State Law and Order Restoration Council junta

1992: Colombia begins shipping high-grade heroin to the USA

1993: The Thai army and US DEA cooperate on destroying opium fields in the Golden Triangle

1995: The Golden Triangle becomes the world's biggest opium producer, with annual yields of 2,500 tonnes

1996-2002: Heroin trafficking continues to be problem with involvement of Chinese, Nigerian, Mexican and Colombian crime organizations

## JUNKIE SLANG

AIP – heroin from Afghanistan, Iran and Pakistan

Atom bomb – heroin mixed with marijuana

Back to back – smoking crack after injecting heroin

Bad bundle – low-quality heroin

Bag – pack of heroin

Ball – Mexican black-tar heroin

Balloon – heroin dealer or balloon containing heroin

Belushi – cocaine and heroin

Bindle – small pack of heroin

Blank – non-narcotic powder passed off as heroin

Bomb – very potent heroin

Channel swimmer – someone who injects

Chasing the dragon – crack mixed with heroin, smoking heroin

Chase the tiger – to smoke heroin

China cat – very pure heroin

Chipper – occasional user

Chocolate chip cookies – MDMA mixed with heroin or methadone

Chocolate rock – crack smoked with heroin

Chucks – hunger following withdrawal

Cigarette paper – packet of heroin

Cook – to mix heroin with water; heating to prepare for injection

Cook down – to liquefy heroin in preparation for inhaling it

Cotton brothers – heroin, cocaine, and morphine

Crap – low-quality heroin

Criss-crossing – snorting up lines of cocaine and heroin simultaneously

# The Little Book Of **HEROIN**

Crop - low-quality heroin

Deck - between 1g and 15g (½oz) of heroin

Dime's worth - amount of heroin that would cause death

Dinosaurs - old users or addicts

Dragon rock - mixture of heroin and crack

Dust - to add heroin to marijuana

Dynamite - cocaine mixed with heroin

Eightball - crack mixed with heroin

Five way - snorting heroin, cocaine, methamphetamine, and crushed
flunitrazepam pills, and drinking booze

Flamethrowers - cigarettes laced with heroin and cocaine

Flea powder - low-purity heroin

Foil - baking foil used to cook up and smoke heroin

Frisco special - heroin, cocaine and LSD

Frisco speedball - heroin, cocaine and a small amount of LSD

Garbage - inferior heroin

Get-off houses - places where users can buy and inject

Give wings - inject someone or teach them how to inject

Glass - hypodermic needle

Goofball - heroin mixed with cocaine

Gravy - to inject heroin

H&C - heroin and cocaine

H-bomb - heroin mixed with ecstasy

Half load - 15 bags of heroin

Half piece - 14g (½oz) of heroin

Homicide - heroin cut with scopolamine or strychnine

Hong yen - heroin in pill form

Horning – to inhale

Hot heroin – poisoned heroin

Hype – addict

Jolly pop – casual user

Jones – addiction

Karachi – heroin, phenobarbital, and methaqualone

LBJ – heroin, LSD, PCP

Lemonade – poor-quality heroin

Load – 25 bags of heroin

Meth speedball – methamphetamine mixed with heroin

Moonrock – heroin mixed with crack

Mortal combat – very pure heroin

Murder one – heroin and cocaine

New jack swing – heroin and morphine

Nod – using heroin

One-on-one house – place to buy heroin and cocaine

One-plus-one sales – selling heroin and cocaine together

P dope – 20–30 per cent pure heroin

Paper – a small dose of heroin

Paper boy – dealer

Polo – mix of heroin and motion sickness drug

Primos – cigarette laced with cocaine and heroin

Ragweed – poor-quality heroin

Red rock opium – heroin, barbital, strychnine, and caffeine

Red rum – another name for heroin, barbital, strychnine, and caffeine

Rider – 5kg (11lb) of free heroin on top of a 100kg (220lb) shipment of
   cocaine

## This Is **HEROIN**

Sandwich – heroin between two layers of cocaine

Scramble – heroin cut with other drugs or non-narcotics

Serial speedballing – doing cocaine, cough syrup and heroin continuously over a couple of days

Shooting up – injecting

Smoking gun – heroin and cocaine

Sniffer bag – £3.45 ($5) bag of heroin intended for snorting

Snowball – cocaine and heroin

Speedball – cocaine mixed with heroin; crack with heroin smoked together; methylphenidate mixed with heroin

Speedballing – shooting up or smoking cocaine and heroin

Spike – heroin cut with scopolamine or strychnine; to inject; needle

Spoon – 1.75g ($\frac{1}{16}$oz) heroin; used to prepare heroin

Tar – crack and heroin smoked together

Taste – small sample of drug

Tecatos – Hispanic addict

Twists – small bags of heroin

Whack – heroin and PCP

Whiz bang – heroin and cocaine

Wicked – very pure heroin

Z – 28g (1oz) heroin

The Little Book Of

# COCAINE

Printed and bound in the UK by MPG Books, Bodmin

Distributed in the US by Publishers Group West

Published by Sanctuary Publishing Limited, Sanctuary House, 45-53 Sinclair
Road, London W14 0NS, United Kingdom

www.sanctuarypublishing.com

Copyright: Nick Constable, 2003

Cover photo: © Getty Images

ISBN: 1-86074-526-1

The Little Book Of

# COCAINE

Nick Constable

**Sanctuary**

# CONTENTS

# INTRODUCTION

There's someone you've got to meet. His name's Charlie and he gets to go to all the best parties. He's the club king of London and New York, mixes with pop stars and celebrities, has loads of contacts on Wall Street and is just about everyone's best friend in TV land. When Charlie's around you feel like a million dollars and when he leaves it's such a let-down. He's totally cool. Just treat him with a little respect.

Respect is about right. Around the world cocaine is more accessible than ever, and yet the social and scientific arguments swirling around it seem to get denser by the year. Coke is not the kind of drug you place in a tidy little box, because everything about it defies simple analysis. Suffice to say that it is a substance of contradiction: of euphoria and despair; of obscene wealth and dire poverty. It knows no social barriers. Use it wisely and you'll be fine. Or maybe not.

## CHARLIE'S FRIENDS

We're talking about the champagne drug of celebrities, yet loads of addicts are beggars and prostitutes. Its chemistry sustains Peruvian hill farmers just as much as sharp-suited banking professionals. You can be an occasional snorter for years and not have a problem but get psychologically hooked with surprising speed if you smoke it. Some say the drug guarantees great sex, others just want to re-organize their mantelpiece. You'll sell a line to your best friend with a clear conscience, yet you know, deep down, that you've joined an industry that maims and kills to protect its markets.

By the way, got any cocaine on you? Bet you have. It may be that the only white powder looming large in your life comes from the vending machine at your local launderette, but Charlie gets everywhere. Especially into your purse or wallet.

### HE'S A POPULAR GUY

In 1999, a BBC survey conducted by the forensic chemists Mass Spec Analytical discovered that out of 500 banknotes circulating in London, 99 per cent carried traces of cocaine. About 1 in 20 produced a particularly high reading, suggesting they had been used to snort it. The rest had probably been contaminated during handling by users and dealers.

Joe Reevy of Mass Spec explained, 'Once you've taken a snort, the compounds will be in the oils of your skin and they'll get transferred to the notes you handle. That's the main way in which the cocaine gets on to the notes. When you test notes that have been used directly to snort cocaine you get a great big reading and the machine takes quite a while to settle down. You don't miss the difference.'

This study came less than a month after the government-backed British crime survey concluded that cocaine was the fastest-growing recreational drug among 20- to 24- year-olds. Two years later, in April 2001, *The Face* magazine published a survey of 1,000 16- to 24- year-olds, which showed that more than half of those questioned had taken it. *The Face* editor Johnny Davis said prices as low as £10 ($14) per gram (that really is bargain-basement stuff) had attracted this new custom.

'Our suspicion, borne out by the findings, is that cocaine users are younger and more varied than ever before,' he said. 'A glamour drug that was once a celebrity and media choice has become cheaper and more accessible.' Mike Goodman, director of the UK drugs advice line Release agreed, pointing out that clubs where cocaine was popular also did a roaring trade in champagne. 'It's all linked to lifestyle,' he said. 'People have got more money, cocaine is cheaper. You can get it for £40 [$60] a gram, which people will club together and buy to share between them on a Saturday night.'

The UN's *Global Illicit Drug Trends* report for 2001 confirms a rising trend in western Europe, South and Central America, South Africa and Australia. What is termed 'occasional' cocaine use has stabilized in the USA (the world's largest market) at 1.7 per cent of the population aged 12 and over. This is a reduction of two-thirds on the 1985 level. Even so, when 'hardcore' (ie at least weekly) users are counted there are currently 6.6 million people, or 3 per cent of the entire US population, who take cocaine. Spin the numbers however you will; this is not a drug bound for oblivion.

## CHARLIE: A POTTED BIOGRAPHY

So where and why do people take cocaine? How can cocaine culture be defined in the 21st century? To break down the big picture, it's worth separating South American chewers (coca leaf) from snorters (powder coke), smokers (crack cocaine or 'freebase'), mainliners (injected coke solution) and drinkers (usually coke dissolved in alcohol). For reasons that will become clear, it's the chewers and snorters who mostly get along without setting up home in the gutter. Mainliners and drinkers are rarer breeds and are probably flirting with trouble. Regular crack smokers generally claim they're not addicted. Generally, they're lying.

### CHEWERS AND SNORTERS

Coca leaf chewing has been going on for thousands of years in South America and only very rarely causes social or health problems. Powder coke has been around in the West for about 120 years and doesn't necessarily affect a user's health. That's not to say it is either safe or harmless. If you've got the money and the lifestyle that allow you to snort ten lines a day (a line is about one-twentieth of a gram or two-hundredths of an ounce) you're fast-tracking towards a serious habit. But a lot of users don't do cocaine this way. They'll take a line or two at a party or during a night out clubbing, and they won't touch it during the week. This is one reason why comparatively few coke and ecstasy users end up in hospital emergency departments.

## SMOKERS

Freebase and crack cocaine are more recent derivatives of the drug and those that plan to fish in these waters need to be much more careful. When a drug is smoked, it reaches the brain in under four seconds. Recent research suggests that this speed of delivery greatly boosts cocaine's addictive qualities and leads to the 'bingeing' so common among crack and freebase addicts.

## WHO IS THIS BOOK FOR?

This book is for users, their friends and parents, and anyone interested in a balanced perspective of cocaine in today's world. It looks at the drug's curious history, its links with music and showbusiness, fashion and pop culture. It explores the extraordinary underworld dealings of drug lords, traffickers and smugglers, and explains why crack has emerged as a key factor in street crime and gang warfare. It considers the power politics that drive world coca-leaf production, and the terrible poverty that afflicts either end of the trade, from growers to consumers. Above all, it explains the science of cocaine addiction, the health implications and ways in which users can minimize risk.

If you're doing cocaine, or you know someone who is, then it's worth taking a look.

**SOMETHING FOR THE WEEKEND?**

For the best part of a century cocaine has been the music lover's drug of choice. The link dates back to the early American jazz and blues scene but it re-emerged strongly in popular culture with the *Easy Rider* generation of the late 1960s, the fast-living rockers of the 1970s and the new romantics of the 1980s. More recently, it has permeated clubland where, though ecstasy remains the market leader, a core of older clubbers see coke as more sophisticated and manageable.

With a rush lasting barely 40 minutes, party lovers know they can pep themselves up on the dance floor and come down whenever they need to resume normal service. As one regular user of both drugs explained, 'With ecstasy you spend 15 hours grinning at everyone. With C [coke] you can buy a £20 [$30] half-gram special and just dip in and out of your emotions.'

Ed Jaram, editor of the British-based Internet club magazine *Spaced*, says that price is also a factor in the drug divide among the country's 1.5 million regular clubbers.

'There is some resistance to powder coke on the scene,' he says. 'First, it's more expensive and so tends to be used by an older, more affluent crowd. Second, clubbers want to know what they're buying. With pills you can see a stamp and you pretty much know what you've got. But with coke you could be buying speed or even talcum powder. You don't know until you try it.

'As a currency in clubs I don't think coke will ever overtake ecstasy, although a lot of people are starting to combine the two. For sure, everyone on the dance floor looks like they've been fuelled by the same ecstasy dealer but, chances are, there'll be quite a few older clubbers in there using coke or taking it cocktail style with Es.'

## CLUBBERS' DELIGHT

London is the unchallenged club capital of Britain and club nights are essentially multimedia fashion statements. And, of course, drugs are part of this show, despite the body searches on the door and the official warning words from police and proprietors.

'Cocaine and ecstasy use is now so widespread, and so accepted by promoters and the police, that the legal position isn't much of a talking point,' says Jaram. 'Everyone has their own view but it is taken for granted in Britain that you can go to a club and do drugs and nobody is going to mind.

'Promoters and owners are very, very tolerant towards this lifestyle. You can buy your stuff, take it in and do it, and you know you're not going to get thrown out. The question of legalization doesn't arise because you're using drugs anyway without hassle.

'As a general rule clubbers are aware of the dangers they face. This is much more important to them than whether some politician somewhere says a drug is legal or not. There certainly isn't the kind of repression found in, say, New York, where clubs are influenced by a zero-tolerance attitude to anything perceived as crime.'

REDUCING THE RISKS?
This may be true, although the British government is beaming out some confused signals. In March 2002 the Home Office launched a booklet entitled *Safer Clubbing*. This called for more effort to stop weapons being smuggled past doormen but also acknowledged that coke and ecstasy were part of the club scene. The booklet urged proprietors to provide more drinking water, cut out overcrowding and overheating, improve ventilation, train staff to spot the effects of intoxication and offer a 'calm environment' where users can chill out or get treatment.

'If we cannot stop them from taking drugs then we must be prepared to take steps to reduce the harm that they may cause themselves,' said Bob Ainsworth, Home Office minister.

This is fine and dandy, except the Home Office also announced proposals for tough new laws aimed at jailing proprietors and nightclub managers who knowingly allow 'dance-scene' drugs like cocaine to be consumed on their premises. At the very least, this is a contradiction in policy. The message to clubs is: 'Keep drug users safe when they're on your premises. And by the way, don't let them in at all.'

A REAL GROWTH INDUSTRY

According to a Home Office study published in 2001 – *Middle Market Drug Distribution*, by Geoffrey Pearson (Goldsmiths College) and Dick Hobbs (University of London) – the clubbing scene is 'a modern system of fraternity that can facilitate drug networks and highly accelerated drug dealing careers'. Pearson and Hobbs interviewed prisoners who started by selling a few tablets around the dance scene and progressed within months to become 'serious middle market drugs brokers'.

One 21-year-old woman told them: 'Once I started, other people got to hear, and that type of thing, it escalates very quickly... I was on the club scene every week, meeting different people, socializing. People come saying, "Can you get me some?" And as soon as it started – phew! – it got out of control, really.'

A 30-year-old man explained how in a typical weekend he would shift 2,500 ecstasy pills, 4kg (9lb) of marijuana, 110g (4oz) of cocaine and various quantities of speed and LSD. He started selling to friends, then friends of friends and a network quickly built up. 'Eventually you've got other people who want to start dealing and then dealers buy from you and it's a sky rocket before you even know it. I don't agree with selling in clubs, it's more like pushing drugs... I didn't push drugs at all. I did a social thing for friends and then it just got bigger.'

Networking is the lifeblood of the cocaine dealer. The sharper ones will sell you a few lines and then invite you to a party to share them. If you run out – no problem: there's plenty more for sale.

AMERICA ONLINE

London's bar and club cocaine culture is rarely troubled by the law. Police busts aimed at users (as opposed to dealers) are rare. However, across the pond in New York there is a much more repressive attitude towards recreational drugs, so far with little deterrent effect. One correspondent working in the Big Apple for a British national newspaper during the 1990s described cocaine as 'the ultimate night-out accessory'. He was not a user but came to regard it as no different to alcohol and tobacco. 'In some ways it's more socially acceptable than both,' he says. 'You get it in little white home-made envelopes, which somehow seems a nice personal touch.

'It can be a pretty undignified method of consumption – bending over a bog seat and sniffing – but once that's out of the way then the result is attractive. Cocaine doesn't poison other people, like tobacco smoke, and it doesn't make your drinking companion vomit 12 lagers over you.

If you're a club regular, or a stock trader, or in the media, then coke comes with the territory. The police keep publicizing these big drugs clampdowns but most New Yorkers on the scene don't even notice. If anything, cocaine is getting easier to buy.'

Today, corporate America remains awash with the drug. There's a dealers' paradise on South Beach, Miami, Florida, every March, when thousands of house-, techno- and electronic-music fans descend for the annual Winter Music Conference. This is supposed to unearth strange new beats and cutting-edge artists, but more recently it has become an exercise in branding, marketing and corporate focus groups. Where full-on music company executives meet the house crowd you can bet your deck blender that cocaine supplies will be somewhere nearby. Usually in a large truck.

Cocaine powers the music business – not just the dance scene – and has done for much of the 20th century. When in 2001 the British rock music TV channel VH1 ran a poster advertising campaign, it used a photo of three children's drinking straws alongside a rolled-up banknote apparently tipped with white powder. The copy read: 'VH1. Music TV that's not for kids.'

**MUSIC, FASHION, WORK...AND A LINE FOR CELEBRITIES**
In 1975, the American rock legend JJ Cale wrote the song 'Cocaine'. It's inconceivable that you don't know the lyrics but here's a brief reminder anyway:

*If you wanna hang out you've got to take her out – cocaine*
*If you wanna get down, down on the ground – cocaine*
*She don't lie, she don't lie, she don't lie – cocaine*

The song became an anthem for the cocaine boom of the 1970s and reinforced the tabloid press view that all filthy-rotten-rich rock stars were on the stuff. As generalizations go, this one was on the button. It didn't apply so much to the punk movement mind, because punks saw cocaine as a bourgeois affectation, completely unnecessary when you could pop speed and ecstasy.

Still, over the last three decades, your typical pop star seems to have been at least an occasional coke-head. Songs like Black Sabbath's 'Snowblind' or Suede's 'We Are The Pigs', the latter written after an experience of coke-induced paranoia according to the band's Brett Anderson, kept cocaine up there as a fashion drug.

CHARLIE'S WITH THE BAND...

*You get up in the morning, surrounded by empty bottles,*
*and the mirror's covered in smears of cocaine and the*
*first thing you do is lick the mirror* – Elton John recalling
the drug days of his early career in the 1970s (according
to John's biographer Philip Norman the singer got such
a megalomaniac buzz from the drug that he once asked
aides to 'turn down the wind' because the sound of
swaying trees was bothering him)

*Cocaine is a very spiteful bedfellow. If you want to lose all the friends and relationships you ever held dear, that's the drug to do it with* – David Bowie, in his 'Thin White Duke' phase

*I take cocaine. Big fucking deal* – Noel Gallagher, Oasis

*There's a fucking blizzard of cocaine in London at the moment and I hate it. It's stupid. Everyone's become so blasé, thinking they're so ironic and witty and wandering around with that stupid fucking cokey confidence. Wankers. I did it, but I can't say I was a cocaine addict* – Damon Albarn, Blur, speaking in 1996

*By the time I was 23 I was addicted but it didn't seem to matter in our business. No one thought it was unusual to be up all night doing lines of coke* – Alan McGee, head of Creation Records

As you can see, cocaine was – and still is – ingrained in music culture. Sir Paul McCartney tried it when he was writing The Beatles *Sgt Pepper's Lonely Hearts Club Band* album in 1966. He got the drug from art gallery dealer Robert Fraser (one of the bastions of trendy London in the 1960s), who was, in turn, supplied by an American designer. In a biography entitled *Groovy Bob*, Harriet Vyner tells how Fraser also introduced The Rolling Stones to coke, along with a beautiful young member of their circle called Marianne Faithfull.

Apparently when Marianne was offered her first line she didn't know the etiquette and snorted in one go everything that Fraser had laid out. At least she didn't go the way of lead guitarist Ronnie Wood, widely reported to have destroyed part of his nose through overuse of the drug. It was said that Wood woke up one morning to discover that he could see the bathroom sink through the top of his hooter.

During the 1970s, when rock 'n' roll excesses were attaining new heights, rumours circulated about a new method of taking cocaine that wouldn't give you a rotten proboscis. The drug can be absorbed into the blood through any membrane (this is why it's sometimes rubbed on gums) and, inevitably, imaginative types explored a variety of techniques. Apparently the rock stars' 'special' involved anal administration, colloquially known as gak blowing, and gossip abounded about bands with a resident gak blower on their tour bus.

Doing cocaine is now practically expected in the music business. We're not quite at the point where record-company executives give superstars a roasting on the grounds that they should snort - or perhaps gak - more lines, but it can't be far off. Just look at Robbie Williams, for whom coke has arguably been career enhancing.

During his years with Take That, Williams signed up to the scrupulously controlled sparkly clean image demanded by record-label bosses. Then in June 1995 he threw his toys out of his cot and headed for the Glastonbury rock festival with Oasis. As he later told music magazine *Select*, he tried 'every drug except heroin'. Since then, Williams has deservedly achieved superstar status – both for his songwriting and singing. As quickly as he took up his bad-boy image he dumped it, attending a rehab centre, slimming down and staying clean of drugs.

## COKE ON THE CATWALK

Cocaine was, at the same time, becoming the unspoken accessory of fashion modelling. There are obvious reasons for this. Like pop stars, models need to keep a good handle on their image. You can't shimmy down a catwalk with puncture marks in your arms or a big gurney grin shaped by too much ecstasy the night before. You can't be drunk because it's not conducive to moving in straight lines. Amphetamines are out because, hell, you'd do the catwalk in a personal best of 7.2 seconds. What you need is a drug that gets your eyes sparkling (by restricting the blood supply to them) and your confidence zooming. Just a little make-up for the mind.

Naomi Campbell tried to sue the London-based *Mirror* newspaper for compensation after it revealed that she was receiving therapy for drug abuse and had attended Narcotics Anonymous meetings. Campbell won rather a pyrrhic victory, receiving only £3,500 ($5,070) on a somewhat technical legal argument. She was also accused by the High Court judge of lying under oath.

The evidence was, as always in these cases, much more interesting than the outcome. In a written statement, *Mirror* editor Piers Morgan argued that publication was justified because Campbell had publicly denied her addiction to drugs while committing a serious offence 'by possessing and using a Class A drug – cocaine – over a period of years'.

The Californian-born icon Carre Otis, who in the 1990s became the face of Calvin Klein, admitted in a 2002 interview with the London *Sunday Times* that she used the drug to help maintain her skeletal figure. She is now clean and an attractively healthy 'plus-size' (as they euphemistically term it in the clothes-horse business).

'The only way that I have ever been a size 10 was when I starved myself,' she said. 'Or I was doing huge amounts of cocaine or just drinking and not eating. That's the only time I have ever been really skinny.' For Otis, use of the drug carried a terrible history. Aged just 15 she had been dating the son of a Californian politician when the boy lost a soccer match, got himself high on cocaine and blew his brains out. The suicide note was addressed to her.

## THE SOCIALITE'S CHUM

In fact, as she later realised, cocaine was the controller of the pain. This was also the experience of queen of the 'It' Girls, Tara Palmer-Tomkinson, who in 1990s Britain became the darling of the popular press – proper posh totty according to the red-top papers. Palmer-Tomkinson's forte was partying and being outrageous – that and the fact that her family knew Prince Charles very well.

In an article for the *Daily Mail*'s Weekend magazine in 2002 she wrote: 'As an It Girl it was simply my job to amuse. I took the role very seriously. I always tried to entertain: to sing for my supper. And sadly, this is how I started to rely on cocaine.

'...It seemed to give me the energy and the confidence I needed to discourse brilliantly with people from all walks of life. To begin with, I took it before an evening out but the habit escalated and soon I couldn't face the world without it. At the same time I realised that the confidence it gave me was illusory. Cocaine began to eat away at my self-esteem. It took away my natural vivacity and made me restless and paranoid. I was still going to three parties a night and I could never sit still.'

She tried to fight this by returning regularly to the family home in Hampshire for drug-free recuperation. But when she got back to London she got back to cocaine.

## ACTING UP

It was the kind of self-deceptive nightmare succinctly summed up by American actor/director and one-time three-grams-a-day coke user Dennis Hopper. Even when he stopped drinking in 1983 and began attending Alcoholics

Anonymous, it took him another year to finally kiss goodbye to cocaine.

'I would turn up at meetings, saying "I'm an alcoholic" with half an ounce of cocaine in my pocket,' he told the London *Daily Telegraph* in 2001. 'And I wouldn't smoke grass, or use any downers or anything because that was going to take me over the edge. I mean, how crazy am I? So, finally, I just burned out again, and the radio was talking to me and the electric wires – boy, I was out of it. So if anybody has any doubts about cocaine – cocaine is just as bad on its own without any help from anything else.'

## SNOW ON THE SMALL SCREEN

The *EastEnders* soap actress Danniella Westbrook was less fortunate. Little known outside the UK, her cocaine habit produced a powerful reminder of how heavy use of the drug can break down human tissue. Photographs of her taken during 2000 showed how her septum (the part of her nose between the nostrils) had vanished, her single nasal orifice a cruel parody of the star's former beauty. This is a condition that can be rectified by plastic surgery, but it shattered her career – at least temporarily.

Westbrook's rumoured £300-a-day ($435) habit revealed an astonishing level of addiction for a woman still in her mid-20s and is untypical of most users. As the journalist and author Julie Burchill put it later: 'I just don't know how she did it. Between 1986 and 1996 I must have

27

put enough toot up my admittedly sizeable snout to stun the entire Colombian armed forces and still it sits there, Romanesque and proud, all too bloody solid actually.'

Other British celebrities have lived to regret cocaine's allure for different reasons. John Alford, a star of the hit TV fire service drama *London's Burning*, was jailed for nine months and lost his £120,000-a-year ($175,000) role after he was caught selling the drug to an undercover reporter. It took four years for him to claw his way back into a minor TV role. But the biggest scandal to hit British television came in March 2001 when Stuart Lubbock, a party guest at the Essex home of TV presenter and comedian Michael Barrymore, was found dead in the star's swimming pool.

In a TV interview with the journalist Martin Bashir, Barrymore denied allegations that he had given cocaine to his guests and said he had merely smoked cannabis on the night, but he also admitted: 'Any time I wasn't working I would immediately start drinking and taking pills just to get me away. I took drugs as well. I smoked pot, [took] cocaine, Es, speed, anything.' After a year-long investigation, Essex police announced that no further action would be taken. Barrymore escaped with an arrest and caution for possession of cannabis and allowing his home to be used for smoking the drug.

AMERICAN HIGH

America, though, remains the spiritual home of the cocaine scandal. Perhaps the best known involved the comedian

Richard Pryor, who on 9 June 1980 had just finished a freebase smoking binge (still a strange concept to most Americans) when he decided to round things off by drinking the high-percentage-proof rum swilling around his waterpipe. After five days non-stop freebasing Pryor was pretty much shot to shreds and he spilled the rum down his highly flammable nylon shirt. Then he decided to light a cigarette, ignited the fumes as well and effectively blew himself up. He needed months of burns treatment but was still able to joke to an audience how he 'did the 100-yard dash in 4.3'.

Pryor was lucky. Not so fellow comedian John Belushi. He was lured by the intrinsically dangerous 'speedball' cocktail of heroin and cocaine, an upper-downer combination that has fascinated habitual drug users for much of the 20th century. The two drugs combine extremely well in terms of their buzz, although the physical effect has been likened to driving at maximum revs with the brakes screaming. For Belushi, loved by millions as the anarchic star of the cult movie *The Blues Brothers*, it was one ride too many. He died in March 1982 of a speedball overdose.

## STREET CRIME

Cocaine and crime are soulmates. Especially in western cities. Nowhere is this more true than London, which in 2001 saw an explosion in inter-gang violence and street crime apparently caused by crack addicts desperate for some rocks. The major crack suppliers in Britain are Jamaican or of Jamaican origin: often described as 'Yardie' gangs. They have Caribbean associates who arrange imports from Colombia while they act as wholesalers in overall control of UK and some European distribution. They are part of a worldwide trafficking operation. They may also organize street dealing and sales to approved dealers.

According to the head of Scotland Yard's Flying Squad, Commander Alan Brown, Yardie-style gangsters are now the most violent and difficult criminals faced by British police. On 16 January 2002 he released figures showing 21 drug-related murders and 67 attempted murders in London the previous year. All but two of the capital's 32 boroughs (districts) had reported drug-linked crime and all but ten had seen shootings. In the previous fortnight police had logged the first two murders of the new year and a further 25 shootings. All of this was 'black-on-black' crime.

The figures for gun crime across England and Wales rose by 9 per cent in 2001 to 4,019 incidents. It's hard to know how much of this was linked to cocaine in particular and drugs in general, but police believe that a significant proportion is down to Yardie in-fighting and feuding. It is all uncannily similar to the extreme violence on the streets of Miami and New York in the 1980s when America woke up to its own crack epidemic.

PSYCHIATRIC TOXICITY?

While London's crack cocaine gangs are not necessarily drug users themselves they certainly seem to be mad about guns. At Scotland Yard, Alan Brown heads the Operation Trident task force, which targets the big players. He has cited specific instances of how easily shootings are provoked in disputes about drugs, territory or 'respect'. Examples include:

- a sarcastic remark made by one black gangster about another's hairstyle
- a man treading on a gang leader's foot by mistake in a nightclub
- a nightclub bouncer refusing entry to a gang enforcer; the man returned with a gun and sprayed bullets at a queue waiting to enter the club; eight people were injured
- a row between a party-goer and a DJ in which the DJ was shot dead; the bullet passed through a wall, killing a second man.

'There are clearly organizations in both Jamaica and [the UK] that have almost a business relationship for supply and retail,' said Brown. 'The drug and gun culture is producing an incredibly narcissistic generation of young criminals. Their reaction to any act of what they see as disrespect is extreme violence.'

TRAFFICK ISLAND

According to Jamaican police there were around 500 known criminals from the island operating in Britain in 2002. The majority are affiliated to some 30 Yardie gangs: organizations with imaginative names such as the Kickoffhead Crew, the Lock City Crew, the Cartel Crew, the African Crew, the British Link Up Crew, Clans Massive, the Black Roses and the President's Click. The Click was apparently formed out of the notorious Shower Posse gang, rumoured to have committed 1,400 murders in the USA.

Just like the New York and Chicago gangsters of the 1920s and 1930s the Jamaican networks began life as election 'muscle', bullies hired to ensure that voters would support either the left-wing People's National Party or the conservative Jamaican Labour Party. Whereas Al Capone and his Chicago associates got rich on bootlegged alcohol, the Yardie leaders realised that cocaine was their ticket to riches. On 10 February 2002 the London-based *Sunday Times* named the leader of the President's Click and quoted a Jamaican police officer as saying: 'He is wanted for everything: murder, drug running, you name it. He is linked to gangs in the UK but he is untouchable because of his political links. That is the culture in Jamaica.'

DEALING WITH IT

British police have responded to the cocaine crimewave. Brown's Operation Trident arrested 441 people in 2001, most aged between 16 and 35. Of the 620 kilos of Class A drugs recovered nearly all was cocaine. Similar operations are ongoing: 'Stirrup' in Leeds, which resulted in 57 deportations to Jamaica in 2001; 'Atrium' in Bristol; 'Ventara' in Birmingham; 'Trojan' in Southampton; and 'Ovidian' in Plymouth.

Although Britain's crack market is Jamaican-controlled there is no evidence that the drug is used mostly in black communities. According to one senior Metropolitan Police detective it has penetrated all social backgrounds, with a 'heartland' of users – mostly beggars – in Soho, central London. This officer, a member of the London Crime Squad, heads an undercover team that buys crack on the street, busts key players and passes intelligence to other units. He has 21 years' experience, the past four in drugs operations.

'There is no great class divide,' he told me. 'Crack cocaine is used by all racial groups although beggars are the big market. If you go to black areas like Brixton you will obviously tend to find more black users. The same is true for white areas – particularly, in outer south-east London. There are several nightclubs where it is used by the black community but crack is not a club drug in the same league as, say, ecstasy.

'In areas of the West End, particularly around Soho, the customers are pretty much all vagrants. These are people who will beg for a quantity of pound coins until they have enough money to buy a stone. There is also a significant passing trade in office workers – men and women in suits – both black and white people.

The Metropolitan Police anti-crack team pays maybe £20 (about $30) a stone (a piece of crack cocaine), which typically weighs about 200mg. Stones fluctuate from 50–60g (1¾–2oz) to around 300g (10½oz) and, like powder coke, they will have varying levels of purity depending on the recipe used to cook them. Maintaining a crack habit without a healthy income or resorting to prostitution is nigh on impossible, however good your sob story to passers-by.

'People talk glibly about smoking a dozen stones a day,' said the detective. 'That means the drug is costing them perhaps £200 ($290) daily, and although there's a discount if they buy in bulk, crime is often the only way to pay. Users become desperate for crack and will do almost anything to get it. This may mean robbing someone in the street, especially if they need a stone urgently and haven't the means of finding money quickly. In the last four years crack crime has been a constant problem and it has escalated in that time.

'There's no such thing as a typical street dealer, but there are very few that have full-time jobs. We did find somebody who worked at a hairdresser's shop in the morning and then cruised the streets selling cocaine in the afternoon. Dealers basically work the hours they want to.

'Some sell straight to the crack houses. There are a plethora of these in London, addresses where users know they can go to smoke out of sight. It is a huge problem but it is almost impossible to estimate the total number of users. From our experience I would say the majority are aged under 30.'

He believes the fight against crack dealing is not hopeless, but demands a rolling review of police tactics. 'There is also an immigration issue here with carriers entering the UK, particularly from Jamaica,' he said. 'We need to look at these drug mules more closely and identify those who sponsor their application to enter Britain.'

Young, homeless, addicted, broke and desperate to service a craving for crack. No wonder cocaine has become synonymous with crime around the world. But if you think this is only a problem for the major cities think again. Crack dealers are businessmen. They thrive on making and defending new markets.

## WHAT'S THE SET-UP?

Street dealers use a variety of business models. The most basic has a single trader buying and selling small quantities, often to fund his own habit. More usually (according to Pearson and Hobbs) there will be a team centred on a leader who buys wholesale and assigns runners to make street deliveries or take payments. This leader maintains the books and keeps the contacts hot. There may also be peripheral employees, eg purity testers, crack cooks and packagers.

The UK Home Office's New English and Welsh Arrestee Drug Abuse Monitoring programme (NEW-ADAM), published in 2000, looked at cocaine and crack purchases in two British cities: Nottingham and Sunderland. Of the 131-strong sample, 82 per cent bought in their local neighbourhood and 75 per cent made contact with their dealer via a pager or mobile phone. Two-thirds were given a collection point (usually in a residential street) while the remainder had it delivered to their door by a courier.

In America cocaine markets traditionally work on a credit system in which the drug is supplied up-front by wholesalers to street dealers. The dealer than pays up over an agreed timescale. In the UK this model is less typical; sometimes cash on delivery is demanded within a network and sometimes it isn't. Either way it makes sense to keep drug and cash runners separate. If there's a bust or a taxing it means there's less to lose.

Dealers who peddle only one type of drug are comparatively rare. Marijuana is an exception because it is seen as all but legal. Why would grass-only suppliers wish to jeopardize a good business by dabbling in a drug like coke, with all the additional hassle from police and rival operators that might bring? Often street dealers will buy from 'multi-commodity brokers' offering club drugs such as speed, ecstasy, powder coke and perhaps a little marijuana on the side. Finally, there is the crack and heroin market, seen as a class apart because it involves 'dirty' habits. Even dealers and traffickers have morals...but not all of them. The level of violence used to extract payments and warn off competitors has no comparison in the criminal underworld. This occurs mostly at international trafficking level, but sometimes also between rival gangs in an individual city. None of the players goes looking for trouble because it stirs up police interest and is generally bad for business. Usually it's the sign of an unstable, disrupted supply chain or a good old-fashioned turf war.

**COKE AT WORK AND PLAY**

To appreciate the forces that drive worldwide cocaine trafficking you first have to crunch statistics. Drugs breed statistics. So this next bit is for all those anoraks who feel comfortable knowing that in Guatemala the annual prevalence of cocaine abuse as a percentage of the population aged 15 or over in 1998 was 1.6 per cent (*Global Illicit Drug Trends*, United Nations, 2001).

The Vienna-based International Drug Control Programme (UNIDCP) is a mine of fascinating facts on cocaine. In 2001 it estimated that the drug was used by 0.3 per cent of the global population with more than 70 per cent of these consumers living in North or South America and 16 per cent in Europe. Abuse levels in North America were seven times the world average, while Asians and eastern Europeans were noticeably abstemious. The continental breakdown is shown in the table over the page.

**NUMBER OF COCAINE USERS (MILLIONS) AS A PERCENTAGE OF POPULATION AGED 15+**

|  | MILLIONS | % OF POPULATION AGED 15+ |
|---|---|---|
| North America | 7.0 | 2.20 |
| South America | 3.1 | 1.10 |
| Oceania | 0.2 | 0.90 |
| Western Europe | 2.2 | 0.70 |
| Eastern Europe | 0.1 | 0.04 |
| Africa | 1.3 | 0.30 |
| Asia | 0.2 | 0.01 |
| Global | 14 | 0.30 |

## WORLD OF COCAINE

More important than the hard data is the trend in consumption levels. Here's what the GIDT report for 2001 has to say about the pattern of cocaine use around the world. Most of the statistics are two to three years old (it takes this long to collect, collate and publish them) and there is inevitably a variation in sampling methods.

### THE AMERICAS

Annual cocaine use (ie taking at least once a year) has stabilized in North America at 1.7 per cent of the population aged 12 and above. This is one-third lower than in 1985, while the number of monthly users fell even more dramatically over the same timespan: from 3 per cent to 0.7 per cent.

One illuminating section of the GIDT report is the 'Use, Risk, Disapproval and Availability' survey 2000, which looks at attitudes to cocaine and crack among American schoolchildren. This showed that just over 4 per cent of twelfth-graders used cocaine powder (down from 10 per cent in 1987). Half of the sample group said they saw 'great risk' in using it once or twice (same as 1987), 85 per cent said they disapproved of using once or twice (same as 1987) and just over 40 per cent said it was easy to get hold of (down from 50 per cent in 1987).

For crack, the figures revealed that 2 per cent of twelfth-graders in the sample had used in the past year (half the 1987 figure). Just under 50 per cent thought there were great risks attached to occasional use (down from 60 per cent in 1987). Around 85 per cent disapproved of using once or twice (slight decline on 1987) and 40 per cent said it was easy to obtain (same as 1987).

On the whole, these figures look encouraging for the US government. However, the report points out that even with a projected decline to 5.5 million users by 2000, the USA will remain far and away the world's biggest coke market.

Elsewhere in the Americas cocaine use is mostly on the increase. Peru and Bolivia – the two biggest coca leaf producers – are notable exceptions. Surveys there show a decline in the number of people experimenting with the drug during the 1990s. Brazil, Argentina and Chile now have the highest percentage of 'lifetime prevalence' cocaine powder abusers outside the USA. In Argentina the percentage of annual users is 1.9 per cent and in Chile 1.3 per cent. Colombia – the 'home of cocaine' – appears to have stable abuse levels (1.6 per cent of the population are lifetime users), although this figure was recorded back in 1996.

EUROPE

Data shows that Europe's two biggest cocaine markets – the UK and Spain – have stabilized. In contrast there is increasing use in Germany, France, The Netherlands, Belgium, Denmark, Norway, Portugal, Cyprus and Turkey. Eastern European countries barely perceive it as a problem. 'Cocaine in Europe – similar to the USA in the 1970s prior to the crack epidemic – is often used recreationally and constitutes less of a social problem than in North America,' says the report.

'However, there has been a trend towards poly-drug abuse ... many heroin addicts consume cocaine, increasingly in the form of crack. Similarly, there have been reports across western Europe of people on methadone maintenance programmes using cocaine to get their "kick".'

Another insight comes from the Brussels liaison department of the United Nations Office of Drug Control and Crime Prevention (UNODCCP). In 2001 it was generally upbeat about the trend in Europe. 'There was an increase in cocaine trafficking and consumption in Europe over the last decade – and this upward trend is probably going to continue. But it has been a creeping increase and there are no indications that this trend is likely to change dramatically in the near future. There are reports of youths who used to take ecstasy changing over to cocaine and there are reports of cocaine spreading from the upper class (or upper middle class) to other sections of society. But all of these trends do not appear – at least for the time being – to result in what could be called a cocaine epidemic.'

The UNODCCP also points out how the political history of a country can significantly affect consumption. In western Germany the number of people taking cocaine at least annually amounted to 0.7 per cent of the population in 1997, whereas in the eastern part of the country, the 'closed' provinces formerly under a communist regime reported a total of just 0.1 per cent. Presumably the Berlin Wall was a bummer for traffickers. Similarly, 'Only Spain, which has traditionally close links with its former colonies in Latin America, including the Andean region, has abuse levels of cocaine which approach those of the USA.' Spain's annual prevalence figure in 1997 was 1.5 per cent of the 15–65 age group.

The UNODCCP report concludes that 'Cocaine use in Europe is already widespread among people in entertainment, in the media and communications and some groups of professionals. There are no indications that the spread of cocaine among these sections of society is on the rise – they are rather ageing while using cocaine. Social security institutions may have to pay in one way or another for the resulting health problems. But use within these circles does not necessarily lead to a spread as members – usually – do not make their living out of drug trafficking.

'If there is an increase in cocaine use it could be expected to arise primarily among ageing groups of the "ecstasy generation" who may try to experiment with other drugs as well, including cocaine. But these groups – though representing potential health problems for themselves and for society at large – are at least less prone to undergo cocaine-related criminal activities than deprived youths living in some ghettos.'

### AFRICA AND ASIA
The GIDT report reveals that cocaine abuse is largely a southern and western Africa phenomena. From the figures available there is increasing use in the Republic of South Africa and, especially, Angola (reflecting trafficking links with Brazil). Most cocaine shipped to Africa is intended for a final destination in Europe. Asian governments regard cocaine as a low-priority social issue. In 1999 only seven countries bothered to report trends in consumption and most of these were stable or falling.

### OCEANIA
Australia is facing one of the biggest rises in cocaine abuse. The number of annual users almost tripled between 1993

and 1998 (from 0.5 per cent to 1.4 per cent of the population aged 14 and above), equivalent to the highest national rates found in Europe. This trend has not permeated to New Zealand, where year-on-year consumption is said to be stable.

## PURER EQUALS MORE

One good indicator of coke availability can be found in the purity of police seizures. According to the 2001 GIDT report, 'As prices tend to remain rather stable in the drug markets, short-term changes in supply are usually reflected in shifts in purities. Higher levels of purities indicate improved supply.' In other words a street dealer with loads of Charlie on his hands doesn't worry too much about cutting. He passes on the improved quality to his buyers: just like any other customer-focused business.

The UNODCCP says that in 1999, mean cocaine purities exceeded 62 per cent in Britain. The last time purity levels topped this benchmark was in 1989 (it has ranged between 47 per cent and 55 per cent throughout the decade). While prosecution and seizure statistics will highlight bits of the story, most analysts agree that there's nothing like good old market forces to get to the nub of things. Cocaine powder 62 per cent pure is not a resounding victory for the forces of British law and order, and is a statistically significant change for the worse...or better, depending on your point of view.

GERMANY

Ah yes, Germany. The nation that first produced cocaine back in the 19th century has never quite ended its love affair with the drug. During the 1990s the decline in its street cocaine price was greater than anywhere else in Europe: it fell by two-thirds between 1996 and 1998. At Europe's busiest air hub, Frankfurt Airport, customs officers seized 780kg (1,720lbs) of the drug in 1995, compared to 421kg (925lbs) the previous year. In the first six months of 1999, according to the UNODCCP, 45 per cent of all cocaine seized in Germany was in transit to other European countries.

In fact, the 1997 report of Geopolitical Drug Watch (you're right, it could only be funded by the European Commission) revealed that cocaine dealing in Germany 'has broken out of its closed circle of distributors and consumers and has taken on the same mass character as heroin dealing. Those arrested include Nigerians, Italians, South Americans and eastern European nationals, but most were Germans; this diversity clearly demonstrates the splintering and democratization of the market.'

Democracy and cocaine is something the Bundestag knows all about. In October 2000 an undercover TV reporter strolled around Germany's parliament building visiting 28 men's toilets and wiping down their surfaces with paper tissues. The tissues were stuffed into airtight tubes and analysed by the Nuremberg-based forensic analyst

Professor Fritz Sorgel. He found that 22 out of the 28 carried traces of cocaine.

Sorgel stressed that his findings might have been distorted by cleaners spreading the drug around on their cloths. Others were less restrained. 'The Parliament of Addicts', declared the tabloid paper *BZ*. Hubert Huppe, the Christian Social Union's narcotics spokesman, pointed out that 'it would be unnatural if parliamentarians were the only group to have nothing to do with drugs'.

THE BUSINESS

One explanation of the tacit acceptance of cocaine among Germany's middle classes is that employers may not necessarily see it as a Bad Thing. At the height of the Bundestag business a leading social scientist, Gunter Amendt, pointed out that whereas marijuana and alcohol were 'employer unfriendly', the big C actually makes staff graft harder. There's nothing new about this idea – for centuries South American plantation owners even paid their workforce with it – but in a nation with Germany's enhanced work ethic you can see how it might appeal.

HARD TO HANDLE?

This is the abiding mystery of cocaine culture. How come some take it without a problem while others watch their personal lives and careers mercilessly shredded? One of the most brilliant economists on Wall Street, Lawrence

Kudlow, was earning $1 million (£700,000) a year when he started snorting as a 25-year-old in 1984. As an adviser to the Reagan administration he was courted and cosseted by the markets to the point that he felt 'indestructible'. Then he began missing client appointments and got himself fired from the investment bank Bear Stearns. The cocaine vice gripped ever stronger; debts mounted; his wife threatened divorce.

In 1995, Kudlow went into five months of rehab. He kicked his addiction, became a devout Christian and, in 2000, regained the giddy heights of Wall Street as chief economist to ING Barings. 'Handling large sums of money can sometimes mislead people into thinking that they are powerful,' he said in one interview in November 2000. 'They are not. I have never blamed Wall Street. It's an attitude, not the pressure. People believe they can turn it on and turn it off and, sooner or later, they realise that they can't.'

Manhattan-based addiction therapist Dr Arnold Washton, founder of America's first cocaine hotline in 1982, sees this all the time. Around a third of his clients work on Wall Street and they tell him they use the drug to feel 'energetic, powerful, sexy and on top of the world'. Washton has little doubt that cocaine is re-emerging as the drug of choice for senior executives. 'It was almost treated as passé for a while,' he told the London *Guardian* (29 November 2000). 'There's a new crop of young, ambitious professionals who find this drug suitable. It fits right in with the tenor of the times.'

It is exactly this attitude that so angers some senior politicians and police officers. On 4 January 1999, Britain's so-called 'drugs tsar', Keith Hellawell, waded into City of London cocaine users. Just because wealth allowed them to buy the drug without thieving, he told BBC Radio 4's *Today* programme, it didn't mean they were innocent of damaging society. 'I wish they'd stop it,' he said. 'There's this arrogance – I call it an intellectual arrogance. If they are dealing with my pension fund on the dealing floors they could be causing me damage. It isn't a joke, it's deadly serious.'

SPORTING SNORTERS

This is another strange facet of the cocaine debate. Sometimes it's funny, sometimes it's not. When the England international footballer Robbie Fowler celebrated a goal at his former club Liverpool FC by kneeling down and running his nose along the white line of the penalty area, everybody under 40 in the crowd had a good laugh. This generation was familiar with cocaine; they knew Fowler was comparing the 'high' of scoring with the 'high' of coke.

Yet for those world-famous sportsmen and women caught using the drug the consequences are stark. When Germany appointed Christoph Daum as trainer of its national football team in 2000 there were widespread rumours that his trademark 'boggle-eyed' expression and legendary short temper were the result of cocaine use. Daum agreed to have a hair sample analysed to prove his innocence. It was the worst result of his career. The test showed he'd consumed large quantities of the drug and the coaching offer was hurriedly withdrawn.

Drug testing has now become so prevalent in sport that for professional players and athletes a line or two of cocaine is no longer worth the risk. American footballer Dexter Manley failed one test while starring for the Washington Redskins in 1989 and then another two years later as a Tampa Bay Buccaneers player. He retired from football but not from cocaine and eventually served 15 months of a four-year drugs sentence.

## FREE-FLOWING TRAFFIC

Cocaine consumers may come from all walks of life but the cocaine business has only one spiritual home. It's true that Peru is probably the largest coca leaf grower, that Bolivia harvests a decent crop, that Mexican drug cartels have grabbed a big slice of the US smuggling trade, and that the Caribbean is a key worldwide transiting centre. There are growers and traffickers in Brazil, Venezuela, Argentina, Ecuador, Uruguay and Paraguay, but you could take down every last one and barely register a blip on world supplies. There is only one undisputed king of the cocaine ring. Ask any law-enforcement agency and they'll tell you: 80 per cent of the world's cocaine moves through Colombia.

According to the UN special conference on the global drug problem (New York, 1998) there has been a big reduction in area devoted to the coca bush worldwide. In 1990 this stood at 288,000ha (710,000 acres); by 1998 it was down to 179,000ha (440,000 acres). Yet the production of coca in tonnes/tons has seen a more gradual decline – from 363,981 tonnes/tons in 1990 to around 300,000 in 1998. A combination of improving crop yields (horticultural science doesn't care who it helps) and the spread of new, unidentified plantations probably explains the discrepancy.

Despite a 40 per cent reduction in its coca crop, Peru is theoretically the biggest grower (118,000 tonnes/tons in 1997) followed by Bolivia (93,000 tonnes/tons) and Colombia (91,000 tonnes/tons). By the time this book is published this league table may well have changed, as Colombian guerrillas use coca growing to fund their continuing civil war against the government. What these statistics don't reveal is the proportion of South American coca bought up by Colombians. Put it this way, they don't miss much.

Assuming a conversion rate in which 1,000 tonnes/tons of coca leaf equals 9 tonnes/tons of cocaine, the UN reckons that the total world harvest was upwards of 800 tonnes/tons in 1997. Government seizures accounted for perhaps 300 tonnes/tons, leaving 500–700 tonnes/tons to be smuggled, shuffled, smoked and snorted around the globe. This is almost certainly a massive underestimate, but then that's the United Nations for you.

The UN's *Global Illicit Drug Trends* report for 2001 has cast a little more light on things. It analysed the amount of cocaine actually seized by government forces in 1999. This predictably showed the world's biggest market – America – way out in front with 132,318kg (291,000lbs). Next came Colombia with 63,945kg (140,000lbs) and way behind in third place Mexico with 34,623kg (76,000lbs).

The rest are also-rans. There's Spain (18,111kg/40,000lbs) Venezuela, Peru, The Netherlands, Ecuador and Guatemala (all in the 10,000–12,500kg/22,000–27,500lbs range) and Bolivia and Brazil (each 7,700kg/17,000lbs). The whole of western Europe accounted for 43,707kg (96,000lbs), while in the Caribbean seizures amounted to 12,133kg (26,700lbs).

The report confirmed what everyone already knew: that the main trafficking routes shoot out from the major South and Central American producers and head straight up Uncle Sam's monster pair of nostrils in the north. Cocaine shipments come via road across the US/Mexican border, in 'go-fast' boats up America's Pacific coast and in sea ferries, pleasure boats or commercial planes via the Bahamas, Haiti, Puerto Rico, the Dominican Republic and various other Caribbean islands.

Jamaica is the main air bridge for Colombian cartels accessing Europe and the Middle East. Since the late 1990s these markets have been particularly good at filling traffickers' boots with cash, at only slightly enhanced levels of risk. Whereas a kilo (2¼lbs) of pure cocaine may sell for $20,000 (£14,000) wholesale in Miami, in London it can be worth three times as much. Elsewhere there is some traditional, international trade: Brazil to Angola, Ecuador to Hong Kong or Japan and Argentina to South Africa and Australia. As for smuggling methods, these range from the ingenious to the downright yucky (see below).

## WHAT'S ON THE MOVE?

At this point we need to be clear about the type of cocaine being smuggled. If it's a bulk shipment it may be coca paste – *pasta basica* – the same, smokable stuff that so excited those early American traffickers back in the 1970s and later sparked the crack epidemic. If it has already been fully processed it'll be pure(ish) cocaine hydrochloride in ready-to-cut powder form.

Paste is favoured by the big cocaine cartels because it's convenient in size and weight, and dead simple to produce in jungle kitchens from raw coca. The recipe varies from country to country, but essentially you harvest your coca leaves, dry them, chop them up, sprinkle them with cement and soak them in petrol for a day. This leaches out the cocaine alkaloid. You then siphon off the petrol and put the mashed leaves through a press to extract the remaining liquid.

Add a bucket of water containing some drops of car battery acid (one bucket per 30kg/65lbs of leaf), stir and allow to rest. Because the alkaloid is more soluble in acid than in petrol it moves into the acid solution. Chuck in some caustic soda, filter the solidifying murky mess through a cloth, strain and allow to dry into a yellowy-white powder. Here's your paste, somewhere between 40 and 60 per cent pure. If anyone ever tells you that cocaine is a 'natural' drug, ask them about the cement, petrol, battery acid and caustic soda.

In fairness, there are two further steps before the cocaine is ready for market. It has to be dissolved in solvents, allowed to solidify and then washed in another, very pure, solvent to produce 90 per cent pure cocaine hydrochloride. This is usually done by the cartel buyers, who process the paste in their own remote laboratories. It's at this point that the traffickers, and the money movers, queue up to make their millions.

## WHO ARE THE MOVERS?

In September 2001 the US Office of Domestic Intelligence (ODI) published a report highlighting recent trends in the Central American cocaine markets. This showed that while Colombia remains the major player, drug cartels there have contracted-out much of their cross-border smuggling business to the Mexicans. Until 1989 Colombians usually paid Mexican traffickers to drive or fly cocaine across the US border (65 per cent of American cocaine enters this way) but had associates in place the other side to take delivery. This ensured that Colombian cartels retained control of wholesale distribution. However, a massive 21 tonne/ton seizure in 1989 led to a new underworld deal.

'By the mid-1990s, Mexico-based transportation groups were receiving up to half the cocaine shipment they smuggled for the Colombia-based groups in exchange for their services,' says the ODI. 'Both sides realised that this strategy eliminated the vulnerabilities and complex logistics associated with large cash transactions. The Colombia-based groups also realised that relinquishing part of each cocaine shipment to their associates operating from Mexico ceded a share of the wholesale cocaine market in the United States.'

According to the ODI there then followed a good old-fashioned carve-up of territory. The Colombians retained control of their lucrative north-east markets and eastern seaboard cities such as Boston, Miami, Newark, New York and Philadelphia. The Mexicans got the west and mid-west, specifically cities such as Chicago, Dallas, Denver, Houston, Los Angeles, Phoenix, San Diego, San Francisco and Seattle. Both sides made alliances with Dominican underworld groups (traditionally responsible for street-level distribution), particularly in New York City.

It's not that Colombian drug lords didn't have the stomach for a turf war. It's just that they didn't see the point. When you make $10 million (£7 million) a day, why worry if it drops to $5 million (£3.5 million), especially if the risks are spread. More to the point, there was that horrible word 'extradition', which had never really been part of the Colombian vocabulary. From 17 December 1997, however, any Colombian mafia boss drug running overtly to the USA knew it was likely to lead to an appointment with an American judge. And a long, long time to think about what went wrong.

When a Colombian or Mexican drug lord dies accidentally or through natural causes no one ever believes it. People just assume the man concerned has faked his own death in order to acquire a clean new identity. This is why good plastic surgeons are never idle in Central America. However, treating mafia bosses is not without the occasional setback, chief among which is the patient dying on the operating table. Drug families are never very understanding about that sort of thing.

So when Amado Carrillo Fuentes – the single most powerful cocaine baron in the Americas during the mid-1990s – apparently died while undergoing liposuction and cosmetic surgery at Mexico City's Santa Monica hospital, the country's response was to look for a set-up. The patient had checked in under the name of Antonio Flores Montes and the bruised and surgically scarred corpse was simply assumed to be some convenient victim hauled in as Carrillo's dead body double. This was not the view of the chief surgeon, who promptly fled the country. Neither was it the opinion of the DEA, FBI or the Mexican police – all of whom declared fingerprint and DNA analysis as conclusive proof that the cadaver was Carrillo. Champagne corks must have popped in Washington DC that night.

The trouble is that killing cartel leaders – even big fish like Carrillo – makes not a jot of difference to cocaine street sales. The DEA admits as much in its website analysis of leading Colombian and Mexican traffickers. 'Until recently, the Colombian trafficking organizations, collectively known as the Cali mafia, dominated the international cocaine market. Although some elements of the Cali mafia continue to play an important role in the world's wholesale cocaine market, events in recent years – including the capture of the Rodriguez-Orejuela brothers in 1995, the death of Jose Santacruz-Londono in March 1996 and the surrender of Pacho Herrera in September 1996 – have accelerated the decline of the Cali mafia influence.

'Other experienced traffickers, who have been active for years but worked in the shadow of the Cali drug lords, have successfully seized opportunities to increase their share of the drug trade...Independent Colombian traffickers are still responsible for most of the world's cocaine production and wholesale distribution.'

This is the problem for western governments. For every cocaine godfather taken down, six more are clamouring to nab his markets. It's the same with the drug couriers. As police and customs technology gets better, so the smuggling gets sneakier.

**DELIVERING THE GOODIES**

Here's the scale of the problem facing the United States Customs Service (USCS). According to its own statistics, 60 million people arrive in America on more than 675,000 commercial and private flights each year. Another 370 million come by land and 6 million by sea. Around 116 million vehicles cross the land borders with Canada and Mexico. Upwards of 90,000 merchant and passenger ships enter American ports carrying a combined total of 9 million shipping containers and 400 million tonnes/tons of cargo. In addition, 157,000 smaller vessels visit the harbours of coastal towns. Would you know the enemy? Exactly.

A quick tally reveals 436 million people arriving every year. The vast majority are good, decent law-abiding citizens, but the task of picking out the bad guys falls to just 7,500 USCS officers at 301 ports of entry. The odds are not great but the USCS, the US Coast Guard, the Navy, DEA, FBI and CIA undoubtedly do disrupt drug smuggling effectively. There are 26 customs jets on interdiction deployment with smuggler 'host countries'. Customs P3 aircraft mount continuous surveillance over the Andean mountains to identify potential drug planes, and over the eastern Pacific to spot suspicious inbound ships. Fast Coast Guard cutters patrol the Caribbean and Pacific trafficking corridors.

Of the 86,700kg (190,000lbs) of cocaine seized in the USA during the fiscal year 2001, 40,000kg (88,000lbs) was being taken across the US/Mexican border. It's easy to see why. The border is mostly desert, unpopulated, unpatrolled, unfenced, and stretches for 3,200km (2,000 miles). The US government does its best with radar balloons and the odd surveillance aircraft but, frankly, you could march a couple of battalions across before anyone noticed. Most smugglers still use the tarmac roads, but as there aren't very many of these congestion causes a different set of problems. At the entry point of San Ysidro, south of San Diego, 20,000 pedestrians and 96,000 car passengers travel across the world's busiest land border post every day.

Among the hi-tech gadgets used by customs officers to monitor this mass of humanity is something called a 'density-buster': a kind of ultrasound scanner that can tell, for instance, whether your tyres contain more than just air. Digital cameras photograph 40,000 car registration plates a day, simultaneously checking them against national databases of suspect cars. On the USA side, metal tyre shredders can be raised from the road to stop drivers crashing through inspection booths. But the best way of rooting out cocaine stashes is to use the most unbelievably sensitive drug-odour detectors known to man: dogs.

In March 2001 one attempt to keep sniffer mutts at bay involved packing 1,000kg (2,200lbs) of cocaine into a trailer carrying pallets of onions. It was stopped by police in rural Hidalgo County on the Texas/Mexico border and escorted to the Pharr port of entry for examination. The powerful smell of the onions didn't seem to worry sniffer dog Scar, who immediately alerted them to the presence of drugs.

Customs officers tell stories of wised-up traffickers vacuum-sealing cocaine, smearing the package in grease, sealing it again and sinking it into a car petrol tank. Doesn't work. Dogs such as German shepherds – one of several breeds used by the USCS – have 220 million sensory cells in their noses, compared to just five million in humans. They can thoroughly check a car in six minutes. Even a cursory search by officers would take 20.

## GO CREATE!

Tried and trusted smuggling methods include false compartments in suitcases and aerosol spray cans, false soles in shoes, swallowing 'bullets' (small amounts of coke wrapped in plastic or condoms and swallowed), solutions of cocaine in wine or brandy bottles, baby powder containers – the list goes on. But as detection techniques are improving, smugglers are having to think more creatively. On 26 February 2001, customs special agents raided a bungalow in Nogales, Arizona, where they found a 7.5m- (25ft-) long hand-dug tunnel linked to the city's sewer system. Given that 198 cocaine bricks were found in the front room, and that Mexico lay three-quarters of a mile to the south, it's clear what was happening.

## THE HIGH SEAS

American successes on land are more than matched by results at sea. In 2000 and 2001 there was a string of record-breaking marine seizures involving cocaine. Using boats is a huge gamble for traffickers because it's obviously impossible to spread risk. You can send 100 drug mules through an airport and if two-thirds make it the losses are manageable. But if your boat gets busted, it's painful – even for a cartel boss.

Yet moving cocaine by sea seems as popular as ever, at least if seizure figures announced by the White House Office of National Drug Control Policy (ONDCP) are any guide. In October 2001 its acting director, Edward Jurith, revealed that 62,800kg (138,334lbs) of the drug was recovered by US Coast Guard vessels over the previous 12 months: almost 2,700kg (6,000lbs) more than the previous record (set the previous year). This can mean one of three things:

- the Coast Guard is getting better or luckier;
- there's more cocaine on the ocean;
- both of the above.

Jurith had no doubt that pooling international resources was the key. He told a Washington DC press conference (5 October 2001) that, 'This increase in seizures takes place at the same time that other data tell us US consumers are using an ever-smaller proportion of the world's cocaine. Seizing more from a smaller universe of drugs is exactly what supply reduction aims to do. Much of the success is due to international cooperation, information-sharing and targeted operations. Foreign governments are also doing better – and for many of the same reasons.'

Of the 2001 successes, by far the greatest was the boarding of the Belize-flagged fishing boat *Svesda Maru* on 3 May 2001. This 45m (150ft) vessel was first sighted on

28 April by one of US Customs' P3 aircraft. Its position in the eastern Pacific was reported the following day by a Coast Guard C-130 patrol plane, and a decision was made to despatch a US Navy guided missile frigate carrying specialist search teams. After five days they discovered a large, unexplained area beneath the fish holds: at least it was unexplained until they found a 12,000kg (26,400lbs) stash of cocaine. This single seizure was the biggest in maritime history, equivalent to one-sixteenth of the entire cocaine haul confiscated on mainland America that year.

It wasn't just American agencies that broke seizure records in 2001. On 27 July Federal police recovered Australia's largest single cocaine consignment soon after it was offloaded from a 30m (100ft) fishing boat in Dulverton Bay, a remote stretch of the western Australian coast some 650km (400 miles) north of Perth. Around 1,000kg (2,200lbs) of cocaine were buried on a lonely beach and soon afterwards the boat sank in what police euphemistically called 'inexplicable circumstances'. Five people were arrested.

In March 2002 it was the British government's turn to celebrate. After a joint surveillance operation and raid by Her Majesty's Customs and Excise and the National Crime Squad (NCS), five marine traffickers were jailed for a total of 99 years. They had been caught red-handed offloading 400kg (880lbs) of cocaine to a safe house on the Isle of Wight, off southern England. This, too, was a record cocaine seizure.

CRACKDOWN

Three months after the attacks on the World Trade Center and the Pentagon, US Customs Commissioner Robert Bonner pointed out that America's war on terrorism was also bad news for traffickers. 'Contrary to what some might believe, the counter-terrorism and counter-narcotics missions are not mutually exclusive,' he said. 'One does not necessarily come at the expense of the other. Everyone...knows that there is a nexus between drug trafficking and terrorism. Everyone in Colombia knows this' (speech to the 2001 National High Intensity Drug Trafficking Areas (HIDTA) conference, Washington DC, 6 December 2001).

The tightening of America's domestic security briefly took its toll on land-based Mexican and Colombian cocaine operations. Cross-border runs were delayed as the underworld waited for things to calm down. 'In the end they got fed up waiting and carried on regardless,' USCS officer Dean Boyd told me. 'We saw cocaine seizures pick up in the fall of 2001 and early 2002. This was partly because we were deploying more people to counter terrorism along our borders. [The events of] 11 September did disrupt road trafficking – but not for long. We soon saw cocaine smugglers back down their usual routes. They knew, and we knew, that they had buyers waiting.'

For the air mules it was a different story. Before 11 September, 50 per cent of all drugs found on passengers arriving in the USA came from flights originating in Jamaica. Given that the island generates less than 3 per cent of US air traffic, this is some achievement. However, after the terrorist attacks, getting drugs through American airports became a nightmare. There was a sense that US air authorities had been too complacent in the past and they sure as hell weren't about to make the same mistake again. In Jamaica supplies built up. European markets, with their traditional high prices and expanding street dealerships, suddenly seemed more attractive than ever.

Superintendent Gladstone Wright of the Jamaican Constabulary Narcotics Division put it like this: 'In terms of what is happening in Britain, the trade has escalated sharply since 11 September. The couriers who would normally be travelling to America are unable to get their drugs through because security at the borders has become so tight. Cocaine is stockpiling in Jamaica and that is no good for the dealers. There is no viable market for the drug here. So it is all being diverted to Britain.

'Becoming a drug mule is the most readily available form of employment in this country at the moment. It is a job that you do not need to be interviewed for, or have any kind of qualifications, but you can earn more money than most Jamaicans see in a lifetime. The economy here is very bad at the moment and unemployment among women is running at 22 per cent. These people are easy prey for the dealers' (London *Observer*, 6 January 2002).

The Netherlands' Schiphol Airport has become another key destination for British and European distribution. Police estimate that between 20,000 and 25,000 mules pass through the terminal each year, most of them Dutch citizens flying on return tickets from the former Caribbean colonies of the Antilles and Surinam. Government figures for 2001 show that 1,200 air passengers were convicted of cocaine trafficking, a 60 per cent increase on the previous year. Those who escaped arrest and made their delivery would have been paid around £2,000 ($2,900) plus expenses.

The situation at Schiphol got so bad after 11 September that, in January 2002, senior customs officers wrote a letter to the Amsterdam daily newspaper *Het Parool* complaining that they'd been ordered to stop arresting cocaine traffickers. The reason? Dutch jails were too full to take any more felons. This was despite the fact that during random checks on one flight from the Caribbean, no fewer than 40 smugglers had been caught. 'At a time when our society is being flooded with drugs,' the customs team wrote, 'we are being forced on the express orders of our superiors to stick our heads in the sand.'

They recounted one ludicrous case in which a woman found with 14kg (30lb) of coke in her luggage was released because no cell was available for her. Her £460,000 ($666,000) consignment was confiscated but she demanded – and got – a police receipt to prove to her drugs masters that she hadn't sold off the goodies herself.

## HARD TO SWALLOW?

Of all the mules, the 'body packers' adopt the most ignominious technique. They prepare for their ordeal by swallowing whole grapes. Shortly before their flight they switch to compressed cocaine encased in the severed finger pieces of latex rubber gloves. These are sealed into pellets by a special machine and coated with honey to help prevent gagging. The sealing part of the process isn't quite perfect. This is probably why at least ten mules died of cocaine poisoning during 2001 while waiting to board flights at Kingston Airport.

Once the pellets are swallowed (payment is per pellet and swallowers are believed to manage anywhere between 30 and 120 in a single sitting) the mule will take a large dose of anti-diarrhoea tablets to induce constipation. After the flight there's then a six-day wait for nature to take its course.

How did it come to this? How did supposedly civilized societies reduce their citizens to swallowing rubber gloves filled with chemically laden drugs to be crapped out and handed to others to mix with yet more chemicals so that different people would pay big bucks to snort or smoke them and feel cool? I mean, you couldn't make it up. All this nonsense over one ordinary little plant.

Time for a history lesson.

## FOOD OF THE GODS

Who knows how it happened: how the very first South American became the very first coke-head? It would have been several thousand, maybe tens of thousands of years ago, that this 'First User' would have ripped off a bunch of coca leaves and taken a tentative chew to check out the taste.

Suppose this Indian – let's call them Charlie for obvious and convenient reasons – tried to improve the flavour and texture by adding a touch of alkali. This could have been burned roots, powdered lime, seashells or anything else in the native diet with a high pH. Alkalis like these leach out the rush-giving alkaloids from coca.

There's no doubt that over the next few hours this primitive equivalent of chewing gum would have made Charlie feel cool about, say, hunting guanaco for that day's dinner. It wouldn't have matched the coked-up buzz enjoyed by today's users as most coca leaves contain less than 1 per cent cocaine. To get a 21st-century-style high Charlie would have had to dry the leaves, pound them up and consume 50g-worth (1¾oz) in one mega-snort.

Even so, the leaves would have produced a gradual onset of euphoria and well-being, a marked lack of hunger and fatigue, and heightened mental alertness. Within a few generations coca would have progressed in Indian culture from unremarkable shrub to food of the gods.

This version of events is admittedly light on fact. But, in essence, it is true. South American Indians were the first people to use coca simply because it didn't grow anywhere else. It has become a defining part of their culture, helps them work longer and harder, performs wonders as an anaesthetic (the Inca seemed very keen on it for brain surgery), treats snow blindness, stomach upsets, headaches and altitude sickness, and even, so it turns out, provides some useful nutrition.

## COCA ROOTS

Coca is a member of the genus *Erythroxylum*, of which there are around 250 species, mostly native to South America and all heavily reliant on wet, frost-free, warm, humid growing conditions. It grows faster at sea level but its cocaine yield increases at altitude and most commercial plantations are found at heights between 450 and 1,800m (1,500 and 6,000ft). As a result, the continent's prime cocaine belt runs from Colombia in the north, down the eastern foothills of the Andes to southern Bolivia and the eastern edge of the Amazon basin. Many, though not all, species contain cocaine although only a few contain enough to make cultivation worth the candle. Of these few, four in particular have cornered the market.

- **_Erythroxylum_ variety _cocacoca_.** Usually known as Bolivian coca, this was for many years the biggest source of illegal cocaine. It still plays a major role in Bolivia's agricultural economy and, according to the United Nations Drug Control Programme, the country's total annual harvest is currently around 93,000 tonnes/tons.
- **_Erythroxylum novogranatense_.** This one is native to Colombia – a region known as Nueva Granada (New Granada) to Spanish colonists – hence the plant's name. This was the first coca leaf seen by white Europeans and its cocaine was later exported all over the world as a legal, medical anaesthetic. For years it never much featured in international trafficking; at least not until the big Colombian cartels decided during the 1980s that they could expand profit margins by growing their own instead of importing from Bolivia and Peru. It was a canny move, given that novogranatense now services 85 per cent of the world's illegal cocaine market.
- **_Erythroxylum novogranatense_ variety _truxillense_.** Better known as Trujillo, this flourishes in the dry, coastal desert strip around the Peruvian city of the same name. Because of the climate, Trujillo can only grow in well-irrigated plantations but its flavoursome leaves and high cocaine content made it well worth the effort for Inca

tribes who knew it as 'Royal Coca'. Mother Nature gets particularly motherly where Trujillo is concerned because its cocaine content is a total nightmare to extract commercially. For this reason it has never been much use to traffickers, although it is the leaf of choice for the manufacturers of Coca-Cola. In case you were wondering, coca leaves are still used to give Coca-Cola its flavour – but only after the cocaine has been removed. So when right-wing politicians and middle-aged golfers finger-wag you at drinks parties and demand to know why the world coca crop can't just be blitzed by the CIA, you can tell them the truth. It's to keep the world's greatest soft drink up there as market leader. Besides, Bacardi doesn't taste as good on its own.

- ***Erythroxylum coca* variety *ipadu*.** Another coca variety which, until the last two decades, rarely interested traffickers because of its fairly low cocaine count. It is native to the Amazon basin and has been chewed by Indians there for aeons. The war on drugs and drug plantations by western governments has increasingly forced growers to look to *ipadu* and the Amazon as a safer, discreet source.

A DIRECT LINE TO THE PAST
There are two sources for the history of coca: archaeological (still somewhat patchy) – and written, which begins when Francisco Pizarro and his conquistadors

conquered the Inca in 1532. For many years the prehistoric archaeology of South America was dominated by a view that human occupation began well after 18000 BC, when an Ice Age Arctic land bridge allowed Asian migrants to colonize what are now Alaska and Canada. The theory was supported by the carbon dating of tools and weapons of the Stone Age Clovis people, whose cultures were widespread further south, to around 10000 BC.

Then, in 1977, discoveries at Monte Verde, southern Chile, by the American archaeologist Tom Dillehay turned all this on its head. Radiocarbon tests showed that much of the material he unearthed was laid down in 11000 BC, opening the possibility that hunter-gatherer people were living in the southern Andes as early as 31000 BC.

The Monte Verde tribe's religion was apparently important enough for labour to be assigned to the construction of a ritual temple. It had gravel footings, wooden stakes strengthening its walls and a central platform. Here Dillehay's team found remnants of medicinal plants (though not coca): an indication that the temple was used for healing ceremonies as well as perhaps ancestor worship.

The word coca is thought by many anthropologists to derive from khoka, which literally meant 'the plant' in the tongue of the pre-Incan Tiwanaku people. Centred on Lake Titicaca, this culture developed a highly efficient agricultural system in which raised beds and shoreline canals lengthened the growing season. For these farmers to christen coca *the* plant – as opposed to any old plant – gives some idea of their regard for it. Tiwanaku dates from at least the 3rd century AD, declining around AD 1000, and its legacy is the Quechuan language spoken by ten million people from Ecuador to Argentina.

By the time the Inca arrived on the scene, coca production had really taken off. The Inca were a remarkable people. They transformed themselves from a 12th-century minor tribe confined to a 30km (20 mile) radius of Cuzco, in Peru's Cordillera region, to become masters of an empire stretching for some 3,500km (2,175 miles) north to south and 800km (500 miles) east to west. And they achieved all this in under 100 years.

It was the eighth Inca (ie emperor) Viracocha who began seizing new territory in 1437. But it was his son Pachacuti, grandson Topa and great-grandson Huayna Capac who really caught the empire-building bug. By the time Huayna died in 1525 Inca influence stretched from what is now southern Colombia, through Ecuador and Peru and on to Bolivia, northern Argentina and Chile: a total population of anything up to 16 million.

Their power was rooted in natural aggression and superb organization. The fact that people worshipped the emperor as a living god certainly helped – no wishy-washy democracy here. Good communications across the empire were crucial: the four administrative areas were linked by a 24,000km (15,000 mile) network of stone roads, tunnels and vine suspension bridges. These were reserved for teams of state-appointed messengers capable of covering 400km (250 miles) per day. Food production was organized on rigid 'communist' lines, with government experts choosing crops, supervising irrigation, terracing and fertilization, and taking a share of the harvest to store in times of need. A healthy percentage of this would have been coca. In fact, coca was key to the whole shebang. It was the centre of religious life.

Inca religion regarded the leaf as divine and magical. Priests used it for offerings, chewed it during rituals (and in the presence of the emperor), burnt it to ensure its glorious aroma pleased the gods, scattered its ashes to keep the fertility goddess Pachamama happy and placed it with the dead to stop spirits returning to the land of the living.

Predicting the future was part of a high priest's job and if there was one thing Inca folk liked in a priest it was divination. Oracles were consulted over everything from sickness to criminal investigations and, most importantly, the timing of sacrifices. Conclusions could be drawn from simple rituals – watching the path of a spider in an upturned bowl – to messier ones such as inspecting the marks on sacrificed llama lungs. Inevitably, coca was right up there as a divination aid. Leaves would be flung into the air or thrown on to liquid and 'read' according to how they landed.

Young men from high-ranking families would sometimes undergo a fearsome initiation into manhood, which could involve flogging, racing and sparring. More commonly this rite of passage took the form of a simple race in which the final straight was lined by young women making suggestive quips and offering coca or *chicha* (weak beer). Finishers, or survivors, were rewarded with a sling and a coca pouch marking their emergence into manhood. Even today, one Colombian tribe still practises an initiation ritual in which candidates 'marry' the coca leaf.

Perhaps because of its special place in Inca society, some historians have argued that coca was restricted to an elite. There's no doubt that it was, literally, close to the heart of the Inca (emperor) himself, because the only object he ever carried was the coca pouch around his neck. Two emperors even named their wives after the leaf, using the sacred title *Mama Coca*. Only two other crops were credited with the *Mama* prefix: maize and cinchona.

Other important state officials would have been allocated coca rations as a perk or necessity of the job: priests, doctors, magicians, warriors, leaders of defeated tribes, memorizers of state records (the Inca never bothered with writing) and those fleet-footed messengers. This is not to say that ordinary people were banned from using it. Given that coca had been around for millennia before the Inca, this would have been a hopeless task. Besides, why ban it? Judging by the huge plantations in the Huánuco Valley and at Yungas in Bolivia, there was no shortage. Far more sensible to concentrate on controlling production and distribution, much in the style of the Chilean government before General Pinochet.

## OLD-STYLE CONSUMPTION

Traditional methods of consuming coca have continued unchanged since Charlie and co first got high. A user grabs a few leaves from his personal coca pouch or *chuspa*, wedges them between his teeth and cheek and starts working in a bit of saliva. Then he takes out his *iscupuru*, a gourd containing a concentrated, highly caustic alkaline like powdered shells or roots, and removes a smidgen with a stick.

This powder, known as *llipta* to the Indians, is then carefully pushed into the middle of the coca wad, raising pH levels in the mouth and increasing the speed with which cocaine alkaloids are leached out of the leaf wad. There's a bit of a knack to it. You're not so much chewing as occasionally manipulating the wad with your tongue to keep it moist and exposed to saliva. And one slip with your *llipta* and you've got an internal mouth burn that makes the world's hottest madras feel like cold yoghurt. To guard against this, Indian mothers introducing their children to coca will often 'mix' the *llipta* themselves before transferring it to the child's mouth.

The most obvious effect is that your saliva turns bright green. However, you tend not to worry about this because your mouth is already tingling pleasantly and your throat feels like it's having an out-of-body experience. You have no interest in food and you feel ready to hit the road running. It is by all accounts a far less intense rush than you'd get snorting a line in your neighbourhood club toilets, but because the coca is releasing alkaloids gradually this 'slow rush' persists for much longer.

There is, incidentally, a continuing medical debate about whether the South American chewer, or *coqueros*, are unreconstructed coke addicts or simply 'social' chewers – much in the way western medics will argue the toss about social drinking and alcoholism. Some say your typical *coqueros* has a daily intake of around 15mg, that's about the amount of caffeine in a strong cup of coffee. Others reckon it's closer to half a gram of pure cocaine, which in western street terms is a hefty habit. There are all sorts of sophistry in this kind of debate, but one thing is certain. To a *coqueros*, coca is as much a part of life as a cold beer is to a steel worker. Two different cultures. Two different drugs. Same outrage if anyone suggests a ban.

## COCA AND THE CONQUISTADORS
One of the great things about the Spanish (and if you were an Inca Indian there weren't many) is that their explorers in the Americas kept detailed diaries. These reveal fascinating early impressions of coca, including the one reprinted below, which was noted down during the fourth voyage of Christopher Columbus, who sailed from Cadiz in May 1502.

*The lieutenant went into the country with 40 men, a boat following with 40 more. The next day they came to the river Urisa, seven leagues west from Belem. The cacique [tribe leader] came a league out of the town to meet him with some 20 men and presented him with such things as they feed on and some gold plates were exchanged here. This cacique and his chief man never ceased putting dry herb into their mouths, which they chewed, and sometimes they took a sort of powder, which they carried along with that herb, which singular custom astonished our people very much.*

The Italian navigator Amerigo Vespucci was also baffled by coca. He came across it when he landed on the island of Santa Margarita, off Venezuela, in 1499, and was immediately revolted by the way its 'loathsome' people chewed it. In one letter, published five years later, he included the following report.

'They all had their cheeks swollen out with a green herb inside, which they were constantly chewing like beasts so they could scarcely utter speech: and each one had upon his neck two dried gourds, one of which was full of that herb, which they kept in their mouths, and the other full of a white flour, which looked like powdered chalk and from time to time with a small stick, which they kept moistening in their mouths, they dipped it into the flour and then put it into their mouths in both cheeks... This they did very frequently. And, marvelling at such a thing, we were unable to comprehend their secret.'

Others were more positive. In 1609 Garcilaso de la Vega's classic account of the history and conquest of the Inca, *Royal Commentaries of Peru*, carried a priest's account of coca medicine. 'Our doctors use it in powdered form to reduce the swelling of wounds, to strengthen broken bones, to expel cold from the body or prevent it entering, and to cure rotten wounds or sores that are full of maggots. And if it does so much for outward ailments, will not its singular virtue have even greater effect in the entrails of those who eat it?'

## THE COCA CONQUERORS

Vespucci was by no means the only European interested in this strange new world. Spanish adventurers were on the hunt for a fast buck – namely gold and silver – and they had the comfort of knowing that God was on their side. They knew this because the pope had given them the Inca empire back in 1493, in a way that only popes can. They therefore wasted no time in claiming vast territories for Spain and sending home horror stories of the unChristian cannibals and barbarians who passed for human beings. This in turn provided a sensible reason to kill as many as possible, a task the Spanish embraced with enthusiasm. Yet they were outnumbered by hundreds of thousands of Inca warriors. How did it happen? How could it happen?

In fact, the Inca empire was on borrowed time from the moment it first encountered white Europeans. The Indians had no natural immunity to the diseases imported by sailors – plague, smallpox and measles all probably figured – and, by 1527, something like 200,000 Inca had died. The Spanish were firmly in control: the only problem for them was to find something worth controlling. The rivers of gold they had expected to find were just not flowing and the only commodity the Indians really seemed to rate was this strange plant called coca.

## CHEWING OVER THE POSSIBILITIES

Coca did nothing for the Spanish. Chewing was a revolting habit and you couldn't export the stuff – even if a European market existed – because it rotted so easily. That said, they were never ones to pass up a business opportunity and it seemed there was very little the Indians wouldn't do for coca. Gradually the settlers saw there was good money in plantations. Production went through the roof and the chewing habit spread even further than it had under the Inca.

Meanwhile, some Europeans began following up old legends about mountains that were made of silver. All these leads pointed to one place, Potosí, in what is now southern Bolivia, a mining area abandoned by the Inca after volcanic rumblings convinced them that the gods were angry. The Spanish had no such fears and when silver was rediscovered there in 1546 it was boom time. Inside a year a new city had been founded and 7,000 Indians were soon digging away, removing 70 tonnes/tons a year. Contemporary records suggest that in 1549 the Spanish crown's one-fifth share was something around 40,000 pesos per week. Potosí expanded exponentially until, by 1611, it had a population of 150,000. Yet all the time the mines got deeper and the Indians worked harder. They needed something that would sustain them. Guess what they chose...?

In 1548 the miners of Potosí chewed their way through more than 1 million kg (almost 1,000 tonnes/tons) of coca. Most wanted to be paid in coca (hard currencies such as the peso were a mystery to them) and so plantations pushed up production to meet demand. Everyone was getting rich, especially the mine owners. They sold silver ore to the smelters and overpriced coca to their workers.

## HOLIER THAN THOU?

While Spain counted her cash, the Roman Catholic Church got increasingly stuffy about the coca business. The First Council of Lima in 1552 heard talk of the plant as the devil's work and a form of idolatry, and demanded it be banned. With a smooth bit of spindoctoring, Philip II's father, Charles I of Spain, absolutely agreed and absolutely refused. The Second Council had another go 15 years later, this time hearing that coca encouraged 'demonic influences' and made women infertile. Again the Crown looked the other way. By the time of the Third Council, Philip II had got the hint and agreed that the Church should take a 10 per cent cut of all coca sales. Suddenly priests were commenting on how useful the leaf was to labourers. And for the next 200 years coca and South America carried on pretty much as usual.

## THE BOFFINS TAKE A TRIP

In 1786 coca was classified by the biologist Jean Chevalier de Lamarck as *Erythroxylum coca*. Now scientists knew what it was. They just didn't know how it worked.

Biochemistry was, at this time, little more than pseudo-science. Biologists were beginning to look at the natural chemicals in plants as potential medicines; the hard bit was to isolate them. In 1803 the German apothecary FWA Setürner successfully extracted morphine from opium. Strychnine, quinine, caffeine, nicotine and atropine were discovered over the next 30 years and science began grouping these and other nitrogen-based organic compounds as 'alkaloids'. The problem with coca, as we already know, is that it was a nightmare to export. There was never enough good-quality leaf on which to experiment.

In 1859 the breakthrough came. The celebrated German organic chemist Friedrich Wöhler arranged for a colleague working in Peru to bring back a 13.5kg (30lb) bale of coca. He then handed this to one of his best students, Albert Niemann, who analysed it for his PhD. He washed the leaves in 85 per cent alcohol with a little sulphuric acid, distilled the alcohol to leave a sticky residue, separated this into a resin and shook that repeatedly with bicarbonate of soda. The end result was a palmful of small, rod-shaped crystals. As all the other alkaloids ended in 'ine' Niemann thought it right to follow suit. He named his compound coca-ine.

Niemann died the following year, aged just 26, not realising the magnitude of what he had done. Initially, neither did anyone else in the scientific community, but when word spread about an Italian doctor called Paolo Mantegazza, who enthusiastically published the results of coca experiments on himself, eyebrows were raised. Mantegazza's paper, entitled 'Coca Experiences', told how after a dose of 12g ($\frac{1}{3}$oz) he began leaping over his desk and felt himself 'capable of jumping on my neighbours' heads'. After 54g (1$\frac{1}{2}$oz), chewed over an entire day, he was really buzzing.

'I sneered at all the poor mortals condemned to live in the valley of tears while I, carried on the wings of two leaves of coca, went flying through the spaces of 77,438 worlds, each more splendid than the one before. An hour later I was sufficiently calm to write these words with a steady hand: God is unjust because he made man incapable of sustaining the effects of coca all life long. I would rather live a life of ten years with coca than one of 100,000 (and here I inserted a line of zeros) without it.'

Gradually, doctors began to suspect cocaine had its uses. Another self-experimenter was none other than Sir Robert Christison, 78-year-old president of The British

Medical Association. He told *The British Medical Journal* that during two 24km (15 mile) rambles, attempted with and without coca, he felt a huge energy boost when using the leaf.

'I was surprised to find that all sense of weariness had vanished and that I could proceed not only with ease but with elasticity,' he said. Later, Sir Robert told how, after leading some students to the top of a 1,000m (3,280ft) Scottish mountain, he had chewed a little coca for the return trip.

'I at once felt that all fatigue was gone and I went down the long descent with an ease which felt like that which I used to enjoy in the mountainous rambles in my youth,' he noted. '... The chewing of coca not only removes extreme fatigue, but prevents it. Hunger and thirst are suspended; but eventually appetite and digestion are unaffected. No injury is sustained at the time or subsequently in occasional trials.'

### THE FIRST COCAINE USERS

While the boffins were somewhat slow off the mark, big business quickly recognized cocaine's potential. Among the first entrepreneurs to exploit the mass market was a Corsican apothecary called Angelo Mariani, who in 1863 hit on the idea of mixing the drug with wine.

The taste was pleasant enough but the real advantage was that alcohol worked as a solvent, extracting cocaine alkaloids from the leaf. Soon everyone in polite society had heard of Vin Mariani.

## COCA UNDER THE MICROSCOPE

While all this was going on, science at last got its act together. A promising young Austrian research student called Sigmund Freud read about cocaine experiments carried out on Bavarian soldiers by a Dr Theodore Aschenbrandt. Aschenbrandt's idea was to look at military applications for the drug and, clearly, an army on wizzo marching powder would be, as early enemies of the Inca discovered, some army.

Freud clearly thought it was a wonderful drug (judging by the free samples he sent out to colleagues and friends) and he found it a great way to alleviate bouts of depression (of which he had many). However, it seems he loved it a little too much. The paper he produced later, 'About Coca', could almost have been written by a coke-head, talking of 'the most gorgeous excitement' shown by animals injected with the drug and referring to 'offerings' rather than 'doses'. It was not exactly scientific language.

## IT'S A KNOCKOUT…

Freud would go on to invent psychoanalysis and be generally considered one of the 20th century's most innovative – or barmy – thinkers, depending on your point of view. But the future of cocaine was entwined with the fate of a younger colleague, the medical student Carl Koller, with whom Freud had been cooperating in cocaine experiments. Koller was obsessed with finding better anaesthetics, particularly for eye surgery. Knocking out patients with ether was hopeless (a) because those in frail condition might never recover and (b) because in coming round patients often vomited violently, tearing fragile sutures.

Koller had noticed that when pure cocaine touched his lips it made them feel numb. He'd mentioned this to Freud with little response, but when another colleague casually remarked that the new drug 'numbed the tongue' realisation dawned. Koller dashed to a nearby laboratory and immediately conducted experiments: first on the eyes of a frog and then on his own eyes. He found that after applying a cocaine solution he could touch the cornea with a pinhead and feel nothing. On 15 September 1884 his discovery of the world's first local anaesthetic was placed before an astounded audience at the Heidelberg Ophthalmological Society's annual convention. One of medicine's most challenging problems had been solved by a mere 27-year-old intern.

Sigmund Freud was frustrated by Koller's triumph but he soon had more important things to worry about. That same year he was attempting to provide pain relief for his great friend Dr Ernst von Fleischl-Marxow, who had an excruciating nerve condition. Fleischl-Marxow had resorted to morphine to help him sleep and had become addicted. Freud offered him cocaine as an alternative. Inside 20 days, Freud reported later, all trace of the morphine craving had vanished while 'no cocaine habituation set in; on the contrary, an increasing antipathy to the drug was unmistakably evident'.

Of course, Freud was wrong. The morphine habit had simply been replaced by a cocaine habit, and in April 1885, barely a year after Fleischl-Marxow first tried the new drug, he was in bits and pieces. Freud discovered he was injecting a full gram of cocaine solution every day and suffered from fits and fainting. Worse, the patient experienced a horrendous physical ordeal in which he believed insects were crawling around underneath his skin. He would sit staring at an arm or leg for long periods trying to pinch one out. Fleischl-Marxow was, in fact, suffering hallucinations caused by cocaine toxosis: the dreaded 'coke bugs'.

To his horror, Freud realised that he had produced the world's first cocaine addict. He began warning friends that they should now be extremely careful with the samples he'd sent them. What he did not know was that Fleischl-Marxow had also created a piece of social history by inventing the 'speedball', a dose of cocaine and morphine (or heroin) taken simultaneously.

He found that the stimulant effects of cocaine worked well alongside the 'downer' offered by morphine and that this combination taken intravenously helped get him through the day. When Freud discovered the truth he hoped and believed that his friend would die in six months. In fact Fleischl-Marxow's tortured body held out for six more years. The fundamentally flawed belief that cocaine could be used to treat morphine addicts persisted well into the 20th century.

## BIRTH OF A GLOBAL BRAND

For a brief time, cocaine was viewed as a wonder drug, both by qualified doctors and the less-scrupulous quack-potions industry. It was certainly seized upon as a potential cure for morphine and opium use (a particularly serious problem in America where many Civil War veterans had returned to civvy street as junkies). An Atlanta pharmacist called John Pemberton was one of these addicts and in 1880 he decided to copy Mariani's idea of mixing coca with wine, producing his own uninspiringly named French Wine Coca. He marketed it as a general tonic and morphine substitute, and claimed it was regularly knocked back by 20,000 of the world's greatest scientists.

Things were looking good for Pemberton until 1885, when Atlanta's politicians banned all alcoholic drinks. Undeterred he went back to his laboratory and came up with a new concoction, mostly coca leaves and caffeine-rich kola nuts, sold through chemists as a concentrated syrup that buyers diluted with water or soda water. Pemberton needed a snappy trade name and by swapping the 'k' in kola for a 'c' he came up with something called Coca-Cola. Sounds vaguely familiar, doesn't it?.

The drink didn't take off as Pemberton hoped and after six years he flogged the rights to an ex-medical student called Asa Griggs Candler for $2,300 (£1,600). It proved good business for Candler. When he took over, sales stood at 40,000 litres (9,000 gal) of syrup a year. Ten years later, at the turn of the century, he was shifting 1.7 million litres (370,877 gal) and, by the time he died in 1929, his personal fortune had topped $50 million (£34.5 million). Most of this success was achieved without the aid of cocaine, removed from the drink in 1905.

## BAD MEDICINE?

Taking the coke out of Coke must have been a big commercial risk for Candler. The quack market had been awash with products such as Dr Don's Coca, Liebig's Coca Beef Tonic and Kumfort's Cola Extract. Because coca dried up the nasal passages it was mixed with snuff as a cure for hay fever and asthma: the first widespread use of sniffing to get a rush. You could buy wonderfully named preparations such as Dr Tucker's Specific or Anglo-American Catarrh Powder. There were cough drops, toothache remedies, chewing 'paste' (the Inca never got proper credit for that one) and even coca cigarettes 'guaranteed to lift depression'. Cocaine could be bought from chemists as a neat solution or even as pure cocaine hydrochloride or 'powder coke'.

As the market expanded, so the price at first increased. Drugs companies such as Merck in Germany, and Parke-Davis of the USA, saw prices per gram quadruple soon after Koller's discovery, to stand at $13 (£9). It couldn't last. More manufacturers flung themselves on to the bandwagon, there was oversupply and the price dropped. By the late 1880s, cocaine was so common that bar tenders were sprinkling it around liberally, what you might call Scotch with Attitude.

## THE MAN WITH THE PLAN

The reason for the explosion in production was simple. In the past the big drugs companies had faced the same problem as the early medical researchers. They couldn't get enough coca leaf. It couldn't be grown in North America or western Europe and exporting bulky good-quality leaves was both expensive and difficult. Parke-Davis decided it needed a man in South America to check out possible new options. It chose Henry Hurd Rusby, recent medical graduate, botanist and, most importantly, a man with a brainwave.

Rusby reasoned that it must be possible to make cocaine on the spot. Trouble was, he didn't have a state-of-the-art pharmaceutical plant handy. He decided to improvise to see if there wasn't an easier, simpler way to produce the drug. The method he hit upon – still essentially the same used in the industry today – involved soaking the leaves in acid, shaking up the muddy brown result in alcohol to extract the alkaloids, adding an alkali like sodium bicarbonate, scooping out the dirty-white paste (known as *pasta basica*, or basic paste) and drying it out. The paste is up to two-thirds pure cocaine, it is compact and easy to transport, and is quickly converted into the final product: cocaine hydrochloride. In Peru, a new cocaine boom was born – 350 years after the Spanish one – in which processing factories as well as coca growers played a key role.

## THE DOWNSIDE

Back at Coca-Cola, Candler wasn't so much worried by the competition as the fact that cocaine had side-effects. Side-effects were not good for business, particularly with the media homing in on a scandal. There had been a public relations disaster in 1902 when a court heard disturbing evidence that children were becoming addicted to the drink. Candler was having none of it and ordered cocaine to be removed from the Coke recipe. Meanwhile public unease was heightened by reports of hospital patients suffering from blackouts and convulsions and even dying as they received cocaine anaesthetics.

Health hazards were one thing, but when reports began to filter through of a link to violent crime, the Great American Public took a collective step backwards. The problem was that cocaine had become so easy to find that it was no longer the preserve of the filthy rich. People on limited incomes had got themselves habits they couldn't fund legally. What did they do? According to the government they robbed and stole to buy the drug, and they robbed and stole while they were high.

In March 1911 the head of America's anti-opium campaign, Dr Hamilton Wright, wrote to *The New York*

*Times* expressing his concern: 'The misuse of cocaine is a direct incentive to crime... It is perhaps of all factors a singular one in augmenting the criminal ranks. The illicit use of the drug is most difficult to cope with and the habitual use of it temporarily raises the power of the criminal to a point where, in resisting arrest, there is no hesitation to murder.'

This was bad enough. Next, some medical journals began reporting that 'the Negroes' in parts of the American South had become addicted to cocaine. Apparently many of them worked long shifts in the New Orleans docks and discovered that a sniff of that magic white powder they regularly unloaded allowed them to work longer and harder on less food. This was obviously fine with the dock management. Soon a vibrant drug market had sprung up, with local plantation workers also getting in on the act. By 1902 *The British Medical Journal* was telling how plantation owners had to issue cocaine rations to keep their men happy.

Soon the newspapers were on the case, with lurid reports of 'coke orgies', rapes and mass murders committed by blacks. One particularly ludicrous account was submitted by a police chief in Asheville, North Carolina, who told how a 'hitherto inoffensive Negro' had been driven mad by cocaine and pulled a knife. The officer placed his revolver over the man's heart and fired. He then fired a second shot into his chest. Neither of these bullets, claimed the cop, had any effect. The only thing that worked was to bludgeon that crazy Negro to death with a club. So he did and promptly headed off to buy a bigger gun.

Not for the first time in the history of this drug – and all drugs – propaganda was accepted as fact.

## KICKS FROM COCAINE...

At the end of the 19th century doctors, dentists and chemists accounted for a huge percentage of coke addicts. This was partly because they could get it easily, but they were also curious to check out its effects on themselves. There was a belief, held among some scientists even until the 1980s, that cocaine wasn't really addictive.

True, the early glut of production never developed into a national epidemic, but this wasn't because the drug was benign. The reality is that new US laws were restricting availability – by 1922 dealers risked ten-year prison terms – and the street price was creeping up. Soon, ordinary American users couldn't afford to acquire a habit. Besides, as the 1930s dawned there were cheap new stimulants appearing, which were legal and, apparently, harmless. They were called amphetamines.

The US cocaine market was perhaps ten years ahead of Europe's experience. Cocaine was still widespread in Paris (where half of all prostitutes were rumoured to be users), Barcelona, Madrid, Brussels, Berne and Rome. Germany, the world's biggest producer, had been ordered to cut back under the 1919 Treaty of Versailles, which ended World War I. The

Germans had been stockpiling supplies, however, and in a country economically devastated by war these inevitably filtered on to the black market. People saw coke as a way to escape the national depression. Dealers cashed in, often eking out a stash by mixing in additional impurities.

In London, the *Daily Mail* reported that the drug was widely used among the West End's professional classes (barristers, politicians, actors and showbusiness types). Members of this young, smart and wealthy set were said to meet in designated flats or houses for 'a few doses of cocaine and a night of revelry'. Here was an early sign of the shifting cocaine culture. People began to see it as a drug of the upper classes and the 'gay young things' (that's gay in the traditional sense) of 1920s London. Cocaine was getting arty...and marching upmarket.

## A KICK UP THE ARTS

Nowhere was this more obvious than in popular music and literature. One verse of the classic Cole Porter song 'I Get A Kick Out Of You' (covered in the 1980s by Roxy Music) opens with the words: 'I get no kick from cocaine'. After some subtle behind-the-scenes pressure – presumably to prevent apoplexy among conservatives – Porter's version was sometimes reworded 'Some get their perfume from Spain'. At least it rhymed.

The final line of a traditional blues song called 'Cocaine Lil' ran:

*They laid her out in her cocaine clothes*
*She wore a snowbird hat with a crimson rose*
*And on her tombstone you'll find this refrain*
*She died as she lived, sniffing cocaine*

And then there was the great 1930s blues classic 'Minnie The Moocher, which tells how the heroine 'fell in love with a guy named Smokey – she loved him though he was cokey'.

Fiction writers such as Agatha Christie and Dorothy Sayers both produced stories featuring cocaine addicts. Proust picks up the upper-class theme through his character the Vicomtesse de St Fiarcie, who destroys her good looks through overuse of the drug. The Russian-American novelist Vladimir Nabokov, whose best-known work was *Lolita*, once complained that his editor rejected a short story called 'A Matter Of Chance' on the basis that 'we don't print stories about cocainists'. But the biggest fictional coke addict of the age was none other than the world's greatest detective, that quintessential English hero Sherlock Holmes.

Holmes is first seen dabbling in the drug in *A Scandal In Bohemia*. Dr Watson tells how his friend alternates 'between cocaine and ambition', bizarrely attributing Holmes's drowsiness to his habit. This is probably because the author, Sir Arthur Conan Doyle, was not quite sure what cocaine actually does. He assumed that because it's an anaesthetic it must be a downer.

## HIGH IN THE HILLS

Music? Literature? It could only be a matter of time before Hollywood also became a player in the cocaine trade. In the 1920s the emerging film industry with its pantheon of rich, hedonistic celebrities was a lucrative marketplace for cocaine dealers. Americans already perceived movie stars as sex-and-drug crazed ne'er-do-wells and the Fatty Arbuckle scandal of September 1921, in which a young actress called Virginia Rappe died during a hotel party thrown by the silent screen comic, simply reinforced this view. In fact there was no proper evidence against Arbuckle, other than that he had consumed bootlegged drink in breach of Prohibition laws, but the popular press tried and sentenced him, and worked in a cocaine angle for good measure.

In fairness, making a link between Hollywood and cocaine was hardly wide of the mark. Arbuckle worked for Mack Sennett's Keystone Studios along with a young actress called Mabel Normand, who became embroiled in a high-profile murder case. She was ruined after being exposed as a cocaine addict with a truly awesome $2,000-a-month (£1,400) habit. Barbara La Marr, who starred alongside Douglas Fairbanks in his 1921 film *The Three Musketeers*, was said to keep a permanent stash of coke in her grand piano, using it to stay awake 22 hours a day (she later overdosed on heroin).

Good breeding made no difference. The acclaimed American actress Tallulah Bankhead, daughter of

Democratic party leader and House of Representatives speaker William Brockman Bankhead, told in her autobiography how she once mistakenly put cocaine solution in her eyes, mistaking it for eyedrops. When a friend at the New York restaurant urged her to call a doctor, Bankhead threw a wobbly. 'I put the cocaine in my eyes and I don't tell that to doctors or anyone else,' she fumed. She is also, famously, the source of the quip 'Cocaine isn't habit-forming. I should know, I've been using it for years.'

In the eyes of middle-class America, Hollywood was built on 'happy dust' and booze. There was a clampdown by the police and a feeding frenzy among the press, resulting in a marked drop in use. Even so, some stars wouldn't leave cocaine alone. America's first 'drugs tsar', Harry Anslinger, tells in his memoirs of the 'swashbuckling' actor who hawked himself around Europe trying to get the drug from doctors. This star – which only a blind Alaskan hermit would fail to recognize as Errol Flynn – claimed he needed the drug to cure everything from an inferiority complex to painful haemorrhoids. Flynn eventually admitted to Anslinger that he used cocaine to heighten sexual pleasure.

## COLOMBIA, COKE CENTRAL

Colombia had a long and lucrative tradition of smuggling, particularly luxury household goods, alcohol and precious stones. It was an undeveloped country with a long, remote coastline and easy access to the Panama Canal free-trade area. No coca or cocaine had ever been produced there but, hey, so what? If it was valuable and you could smuggle it, you could count the Colombian underworld in. Corruption was rife, drugs law enforcement negligible.

At first the Colombians simply set themselves up as middlemen, servicing both their Cuban and Chilean partners. Then they began to muscle in on their customers' territory, bidding for unrefined coca paste in Bolivia and Peru, cooking it up and distributing it across the USA. By 1970 the Colombian cartels had come from nowhere to challenge Cuban domination. Millions of young Americans revelling in the rebellion culture of the day decided cocaine was the new Big Thing: less dangerous than heroin or speed, more predictable than LSD, more exciting than marijuana and dead simple to take. Besides – and this was the clincher – it was supposed to take sexual orgasm to new heights.

Almost overnight – its image boosted by a plethora of rock songs and films such as *Easy Rider* – cocaine became easily accessible. *Rolling Stone* magazine declared it 'Drug of the Year' for 1970. *Newsweek* famously reported that 'orgasms go better with coke'. Students looking to make their fortunes worked out that you could buy a kilo (2¼lb) in Peru for $4,000 (£2,750), cut it, and sell it back home for $300,000 (£200,000). Oh, and in case there were any doubters one police narcotics chief told how cocaine produced 'a good high… and you don't get hooked'.

## THE DRUG LORDS OF COLOMBIA

The 1970s cocaine boom in America coincided with a major shift in production. Chile had always been a major supplier to the USA, but the coup by General Pinochet in 1973 was bad news for traffickers. Literally hundreds were rounded up and despatched on planes to America. It was Pinochet's way of saying thanks to the CIA for helping ease him into power.

Colombian drug barons moved quickly to full the vacuum. They had no shortage of muscle (the country was awash with guns after a civil war) and they were not afraid to use it, especially on foreigners and gringos trying their luck as cocaine smugglers. Soon any serious competition from American gangs was seen off, sometimes violently.

The leading cartels sent representatives to Bolivia and Peru to jack up coca production and ensure a steady supply. They bribed local cops and politicians to stop domestic interference. They also began sounding out Colombian nationals resident in America to see if anyone fancied making an easy buck as a distributor. The ex-pats usually did. Ever since Colombia's textile industry went belly-up in the 1960s there has been a steady stream of emigrants seeking a new life in the US of A. Unfortunately, that new life was uncannily similar to the old one: namely poverty and unemployment. For these people cocaine was a way out. They were well-placed to co-ordinate supply.

By the mid-1970s the minor players in Colombia had fallen by the wayside, often quite literally, courtesy of 100

.rounds or so from a machine pistol. There was vicious fighting between the Colombians and the Cubans (the latter coming a distinct second) but DEA agents noted with interest that there was not always all-out war between the big cartels. On the contrary, they sometimes struck alliances, combining shipments to share profits and swapping intelligence to guard against informers. The cities of Medellín and Cali became the centre of the cocaine business. Each had their own, notorious drug families.

In Cali, names in the frame included Helmer 'Pacho' Herrera, Jose Santacruz-Londono and several members of the Rodriguez-Orejuela clan. In Medellín one of the first high-profile gangsters was a former prostitute called Griselda Blanco, aka the Black Widow (on account of her three husbands who had been killed in drug wars). Her other nicknames included the Godmother, La Gaga (the Stutterer) and Muneca (Dollface).

## GRISELDA BLANCO

In 1979 Blanco was the best-known – and most feared – cocaine trafficker in the United States. Then aged 36, she had transferred the hub of her operation to Miami. She was attractive, flamboyant and tried to work wherever possible with other women, especially widows. Drug folklore has it that she even designed her own knickers with hidden pockets suitable for carrying coke stashes through customs.

Her gang was known as Los Pistoleros and she had several hundred names on her payroll. These hitmen were credited with inventing a crude, but effective, assassination method in which a motorcycle driver and pillion passenger would draw alongside their target car in a busy city street. The pillion man would then empty his machine pistol into the occupants and the pair would hightail it through traffic queues. But let it not be said that Blanco's killers were unimaginative. One was rumoured to tape shut the eyes and mouths of his victims, drain off their blood in the bath and neatly fold remaining skin and bone into old TV or hi-fi boxes.

Soon the DEA and the DAS (Colombia's equivalent of the FBI) were watching other major drug lords. There was Jorge Luis Ochoa Vasquez (the Fat Man), Jose Gonzalo Rodriguez Gacha (the Mexican), an underworld enforcer whose hobbies were – in order – violence, soccer (as in buying teams) and horses. There was the legendary Caribbean drug transporter known as Carlos Lehder. And then there was El Padrino (the Godfather), otherwise known as Pablo Escobar Gaviria. Together, these four were the brains behind the notorious Medellín cartel.

The DAS knew that rival traffickers would occasionally blow each other away, although they had no real conception of the term 'cocaine wars' until 22 November 1975 when air-traffic controllers at Cali spotted a light plane trying to land under cover of the radar clutter surrounding an Avianca Airlines commercial flight. Police arrested the two pilots and recovered 600kg (1,320lbs) of cocaine, then the biggest seizure on record. There was mayhem on the streets, with 40 gangsters wiped out in a single weekend. Curiously, all the killings were in Medellín rather than Cali. Medellín was declared cocaine capital of the world.

## EL PADRINO

The Medellín bosses were all ruthless, murdering, millionaire villains, but history will record Escobar (El Padrino, the Godfather) as the most successful. In fact, he was arguably the greatest criminal the world has seen. Born into a middle-class background (his mother was a teacher and his father a farmer) he left high school with enough wit and intelligence to run a legitimate business. Instead he started work as a hi-fi smuggler's enforcer and graduated to kidnapping (a growth industry in 1970s Colombia).

When in 1976 he was arrested in possession of 39kg (86lb) of coke the DAS believed he was merely a drug 'mule' or delivery man. This view rapidly changed. First, Escobar's arrest order was mysteriously revoked. Then the head of the DAS got a death threat. The two arresting cops were murdered along with their regional commander. The judge who ordered the arrest was murdered. A newspaper editor who wrote the story eight years later was murdered and his newspaper bombed. The moral of this tale? Don't bust Pablo Escobar Gaviria.

By the turn of the 1980s Escobar was wallowing in money.

A cool $500,000 (£345,000) per day according to some estimates, rising to $1 million (£700,000) a day by the mid-1980s. These kind of sums are not easy to spend but Pablo did his best. He bought 2,800ha (7,000 acres) of land east of Medellín, built a luxurious ranch complete with swimming pools and, obviously, mortar emplacements, and hung a Piper Cub light aeroplane above the entrance gate. Everybody knew, especially the drug agents, that this was the plane in which he had flown his first cocaine shipment to America.

Escobar didn't stop there. He bought dozens of wild animals, turned them loose in the ranch grounds and opened the place as a public zoo. He became Public Benefactor No.1 by building 500 houses in Medellín and giving them to poor families. He mended roads, built churches, wired in street lamps, paid for food wagons to tour poor estates and ensured that the residents got free private healthcare. Every year, at Christmas, he handed out 5,000 toys to underprivileged children. He even formed his own political party, called Civismo en Marcha (Good Citizenship on the March). In 1982 he got himself elected as a member of the Colombian parliament, a position that, under the constitution, guaranteed him immunity from prosecution.

## JORGE OCHOA

That same year Colombia was reeling under a new threat from a revolutionary Marxist group calling itself M-19. It was raising cash for the cause through kidnapping and on 12

November 1981 its terrorists abducted Marta Nieves Ochoa from outside Medellín's Antioquia University. This was a bad mistake. It was one thing to target industrialists and politicians. It was quite another to lift one of the five Ochoa sisters. Jorge Ochoa was suitably unimpressed and, within a couple of weeks, a summit of all the major drug cartels had formed a vigilante group known as Muerte a Secuestradores (MAS) (Death to Kidnappers).

Three weeks after Marta's kidnap, a light aeroplane banked gently over a crowded football stadium in Cali and dropped some leaflets announcing that 233 'businessmen' had formed the MAS to stamp out kidnapping. The wording of the leaflet suggested that Jorge and his mates weren't messing about: 'The basic objective will be the public and immediate execution of all those involved in kidnappings beginning from the date of this communiqué ... [they] will be hung from the trees in public parks or shot and marked with the sign of our group – MAS.'

The statement warned that jailed kidnappers would be murdered or, if this proved impossible, 'retribution will fall on their comrades in jail and on their closest family members'.

Within six weeks 100 M-19 members had been captured and handed over to the police. No one knows precisely how many were murdered, but judging by the speed with which Marta was freed, M-19 was clearly anxious to end this little spat. The word on the street was that the Ochoa family never did pay the $12 million (£8.3 million) ransom.

It looked as though Escobar, Jorge Ochoa et al were the unofficial rulers of Colombia. With their private armies and huge resources they feared no one. Occasionally there was an inter-gang feud but nothing they couldn't handle. As for the government, its efforts at drug control were barely even irritating.

ENTER THE ENFORCERS

Until, that is, in August 1983, when newly elected president Belisario Betancur appointed a determined young congressman called Lara Bonilla as his Minister of Justice. Bonilla recognized that drug money was destroying his country's economy because it required a vast black market to prosper. He began by asking awkward questions: how did Colombia's mega-millionaires make their money? Why did they need all those aeroplanes? Escobar's people tried bribes to keep him quiet, then death threats. But it made no difference; Bonilla publicly branded Escobar a trafficker and ordered his chief of police Jaime Ramirez to bust every cocaine laboratory in the country.

Ramirez was a rare jewel in Colombian law-enforcement circles. He was incorruptible. So when in 1984 he was informed by the DEA of a major cocaine plant deep in the Colombian jungle he organized an attack so secret that none of the police and army officers knew where they were going until they were actually in the air.

The DEA's intelligence was spot on, not least because their undercover people had sold a huge consignment of anhydrous ethyl ether – a key ingredient of the cocaine production process – to a Medellín cartel representative called Frank Torres. In with the ether barrels were some satellite beacons, and soon the DEA was analysing satellite photos of a 1km (0.6 mile) airstrip in the middle of nowhere. The photos didn't need much analysis. Neither did the amount of radio traffic beaming out of the place.

The lab was called Tranquilandia and once the Colombian SWAT team had seen off its guards they knew they had hit the mother lode. It looked like something from a James Bond set: a huge complex with quarters for guards, chemists, pilots and cooks; there were hot showers, flushing toilets, mains electricity and weapons stores; and everywhere lay thousands upon thousands of chemical drums. One logbook showed the place had processed 15 tonnes/tons of cocaine paste in January and February that year.

Ramirez's men also found a pilot's notebook containing a convenient map of labs in the area with radio frequencies. Over the next few days the raiders visited each of them: Cocolandia, where a tonne/ton of the drug was wrapped in waterproof packaging; Cocolandia 2 (500kg/1,100lb); Tranquilandia 2 (4 tonnes/tons); El Diamante (half a tonne/ton). Over the next fortnight Ramirez recovered 8,500kg (18,700lb) of pure cocaine and 1,500kg (3,300lb) of cocaine base. He seized seven planes, nine labs and

12,000 chemical drums. The whole shooting match was worth over $1 billion (£0.7 billion). Even by Medellín standards this was serious spondulicks.

Lara Bonilla rightly took the credit for the operation. He also knew he was a dead man walking. He told a journalist friend that he would be killed on 30 April 1984 and, sure enough, that afternoon two young hitmen hired by the cartel roared alongside his official car on a Yamaha motorbike – in classic Los Pistoleros style – and sprayed the back seat with bullets. Lara's bodyguards opened up immediately, killing one and injuring the other. But it was too late. Colombia had lost the one man truly capable of striking back at the drug lords.

President Betancur responded in a national radio broadcast at 3am the following morning. He described the drugs business as the most serious problem in Colombian history and pledged a 'war without quarter' against traffickers. Escobar and his friends weren't unduly worried. They'd heard this kind of stuff before. But Bonilla's memorial service wiped the smiles off their faces. During his address Betancur announced that, 'Colombia will hand over criminals wanted in other countries so that they may be punished as an example.' He got a standing ovation from the congregation.

Reintroducing extradition was a brave move. Escobar, Ochoa and their lieutenants knew that if ever they got hauled before an American court they would never taste freedom again. Bribes and escape plots would be useless. So, like

Betancur, the Medellín cartel also prepared for war without quarter. The result was an unprecedented level of bombings and killings on the streets, an increasing cycle of violence in which American diplomats, DEA officers and their families also became prime targets.

The country was now quite literally a war zone. At one point, anti-tank rockets were fired at the US Embassy and government tanks were deployed to end an M-19 terrorist siege at Bogotá's Palace of Justice. Almost 150 people died in the subsequent shoot-out. Judges, journalists and their families were threatened or murdered, and in 1986 the main cause of death for adult males in Colombia was not heart disease or cancer but murder. Shootings in Medellín alone were reported at an average of almost ten per day. In 1988 and 1989 it is estimated that death squads accounted for 40,000 citizens. And amid all this death and destruction, the Medellín and Cali cartels began fighting a turf war.

For the Colombian government the killing was too high a price. Extradition had to end. In 1990, after an election campaign in which three presidential candidates were murdered, Liberal Party leader César Gaviria Trujillo, was elected. Two months later his new constitution banned the extradition of Colombian citizens and Gaviria offered an amnesty to drug traffickers who turned themselves in. Pablo Escobar was among those who obliged.

He was sent to prison to await trial. But it was a funny kind of prison because, well, Pablo owned it. There was a health club, a marijuana plot, a disco, a motorbike scrambling track, chalets for entertaining women visitors – even an underground bombproof bunker. The prison 'cells' all had videos, TVs and hi-fis. Escobar had the telephones and fax lines he needed to run his business, and enjoyed the occasional trip to a soccer match – under police escort, of course. It was all quite hunky-dory, until he got too cocksure.

Perhaps to emphasize that he was still in charge, Escobar tortured and killed two former associates who had been trying to negotiate a reduction on the monthly $1 million (£700,000) 'tax' he'd levied on their cocaine trafficking. The police decided this was too much. Pablo should go to a proper prison. Inevitably, though, he was tipped off and in July 1992 simply discharged himself. He went into hiding in the heart of Medellín, moving from house to house and communicating from moving cars to prevent his phone calls being traced.

Had he not ordered those last two gangland killings he might have pulled it off. But now even Pablo's own people feared he was going insane. They wondered if he would turn on them next and some key aides defected to the Cali cartel – then headed by Pacho Herrera and the Rodriguez-Orejuela brothers – for protection. Now Escobar had not only the DAS, DEA and CIA after him but a new organization called Los PEPES (People Persecuted by Pablo Escobar). It was run by the Cali boys.

By November police mobile tracking units had pinpointed Escobar's phone calls to a 200 sq m (2,000 sq ft) area of the city. It was far too densely populated to surround, so they played a waiting game hoping his guard would slip. On 2 December it did. He stayed put rather than talk on the move and he spoke for six minutes, long enough to get a secure signal fix. Then he was seen at a window and commando-trained police moved in. Pablo was not the kind of guy to be taken alive. And he wasn't.

Escobar is now a distant memory, yet for Colombia's new cocaine kings the past decade has been business as usual. When you hear politicians talk of the 'war on drugs' they usually forget to mention that it's a war that patently isn't being won. Certainly not by destroying coca fields or raiding traffickers. Not by prosecuting dodgy chemical manufacturers and money launderers. Not by busting backstreet labs and dealers. Deep down, law enforcement agencies know and privately accept this. The cocaine trade abhors a vacuum and there'll always be someone willing to blow in and make a fortune. In reality, all the cops can do is make life tough for the bad guys.

Cocaine will always be in circulation. The question is, will it be in your circulation?

## COCAINE, SEX AND THE FEEL-GOOD FACTOR

If you've ever had a sexual orgasm you'll know how wonderful it feels. That's because your unconscious brain regards the reproductive act as the single most important thing you can do with your life. Forget global warming, democracy, human rights, scientific discovery, justice, racial equality and all the other great issues of the day. As far as your brain is concerned, pal, your number one duty is to get laid.

Unless, of course, you are a regular cocaine user.

### BETTER THAN SEX...

Dr Bill Jacobs, assistant professor of addiction medicine at Florida University's Department of Psychiatry, explains it like this: 'When you take cocaine you create an artificial stimulus to your brain's reward pathway. The pathway is there to keep our species alive: it's food, water, nurturing the young and especially sex. These are all natural rewards which turn on the reward pathways and tell us, "You did good, do that again."

'If those natural rewards turn on the pathway to a value of one, well, cocaine turns it on to a value of 1,000. That is just not a natural phenomenon. Our brains are not made to run like that. When you remove the cocaine you immediately start to fall from a much higher place.'

Aidan Gray, national co-ordinator for the UK charity Conference on Crack and Cocaine (COCA), describes the buzz in more colloquial terms. The former drug-project worker has specialized in cocaine since 1994 and is among Europe's leading authorities on its effects.

'Is cocaine an aphrodisiac? I'm not sure that's the right word. It certainly does increase anticipation and if you've ever been to a theme park like Disneyland and you're waiting for the big ride you'll know that sense of "Ohmigod! What am I doing?" That's your fight or flight response. It's where craving comes from. It's your heart beating, the funny churning in your stomach, the sweating – all that stuff. It is rooted in anticipation. Like at school when you have a first date with someone you really fancy, there's that strange giddy feeling. Anticipation and sex are very closely linked.

'The other connection is the brain's pleasure-giving neurotransmitters. There's a definite tick alongside cocaine's effect on dopamine and a lot of scientists think seratonin is also a factor. Cocaine works on reward. When you have lunch and you enjoy it you get a small release of neurotransmitters and that reinforces your behaviour. Your brain knows that eating is good for you.

'The biggest high from your brain's neurotransmitters is meant to be sex. That's your orgasm. When you are taking cocaine you are leap-frogging way over that. The brain mechanisms are very similar for sex and coke. So when you combine a sexual partner, a gram or two and perhaps a bottle of champagne you can see why people think there is an aphrodisiac effect. The pleasure is both physical and neurological.'

Dopamine, seratonin – let's face it, these aren't names to concentrate your mind as you snort a line or achieve sexual ecstasy (unless you are an unbelievably sad person). But neurotransmitters seem to be at the core of cocaine addiction, and the reason why taking the drug is so much fun. Thanks to scientists such as Dr Nora Volkow, we now know a lot more about them.

## ALL IN THE MIND?

During studies at the University of Texas, Houston, in 1984 Volkow noticed that the brains of cocaine users showed severe changes. She began photographing them using a positron emission tomography scanner, a process that involves tagging molecules with radioactive particles (positrons), injecting them into the blood and monitoring their voyage around the brain. She quickly discovered that cocaine has a special relationship with neurotransmitters such as dopamine.

First, what's a neurotransmitter? Imagine the wiring in your house. You switch on a light and because this completes an electrical circuit, the bulb is powered into life. Your brain also uses electrical circuits but it doesn't mess about with cumbersome physical connections. Instead it completes circuits by sending chemicals – neurotransmitters – from one nerve cell to another. This happens almost instantaneously. Neurotransmitters make your body perform physical functions – talking, sneezing, cutting toenails – but they also handle emotion and instinct for survival. Eating chocolate, taking a hot shower, drinking ice-cold beer in a heatwave, cuddling your kids and (especially) having sex: dopamine makes all these experiences feel good for various evolutionary reasons.

Dopamine messengers are being released into synapses (the spaces between nerve cells) all the time. But they don't hang around because your brain immediately sends out transporters to round them up and shepherd them back to their cells ready for next time. This is called re-uptake. If it didn't happen, your orgasm would last all afternoon and disturb your post-coital nap.

Cocaine uses sneaky tactics to disrupt this mechanism. It attaches itself to perhaps two-thirds of your dopamine transporters and disables them. The stranded dopamine keeps swirling around the spaces, or synapses, between nerve cells, and does its genetic duty by dispensing euphoric joy. That's your cocaine high and it will last for between 40 and 60 minutes, depending on the method of consumption.

What happens then is unpleasant. After attaching itself to a dopamine transporter the cocaine detaches fairly quickly (although traces remain in the brain for two to three days). If no more arrives the dopamine is duly rounded up, except now the process becomes much more rigorous. It's as though the brain is a fussy mother, angry that her kids have been out too long. Dopamine levels fall below normal – below the level they existed prior to cocaine intake – and, sure enough, that's your crash. The immediate urge is to take more cocaine, to 'binge' until either supplies run out or exhaustion takes over.

All this happens within your medial forebrain bundle, the structures of which are your frontal cortex, nucleus accumbens and ventral tegmental area. Most recent research has focused on what happens when dopamine leaves the ventral tegmental area and heads for the nucleus accumbens. In this area of the brain lie the roots of addiction. Scientists can argue about whether it's a physical or psychological addiction, but addiction it is. When you take cocaine regularly your brain physically alters.

The most obvious change is a drop in the number of dopamine receptors on nerve cells. With fewer receptors, those nerves are denied normal levels of stimulation and so pleasurable experiences other than cocaine no longer induce familiar feelings of 'natural' happiness. This is why some of Aidan Gray's clients preferred coke to sex.

For reasons not fully understood it seems that taking cocaine irregularly may sensitize some people (they become more responsive to the same dose). But regular use leads to tolerance and so more of the drug is needed to reach the same level as a previous high. Evidence suggests that, for regular users, dopamine receptors become permanently damaged and the brain never manages to restore them to pre-cocaine levels. This creates a huge problem for those seeking treatment because their desire for the drug is never quite diminished. They remember it as the only thing that delivered true pleasure. The best they can hope for is to resist their craving until enough dopamine receptors come back into play, allowing other things in life to feel pleasurable again.

According to Dr Volkow, the bingeing tendency may be caused by cocaine's ability to dabble in other areas of the brain, specifically the bits that tell us when we've had enough. This is our 'satiety' response. Volkow believes that in switching it off, cocaine ensures that users binge even though they know they will suffer at the end of it.

'Pleasure is a natural reinforcer to increase the probability that a species will engage in a given behaviour and continue that behaviour,' she told a National Institute on Drug Abuse research briefing in July 1998. 'Once these urges have been satisfied the body's normal response is satiety or "that's enough". When satiety is suppressed, the pleasurable properties of cocaine serve as a trigger for activating brain pathways that will then maintain the drug-consuming behaviour.'

Cocaine experiments on animals support this view, even though the behaviour of caged creatures is unlikely to mirror that of free human beings. In the 1960s researchers gave one group of laboratory rats unlimited access to heroin while another group got unlimited coke. Heroin is a sedative or 'downer' and so these rats tended to sleep more. Their consumption became routine and regulated. The cocaine rats on the other hand didn't stop self-administering hits until they became physically exhausted. They didn't sleep or eat and after waking from a collapsed state they immediately took more of the drug. They were all dead inside a month. The heroin rats by this time had developed a habit, yet groomed, slept and ate fairly normally.

There are plenty more examples of animal experiments that demonstrate cocaine's extraordinary power over brain function. In one case a chimp was trained to hit a bar to receive a single dose of coke. Once he'd worked this out, researchers began increasing the number of times he needed to hit the bar to get the same dose. The aim was to measure the addictive potential of the drug and scientists assumed there would come a point where the chimp had to press the bar so many times for his fix that he'd get bored and find something else to do. He didn't. They stopped the experiment after he pressed the bar 12,800 times for a single shot: 100 – 1,600 per cent more than for any other drug.

**WHAT'S THE CRACK?**

Ever wondered why you can't get hooked on nicotine quit-smoking patches? Why no one ever pleads with their neighbourhood pharmacist for 'just one more patch' to get through the day. After all, this is the same drug smoked by billions; the drug that is so seductive when inhaled. A patch contains as much as a few cigarettes. How come nicotine hooks you one way but not the other?

It's simple. The reason people like recreational drugs is that they crank up the pleasure centre of the brain. The more drugs you take the greater the pleasure rush, at least up to the point where you overdose. But, more importantly, it's the speed with which these drugs hit the brain that really counts. If you inhale them they go straight into your main blood vessels and you're in the fast lane to Pleasure City. If you snort, drink, eat or 'patch' them, then they have to trog around the back roads of your circulatory system before they find the freeway. The eventual rush will be more gradual and less intense, although it'll last longer.

This is the essential difference between a patch and a cigarette. It's also the difference between snorting powder coke and smoking crack cocaine. Because the high is more intense there's a powerful incentive to light up again as soon as the (equally intense) crash takes over. But before we tell the story of crack we need to know more about its parentage. That means a trip back to the

1970s and the amazing new wonder drug of America's *Easy Rider* generation. Cocaine freebase.

## FANCY FREEBASE?

When you sniff cocaine you're actually consuming cocaine hydrochloride (or cocaine salt). The production process for this has essentially remained the same since a young student called Albert Niemann discovered it while working at the University of Gottingen in 1859. Niemann washed coca leaves in alcohol and sulphuric acid, distilled off the alcohol and separated out a resin, which he shook with bicarbonate of soda. This substance was again distilled to produce the now familiar, rod-shaped white crystals.

A quarter of a century later, drugs companies discovered a simpler method, which could be carried out on-site in South America's coca plantations (avoiding the problems associated with exporting fast-rotting coca leaves). They dowsed leaves in acid, shook up the sludgy result with alcohol, added a strong alkali such as bicarbonate of soda and, hey presto!, basic paste or *pasta basica*. This is between 40 and 65 per cent pure and is still the form most favoured by traffickers. It is a rough mixture of contaminated cocaine compounds, which is designed to be further refined into cocaine hydrochloride higher up the trading chain. As paste it can be smoked because it vaporizes quickly when heated. Ordinary powder coke just degrades. Light it and you might as well burn money.

Now the freebase story gets a tad speculative and confusing. According to the world's leading authority on the history of cocaine science, the University of California's Professor Ron Siegel, here's what probably happened.

Around 1970 a pioneering American cocaine trafficker in Peru notices production workers puffing away at something they call base. He tries it, likes it and, back in the USA, he smokes a bit of his usual cocaine hydrochloride mixed with tobacco. But something is wrong. There's no big rush. So he calls a friend with some chemistry know-how and asks why base might be different. They check out a textbook and discover the definition of a chemical 'base'.

They establish that cocaine hydrochloride (cocaine salt) can easily be converted back to base form by removing the hydrochloride molecule. This involves adding a strong alkali and dissolving everything in a solvent, such as ether. The ether stage is a bit dodgy because the fumes ignite so easily, but once the cocaine dries and crystallizes out it's in a stable form ready for smoking. The amateur chemists call this 'freeing the base' or freebasing.

Their one error is to assume that what the Indians call base and what their textbook calls base are one and the same. Not so. What they end up smoking is close to pure cocaine, not some mishmash of coke-plus-impurities. In drinking terms it's the difference between a light beer and a similar quantity of 90-per-cent-proof Polish vodka. In other words, completely different.

By then, users and scientists alike had realised that freebase was a new phenomenon. Smokers developed bizarre traits, such as constantly staring at the floor searching for a mislaid bit of base. When sharing a pipe they would bicker like children over sweets. Siegel's book *Intoxication* tells how he usually had to provide lab monkeys with a reward to persuade them to smoke drugs. With freebase they needed no reward. One monkey would even try to lick the smoke she exhaled. When Siegel conducted tests on men who had never smoked freebase they spontaneously ejaculated, even though their penises were flaccid. Euphoria was being redefined.

Some cocaine dealers, such as the notorious Ricky Ross – aka Freeway Rick – of South Central, Los Angeles, began offering clients prepared freebase to save them the trouble of cooking up powder coke. Because freebase comes in chunks, and because Ross had natural marketing flair, he called his product Ready Rock. When demand went ballistic he bought and converted houses into fully equipped freebase factories. In 1982 he was processing 15kg (33lb) per week. Two years later production hit 50kg (110lb) per week. As his buying power increased, so the price plummeted: from $25,000 (£17,250) down to a low of $9,500 (£6,500) per kilo (2¼lb). From being an expensive, white middle-class kind of drug, freebase was suddenly available to poorer Hispanic and black communities. At his peak, Ross cleared profits of $100,000 (£70,000) a day.

As the *Los Angeles Times* reported on 20 December 1994, 'If there was an eye of the storm, if there was a criminal mastermind...if there was one outlaw capitalist most responsible for flooding LA's streets with mass-marketed cocaine, his name was Freeway Rick.'

There was another factor, though, for which Ross couldn't take the rap. As more people became familiar with freebase so they experimented with new ways to prepare it. Soon cooks discovered a method that avoided fiddling with beakers and dodging ether fireballs. They just heated ordinary coke powder in a solution with baking soda until the water evaporated. Dead easy. When this type of freebase was lit and smoked it made a crackling sound. If you were a drug dealer what street name would you have come up with?

## AMERICA GETS CRACKING

On 17 November 1985, *The New York Times* told the world: 'Three teenagers have sought treatment already this year...for cocaine dependence resulting from the use of a new form of the drug called "crack", or rock-like pieces of prepared freebase.' The media descended like vultures. Rightly or wrongly, 'crack' became the hyped-up horror story of the 1980s.

According to Dr David Smith at the Haight-Ashbury Free Clinic: 'When you snort cocaine you are actually snorting cocaine hydrochloride. With freebase you have an extraction process in which you "basefy" the drug, that is, you extract the hydrochloride using an organic solvent and you dry it. This lowers the vaporization point. When people talk about smoking cocaine what they really mean is vaporizing it. When you freebase, you heat the drug, vaporize it, inhale and you get a blood and brain level similar to an injection.

'With crack it's all pre-prepared. You don't extract it yourself or do any of that. The supplier mixes it with baking soda, which is the base, puts it in the microwave and then cracks off pieces – they call them rocks – to sell. That's one explanation for the drug's name. The other is that it crackles when you smoke it. Either way, it's the fast food of drug culture.

'The analogy I use sounds very simplistic but it gets the message through. Freebase is like a barbecue party. You have your barbecue pit and you go get a bun and a burger, you get all your condiments lined up and all your cooking utensils, and away you go. That's the kind of ritual the middle and upper classes follow.

'Crack cocaine is like going out for a McDonald's takeaway burger. It costs a lot less and it's all pre-prepared. We saw the crack-cocaine epidemic explode and it moved immediately into the lower socio-economic non-white populations. It was no longer a drug of the white middle class but of the lower-class black culture.

'With crack you buy a rock for $20 (£14) and away you go. It's a street drug and you can easily carry it around.

With freebase you've got to have all the equipment – which means paying out around $100 (£70) – and it requires a lot more skill. You have to be careful that you don't produce something that will make you lose perspective and burn yourself up like Richard Pryor.

'Crack has become very much a contributor to sexually transmitted diseases because of the prostitutes, the so-called "crack whores". They use crack cocaine repeatedly to the point that they are offering sex for a rock. They are in a cycle of drug use that, for many, is impossible to break.'

One Miami, Florida, user four months into treatment agreed to explain the lure of the drug. He was in real estate, young, wealthy and a former powder coke user. A business acquaintance showed him how to heat crack on aluminium foil and inhale the fumes.

'If you haven't experienced crack you can't know what ultimate pleasure feels like,' he said. 'It goes beyond any other human experience; you can't even begin to compare it to an orgasm. The first couple of minutes are a new level of consciousness. Your senses are alive in a way you cannot understand.

'After this you get maybe 10 to 15 minutes of feel-good feeling. Then you start to come down and it's a heavy down. You feel depressed big-time, tired and anxious. You know that the quickest way to deal with it is to smoke more crack and so that's what you do. And gradually the highs don't seem quite so high but the lows just keep getting lower. I did this on and off for six months and I was spending God knows how many hundreds of dollars. But at the time I wouldn't have said I was addicted.'

## A GUIDE TO THE SIDE-EFFECTS

The side-effects of cocaine fall into short- and long-term categories. Each of these can be subdivided into psychological and physiological effects. Sources for the information outlined below include America's National Institute on Drug Abuse (NIDA) website and Dr Mark Gold MD, distinguished professor at the University of Florida Brain Institute and a leading authority on addiction medicine (from both personal interview and published papers). While this section isn't really intended as 'A Spotter's Guide to Coke-heads', concerned friends and parents of users may find it helpful.

### POSSIBLE SHORT-TERM PHYSICAL AND PHYSIOLOGICAL EFFECTS

- A tendency to become talkative and energetic
- An apparent heightening of the senses, particularly sight, sound and touch
- A decreased need for food, water or sleep
- Dilated pupils, constricted blood vessels (the anaesthetic effect) increased temperature, blood pressure and heart rate
- Nausea, headaches and sweating
- Chest pain and breathing difficulties

- Urinary and bowel delay
- Large amounts (eg several hundred milligrams ) can trigger onset of tremors, vertigo, muscle twitching
- Large amounts – regardless of whether snorted, smoked or injected – can lead to acute overdose effects such as heart seizures and strokes

POSSIBLE LONG-TERM PHYSICAL AND PHYSIOLOGICAL EFFECTS

- Damage to the nasal septum, causing nosebleeds, sense of smell loss and the 'cocaine sniff'
- Total destruction of the septum (single-nostril syndrome)
- Irregular heartbeat – leading to heart attack (rare); caused by increased oxygen demand on the heart (stimulant effect) and decreased oxygen flow to the heart (blood vessel constriction)
- Temporary paralysis of a limb
- Aortic dissection – the lining of the major vessel carrying blood from the heart tears under increased blood pressure
- Burst blood vessel in the brain (stroke) caused by increased blood pressure
- Overcompensation for the anaesthetizing effect on vocal chords, causing permanent hoarseness
- Bulging eyes; gaunt appearance
- Heart valve disease (linked to needle users)
- 'Black lung' and severe phlegm (crack smoking)
- Increased risk of HIV/hepatitis C (see below)

POSSIBLE SHORT-TERM PSYCHOLOGICAL EFFECTS
- Intense euphoria, sense of well-being, total control over destiny – the 'Superman Syndrome'
- Increased libido (low doses)
- Decreased problem-solving ability
- Restlessness, irritability, vertigo and suspicion of others
- A sense of doom and being out of control (during the crash); feelings of anxiety and panic
- Obsessive behaviour – eg crack smokers picking at scabs or hunting for cocaine fragments

POSSIBLE LONG-TERM PSYCHOLOGICAL EFFECTS
- Coke 'bugs' – a form of cocaine toxosis in which the sufferer believes insects or snakes are crawling beneath his/her skin
- Hallucinations
- Dulling of emotions and feelings of 'natural' pleasure
- Intense paranoia; a mistrust even of family and friends
- Feelings of isolation
- Suicidal thinking and behaviour
- Feelings of impending death
- An (unproven) link to Parkinson's disease

SNIFFING OUT THE STATISTICS
In looking over this list it seems incredible that the 'cocaine is safe' lobby ever gets taken seriously. Measured in the numbers of deaths, you could perhaps argue that the drug

has a low mortality risk (which is not the same thing at all), but official drug-related death statistics don't paint the full picture.

In America, hospital emergency room deaths linked to cocaine are running at around 10 per 1,000, a figure that has remained fairly constant for a decade. In Britain, however, the number of cocaine-related deaths has risen alarmingly from 19 in 1995 to 87 in 1999. Is this because there were more users? Are post-mortem detection techniques better? Are coroners being more forthright in their conclusions? At the University of Florida's Brain Institute, Dr Mark Gold believes cocaine death rates are a poor indicator of the true problem.

'When you look at coroners' reports they often don't tell you precisely what the person died of,' he said. 'Maybe they want to protect the family, sometimes they don't have the right tests to make a diagnosis absolutely and other times they just don't bother reporting the detail at all.

'I'm sure there are people around who'll say that powder cocaine isn't really a problem. It would be very hard to find a professor in any faculty in the United States who agrees with that. If you look at the people who smoke and inject cocaine, they started by doing something. We've seen people here who have become addicted to drinking cocaine as a means of weight loss.

'That doesn't mean everyone becomes addicted. Nonetheless, the problems associated with this drug are very great. We've all heard stories of grandmothers who smoked for 80 years and never got lung cancer so it doesn't surprise me that people come up with single-case studies to show that cocaine is really OK.

'Here we have a drug which can hijack the brain, which in essence creates itself as the new drive state. Most experts would say that, particularly when smoked, its specific interaction with the reward circuitry is both unique and compelling. This is why when they take it people feel great, powerful, omnipotent, like the typical laws of nature don't apply to them. If you accept the original dopamine hypothesis you'd say that in the cascade of brain rewards cocaine comes closest to the endgame. It's the ultimate reward.'

He points out that the long-term effects of the drug are poorly understood. Heart problems, heart attacks and strokes are all under suspicion, but suspicion and proof occupy different medical galaxies. Even tobacco has only relatively recently been branded harmful by the Surgeon General – 300 years after it arrived in Europe. Gold says that the most common cause of strokes in young people used to be tumours and 'arterial venous malformations'. Now, according to new British research, the commonest causes are cocaine, amphetamines and ecstasy.

'We need more long-term research,' he said. 'Medicines are viewed by everyone as dangerous until proven absolutely and completely safe and effective. And so we let the pharmaceutical companies and governmental agencies do extensive tests. Everyone complains about how long this takes but you do need 10 or 20 years to bring a drug to market.

'Then you have the drugs of abuse, which are viewed by many as safe until proven dangerous. With cocaine there's no silver bullet to treat addiction. Some groups are looking at vaccines and we've been trying a pharmacological approach without great success. We've also treated addicts who are health professionals – doctors, nurses and the like – and in that setting we use group therapy and support. But if you compare the doctor who's an alcoholic with the doctor who's a cocaine addict, the outcome for the cocaine addict is worse.'

LOOKING FOR A CURE

The quest for a cocaine cure has made some progress. NIDA researchers have focused on dopamine, seratonin and another neurotransmitter – norepinephrine – to produce genetic clones of their various transporters. The hope is that drugs can be designed to chemically alter transporters so that they resist the attachment of cocaine molecules. This would prevent the euphoria of a coke rush. Another idea is to disrupt the mechanisms of cocaine and neutralize it in the blood before it even reaches the brain.

Alternative therapy is also making a case. A study of auricular acupuncture at Yale University, published in the *Archives Of Internal Medicine* journal (August 2000), involved the insertion of needles into the outer ears of 82 volunteer addicts. The group was treated for 45 minutes five times a week and, after two months, was tested for cocaine use. More than half the patients returned negative urine samples compared to 23 per cent and 9.1 per cent in two control groups.

Until a major breakthrough comes, most recovering addicts will have to make do with antidepressants and one-step-at-a-time group therapy similar to the process endured by alcoholics. The essence is to concentrate on avoiding cocaine for a day at a time – even ten minutes at a time – and to reject thoughts of tomorrow. Isolation from cocaine-taking friends and old haunts is key to the strategy because any reminder of coke can trigger its craving.

## THE UNPALATABLE FACTS

'When you're taking a drug you never want to understand the full consequences and dangers involved,' says Aidan Gray of COCA. 'It's pissing on the bonfire, it spoils the high. There's this strong image that powder coke is OK, it's pure, it's fine, but there's also this thing about the word "cocaine". I've come across people saying, "I just take cocaine. I don't do crack." Very often they are playing with words.

'There are a number of dance clubs where people openly do crack and freebase. Everyone calls it cocaine and technically, of course, they're right, it is. That's the term they've learnt. But this group is not getting any attention from drug agencies and neither are they getting independent information. I've worked exclusively with cocaine users longer than most professionals in this country – since 1994 – and what I've come across is incredible ignorance. There's been a load of initiatives in the UK on the dangers of heroin, safer use, all that kind of stuff. But there's been nothing like that for crack and cocaine.'

Gray's comments have massive implications for cocaine users everywhere. Over the years part of the drug's appeal has been that it is quick, clean and simple to take. In contrast, the AIDS epidemic has reinforced perceptions that needles represent a seedy, dangerous lifestyle. If you smoke or snort coke there can't be an infection problem with HIV or hepatitis C, right? Wrong.

'When you snort cocaine it damages the mucus membranes inside your nose, where the drug is being absorbed into the bloodstream,' said Gray. 'The more snorting you do, the more you damage the septum. When that damage is done your nose bleeds frequently. It's a classic sign of a cocaine user that they will blow their nose and produce fresh blood.

'Imagine you're at a party. There's a group of people ready to take cocaine and they're telling themselves, "This is a safe drug, it's not in the same league as, say, heroin." So there'll be someone drawing up the lines and that person will often be the first to take a snort. If he or she is a regular snorter you could have fresh blood at the end of the straw.

It's commonplace for the straw to be passed on, especially if it's in the form of a rolled-up banknote. There's some stupid thing about trust, about passing the note around the group.

'If there's another regular in the group then the chances are there'll be fresh blood to fresh blood contact. Hepatitis C, according to the latest tests from Australia, can stay alive outside the human body for up to three months. The risks are obvious. It's like sharing a needle, and of course injecting cocaine with somebody else's needle is another route for this disease to enter the body.

'The third route is smoking. People will quite often burn their fingers using a lighter. The type of crack pipe is important – some of them burn your lips or cut your mouth – and actually smoking crack cocaine dehydrates you a hell of a lot. One of the things you notice about someone emerging from a crack house is that their lips are really chapped. There's something about cocaine that makes people pick at broken skin or sores. They've got open weeping wounds on their mouths and they're passing around a crack pipe. Again, they can be passing on hepatitis C.

'Crack cocaine, because of the way it works on the brain, creates an incredible compulsion among users. You may know about the dangers but you ignore them. You get instances of people injecting cocaine and saying, "I don't care if it's a dirty spike; I don't care if you've got HIV. I just want my hit." That attitude is increasing. We have to wait and see what the impact will be on HIV and hepatitis C statistics among cocaine users. The tragedy is that – especially among the snorters – there are a lot of people out there unaware of the risks.'

Coke and HIV is a nagging worry for public health workers. Not just because cocaine offers the disease a route into the body but because of the biochemistry that unravels once it's there. A study by scientists at the University of California Los Angeles (published by NIDA, 15 February 2002) looked at the direct relationship between drug and virus and discovered a 'double whammy' effect.

The researchers took mice genetically bred to have no immune system and injected them with human cells. They then infected the cells with HIV, gave half the animals daily liquid injections of cocaine and the other half a saline solution. Ten days later they found that the cocaine mice had a 200-fold increase in HIV-infected cells coupled with a nine-fold decrease in CD4 T-cells: the cells HIV attacks to destroy its host's immune system. In other words, cocaine helps HIV to breed as it destroys the body's natural defence against the virus. Given that crack smoking and prostitution often go together, the implications are obvious.

Gray believes that governments and drug agencies should be doing more to identify cocaine addicts at an earlier stage in their illness. 'Part of the problem is that addicts do not come into services until they're in crisis,' he said. 'You'll see heroin users because they'll at least come in to get clean needles, and you can help them stabilize and manage their dependency. With crack and cocaine you'll usually see people only when the shit has really hit the fan, they're on the doorstep saying, "I need help and I need it now." We haven't got a lure to get them into services. We give out needles but we don't give out crack pipes. Maybe we should.'

Keeping cocaine addicts clean of the drug is now a huge industry. But while the theory of recovery is similar worldwide, the style can be worlds apart. If you're rich, boy can you enjoy therapy in style. If you're poor and readjusting in some backstreet halfway house, then humility is the word.

## REHAB… AT A PRICE

One of the world's newest and most luxurious rehabilitation clinics is Promises Malibu in California's Santa Monica mountains. If you log on to its website you'll find it set in stunning gardens fringed with palm trees. There are idyllic sandy beaches, tennis courts, a swimming pool and stables (where you can, naturally, experience equine therapy), and the chance to take guided walks in the hills. Lunch is created by a gourmet chef and celebrity guests such as Charlie Sheen and Robert Downey Jr can relax in the knowledge that their needs are serviced through a one-to-one ratio of staff to clients. The bill? Around $29,000 (£20,000) per month.

Inevitably, questions are being asked in the media. Under the headline 'Is Rehab A Rip-Off?' (14 April 2002), *The Sunday Times' Style* magazine pointed out that five-star country retreats are not absolutely crucial to recovery. Especially at that price. It quoted Nick Heather, professor of alcohol and drug studies at Britain's University of Northumbria, who suggested that luxury surroundings might even be counter-productive.

'There is a mountain of evidence to show that you get equally good results from outpatient treatment for one-tenth of the cost,' said Heather. 'People abuse alcohol and drugs in a particular social environment. Getting them to sit around talking about problems and then throwing them back into their old world, full of temptations and opportunities to relapse, is not helpful.'

'Ritzy rehab supporters argue that the clinics carry huge staff overheads and compare favourably in price with, say, a private heart bypass operation. Robin Lefever, a former addict who runs the £12,000-per-month ($17,500) Promis Recovery Centre in Kent, England, told *The Sunday Times*, 'I make no apology for it. I believe that your surroundings have an impact on the quality of your recovery. I know what it's like to come out of detox and be sent to a really grim halfway house: it's incredibly hard. Being relaxed and having time and the right atmosphere to think in is incredibly important.'

Perhaps both sides are right. All addicts are not the same and if you're a Hollywood superstar you might feel reluctant to shuffle along to Joe Public's group therapy session if there's a chance that fellow addicts will phone the press faster than you can say celebrity coke-head. 'Private hospitals have their place,' says Aidan Gray, 'though personally I think there's an assumption from richer users that because they're paying £2,000 ($2,900) a week they're getting the best service, which isn't true. In a way it doesn't matter. A big element in recovery is belief and if paying money allows you to have more faith in the process then why not?'

## THE MONEY LAUNDRY

Imagine you're a drugs baron, running cocaine from Colombia to wholesalers and street dealers in north-east America. You've contracted-out the smuggling and transport business to a Mexican cartel, which gets to keep a third of all consignments as payment. You've bribed a few police chiefs and politicians along the way and you've settled the pittance you pay coca growers. You're share is still $1 million (£700,000) a day in profit. But there's a problem.

All your income is in cash: small denominations handed over by cocaine users. The USA, along with most major western economies, insists that banks report any cash deposit of more than $10,000 (£7,000) under a process called Currency Transaction Reporting (CTR). Given that, according to the US Customs Service website (March 2002), the total American narcotics market is worth $57 billion (£39 billion) a year, and there are around 255 banking days per year, this would mean drug dealers depositing around $223.5 million (£154.2 million) per day. Even if depositors managed to make three drops a day without raising eyebrows, there would need to be 7,450 of them on the combined payroll. This is not the way drugs barons like to do business. It would be a turkey shoot for the DEA.

Depositing drug profits like this sounds farcical but, actually, isn't. When the cocaine boom hit America – and specifically Florida – in the late 1970s, US Treasury officials discovered an anomaly in their sums. Why was the Miami Federal Reserve Bank reporting a cash surplus of $5.5 billion (£3.8 billion) in 1979 – more than the surplus of the other 12 Federal Reserve Banks put together? The answer wasn't long coming. All over the state, Colombian couriers were handing in dollar bills by the bagful. Some even turned up carrying cash in supermarket trolleys.

The Bank Secrecy Act (which enforced CTR) temporarily halted this practice. Then DEA agents began reporting a curious new phenomenon in which dozens of cash couriers, each carrying amounts not dissimilar to $9,999 (£6,999), were being bussed around the banks on a daily basis. They looked so like caricatures – queuing to get off the bus, queuing to get in the banks, shoulder bags full to bursting – that the DEA nicknamed them after those much-loved cartoon characters, the Smurfs. To this day, 'smurfing' is the DEA's technical term for multiple deposits of drug money.

There are dozens of methods used to launder cash but they all involve three essential steps:

- getting the money into commercial financial systems,

    either through a bank or front company
- 'layering' that cash by moving it to different accounts (so obscuring the original source)
-   pumping it back into the economy as 'clean' money.

In theory, the simplest way is simply to export drug dollars in bulk to a country where banks have no CTR. The problem here is that $1 million (£700,000) in small denominations is not easy to conceal. Customs officers deploy the same techniques as in detecting drug trafficking, even training sniffer dogs to recognize the smell of money. Latest DEA figures show a doubling of currency seizures (up to $12 million/£8.3 million at a time) from $38 million (£26 million) in 1995 to $77 million (£53 million) in 1998.

    Given the risks associated with bulk shipments, some cartels set up legitimate businesses as cover. Flea markets and restaurants deal in bucketloads of cash and their legal earnings can easily be pumped up with cocaine money. Front or 'shell' companies (those that are registered but don't trade) are also popular, masquerading as art dealerships, precious-metal brokers, real estate, hotel and restaurant businesses or construction companies. Fake charities and even religious organizations have been used as dirty-money conduits and you could always buy a bank or corrupt its officials. But of all the methods employed by the cocaine cartels one stands out as a perennial favourite. It is the BMPE: the Black Market Peso Exchange.

According to the US Customs Service it works like this.

- Colombian drugs bosses export their cocaine and sell it to wholesale dealers for US dollars;
- They call in a Colombian-based money changer or 'peso broker', who agrees to exchange pesos he owns in Colombia for dollar bills owned by the cartel in America;
- The cartel has now laundered its profits into 'clean' pesos and can get on with the business of trafficking cocaine;
- The peso broker meanwhile uses American contacts to channel his drug dollars into the US banking system (some or all of the above methods will be used);
- Colombian importers seeking to buy US goods and commodities place orders through the peso broker. He again uses his American associates to make the purchases, paying with the drug money now nestling in legitimate bank accounts;
- Purchased goods – typically hi-fis and TVs, household appliances, alcohol and tobacco – are exported via Europe or the Caribbean, and then smuggled into Colombia, often through the Panama Canal free trade zone. The Colombian buyer avoids hefty state import tariffs and pays the broker in pesos. The broker, who has by now charged both cartel and importer for his services, then has more pesos to buy drug dollars.

So why is this a government problem? Black markets exist everywhere – not just in Latin America – and still life goes on. The answer lies both in the fragile state of developing economies, such as Mexico, Colombia, Peru and Bolivia, and in the astonishing amount of dirty currency swilling around the system. This is money that can't be taxed, buying goods that officially don't exist and paying wages that can't be traced. You don't need to be John Maynard Keynes to realise it's bad news for national treasuries.

## INVISIBLE EARNINGS

Take Mexico, for example. In 1997, before the recent government offensive against cocaine cartels, its drugs trade was worth $30 billion (£20 billion) a year: that's the equivalent of the rest of the country's gross national product (GNP) put together. The second biggest earner was the oil industry, which managed a mere $10 billion (£7 billion). By coincidence, $10 billion (£7 billion) was then the annual personal income of the drugs baron Amado Carrillo Fuentes who, you'll recall, died undergoing plastic surgery in July that same year (London *Daily Telegraph*, 18 October 1997).

Among the $800 million (£550 million) per year handed out in bribes was the purchase of unfettered air access for Carrillo's drug planes. According to one contemporary legend he would take an hour-long 'window' in Mexico's air-defence network and use it to fly through as many planes as he could, including a cocaine-laden Boeing 727. No wonder his nickname was Lord of the Skies.

Carrillo knew that his earnings were effectively keeping the Mexican economy afloat. He said as much in a letter to President Ernesto Zedillo dated 14 January 1997, which was later leaked to the press. 'Leave me alone to run my business,' it warned, 'otherwise I'll withdraw its benefits from the nation.'

US Customs officer Dean Boyd, who specializes in analyzing drug dollar laundering, believes Latin America is slowly accepting the need to challenge the economic muscle of the cartels. The BMPE, he says, acts like a parasite on a nation's wealth.

'This scam has been in place for decades; in fact, it pre-dates the drug trade altogether,' he told me. 'It is just about the largest money-laundering system in the western hemisphere and primarily sucks in Colombia, Panama, Venezuela and the United States. The only way to tackle it is for these countries to act together using every agency at their disposal. Our best estimates suggest that BMPE alone launders between $3 and $6 billion (£2 and 4 billion) every year.

'Colombia is well aware of the problem and has been for a long time because it directly affects that country's economy. It results in a huge quantity of lost tax revenue for them because, in effect, goods are smuggled in as contraband and no import taxes are paid. This has had a devastating effect on their treasury and they have really stepped up their efforts to stop it. It isn't easy because a lot of the goods go through the Panamanian free-trade zone. That can be hard to police. It is in the interests of the United States to help them because the end result is that our companies get paid in drug money. Nobody wants that.'

There is certainly plenty of US help.

OPERATION WIRE CUTTER

In September 1999 the 'El Dorado' multi-agency task force in New York launched an ambitious strike against Colombian money brokers with Operation Wire Cutter. This saw undercover Customs officers posing as American-based money launderers to penetrate the Caracol cartel on Colombia's north coast. Over several months they picked up drug dollars in cities such as New York, Miami, Chicago, Los Angeles and San Juan, Puerto Rico, wiring the cash to accounts specified by the brokers. As the net grew bigger both the DEA and Colombia's equivalent, the Departamento Administrativo de Seguridad (DAS), were called in to monitor the dirty money emerging as 'clean' pesos and then as smuggled goods in Colombia.

On 15 January 2002, the DAS arrested eight brokers in Bogotá to face currency charges in New York. Between them they had 50 years' experience in the money-laundering business and allegedly offered their services on a contract basis to several different cartels. More than

$8 million (£5.5 million) in cash and 400kg (880lbs) of cocaine was recovered. A further 29 people were held in various US cities (according to a USCS press release).

In a press statement released later, DEA administrator ASA Hutchinson said, 'By integrating electronic surveillance with investigative intelligence, US and Colombian officials tracked millions of dollars laundered through the Black Market Peso Exchange and arrested the principal money launderers involved in the conspiracy.' Colombia's US ambassador was equally chipper, describing the operation as 'a model for how other nations around the world will have to work together if we are going to be successful in shutting down global narco-trafficking and terrorist networks.'

Wire Cutter was a major coup, although no one is pretending that it will deter the cartels for long. 'All we can do is make it as difficult as possible for them to use the BMPE system,' says Dean Boyd. 'What's amazing is that the traffickers are prepared to lose so much of their profits to these brokers. If I'm a cartel boss down in Colombia and I have $10 million (£7 million) sitting in New York I'll happily sell that for $8 million (£5.5 million) worth of pesos.

'That's indicative of how lucrative the whole business is. If we can make the cost of laundering more and more expensive then we are getting somewhere. Part of our job is to make life difficult for these people and if we can make them try another system then that's a victory. One thing is for sure. Whatever else they do, they always want to get their hands on the money.

'Typically, when we mount a major operation to disrupt money laundering they go back to bulk cash smuggling. That is a risky situation for them. Carrying millions of dollars in cash weighs a lot; it's very unwieldy, difficult to transport covertly and our sniffer dogs are trained to find it. After we complete an operation we alert our people on the borders to expect more cash smuggling and, sure enough, it always happens.'

In Europe the system works in exactly the same way, with drug money converted into various national currencies and cleansed through the purchase and smuggling of black-market goods. Life may prove harder for the money launderers in future because the introduction (and inevitable adoption) of the euro as a European-wide currency will make wire transfers more transparent. Until that time comes there's always Liechtenstein as a safe haven for dodgy money.

## HAVEN IN THE HILLS

This little Alpine statelet has long been famous for its secretive banking, lax regulation and negligible tax regime. That's why crooks such as the disgraced (now deceased) British publisher Robert Maxwell liked doing business there. But in January 2000 a report by Germany's Federal Intelligence Service (FIS) painted an alarming picture of the extent to which the 160 sq km (62 sq mile) principality has courted mafia bosses and drug barons, including our old friend Pablo Escobar. Through its 'cyber-spying' division, the Bundesnach- richtendienst (BND), the FIS claimed it had hard evidence that underworld figures across the world had been tapped up by men in suits from Liechtenstein.

It described meetings with the 'financial managers of South American drug clans' over many years and highlighted 'a network of relationships between high-ranking officials, judges, politicians, bank managers and investment advisers, who assist each other with illegal financial transactions on behalf of international criminals.' The German news magazine *Der Spiegel* was rather more blunt: 'The secret document reads like the worst nightmare,' it fumed. 'An entire country in the middle of Europe appears to be in the service of criminals from all around the world. The findings destroy once and for all what was left of Liechtenstein's battered reputation.'

It should be said that in the wacky world of drug money, Liechtenstein doesn't have a monopoly on battered reputations. For all its talk of consensus and multinational approaches, the White House has an undistinguished record of playing fast and loose.

## PANAMA SPAT

The politics of cocaine never fail to dog the US when it blunders into South America. In Panama, their bête noire was one Manuel Noriega, a particularly loathsome bully who had been protected from child rape charges to rise to the top of the Panamanian armed forces. Panama had a reputation as a drug smuggling and money-laundering centre, but the Americans tolerated Noriega because he seemed to be on the right side. After all, Panama was acting as a pipeline for Contra guns...

Noriega was playing a dangerous game. He allowed Colombia's Medellín cartel to build a huge cocaine laboratory in the Darien jungle, accepting something between $2 and $5 million (£1.4 and £3.5 million) in bribes. He also permitted the cartel to channel coke through Panama on payment of a $1,000 (£700) per kilogram (2¼lb) tax. Things started to go wrong when Panamanian army officers heard whispers about the Darien laboratory and staged a major raid to shut it down. The Medellín bosses are rumoured to have responded by sending Noriega a gift-wrapped coffin. The White House was more restrained but began to see clearly the monster it had helped to create.

As the 1980s rolled on, Noriega lost the plot completely. He had his main political opponent assassinated for publicizing the drug deals. He was accused by his second-in-command, General Robert Diaz, of stuffing ballot boxes to secure re-election. Stupidly, he began targeting US citizens in Panama as suspected illegal aliens. And, really stupidly, he hinted that American access to the Panama Canal might not be guaranteed.

By the time Panamanians began street protests demanding Noriega's removal, Washington was on the case. On Wednesday 20 December 1989, the US military launched

Operation Just Cause against a man Senator Jesse Helms described as 'the biggest head of the biggest drug-trafficking operation in the western hemisphere'. More than 24,000 airborne US troops invaded Panama with the intention of bringing back Noriega to stand trial in Florida. Unfortunately, they couldn't find him straight away because he was busy in a brothel in Tocumen.

Soon after the invasion, Noriega tipped up at the offices of the papal ambassador in Panama City demanding sanctuary courtesy of the Catholic Church. The building was surrounded by US Special Forces, who spent a sleepless festive season blitzing the building with loud pop music. Noriega emerged on 3 January 1990 and was brought to Florida for trial. He was found guilty and will remain in jail for the foreseeable future.

You might think the lessons of Panama and Nicaragua would deter the White House from dabbling further in cocaine politics. You'd be wrong. The big three coca countries – Colombia, Peru and Bolivia – are all taking Uncle Sam's dollar as an incentive to restrict cocaine production. The hard statistics trotted out by the White House ONDCP seem encouraging.

LIES, DAMNED LIES AND ...
On 22 January 2001, ONDCP director Edward Jurith revealed that coca production had dropped 33 per cent in Bolivia and 12 per cent in Peru over the previous 12 months.

Over five years the harvest was down even more dramatically: from 94,400ha (233,200 acres) to 34,200ha (84,500 acres) in Peru and from 48,100ha (118,800 acres) to 14,600ha (36,100 acres) in Bolivia. At a press conference, Jurith presented this as a major victory.

'Bolivia and Peru have demonstrated a sustained commitment to counter-drug efforts,' he said. 'Their ability to sharply reduce coca cultivation illustrates that a long-term commitment and a solid strategy bring positive results. We look forward to continuing to work with their governments towards further reducing illicit coca production. These successes underscore that when political will is combined with comprehensive alternative economic development and the rule of law, drug cultivation and production will plummet. This is also our objective in Colombia, where Plan Colombia envisions a 50 per cent reduction in coca cultivation in five years.'

Sounds like bad news for the cartels, doesn't it? America taking the war on drugs to the enemy; being proactive instead of reactive; preventing a white wave of cocaine from breaking over its people. Doing something must surely be better than doing nothing, right? Let's probe Jurith's statement a little further. Let's start with 'Plan Colombia'...

This is a $1.3 billion (£0.9 million) military package introduced in 2000 by President Clinton to help the Colombian army destroy illegal coca plantations, fight cocaine trafficking and target rebel guerrillas in the country's heartlands. Over two years the Americans have provided more than 100 Black Hawk and Huey 2 helicopters, and hundreds of US troops acting as trainers and advisers. This intervention was a bold policy, which the European Union and most of South America refused to back.

European leaders were concerned that Colombia's appalling record on human rights had not been addressed. The 12 South American presidents (some of whom represented nations with equally grim records), meanwhile, reckoned that Plan Colombia missed the point altogether. At their August 2000 summit in Brasilia they argued that the USA should reduce market demand for cocaine, restrict the chemicals used in its production and do more to help peasant farmers grow different crops. Venezuela, Ecuador, Peru and Brazil all tightened security along their borders with Colombia, fearing a refugee crisis and a spill-over of military action.

In February 2001 the US Army delivered an interim report claiming that the coca destruction programme was going swimmingly. Nearly a quarter of Colombia's plantations had been destroyed in two months of aerial fumigation. However, commanders were cagey about the remaining three-quarters, most of which are in jungle territory controlled by the powerful left-wing guerrilla group FARC (the Revolutionary Armed Forces of Colombia).

Since 1999, FARC has effectively governed a 3.8 million ha (9.4 million acres) 'de-militarized zone', offered by President Andres Pastrana in a desperate attempt to end the country's debilitating civil war. Known unofficially as Farclandia, the world's newest nation, it includes some of Latin America's most productive coca plantations. The problem for the USA is that FARC fills its war chest with drug money. It taxes paste makers and has set itself up as a monopoly buyer of coca leaf.

According to *The Sunday Telegraph* (3 September 2000), FARC earns around £600 million ($870 million) a year from cocaine. It controls 70 per cent of the coca fields and sets the price (around £700/$1,000 per kilo/2¼lb of leaf). Although it has other methods of fundraising – Farclandia law 002 states that anyone worth more than $1 million (£700,000) must hand over 10 per cent for the rebel cause – it needs the drug trade for its political ambitions. It is unlikely that American crop-eradication helicopters will be invited in to spray a genetically modified anti-coca fungus. As General Fernando Tapias, head of the Colombian armed forces, told the newpaper: 'There will be peace. But first there will be war.'

FARC is not the only player in Colombia's coca market. Its sworn enemy, not counting the government, is the Self-Defence Forces of Colombia (AUC), which controls some 7,000 right-wing paramilitaries based around the bustling market town of Puerto Asis. This is also good coca country, with around 60,000ha (148,000 acres) devoted to the leaf. Predictably, the AUC is equally cautious about its cash crop being zapped by US chemical sprayers. According to one peasant farmer in the region, Jose Sonza, 'the paras [AUC] are offering 2.4 million pesos [£800/$1,160] for a kilo of coca base whilst the guerrillas in the jungle [FARC] only pay 1.8 million [£600/$870]' (London *Daily Telegraph*, 24 August 2000).

The reality is that Plan Colombia may actually be fuelling coca production and cocaine prices elsewhere. On 17 February 2001, the British Broadcasting Corporation (BBC) carried a report on its website that began, 'Fears are growing that Peru could soon regain its title of being the world's number one cocaine supplier. It is because of the huge US-financed anti-drugs operation in neighbouring Colombia.'

This report went on to reveal that new coca fields had been sighted in south-east Peru. It quoted the UN Drug Control Programme representative, Patricio Vandenberghe, who predicted that a shift in coca production from Colombia to its neighbours was a 'logical move'. A UN investigator, Humberto Chirrinos, said Peruvian farmers were being lured back to the industry as leaf prices rose 100 per cent: from $2 (£1.40) to $4 (£2.80) per kilogram (21/4lb) over the second half of 2000. This is basic economic stuff. Restrict supply of a desirable commodity and – everything else being equal – buyers will pay more.

AN UNWORKABLE SOLUTION

As the world's 'boilerhouse' economy, the United States knows all about wealth. What's not so clear is whether Jurith and the White House have got to grips with the politics of poverty. The idea that all South American coca farmers can switch seamlessly to new crops subsidized by US dollars is not credible.

Sanho Tree is a fellow of the Institute of Policy Studies (IPS), a respected Washington DC think-tank that prides itself on 'unconventional wisdom to public policy problems'. Tree heads the IPS's Drug Policy Project. He is scathing about White House claims of success in the coca fields.

'The eradication programme is absolute folly,' he told me. 'It doesn't take into account how much land there is for potential cultivation, nor does it appreciate the reserve army of the poor, the people who are prepared to defy the US and take a risk on growing coca.

'The bureaucrats are concerned only with Congressional mandates such as how many hectares have been eradicated in a year. They can't see that crop eradication is actually a great form of price subsidy. It takes a lot of coca off the market and ensures a high price for everything that's left. This is essentially what we're doing when we pay American farmers not to farm legal crops such as soya beans and maize.

'In countries like Bolivia, eradication has had a quite brutal effect on local people. This is because no money or thought is put into alternative development – or indeed any basic development. Bolivia is the poorest country in Latin America and it is now suffering great social upheaval.

'We have taken a relatively peaceful country and pushed it to the brink of civil war. Civil war isn't quite the right description because one side is well armed and the other has virtually nothing. But the *campesinos* [coca farmers] are now starting to ask, "Where can we get guns, we can't take this any more." They've tried peaceful protests, they've been shot at, they've been killed, and they are told to go and grow other crops that no one wants.

'The idea has been an utter failure. The United States asks peasant coca farmers to switch to fruit, which they must transport in vehicles they don't have, down roads that don't exist, to sell in markets with no buyers. Even if there were customers the idea that the *campesinos* could compete in an international global economy is truly farcical. They wouldn't stand a chance.'

But peasant farmers are not all angels. They are allowed to grow coca for 'traditional use' and the White House is surely right to suspect that some of it reaches paste makers for conversion into cocaine. Again, Tree is unconvinced.

'Even if some legally grown coca is ending up in illegal markets – and I don't see much evidence yet for this – getting rid of it is not going to make any difference,' he said. 'Certainly not in terms of reducing street cocaine in the USA, which is ostensibly what eradication is supposed to be all about. Colombia's output is more than adequate to make up the difference and in Peru they're already replanting. The whole policy is a horrible failure.

'In Colombia FARC is now forcing farmers to grow coca whether they want to or not. Our interference there is actually helping to increase cultivation. FARC will fund their war no matter what it takes. They don't have a choice. I'm really not sure what the US government expects here.

'There is growing alarm in Congress about the transition from a counter-narcotics mission in Colombia to counter-insurgency and now to counter-terrorism. A lot of Congressmen are prepared to go along with the global war on terror because they're afraid to oppose it. But it is worrying that both parties, the Clinton administration, and even the Bush administration until recently, had promised the American people: "Don't worry, we're not getting sucked into this four-decade-old civil war. We're just fighting drugs." And now suddenly we're protecting an oil pipeline and we're fighting guerrillas and we're not looking at mission creep* any more, we're looking at mission gallop.'

Kathryn Ledebur agrees. As co-ordinator of the Andean Information Network in Cochabama she spends her time highlighting 'US folly' in Bolivia's coca fields. She says the American eradication programme – 'Plan Dignity' – has been anything but dignified since it began in 1997. Instead there has been an escalating series of conflicts, culminating in the deaths of ten coca growers and four members of the security forces between September 2001 and February 2002. More than 350 other farmers have been injured or detained.

* military term for the way in which politicians expand clear military objectives into a range of complex ones

BITTER HARVEST

'The plan has targeted the very poorest people in Bolivia, the peasant farmers who grow coca leaf for survival,' said Ledebur. 'It doesn't significantly attack high-level drug traffickers or money launderers. The Bolivian government has eradicated huge amounts of coca in the Chapare [one of the main growing regions] but promises of alternative crops and employment are proving slow to deliver. As a result, levels of poverty and malnutrition in an already poor tropical region have soared.

'This is the first time the Bolivian military has ever taken a role in anti-drug operations. We have a country that has been democratic for less than 25 years and, at a time when we should be strengthening that democracy, we are instead creating strong, well-funded roles for the Bolivian military. There are conscripts who have to pull up the coca and there's a huge military police presence in the Chapare. This has led to a series of violent conflicts, many involving the so-called Expeditionary Task Force, which is a very strange group funded almost exclusively by the USA. These people are non-military; they are hired hands working under military command and they have been implicated in some of the most serious human rights violations to have occurred.

'It is true that nothing will be able to replace the income from coca in the Chapare but, as stipulated by the law, there needs to be something that provides an income for 35,000 families. What we've seen by aggressive US eradication is that they have pushed coca production around the Andean region. You have these big advances in Bolivia – it's heralded as the great anti-drug success – and yet Colombia is easily filling the gap in the market and Peru is planting again. We're actually seeing a net increase in the amount of coca grown and no noticeable impact on the price, purity and availability of cocaine on American streets.

'There is going to be a permanently funded US military presence in the Chapare. It will cost $10,000 (£6,900) a day to keep this force and that's roughly the cost of building a school. There is no exit strategy here. The farmers have no alternative, so they replant coca leaf. Governments say that justifies a military presence. The coca gets pulled up by the military, the farmers replant and so the cycle goes on.'

These views are echoed by peasant farmers across the Chapare. One, Zenon Cruz, told the London Guardian (25 August 2000) how he had been forced to grow beans and oranges instead of coca. Plan Dignity meant that he and his family had to live on a fraction of their former income. 'My father sowed coca and his father sowed it before him,' he said. 'What the Americans do not understand is that this leaf is a gift from mother earth to our people, an ancient tradition. They do not understand its sacredness. They think it is all about drugs.'

More pragmatically, he added, 'You can fill a lorry with oranges and not sell any of them at market. But coca always sells like hot bread. I was making 150 bolivianos [about £20/$29] a week before they cut down the coca. Now we sometimes struggle to make 20 [£3/$4.50]. How can you feed a family on that?'

Another farmer, Celestino Quispe, was interviewed by BBC news in La Paz in June 2000. Reading his words you can't help but question the standard western government propaganda that brands everything about the drugs business evil. Quispe patently isn't evil. Like most parents, he's just trying to do his best for his kids.

'Coca is a means of survival for us,' he said. 'Because the soil is very tired, very eroded. Coca leaves are the only option we have for earning a living to feed ourselves and our families. We can't substitute it with other products like citrus fruits or coffee. Citrus fruits are very cheap. There are supplies sitting there rotting. I would not be able to feed my family by growing citrus fruits.

'Coffee is annual, whereas I can harvest coca leaves three times a year. It does go down in price sometimes, but we always manage with coca. True, we have to replant every five or six years because the soil has to be renovated. But we can earn a living. You get much more money from coca leaves than you do for oranges. It's a very big difference in price. And oranges are heavy, so by the time you've paid for the transport to get them to the market there is nothing left for the producer.

'I have five children. Coca leaves allow me to pay for

their education. My children are able to study, which I was not. I have little choice in what I can do for a living now but I am trying to make sure that they get qualifications. I would like for them to be able to choose what they want to do in the future. An education is very important because it will give them choice: they will be able to decide whether they want to grow coca like me or do something different, something better.

'Also, remember that coca leaves are not all bad. They are not only used to feed a habit. Coca leaves are also medicinal and a source of a traditional, legal beverage. There are no *cocalero* [coca grower] drug addicts. It is the gringos who have processed the coca leaves with chemical products as a drug.'

This is the argument now being drummed into a new generation of Indians. When families in Bolivia's fertile Yungas valleys gather to make their traditional offering to Pachamama, the earth goddess, they sprinkle coca leaves and alcohol on the ground next to burning incense. Their children then sing in Quechua:

> *Green coca you are born of our land*
> *Your fragrance makes us sing happily*
> *In the fields among the mountains*
> *My little coca leaf is sweet medicine*
> *Not a drug that does damage*
> *We suck your juices for help in our work*

For the poorest of rural Indian families, coca offers comfort in a harsh world. The irony is that their much-loved leaf – worth so much in the world's wealthiest nation – has never, and will never, rescue them from poverty. That's the sad thing about the cocaine business. The few who get rich are ruthless murdering bastards. Most of the rest stay poor.

BROKE ON COKE
Here's some food for thought. In 1969 the White House ONDCP spent $0.65 billion (£0.45 billion). By 1981, Ronald Reagan's first year as president, this had risen to $1 billion (£0.7 billion). In 1999, under Bill Clinton, it had reached $17.1 billion (£11.8 billion). This is serious money even by US Treasury standards. And still, every 30 seconds, someone in America is arrested on drug charges.

One in five inmates in a prison is there for a drug offence. Almost two out of three Federal prisoners are serving time for drugs. The total annual cost of keeping drug violators locked up is around $8.6 billion (£6 billion). Counting the ONDCP budget, that adds up to $25.7 billion (£17.7 billion) a year to 'control' drug use. God alone knows how much this increases if you factor in time spent by police, DEA, US Customs, the Coast Guard, Army, Navy, Air Force and assorted ranks of government bureaucrats. If you were running America would you call this drug control? Only if you were as high as a space cadet. (The above statistics were cited in *The Social Impact Of Drugs And The War On Drugs*, Professor Craig Reinarman, IPS May 1999)

Now relax. We are not about to plunge into the dreaded quicksand of social science. Besides, any argument that there's some neat and squeaky-clean answer to recreational drug use is absurd. No country has ever won a war on drugs, except accidentally when it happened to be fighting a proper war at the time. Even then success proved to be short-lived. As for decriminalization...no, I can sense you glazing over. However, cocaine's relationship with crime, poverty and – especially – racism in the USA is interesting. We know how scare stories of the early 20th century shaped hysterical legislation (remember the indestructible 'cocaine nigger'), but what's really scary is the way US courts still see poor, black, crack cocaine users as more deserving of harsh punishment than rich, white powder cokers. Scarier still is the view among many black community leaders that this strategy is right.

In the USA, sentences in crack cases are far longer than those for powder-coke offences. Smuggling or dealing 100g (3½oz) of powder attracts the same penalty as an offence involving just 1g of crack (cited, again, in Prof Reinarman's report). Why so? It's the same drug. Crack is more popular in poor neighbourhoods (because it's cheap), but you can't start banging people up for longer just because their drug of choice happens to be popular. On that basis just about every American citizen would end up doing 12 years for marijuana offences. There is an argument that crack is more addictive, and more likely to provoke street crime, but then converting powder to crack is a cinch anyway.

Dr David Smith at Haight-Ashbury Free Clinic (HAFC) in San Francisco despairs of the 'lock 'em up' fraternity. 'I have found that politicians and public officials are often wrong but never in doubt,' he says. 'They will stand up and say, "You can't treat crack-cocaine addiction. That's why we have to put them in jail." Well, actually, we have large numbers of successes with crack cocaine.

'Early intervention is the key. If you criminalize the drug, then this becomes so much harder. You can't tell some politicians that because they just want to lock up all the drug addicts. We are talking penny wise pound foolish here. If as a society we don't pay straight away we will surely pay later.

'We have a fundamentally racist system in that we put all the black crack addicts in jail and all the white cocaine addicts in treatment centres. There's been an increased government emphasis on criminalization and a decreased emphasis on early-intervention programmes such as at HAFC. I actually don't include San Francisco in this because we're almost a different country as far as drug treatment goes. We have a much broader base of support for our efforts.

'Europe needs to learn from America's experience. We need to share this globally and understand the dynamics of drug culture. There is so much uninformed opinion that serves as a basis for policy. These epidemics and why they happen and what we can do about them: this all needs to be studied in an objective, professional manner.'

## CLASS DISTINCTION

In May 1999 the Institute for Policy Studies looked at the class-and-crack issue as part of its Citizens Commission on US Drug Policy, held in Los Angeles. These hearings brought together senior judges, law professors and prison reformers to take evidence from experts. One of the witnesses was Franklin Ferguson Jr, a black civil-rights attorney.

'This problem begins not with race but with class,' he said. 'Like a range of other crimes past and present the drug trade consists of consensual transactions that take place within organized sales and distribution networks. These networks tend to segment by economic class. The rise of crack in the 1980s produced a class divide in the cocaine market that was unusually visible.'

He then listed the 'retributive' factors that have persuaded judges in cocaine cases to be tougher on poor crack smokers and dealers than they are on rich powder snorters and dealers.

'The former are certainly perceived to cause greater social harm than the latter and therefore seem to deserve harsher treatment,' he said. 'Lower-class criminal markets tend to be more violent than their upper-class equivalents, at least in terms of the manner in which our society typically measures violence. It is easier to catch and punish sellers and buyers in lower-class markets than it is to catch and punish their higher-end, white-collar counterparts. The lower-class markets are eminently more visible. Lower-class constituents simply possess a much lower expectation of privacy, in direct proportion to their possession of land and property. This does not, however, justify the practice.

'Many have come to believe that because whites disproportionately use powder cocaine while blacks disproportionately use crack cocaine, a two-tier system of punishment has developed. The disparity between the amount of powder cocaine and crack cocaine required to warrant the same penalty for drug trafficking is 100 to 1.'

Ferguson quoted figures showing how the legal system's crusade against crack had significantly increased the proportion of black prisoners in US jails. In 1997 the prison population was estimated at 1,725,842, 51 per cent of whom were African-Americans. Yet African-Americans made up just 13 per cent of the total US population.

Of the 2,100 federal prisoners doing time in jail for crack, 92 per cent were African-American, compared to just 27 per cent of the 5,800 federal prisoners sentenced for powder coke. Finally there's the 'killer' fact that sentences in crack cases 'average three to eight times longer than sentences for comparable powder offenders'.

In his evidence Ferguson said, 'Even amongst staunch advocates of the black urban poor community there is support for this apparent disparity in enforcement. The crack trade destroys not only those who engage in it but also the neighbourhoods in which it takes place. Those neighbourhoods are filled with predominantly honourable black citizens who do not buy and sell crack. These citizens...may benefit from sentencing and enforcement policies that target crack relative to other drugs since crack's residual, often violent, criminal activities are simultaneously targeted.'

In other words most black people living in areas rife with crack dealing don't care that the majority of arrests involve other blacks. Nor do they care about hefty sentences. They just want these people run out of town.

Naturally, politicians notice this mindset. Nobody, they tell themselves, ever got kicked out of office for talking tough on drugs. Locking up crack users is easier to sell to the voters than funding new treatment centres. Crack cocaine is good for scare stories and scare stories are good for talking tough. QED: lock the bastards up.

## SNOUTING OUT A SCAPEGOAT

This brand of political logic was addressed by Prof Reinarman, professor of sociology at the University of California, Santa Cruz, at the 1999 LA Citizens' Commission hearings. There he delivered a paper entitled 'The Social Construction Of Drug Scares', which among other things considered that old election chestnut: the scapegoat. Scapegoating was defined by Reinarman as 'blaming a drug or its alleged effects on a group of its users for a variety of pre-existing social ills that are typically only indirectly associated with it'. Reading his paper you realise that, with some half-decent spin doctoring, absolutely anything can be blamed on drugs.

'To listen to the Temperance crusaders,' said Reinarman, 'one might have believed that without alcohol use America would be a land of infinite economic progress with no poverty, crime, mental illness or even sex outside marriage. To listen to leaders of organized medicine and the government in the 1960s one might have surmised that without marijuana and LSD there would have been neither conflict between youth and their parents nor opposition to the Vietnam War. And to believe politicians and the media in the past six years is to believe that without the scourge of crack the inner cities and the so-called underclass would, if not disappear, at least be far less scarred by poverty, violence and crime.

'There is no historical evidence supporting any of this. In short, drugs are richly functional scapegoats. They provide élites with fig leaves to place over unsightly social ills that are endemic to the social system over which they preside. And they provide the public with a restricted aperture of attribution in which only a chemical bogeyman or the lone deviants who ingest it are seen as the cause of a cornucopia of complex problems.'

The truth is that crack cocaine is directly linked to poverty, both for those who grow it and those who take it.

But it's not the cause of crime and poverty in the ghetto any more than powder cocaine is the cause of fraud and wealth on Wall Street. The distinguished Harvard law professor Derek Curtis Bok once famously observed that 'if you think education is expensive, try ignorance'. Ignorance breeds poverty. Ignorance of cocaine breeds addiction.

## ADDITIONAL INFO

**COCAINE: THE NEXT HIT**

Cocaine will always be with us. It's better than sex (at least, that's what it tells your brain) and about as easy to ban. Given that it can't be uninvented, expunged from the face of the earth or chemically altered to be user-friendly, the only issue is how to manage its presence. The smart-arse answer is to try anything that hasn't already proved a failure. The overall result may not be a triumph, but it is hard to see how things will be worse.

In political circles buzz phrases like 'blue sky thinking' and 'thinking outside the box' are trendy at the moment. Like all the best doctrinal clichés, they have wonderfully flexible meanings. Even so, the clear impression delivered to voters is that shibboleths are OUT, creativity is IN and no idea is off-limits. As politicians, police officers and editors raise the stakes in the war on drugs, we're seeing new initiatives taken up like nose candy at a Wall Street executive's leaving party.

Among the most radical of these ideas supported, worryingly, by both the liberal left and rabid right, is the decriminalization of 'hard' drugs. This book hasn't touched on this subject, because 'decriminalization' is an offensively bureaucratic word and the arguments for and against it are tediously polarized. The same applies to the debate on making drugs legally available over the counter. Let's get this over with quickly.

DOUBTS ABOUT DECRIMINALIZATION

The three big advantages cited in favour of legal use are:

- the market for drug trafficking would collapse;
- the police would be able to focus on other crimes;
- users could be properly monitored and educated.

Sure, a few dealers would struggle on, undercutting state prices or offering something that bit stronger. But the real drug money would be gone for good. Coke use would be up front and manageable.

Unfortunately, from what we know about cocaine, there are moral and practical problems with these arguments. For a start, who's going to decide when a crack addict has had enough crack? Certainly not the addict: he or she will want to smoke until death intervenes. Of course, you may feel that crack-heads have a right to decide to die this way. But are they really deciding? As Jodie, a former crack user puts it, 'People talk about using cocaine as a question of personal choice but, eventually, choice is denied you.'

Then there's the dilemma of younger users. Do we say coke is OK at the age of 18, 16, 14 or 12? What's wrong with a five-year-old trying it? Who decides on 'safe' purity levels? As soon as you dilute cocaine or make it off-limits to anybody you instantly create a new black market. Maybe not so big, but still there. That means more trafficking and more policemen hunting traffickers. As for making powder coke legal but continuing to proscribe crack – please, do pay attention at the back there!

BACK IN THE REAL WORLD…

Assuming that cocaine will always be with us and always be recreationally illegal, what might world governments usefully do? They could help America eradicate coca crops, making life harder for producers and traffickers. Harder, sometimes, but also more profitable (remember, destroying coca supports its market price). And not as hard as the life facing peasant farmers for whom coca is the only practical means of survival. Crop eradication as it stands is becoming more discredited by the day.

Perhaps the war on drugs could be intensified. More gunships and attack helicopters, more soldiers and armed agents, more nifty electronic surveillance, bigger rewards for informers…all could inflict serious damage on the trafficker. But not all traffickers. And when you've hit so many that cocaine supplies become scarce, up goes the price and in comes a new generation of millionaire coke kings.

There's the laughingly named deterrent factor, of course. This means locking up drug users and dealers for long stretches. It's great news for prison officers seeking job security but a real bummer for the rest of us who pay the bills. Drug users get to use more drugs in prison. Traffickers on the outside cheer loudly because the competition's out of action. As for the deterrent factor, there's not been much success there in half a century.

Finally there's that old favourite in the politician's armoury: the scare tactic. This essentially involves middle-aged, stressed-out people telling young carefree people that having fun is no good for them. All right, they can have fun reading or listening to music (quietly) but certainly not doing drugs. Alcohol doesn't count because lots of middle-aged, stressed-out people enjoy the odd drink.

Scare tactics never work in the long term. The classic response of parents to the first big wave of cocaine use that hit in the 1980s was to tell their children:

- 'You don't want to know about this';
- 'You will do yourself harm if you try it';
- 'We will do you harm if you try it'.

Funnily enough, these responses pretty much reflected US government policy. Telling young people that cocaine will either kill them or get them jailed is not a sensible plank on which to base an entire policy.

Most studies suggest something like 80 per cent of powder-coke users never report health problems. Users themselves aren't stupid. They know this. What they really need is clear, unbiased information about the true level of risk to the best of current knowledge. How much more effective would it be for governments and the mass media to put health risks into perspective. But then 'drugs', 'politics', 'media' and 'perspective' are not words that sit easily together in the same sentence.

As in most things, balance is the key. It's probably right to reduce coca crops as long as farmers are offered a realistic new living. It's right to lock up murderous traffickers and dealers, but sensible to keep addicts out of jail and in publicly funded treatment centres. It's right to stress the dangers of coke and also to accept that many users never become ill or addicted. If we are going to fight a drugs war let's at least stop truth becoming the first casualty.

Next time you're introduced to Charlie, by all means enjoy his company. But don't arrange to meet regularly. He can be so two-faced at times.

# The Little Book Of **COCAINE**

## ABC OF STREET NAMES FOR COCAINE

(Note that this is not a definitive list; new street names are emerging all the time.)

Angie

Aunt Nora

Base (used for cocaine and crack)

Batman (also used for heroin)

Bazulco

Bernie's flakes

Big bloke

Big C

Bolivian marching powder

Bouncing powder

California cornflakes

Carrie

Cecil

Charlie

Cholly

Double bubble

Dream

*Esnortiar* (Spanish)

Everclear

Flake

Florida snow

Foo foo

Friskie powder

Gift-of-the-sun-god

Gin

Girl

Happy dust

Heaven

Her

Icing

Jejo

Jelly

King

Lady

Late night

Love affair

Mama coca

Monster

Movie star drug

Nose candy

Oyster stew

Paradise

Pearl

Pimp

*Polvo blanco* (Spanish)

Quill (also heroin; methamphetamine)

Ready rock (crack cocaine)

Roxanne

Scottie

She

Sleigh ride

Snow/snowbird

Speedball (cocaine/heroin mix)

Teenager

Teeth

Thing

Toot

Whizbang (cocaine/heroin mix)

*Yeyo* (Spanish)

Zip

## GLOSSARY

Alkaloid – mind-altering nitrogen-based organic compound found in many drugs, including cocaine

Balling – vaginally implanted cocaine

Base crazies – people who search on their hands and knees for cocaine/crack

Based out – crack or freebase user unable to control usage

Beiging – chemicals that alter the appearance of cocaine to make it look as if it is of purer quality than it actually is

Bipping – snorting heroin and cocaine simultaneously

BMPE – Black Market Peso Exchange (method of laundering drug money)

Body packer – smuggler who swallows packets of cocaine

Break night – staying up all night on a cocaine binge

C joint – place where cocaine is sold

Campesinos – coca leaf farmers

Chalked up – under influence of cocaine

Chuspa – coca pouch carried by leaf chewers

CIA – America's Central Intelligence Agency

Cocaine hydrochloride – chemical name for powder coke; sometimes called cocaine salt

Cocalos – coca leaf plantations

Coke bar – pub or bar where cocaine is taken openly

Coke bugs – form of toxic psychosis in which cocaine addicts believe insects or snakes are crawling beneath their skin

Cooking up – processing powder coke into crack

Coqueros – coca chewers

Crash – feeling of dismay/depression that follows the cocaine 'high'
   or 'rush'

Cutting – process in which powder coke is chopped into lines using
   credit card or razor blade; process of diluting cocaine with other
   substances, eg glucose

DEA – America's Drug Enforcement Administration

Dopamine – chemical messenger in brain closely associated with
   euphoric feeling produced by cocaine

Drive-by shooting – popular gangland assassination technique in
   which the gunman opens fire from a moving car

Drug dollars – money earned through illicit drug sales

Flame cooking – smoking cocaine freebase by placing the pipe over a
   stove flame

Freebase – powder coke converted by chemical process to a
   smokable form

Gak-blowing – taking cocaine anally

Ghostbusting – searching for any white particle in the conviction that
   it is crack

Hash – cannabis or marijuana

High – euphoric feeling produced by cocaine

Horning – inhaling cocaine

Iscupuru – container, often a gourd, containing llipta, an alkaline
   substance (see below)

Line – powder coke laid out ready for snorting

Llipta – alkaline, such as lime or powdered shell, used to leach out
   alkaloids from coca leaf during chewing

Los Pistoleros – assassination technique in which the gunman sits as pillion passenger on a motorbike; the favoured method of Colombian cartels

LSD – lysergic acid diethylamide – potent hallucinatory drug

Mule – smuggler who carries drugs in the body or in luggage

Neurotransmitter – chemical messenger that allows brain cells to communicate with each other

NIDA – National Institute on Drug Abuse (US research organization)

ONDCP – Office of National Drug Control Policy (based at the White House, USA)

Paste – crudely processed cocaine, often in brick form

Reinforcer – brain mechanism that urges that an action be repeated

Reward pathway – method by which the brain decides that an action is good and should be repeated; sex, food, warmth and child-rearing have strong reward pathways – none of these is as strong as a cocaine habit

Rock – piece of crack cocaine

Rock starring – sex with a man/woman who takes crack cocaine as payment

Rush – euphoric feeling produced by cocaine

Satiety – brain mechanism that decides when an enjoyable experience should end

Septum – area between nostrils, sometimes destroyed by prolonged cocaine use

Seratonin – chemical messenger in brain linked to euphoria caused by cocaine use

Shebanging – mixing cocaine with water and spraying it up the nose

## The Little Book Of **COCAINE**

Smurfing – laundering drug money by depositing large quantities of
   cash in banks

Spliff – cigarette containing crack cocaine

Stone – piece of crack cocaine

Synapses – spaces between brain nerve cells in which cocaine causes
   build-up of dopamine and consequent euphoria

Taxing – process in which one drug gang robs another

Yardies – general description for Jamaican underworld gangs

## COCAINE: A LINE THROUGH TIME

Prehistory: Andean Indians discover properties of coca

12th century AD: Rise of the Inca; coca established as a key element of religious life in South America

1502: Columbus expedition makes contact with coca-chewing Indians

1532: Francisco Pizarro's private army invades Peru

1546: Spanish rediscover the silver mines of Potosi; paying miners in coca leaf becomes more widespread

1552: Roman Catholic Church makes first attempt to ban the 'evil' herb coca

1609: Contemporary accounts show that the Church is getting a slice of coca profits and no longer makes a fuss

1786: French biologist Jean Chevalier de Lamarck classifies the leaf as Erythroxylum coca

1859: Research student Albert Niemann extracts the cocaine alkaloid from coca, so 'inventing' cocaine

1863: Vin Mariani – a wine containing cocaine – is launched to wide acclaim in Europe

1884: Sigmund Freud begins experiments with the drug

1884: Freud's student colleague Carl Koller discovers cocaine's use as a local anaesthetic

1884: Freud tries to cure morphine addiction in his friend Ernst von Fleischl-Marxow by administering cocaine

1885: Fleischl-Marxow becomes the world's first coke addict

1885: American John Pemberton comes up with a cocaine drink syrup he calls Coca-Cola

1905: Amid mounting public concern, the Coca-Cola company removes cocaine from its drink

1914: The New York Times carries reports of a 'cocaine nigger' turned into a crazed killer by the drug

1921: The Fatty Arbuckle scandal highlights widespread cocaine use in Hollywood

1922: New laws in America impose ten-year jail sentence on convicted cocaine dealers

WWII years: Cocaine use all but disappears in America

1949: United Nations begins process of closing legal coke laboratories in Peru

1950s: Cuba emerges as the centre of global cocaine trafficking

Late 1960s: Colombia begins to challenge Cuba for control of world markets

1970: Rolling Stone magazine declares cocaine 'Drug of the Year'

1973: Pinochet gains power in Chile; hundreds of Chilean traffickers extradited to America

1975: Full-scale cocaine war breaks out between rival cartels in Colombia

Late 1970s: Pablo Escobar emerges as Colombia's most powerful drugs baron

1979: Huge cocaine money-laundering operation identified in Florida

1979: US officials begin covert support for Contra rebels in Nicaragua; turn blind eye as drug running to America helps finance the war

Mid-1980s: Escobar's cocaine profits estimated at $1 million (£700,000) a day; number of American coke users tops ten million; crack cocaine becomes widespread in USA

1984: Colombian anti-drug crusader and justice minister Lara Bonilla assassinated

1986: CIA-Contra scandal exposed by US press

1989: US launches Operation Just Cause against Panama's Manuel Noriega

1992: Escobar shot dead by Colombian police

2000: President Clinton launches Plan Colombia to wipe out coca plantations in the country

2001: Jamaica highlighted as new centre for cocaine trafficking

2002: British and European press highlight crack cocaine wars among underworld gangs

2002: Coca farmers battle US-backed forces eradicating coca crops in Bolivia

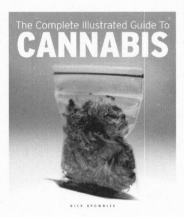

The Little Book Of
# ECSTASY

Printed and bound in the UK by MPG Books, Bodmin

Distributed in the US by Publishers Group West

Published by Sanctuary Publishing Limited, Sanctuary House, 45-53 Sinclair
Road, London W14 0NS, United Kingdom

www.sanctuarypublishing.com

ISBN: 1-86074-528-8

The Little Book Of
# ECSTASY

Gareth Thomas

**Sanctuary**

# CONTENTS

# INTRODUCTION

The older generations are no strangers to the drug scene. Today's parents may well have spent their own rebellious youth dropping acid to ABC, speeding to The Smiths or toking to T'Pau. Younger parents may even have formed the vanguard of the very rave culture that now corrupts their offspring. Their drugs, though, were known quantities. The dope heads of previous generations had a fair idea of how their head was being done in, and the likelihood of recovering afterwards.

The upstart ecstasy will have none of that. Ecstasy flips off its narcotic peers and dares to be all things to all people. The consequence is that no one really knows the slightest thing about it. Ninety years of age it may be, but that's just a kid in the family of narcotics. The trouble is, E is a problem child, and modern parents can't cope with it. Parents know no more about ecstasy than their kids, and therefore tend to acquire their knowledge via rumour and shock journalism. Their kids, conversely, listen to their encouraging peers' assurances, but ignore much sound scientific caution in doing so.

Ecstasy is both a young drug and a drug embraced by the young. If ever there was a drug-culture equivalent to the new phenomenon of Internet chat rooms and bulletin boards, then ecstasy/rave is it. Like one, you'll probably like the other. But, as the remarkable scientist Alexander Shulgin – who dared to nurture ecstasy when it was an infant called MDMA – said not only about ecstasy but other drugs too: 'Be informed, then choose.'

*CULTURE*

**SPANISH HIGH**

A short time ago on an island moderately far away, there was born a dance drug called ecstasy. The island was Ibiza, lying 90km (55 miles) off the east coast of Spain in the western Mediterranean, which tourist operators still describe as a place of 'peaceful countryside and secluded beaches'. Fat chance. Ibiza is, and will remain, the place where an upbeat music genre called 'house' once seduced a marriage-guidance drug called MDMA and produced 'rave' as its bastard offspring. Rave is a youth subculture comprising all-night dancing fuelled by the drug now known as ecstasy. But it is impossible to understand ecstasy without first examining the rave culture that it inspires.

Rave is nothing new. The Ancient Greek bacchants reduce present-day ravers to abject shame by comparison. Bacchants began as mixed-gender celebrants, but in time the stronger sex took over and their parties became strictly women-only affairs. Any unfortunate male that strayed into their path would soon become legless, but not in the usual sense. In *The Sacred Mushroom And The Cross*, John M Allegro writes of the bacchants:

*They were characterized by extreme forms of religious excitement interspersed with periods of intense depression. At one moment whirling in a frenzied dance, tossing their heads, driving one another on with screaming and the wild clamor of musical instruments, at another sunk into the deepest lethargy, and a silence so intense as to become proverbial. The Bacchants both possessed the god and were possessed by him; theirs was a religious enthusiasm in the proper sense of the term, that is, god-filled. Having eaten the Bacchus or Dionysos, they took on his power and character...*

True, the spiritual influence of the god Dionysus was really the chemical effect of *Psilocybe* mushrooms upon brain synapses; true, the bacchants' tendency to rip the limbs off human sacrifices has been honed into peace and love ideals over the millennia: but the essence of rave – drug-induced partying – was very much present and correct.

It wasn't just the definitively civilized Greeks who raved on drugs, though: orgiastic fervour has no pretensions to class or civility. Those from all parts of humankind – from the pampered sons of lords to plate-lipped Aboriginals who've never even seen cities – do, and always have, dropped drugs before dancing the night away.

The Hidatsa tribe of North Dakota, for example, used to perform the ceremony of Midhahakidutiku (Taking Up

The Bowl). This comprised not only drug-fuelled dancing but also the body ornamentation/mutilation that modern countercultures have claimed as their own. In *The Ceremony Of The Bowl*, Edward S Curtis writes of the Hidatsa:

> The fasters now divided the food, and each of them took a bowl of it to one of the medicine men, a clansman of his father. When the latter had finished eating, the faster placed his hands on the medicine man's shoulders and stroked his arm to the wrists, as though receiving some power or virtue from him. His relative then sang to the spirits, imploring them to aid the faster.
>
> The fasters next carried food to the spectators and the medicine men, while the suppliant provided for the singers and the Keeper of the Bowl. Before eating, each one offered the food to the Four Winds and the altar. After the others had eaten and smoked, the Bowl and the suppliant and such of the fasters as chose came to the Keeper and the singers and were pierced as in the Dahpike. Slits were cut into the flesh of each breast and the inserted rawhide ropes were fastened to the cross timbers of the supporting posts of the lodge.
>
> The devotees in a frenzied dance made violent efforts to free themselves. Buffalo skulls were sometimes hung by thongs passed through slits in

*the thighs or shoulders, and other fasters were pierced through the flesh of the shoulders and suspended, their feet clear of the ground.*

*The singers encouraged the dancers and kept their spirits at the highest pitch by wild singing and drumming. The fasters endured the torture as long as they were able; if they failed to tear themselves loose, or fainted with the intense pain, the Keeper of the Bowl and the singers cut the thongs and laid the exhausted dancers on their beds of sage, where they remained until the end of the ceremony, fasting and praying for visions.*

It was left to Middle Ages, ravers to show where dancing was really at. *The Skeptical Enquirer* of July/August 1999 writes of St Vitus' Dance:

*A variation of tarantism [manic dancing allegedly caused by a tarantula bite] spread throughout much of Europe between the 13th and 17th centuries, where it was known as the dancing mania or St Vitus's dance, on account that participants often ended their processions in the vicinity of chapels and shrines dedicated to this saint... [Outbreaks] seized groups of people, who engaged in frenzied dancing that lasted intermittently for days or weeks... These activities were typically accompanied by symptoms similar to tarantism, including screaming, hallucinations, convulsive movements, chest pains, hyperventilation, crude sexual gestures and outright intercourse. Instead of spider bites as the cause, participants usually claimed that they were possessed by demons who had induced an uncontrollable urge to dance. Like tarantism, however, music was typically played during episodes and was considered to be an effective remedy.*

## 20TH-CENTURY WHIRL

Drop-outs were more comprehensively recorded in the 20th century. During each decade or so there were separate and distinctive bands of young people, from all social classes, who stuck two fingers up at authority, then went out and got inebriated together. Uniting each class was a particular ideal, accompanied by an image, drug and music conducive to it. Here's a list:

1910S/1920S
BOHEMIANS

- **Identity** - Artists, writers, workers, anarchists and socialists would debate art, writing work, anarchism and socialism; and drink in cafés.
- **Drug(s) Of Choice** - Coffee, absinthe.
- **Musical Influences** - Debussy, Ravel, Rachmaninov.

**1930S**
WEST END JAZZ FIENDS
- **Identity** - Idle rich folk would congregate in London's West End, get high and listen to the latest swing sound.
- **Drug(s) Of Choice** - Cocaine.
- **Musical Influences** - Louis Armstrong's Hot Five, Cab Calloway And His Orchestra, Bix Beiderbecke And His Gang.

**1940S**
CONSCIENTIOUS OBJECTORS
- **Identity** - Left-leaning poets who sat out World War II.
- **Drug(s) Of Choice** - Spirits, tobacco.
- **Musical Influences** - Benjamin Britten, Michael Tippett.

**1950S**
BEATNIKS
- **Identity** - Pretentious young people would hang out in retreats, debate existentialism and revere Ginsberg.
- **Drug(s) Of Choice** - Marijuana.
- **Musical Influences** - Charles Mingus, John Coltrane, Thelonious Monk.

**1960S**
MODS AND ROCKERS
- **Identity** - Teds on Harleys would line up against Mods on scooters and reduce the natives of Brighton to collective apoplexy.

- **Drug(s) Of Choice** - Alcohol, speed.
- **Musical Influences** - The Rolling Stones, The Who.

HIPPIES
- **Identity** - Spiritual young folk would paint their faces, wear flowers in their hair and avoid such luxuries as soap and shampoo.
- **Drug(s) Of Choice** - Hashish, LSD.
- **Musical Influences** - Jefferson Airplane, The Grateful Dead, later Beatles.

1970S
PUNKS
- **Identity** - Middle-class youths would dress down, attend concerts and spit at the band.
- **Drug(s) Of Choice** - Alcohol, speed, poppers.
- **Musical Influences** - The Sex Pistols, The Damned, The Clash, The Buzzcocks.

1980S
ACID HOUSERS
- **Identity** - rebellious teenagers would break into warehouses, drop tabs and occasionally jump from upstairs windows while flapping their arms.
- **Drug(s) Of Choice** - LSD.
- **Musical Influences** - Happy Mondays, M/A/R/R/S, Jim Silk, Black Box.

## MEDIA MUDDIES

The rave culture – and, by association, the ecstasy culture – is but the latest of dropout fads originated by genuine young people with a message, but named and therefore given identity by the populist and media press of the time.

The media loves a good subculture. The more depraved the subculture – the more faces are slashed and brains are fried – the better it is, and the more the media loves it. To ensure a constant supply of subcultures, the tabloid press and populist TV documentaries help them develop: they root out a localized craze and mass-publicize it to a national epidemic. Had Elvis not gyrated his pelvis, the audience seats at *The Ed Sullivan Show* would have remained dry from teenage girls; had the Stones not been caught pissing on a garage wall, they may still be remembered as 'that band that might have done all right if they'd ditched the ugly rubber-lipped bloke'; had the Pistols not been goaded to call Bill Grundy a 'dirty fucker' on early-evening television, Sid might never have met Nancy and still be alive and managing a pub; had The Beastie Boys not shared the stage with caged go-go dancers and a 1.5m (5ft) hydraulic penis, Volkswagen logos would never have been pulled from Passats for use as pendants.

## YOU SCRATCH MY HACK

The media and subcultures feed upon each other. The tabloids offer more titillating subject matter than budget predictions or the DOW index. Nothing titillates better than a feeling of superiority, and a nice scare story about current youth fads makes the residents of Middle England and the US Bible Belt feel very superior indeed. Things need names to exist, so the media has to apply labels to fads: t he terms 'acid house' and 'rave' are inventions of the media.

'This is a big generalization,' said one US raver. 'There's no specific style for party kids or ravers. But most party kids listen to house and wear phat pants and sweatshirts. Just because they use a certain drug doesn't mean they automatically conform to a style that goes with that drug.'

**HISTORY OF RAVE**
THE ROCK 'N' ROLL (AND DISCO) YEARS
There is no abrupt change between youth movements: John Lennon did not wake up one sunny late-1960s morning, see trees of green and skies of blue, and think to himself, 'What a wonderful day to begin flower power'; Malcolm McLaren did not write 'invent British punk' into his long-term diary for 1976.

Rather, there is an overlap, with one movement gradually dying out while another gains ascendancy. They segue into each other. The acid house and rave movements of the late 1980s and early 1990s followed on the spit-drenched tails of the post-punk movement, but they didn't kick it from the limelight. Far from it – different styles continued side by side; indeed, post-punk is an essential movement to consider if one is to witness the rave phenomenon in context.

Post-punk bands encompassed such diverse sounds as the retro-glam-rock posturing of Duran Duran and Adam And The Ants; the life-affirming ska of Madness and The Specials; the comedy punk of The Undertones and The Toy Dolls; the gloomy ambience of Magazine and Bauhaus; the angst of the later Buzzcocks and The Smiths and the avant-garde noise of Sonic Youth and Wire. Although sounding drastically different from one another, these groups retained punk's aggression but either rejected the out-and-out nihilism of bands like The Sex Pistols and The Dead Kennedys or expressed it more poetically.

Post-punk appealed to students, former prog-rockers and sophisticates, who retrospectively accepted the original punk bands as the forerunners of their 'scene'. Post-punk therefore became the established 'arty-farty' scene that house attempted to subvert, in the same way that punk's first wave had threatened progressive rock. House didn't succeed, as the 1990s mainstream successes of bands like Nirvana, Pearl Jam and Garbage would testify, but it did crucially revive a music scene that was starting to stagnate.

New trends emerged in counterpoint to post-punk. The soul and funk that dominated 1970s discos increasingly developed the synthesizer-based electronic sound pioneered by Giorgio Moroder on Donna Summer's 'I Feel Love'. Simultaneously, the High Energy (Hi-NRG) movement invaded US gay clubs: this was an upbeat sound characterized by speeded-up dance cuts and strong melody lines typified by songs like Aimi Stewart's 'Knock On Wood' and Patrick Hernandez's 'Born To Be Alive'. Bobby Orlando, also known as Bobby O, a seminal Hi-NRG songwriter and producer, said that the purpose of the Hi-NRG scene was 'to feel good and positive'. Not a world of difference from the ethic of a later ecstasy-fuelled dance movement...

Meanwhile in New York labels like Salsoul introduced remixes and versions of inherently upbeat gospel songs; while in the UK, genres like hip-hop and individual songs like Lipps Inc's 'Funkytown' made their dubious presence known in nightclubs and discotheques. These were joined by edgier disco records from the US underground scene like D Train's 'You're The One for Me' and The Peech Boys' 'Don't Make Me Wait', which introduced dub and dropouts to the existing drum track.

At the time post-punk reached its apex and finest moment with The Smiths' 1986 album *The Queen Is Dead*, another Manchester band, New Order, were developing their definitive sound, culminating in their magnum opus *Technique* in 1989. This superlative record – the first great album of the rave era – is the antithesis of the band's early output. Indeed the ten-year transition between their two albums *Unknown Pleasures* and *Technique* exactly mirrors the changeover from post-punk to rave. When lead singer Ian Curtis hanged himself in 1980, the band began its nine-year fashioning of the UK rave sound. Each successive album *Power, Corruption And Lies, Low Life* and *Brotherhood*, as well as singles like 'Blue Monday' and 'True Faith', moved more toward the definitive rave sound pioneered by *Technique* – a record so redolent of Ibiza that you can taste the paella.

New Order's development reflected the general trend of the 1980s. Post-punk, New Romantic and Goth bands like Echo And The Bunnymen, The Teardrop Explodes, The Cure and The Mission were gradually accompanied in the charts by the electronic music of Kraftwerk, Depeche Mode and New Order; and by the faster and happier music from the likes of T'Pau and The Communards.

They were soon joined in the charts and (especially) nightclubs by a seminal sound from the States: house music.

NEW HOUSE
Punk's less street-cred partner in crime, disco, was in the sorriest of states at this time. Although gobbed at both figuratively and literally by the punk movement, disco had slogged it out for ten years and – while the 1970s stereotype of white men with Afros, bell-bottoms, and shirts that were even louder than the music, did its image no good at all – it had produced genuinely fine numbers like Sister Sledge's 'He's The Greatest Dancer' and Odyssey's 'Native New Yorker'. It didn't last. During the 1980s, disco reached its butt-end and produced musical atrocities like Ottawan's 'D.I.S.C.O.'

Disco had become an embarrassment, so it's just as well that it bred house music.

Ravers worldwide should tip their hats to Chicago, for it was the Windy City that both created and named house music. In the disco era it was Chicago that forged the electronic drum track and pioneered the 12" 45rpm EP (Extended Play) record intended specifically for disc jockeys. These, though, were inconsequential compared to Chicago's greatest attribute. Chicago had an asset that was absolutely fundamental to the creation of house – a nightclub called the Warehouse.

It was not until the Warehouse opened in 1977 that Chicago became remotely a dance city. Until then Chicago was known as the home of the greatest blues acts around and was home or host to such iconic figures as John Lee Hooker, Howlin' Wolf, Muddy Waters, Elmore James and Willie Dixon. Chicago dance clubs, in as much as they existed, used jukeboxes rather than live disc jockeys and, in common with the rest of the US, tended to segregate different races and sexual preferences into their own distinct clubs.

When disco hit its apex in 1977, a successful New York disc jockey, Frankie Knuckles (not to be confused with his skeletal near-namesake Frankie Bones, whose time would come later), noticed the Windy City's live-music vacuum and determined to fill it by opening the Warehouse, which was revolutionary for two reasons.

First, it ditched the racism. The Warehouse welcomed people from across the race (and sexual preference) barriers, and played an eclectic mix of musical styles. Knuckles alternated the disparate genres R&B (rhythm and blues), disco and punk, with results that were beneficial to all three. 'When we first opened in 1977, I was playing a lot of the east coast records, the Philly stuff, Salsoul,' he recalled. 'By '80/81, when that stuff was all over with, I started working a lot of the soul that was coming out. I had to re-construct the records to work for my dancefloor, to keep the dancefloor happy, as there was no dance music coming out! I'd take the existing songs, change the tempo, layer different bits of percussion over them, to make them more conducive for the dancefloor.' By 1981, Knuckles had built the prototype of the house sound by remaking and remixing records with added percussion tracks live in the club – in effect becoming a live musical performer. He would perform such spinning salaciousness as playing a Roland 909 drum machine under old Soyl records – thus emphasizing the beats or mixing in rhythm tracks from reel-to-reel tape recorders.

Second, its name was shortened to 'house' - a useful name for a new music genre...

Other DJs and music-industry figures joined the house bandwagon and contributed to the new hybrid sound. One outlet for the trend was Chicago's WBMX radio station – which featured such DJs as Farley 'Jackmaster' Funk (who later hosted dances at a rival Chicago club called The Playground) and Ralphie Rosario.

House music started off as familiar disco music given a persistent and pounding beat; this rhythm becoming of far more significance than any odd lyrics that might wind their way coherently to dancers' ears. Gradually other DJs, courtesy of Knuckles' example, realised the live-performance potential of their job and began the unofficial game of 'Who can mix the weirdest sound into a classic soul track?'

House music was not initially assigned to vinyl but recorded on cassette tape for exclusive use in clubs, and opinion is divided as to which was the first house record released, though it was probably an obscure track called 'Fantasy' by Z Factor.

Chicago DJ Steve Hurley was another vinyl house pioneer: his seminal release, 'Music is the Key', spurred the formation of record label DJ International which, along with Larry Sherman's Trax Records, dominated the house market in its early years. Artists developing the house sound during this time included Chip E, whose song 'Like This' introduced the sampled stutter technique that is now as big a part of rave as baggy trousers and body odour.

In 1986 disc jockey Marshall Jefferson earned his anointment as 'King of House' by synthesizing the 'deep house' sound that was to become the quintessential club vibe. Meanwhile gay disc jockey Ron Hardy was dabbling with dark forces in the form of raw and wild rhythm tracks that made Jefferson's sound seem like Flanders and Swann by comparison. Hardy's club, the Music Box, introduced singers of the calibre of Liz Torres and Keith Nonally to the dancing public's ear, though it was another of Hardy's innovations that had the greatest long-term effect on house: he held open forums for aspiring disc jockeys, inviting newcomers to test their home-grown compilation tapes on a live audience. As with British punk of the 1970s, this 'do it yourself' approach reaped phenomenal benefits for the spread of the genre.

The two primary house hits of 1996 held titles that might be said by an aerobics instructor: Eiffel 65's 'Move Your Body' was the original 'house anthem', while Jim Silk's 'Jack Your Body' (actually January 1997) achieved the feat of transforming a paucity of lyrics and a stuttering 'J' sound into something approaching iconic. Such profundity earned it the honour of being the first house number to top the UK pop charts.

However, it was the 'Jack'-less 'Move Your Body' that initially catapulted house music into the UK. The song was a mainstay of pirate radio stations like disc jockey Jazzy M's London Weekend Radio (LWR), and other songs in the oeuvre soon followed. London's Delirium Club became the first UK nightclub dedicated to the house sound. Soon, a combo called the Chicago House Party toured the UK; and included Marshall Jefferson himself amongst its array of disc jockeys.

There may be an element of rose-tinted-specs-wearing in reminiscences of early ravers. 'I sadly can't say that I was there in the very beginning,' recalls one raver. 'Clubbers who witnessed those select gatherings in dodgy warehouses or parties on the beach in Ibiza still reminisce like war veterans, almost wearing their "smiley" badges like campaign medals. Although aware of the growing scene through friends I passed on it as they tended to be more into speed and "animal" (amyl nitrate). Although I attended a rave they had organized back at the end of the '80s, it was more notable for some local violent score-settling than any loved-up euphoria. The hard-house menacing energy reminded more of local village-hall punk gigs from a decade before. A mate of mine recalls cruising endlessly round the M25 until the mobile call came in, arriving in a field only half an hour before the police shut everything down, and then getting back into a car full of people grinding their teeth and babbling like hardened speed freaks. I stuck to beer and hash.'

## LANCASHIRE HOT SPOT

It was 300km (200 miles) northwest in Manchester that house music really took off in the UK. In particular the legendary Hacienda club, with its disc jockey Mike Pickering, devoted whole nights to house music, and would later become synonymous with the UK rave scene.

It's appropriate that the manager of New Order started it all off. The Hacienda was the direct descendent of

Manchester's punk venue the Factory club, run by Tony Wilson, who also owned the Factory record label on which Joy Division/New Order released their records. When the Factory club closed in 1981, Wilson, along with Joy Division manager Rob Gretton, planned to replace it with a purpose-built club to rival New York venues like the Danceteria, Fun House and Paradise Garage. Funded by New Order, Factory and the brewers Whitbread, the new club was designed by Ben Kelly within the deserted International Marine Centre.

The Hacienda was opened on 21 May 1982, with Hewan Clark as the disc jockey. Clark would return the following night – and every subsequent one for the next four years.

The Hacienda was a multi-levelled affair, with a dancefloor, galleries, a basement and ornaments that included road bollards to prevent girls' high heels getting stuck in grooves at the dancefloor's edge. It adopted a multicultural approach akin to that used by Frankie Knuckles at the Warehouse. It wasn't a house venue at first: typical pre-house artists included Erasure, The Jesus and Mary Chain and, topping the bill, Coronation Street's Vera Duckworth, singing a medley of her favourite songs.

That all changed when the Chicago House Party visited the club in 1987, and the new genre took precedence. 'House certainly sounded new back then but it was still polite,' says journalist John McCready.

'Acid was a different sound altogether – menacing, growling, ungrateful and volatile, at its best like a starved dog prowling in circles. But acid sounded like coded radio signals, a kind of dance instruction from another planet.'

Twelve years later, following the 1992 crash of Factory Records and subsequent incidents of violence and drug dealing, the Hacienda closed down. The Urban75 Rave website gives this account of the iconic venue's final rave-cum-squat in June 1999:

> *The thousand or so party-goers inside were matched by almost as many again outside, as police moved in at midnight to prevent any more people from gaining entrance to the building, squatted since the previous day. When their cheeky attempt at storming the building was repelled by vigilant party people, the cops went wild outside, randomly batonning anyone who seemed most lively. One particularly excited six and a half foot [2m] uniformed officer struck someone straight across the back, before this plain clothes guy cried out, 'I'm a copper, you idiot!'*
>
> *The sound system eventually was negotiated out at 8am. Until then overhead, the police helicopter spotlight swept over determined party-heads getting hauled up into windows or shuffling along ledges, and all those still circling the building.*

## FIRST WAVE OF RAVE

In 1987 the first in a succession of tabloid scares appeared in the newspapers of Britain's middle classes. Young, clearly demented people were breaking into warehouses, playing loud music and dropping tabs of LSD. This depravity was traced to the Spanish island of Ibiza, formerly a favourite resort where retired Britons would stretch their legs, but now a veritable vice den; a throwback to the days when various invaders would try and make the island their own, though the earlier ones were less subtle, using battleaxes rather than beatboxes as their mode of persuasion. The *Daily Mail* recorded:

> *The drugs culture took a disturbing new turn at the weekend when the biggest ever 'acid house' party was held... As 11,000 youngsters descended on a quiet airfield in the middle of the night, drug pushers were waiting to tempt them with an evil selection of narcotics.*

Despite the shock journalism, this was low-key stuff – low-key, that is, until the media distorted it into something endemic and promptly set about a self-fulfilling prophecy by calling the trend 'acid house'. At first it just consisted of two unrelated groups throwing all-night dance parties. Psychic TV, fronted by the redoubtable Genesis P Orridge, had a hardcore edge – but the ones that mattered were

Schoom, because they partied to the newfangled music called house.

Acid house was to UK farmers of the late 1980s what foot-and-mouth disease would become in 2001: it took over their holdings and made them uninhabitable until the pestilence was cleared. Bizarre young people wearing smiley-face T-shirts would occupy their fields all night long, playing music and shouting, 'Acieeeeed!' in high-pitched voices. What the media dubbed the 1988 Summer of Love had begun. So had rave.

Meanwhile, in Germany, young Berliners were breaking into warehouses, too. Curiously, the Berlin rave culture exactly mirrored that of the UK – including its rapid commercialization.

Back in Britain, after farmers had sent a combination of the law, shotgun pellets and rutting bulls after the trespassing partyers, they were forced to seek out alternative venues with at least some chance of covert activity.

In 1989–90, the British government responded to the Middle England hysteria by introducing new laws to shut down the raves. Following the mandatory abandonment of warehouses – once the constabulary had visited and declined to embrace either the ravers' love-and-peace ideals or the ravers themselves – the all-night parties relocated to Manchester, sparking what 'hilariously' became known as the Madchester scene, which focused on the aforementioned Hacienda club.

Manchester never used to have the sunniest of images. The opening titles of *Coronation Street*, the music of Joy Division and The Smiths, stock footage of rain on terraced houses – that was the 'Manchester scene' prior to the late 1980s. Then Joy Division became New Order, the International Marine Centre became the Hacienda and The Stone Roses became the new Beatles, Rolling Stones and Sex Pistols combined. Manchester became Madchester, the UK focus for the rave scene, where students, pseudo-hippies and proto-new-agers would converge to dance, drop E and occasionally collapse from dehydration. The overall mood was that of a unity and optimism that the UK hadn't felt as a subculture since the hippie days of the 1960s.

The familiar musical London versus Manchester rivalry now decidedly favoured the mop-haired northerners, with three bands in particular – The Stone Roses, Happy Mondays and The Inspiral Carpets – leading the nationwide music scene. It was the first of these bands that as good as proclaimed themselves the 'messiahs of Madchester', with their song 'I Am The Resurrection'. They more or less got away with this Mancunian messianic posturing until their turgid follow-up album Second Coming revealed their real status as less the 'new Beatles' than the new Emerson, Lake And Palmer. Nonetheless, during the Madchester years, they defined the times – cocky, optimistic and anti-materialistic.

Inevitably England's capital muscled in on the act and the rave scene spread to the clubs and open areas of

London. In March 1990 the Criminal Justice March took place in Trafalgar Square, beginning with the UK's biggest riot in years and culminating with 'Biology', its biggest ever illegal party. This assured London's place as a rave city, and house/techno became pretty well ubiquitous in its clubs. Venues such as Club UK and the Ministry of Sound became prime rave venues during the early to mid-1990s.

House's small record labels, plucky as they were, couldn't hope to compete with the big boys, and duly the school bully of commercialization administered a short, sharp blow to the UK house scene. Bastardized house songs, like M/A/R/R/S' 'Pump Up The Volume', infested the charts, while PLCs organized 'commercial raves', in London's surrounding countryside. These introduced anthemic songs like 808 State's 'Pacific State' to the market consumers. While the experience of these open-air raves was authentic enough, the motivation behind them was anything but: they were moneymaking ventures pure and simple. So were a succession of cynical and substandard record releases that included Big Fun's appalling cover of the Jacksons' 'Blame It On The Boogie'.

By the early 1990s, the UK rave scene was stagnating, so the resident US disc jockeys – along with some British colleagues who fancied making it big Stateside – traversed the pond and took rave with them. One of these American DJs was the soon-to-be-infamous Frankie Bones. And this is when the fun really started.

The first US raves took place in the Californian hippie havens of San Francisco and Los Angeles. If that's where they'd stopped, they'd not have caused a ripple in the dessert course. Californians put up with any old weirdness; that's their job.

It's when Frankie Bones took rave on tour that it became a US phenomenon. First he took rave to Brooklyn and held the Stormrave parties of 1992, where budding disc jockeys like Doc Martin, Kooki, Sven Vath and Josh Wink made their debuts. On to New York, where a crowd of 5,000 kids gathered at a Queens loading dock for the biggest rave to date. It was at this seminal ecstasy-soaked event that the four keywords of both rave and ecstasy use were first uttered: 'Peace, Love, Unity, Respect' (PLUR). Disciples carried the gospel across the 50 states, and thousands of kids invited rave into their lives.

Back in the UK, and in the true spirit of the European Union, Italian bands were attempting to resurrect British house music. Mostly they failed, because their releases were just substandard covers of UK and US releases, but with the song 'Ride On Time' by Black Box – an excellent track whereby the vocals of Loleatta Holloway's 'Love Sensation' were applied to a keyboard background – the Italians really came up with the goods. The British public duly rewarded Black Box by keeping their song at Number One for a phenomenal five weeks.

The British record-buying public was not always so

discerning: 'Ride On' Time had to usurp a four-week run of Jive Bunny to gain chart ascendancy.

## IT ALL SOUNDS THE SAME

Something subcultures have in common is the axiom from outsiders and old folk that the music 'all sounds the same', a stance that only fortifies the culture to its adherents. To an outsider there is a far greater difference between Black Sabbath's 'War Pigs' and Metallica's 'For Whom The Bell Tolls' than there is between 'War Pigs' and Louis Armstrong's 'What A Wonderul World'. However, for your common or garden headbanger the similarities between the decade-apart metal songs are equivalent to those between orange chalk and a markedly blue brand of cheese.

However, it doesn't take old-fashioned values to find rave tracks indistinguishable from one another. Even open-minded individuals can leave a rave with the impression of having listened to just the one song, nay the one beat, over its eight-hour duration. In a sense that's exactly what they have done – if the disc jockey's any good.

Disc jockeys have come a long way since they didn't jockey discs. The original Jamaican DJs had an assistant, the 'selector', to handle the trivial matter of choosing and playing records. While the selector spun his favourite ska and reggae tunes, the DJ would 'toast': add vocal effects to the pre-recorded track. Looking towards posterity, DJs soon started to make recordings of their toasts over their selectors' mix. This became known as dub, an abbreviation of 'double'.

Disc jockeys have moved on, and moved their audiences, in leaps and bounds since those voiceover days. Since then they have divided into three types, which of course can overlap, with one DJ participating in different areas, as follows:

- **Radio DJ** – Segues between radio tracks and, more importantly, gives a personality and identity to the radio station. It is usually the marketing committee in overall charge rather than the DJ himself/herself who selects the tracks that are played. The radio DJ is therefore more an artiste (performing artist) than artist (creative artist).

- **Travelling DJ** – The ultimate improviser, the travelling DJ travels around emceeing raves and choosing tracks, and therefore must make a good first impression every time.

- **Club DJ** – Employed by a rave venue to entertain its particular crowd, and is therefore well-known by his/her collective audience and knows the particular 'crowd pleasers' that get it bopping. The easiest method to allow self-marketing by the DJ and develop him/her a reputation.

Although all three categories of DJ are relevant to the history of rave it is the third – the club DJ – that is the absolute essence of the rave culture itself.

Rave DJs are the equivalent of the live band at a gig. At a rave, the DJs are the act. They don't just put on records and listen through headphones, they are musicians in their own right. The good rave DJ is an improviser par excellence: every bit as adept at thinking on their musical feet as Dizzy Gillespie on his favourite trumpet. They will spin the records with all the agility of a Neapolitan pizza chef handling a sticky lump of dough. They will pick up the vibes of that night's particular crowd and mix the music to match its mood; they will cause the songs to segue into one another, adjusting the speeds and pitches to produce, in effect, a single and original multi-hour musical track.

The individual ravers, in turn, will also improvise, interpreting the music with their bodies. In this sense there is a dichotomy at the heart of the rave experience: for all the documented spirit of comradeship – PLUR – the essence of rave dancing is one of solitude, of losing oneself in the music.

To these people there is a seismic difference between tracks within a single genre, let alone those between different ones. Those coming to rave anew from, say, Blur and Oasis, would have no chance of telling house from Detroit techno, let alone Tortoise apart from Jazzanova. For these people, here is a potted history of electronic music.

ELECTRIC MUSIC UNTIL THE CURRENT TIME

Electronic music dates to the ondes martenot used by classical composers like Olivier Messiaen in the 1940s but was pretty much a curiosity until Robert Moog invented the analogue synthesizer in 1965. Synthesized music inhabited the pretentious soundscapes of avant-gardes like Karlheinz Stockhausen and Steve Reich, until the late-1960s when bands like King Crimson and Pink Floyd brought it to the attention of students and the art set.

They may have resembled chartered surveyors, but the Herrn that comprised Kraftwerk have the entire electronic sound in their favour, because they introduced electronic sounds into mainstream popular music with their albums Autobahn and The Man Machine, as well as individual tracks like Trans Europe Express. Other European artists like Tangerine Dream and Jean-Michel Jarre leaped aboard this electric-powered bandwagon, and paved the way for late 1970s/1980s artists like Brian Eno, The Human League, Ultravox and Gary Numan to do their electronic thing.

Electronic rave music comprises one or more of the following components (some of these definitions are decidedly different from the usual ones):

- **Drums** – Any sounds (other than the bass ones) that give rhythm to a song – in rave music that is just about all of them;

- **Samples** - Short extracts mixed into a different backing track, or recorded sounds fed into a synthesizer to be replayed at differing pitches. Sampled sounds are often harvested from perversely differing sources: for example, Beats International's 'Dub Be Good To Me' includes both the bassline of The Clash's 'Guns Of Brixton' and Charles Bronson's harmonica theme from Sergio Leone's western *Once Upon A Time In The West*;
- **Computer-Generated Drums (CGD)** - Not to be confused with the generic 'drums' category described above, these are specific synthesized drum sounds from a computer or electronic drum machine;
- **Traditional Bass** - Synthesized electric or acoustic double-bass sounds, used in nearly all rave tracks;
- **303 Bass** - Bass sounds that don't try to emulate non-electronic instruments - again, used in nearly all rave music;
- **Traditional Keyboards And Strings** - Synthesized piano, organ, guitar and violin sound used to give melody and substance to the music's drum and bass beat;
- **Synth Sounds** - Specifically, those that resemble nothing else bar a synthesizer - the synthesizer saying, 'Screw this for a lark' to emulation, and producing its own sounds for its own sounds' sake;
- **Traditional Vocals** - Some girl or geezer singing into a microphone;
- **Computer Voices** - Robotic lyrics (ie when it sounds like Doctor Who's Davros is spinning the discs).

## RAVE CATEGORIES

- **Acid House** – House with the addition of Roland 303 synthesizers that produces different pitches and layers.
- **Detroit Techno** – Influenced by European electrobeat: high bass levels, fast pace of 115–300 beats per minute (bpm). In two words, 'fast' and 'pounding'. Too pounding to retain the soul of house, according to purists. It certainly severed the link between house and disco.
- **Hardcore Techno** – As Detroit techno, but even faster and even more pounding.
- **Gabba Techno** – Of Dutch provenance, this is the fastest and most pounding of the techno trinity. The very soul of 'fast and pounding', with speeds that can exceed 1,000bpm. The disturbing samples added to this subgenre – screams of terror reminiscent of snuff movies and suchlike – tend to detract from any feel-good factor.
- **Breakbeat** – Hip-hop samples and reggae tunes with fast beats and high-pitched samples.
- **Jungle** – Percussion, bongos, ragga vocals and samples.
- **Darkside** – Choral progressions that create a dark urban sound.
- **Trance** – Slow, melodic and hypnotic. Take out the pacifier/dummy and smooch your smelly friend. Halfway house between the hardcore of Moby and the ambience of Brian Eno. Each new day seems to see a lengthening of the list of 'silly subgenres with trance in the name':

hard trance, acid trance, trancecore, Goa trance and psychedelic trance are some of the current ones.

- **Drum And Bass** – Hardcore techno spiced up with hip-hop, industrial sounds, ragga, jazz, funk and a speeded-up breakbeat sound. The return of 'fast and pounding', just when you thought it was safe to go back in the dance hall...

Of course, rave music is in a constant state of evolution, with new styles always being created.

RAVE IN THE US

Rave in the US is a part-time subculture for Generation X. Just as folk no longer see a job as a career and incline toward part-time or job-share work, the rave generation will tune in, turn on and drop out for the weekend, then turn up to work on Monday. (Then put in a poor working week until Wednesday due to the extended hangover that is peculiar to E; see Chapter 4.) Accordingly the US rave scene typically comprises white, middle-class youths in the 17- to 25-year-old age bracket, with an equal divide between boys and girls.

Of course, a subculture is nothing without some anti-Establishment sticking-up of the erect middle finger toward authority. In US rave, the behind-the-bike-sheds combined naughtiness of breaking into warehouses and consuming a Class A drug gives rave its *raison d'être*. Breaking into US warehouses is an out-and-out crime in the US, as opposed to its UK trespassing equivalent that merely lands the perpetrators with rapped knuckles. This has led to the US 'rave hop', whereby one rave can take place over several venues over a single night: 200 kids may set up speakers on a private beach, drop some Es, crank up the volume and bop till the cops come calling. They then move on to the next venue – a warehouse say – and so forth, until daybreak puts an end to the hide-and-seek japery.

The subtext of rave fashions is one of regression to childhood. Clothing and accessories are chosen to reinforce these kindergarten capers, though there is also a practical dimension to some of these clothes preferences. Typical boys' attire includes baggy pants and cartoon-character T-shirts. Girls favour tomboy cropped hair and baby-doll dresses. Accessories would be more suited to the floor of a crèche in late afternoon – ravers will happily wield cuddly toys, glowsticks and babies' pacifiers without the slightest concern that they personally might look ridiculous.

The rave culture in the UK is both the same as and different from the US one. The fashions and 'reversion to childhood' theme is present in all its juvenile glory, and the social demographics are also similar. Research at Glasgow University suggests that 14.5 per cent of children from professional-class families had tried ecstasy and similar drugs at least once, as opposed to 7.5 per cent of children from skilled working-class families.

Unfortunately, some inherent differences between the US and UK societies have trickled down to the UK rave scene.

The UK rave culture has diverted from open-spaced venues like out-of-town warehouses to city nightclubs of varying pokiness and ventilation. This has immense health consequences and contributes to the far greater incidence of ecstasy-related fatalities in the UK than the US. There is also a greater booze culture in the UK; a consequence of counterproductive licensing laws, whereby people have to drink several pints of beer between the hours of 11pm and 11:20pm before tanking up again in a nightclub. This also has immense health consequences because, even by drug-mixing standards, a cocktail of booze and ecstasy can have disastrous (if not fatal) results.

Drinks manufacturers thoughtfully opened the booze culture to young, even under-age, ravers by introducing a type of drink called an 'alcopop' that tastes like a fizzy drink but carries the same alcoholic kick as a large Scotch whisky. Promotion campaigns that exactly mirrored the 'reversion to childhood' rave motif of the E culture were devised to sell the drinks to youngsters. Brands known as Hooch, Two Dogs and Jammin' appeared in off-licences; advertisements featuring two border collies or a giant leering lemon were posted on hoardings. The latterday alcopop demographic has become synonymous with the rave culture. This, despite government efforts to enforce drinks companies to target a more mature market, has decidedly unhealthy ramifications.

It's not all bad, though. The UK rave culture has in effect joined two generations or rather both ends of the same one – the Generation X – in the PLUR ideals. An historical headstart over the US has resulted in people from the first wave of rave – when 'Ride On Time' and 'Dub Be Good To Me' were the dance tracks of choice – who are now in their 30s but still attend clubs to bop alongside the young'uns. A 36-year-old, London-based charity worker has this to say on the subject:

> I like to think I've covered most types of clubbing. I've gone to free festivals. In a squat party in Farringdon I came across the toilet to challenge [Irvine Welsh's book] Trainspotting's 'Worst Toilet in the World' – and when you've taken E sometimes you've just got to go! I've had the joy of feeling like one of the chosen people of God as the sun has come up on a Welsh valley having danced through the night (although seeing what your fellow dancers look like 'when the lights go up' is always a frightening experience). I've danced with the beautiful people in the Ministry of Sound, somehow managing to smuggle myself past the fashion police on the door. Most of the time, however, I tend to go to smaller clubs that play hard house (music that is stripped down to very basic repetitive beats) like Mass or the

*414 Club in Brixton. These tend to have small chill-out rooms where you can smoke dope and chat to people who are affable in the true rave-scene stereotype. Although the clubs tend to be mainly male (hard house seems to be much more a 'man thing'), and some look like they've just piled out of the pub the club still gives off a pleasant vibe so that you can chat to people. The majority are nearly all modern, urban hippies in one form or another (girls in short tie-dyed dresses and big boots, guys in T-shirts and combat pants). It is still refreshing how no one really dresses up to go to these clubs (unlike some of the bigger London clubs). It is even more refreshing that despite being predominantly the home of people in their 20s, or even teens, that there are still enough veterans like ourselves around to not stand out (maybe it's the chill-out area that attracts us in larger numbers). I hear that the big London super-clubs have become more the home ground of mid-30s coke-snorting executives (many still in their suits).*

## THIS REALLY IS ECSTASY

Of course, the point of discussing the rave culture is that it is – or at least was until recently – effectively the same thing as the ecstasy culture. You cannot understand one without the other.

In the one sense, ecstasy carries the least confusing nomenclature of all the street drugs. Unlike the multitude and ever-growing number of slang terms for, say, cannabis, generic ecstasy is only known by the names 'ecstasy', 'E,' 'adam' and MDMA. In another esoteric sense, it does no such thing. Any punter looking for technical information about the drug might have these beauties to contend with:

- MDMA;
- MDM;
- N-methyl-MDA;
- 3,4-methylenedioxymethamphetamine;
- N-methyl-3,4-methylenedioxyamphetamine;
- N-methyl-3,4-methylenedioxyphenylisopropylamine;
- N,alpha-dimethyl-3,4-methylenedioxyphenethylamine;
- N,alpha-dimethyl-1,3-benzodioxole-5-ethanamide;
- N,alpha-dimethyl-homopiperonylamine;
- N-methyl-1-(3,4-methylenedioxyphenyl)-2-propanamine;
- 2-methylamino-1-(3,4-methylenedioxyphenyl)-propanamine;
- N-methyl-beta-(3,4-methylenedioxyphenyl)-isopropylamine;
- N,alpha-dimethyl-beta-(3,4-methylenedioxyphenyl)-ethylamine;
- EA-1475;
- DEA Control #7287: MDMA HCl;
- DEA Control #7405: MDMA;

- DEA Control #7406: MDMA;
- Chem Abs: [66142–89–0] S-(+)-MDMA;
- Chem Abs: [69558-32-3] S-(+)-MDMA HCl;
- Chem Abs: [81262-70-6] R-(-)-MDMA;
- Chem Abs: [69558-31-2] R-(-)-MDMA HCl;
- Chem Abs: [69610-10-2] MDMA;
- Chem Abs: [64057-70-1] MDMA HCl.

There is no longer such a thing as an ecstasy trip. There used to be, when the drug was in its early dance days and ravers were too caught up in their own euphoria to compare notes, but no longer. The experience is still there, of course – MDMA hasn't suddenly lost all its narcotic qualities – it's just that seasoned ravers reckoned that the name didn't fit the experience and changed it to 'roll'. One ecstasy user explains: 'God only knows where it started, but the term really fits...rolling, as in moving along with little effort on sheer momentum. Once the drug's effects start it usually just...well, rolls right along on its own...you don't feel like you're really making an investment of effort in whatever you're doing.'

The rave culture is inexorably linked with ecstasy. The two are symbiotic; they effectively inhabit the same cultural gaff. There are exceptions, but these are of the type that apparently proves a rule. Most notable are the 'raves in the nave' organized by trendy vicars. Here young Christian folk (by invitation) break into cathedrals and hold a sweaty bop. They class it as an act of worship: it is their equivalent of sleeping during the sermon and mouthing the hymns because you can't reach the pitch of the women around you.

A Methodist minister, the Reverend Jeff Reynolds, raves over the holy antics to be had in the aisles:

*After many years of being involved with various events as an organizer and performer it was good to visit Ely Cathedral as a 'punter'. It was my first visit to 'Rave in the Nave' and it was a very pleasurable experience. From wondering whether I would squeeze my six-foot-three [1.9m], 15 stone [95kg] frame into a Velcro suit, to not being particularly turned on by my blackcurrant cordial and orange juice type cocktail (enough to turn anyone to drink!), to casting a musician's eye over the band, to being particularly moved by the different types of worship in the Lady Chapel, I found the event stimulating and refreshing. It was great to stand in that beautiful building and realise that for centuries worship has evolved and provoked a response from worshippers. This event was no different and, thank God, that we can worship in a style that is relevant to our modern culture. Yes, I'll definitely be back, all I need is a bigger Velcro suit, a stamp that actually works on my hand and more imagination in the cocktail line!*

So, is ecstasy a delinquent's drug? Does it involve internecine ghetto gang warfare, muggings, pimping, prostitution, selling your grandparents to feed the habit? Nope, ecstasy will have none of that. Not at the user level. Not until recently.

Is ecstasy a hippie drug? Does it favour abandonment of material wealth, 'tuning in, turning on and dropping out' and open-air festivals in the rain? Yes, but only half-heartedly. Like rave, ecstasy is a part time pursuit. One Hacienda veteran says:

> So is E addictive? Well, in my experience raving certainly is. My friends and I early on vowed to sensibly manage our raving. The anticipation and high was so great, and the washed-out feeling from dancing all night potentially so low that it required limits on how frequently we would rave. Most of this was down to the fact that we mostly had jobs requiring responsibility during work hours (our group includes everything from a company director to a barrister). This certainly meant that money wasn't a problem (we'd hardly be stealing off old ladies to fund our rave habit), but coping with the come-down on Monday was. For the same reason we never took too many Es in one night (there is always a temptation in a long night to take another as the first is wearing off, and then inevitably another, or just to increase the dose). I remember being with someone at an

*outdoor rave whose middle-distance stare and brain-dead responses in the morning showed the dangers of taking too many.*

Ecstasy is not heroin: its users do not base their entire lives around the drug, living in derelict council estates, claiming social security and stealing stereo systems. No, they take the drug at weekends, then turn up to work on Monday. This involves a sleep-deprivation hangover of phenomenal proportions.

Alternatively, some ecstasy users attempt to prolong the euphoria; to continue the rave into Monday. Unfortunately, there's a minor irritant called work that gets in the way.

One 18-year-old shop worker revealed:

*This was yesterday; I can't believe we got away with it, me and a girl at work on half an ecstasy each! I don't think I'd get away with it again though. NEVER again. The girl who I'll call 'I' suggested doing a pill at work, I said half each, we agreed. It was one of those 'I'll do it if you will' type things. I went for my break at around 10:40am and ate as much as I possibly could. Went to the kitchen to get a knife, took that to the toilet to cut the pill. Did that, swallowed half, and put the other half back in the bag, which went in my pocket. Back to work, spoke* to 'I', handed her the contents of my pocket. I don't think she was expecting me to do it, but she followed my lead and went for a break. As 'I' left, the duty manager arrived and was on the till with me. How ironic! There I was, taking E at work for the first time, and the most anti-drugs person I know was standing six inches [15cm] away serving customers with me! I felt okay so far, I could feel the effects of it, but because I was concentrating it wasn't overpowering. I didn't get stressed at all. The great thing about my job is the ability to play what I like. I'm not really bothered if the customers don't like it! 'I' was shelf filling, obviously staying away from the tills. Every time I looked at her, she would smile, giggle a bit and I would smile back; it was like that all afternoon. The duty manager had no idea whatsoever. I was nice and friendly to all the customers all day, and got no complaints about my attitude or music selection. And the best thing about it? Well, at 5:30pm, just as we were leaving, the new manager came over and praised us for our hard work, the first time I have been thanked for doing a good job in three and a half years!

## SYNONYMITY

With exceptions like 'rave in the nave', rave is ecstasy and vice versa (though that 'is' is worryingly becoming a 'was' in this third millennium). Like LSD to the hippies and speed to the punks, ecstasy is a drug whose effects exactly induce the emotions carried by the subculture's ideals. Whether ecstasy or rave came first is to invite recursive comparisons between chickens and eggs. However, it is clear that ecstasy and PLUR go together like the (brand of E tablet) 'strawberries and cream'.

John McCready writes of the first encounters of Hacienda patrons to the new drug:

> *According to Shaun and Bez [respectively Shaun Ryder, the singer with, and 'Bez', the dancer with, seminal Manchester indy band Happy Mondays], interviewed some time after the event and not usually known for being good with dates, some of their mates had been away on holiday in Valencia and Ibiza and had brought back some ecstasy tablets. People tried them out and they seemed to fit the music perfectly. Many lost their inhibitions overnight – feeling comfortable enough to get on stages and podiums and wave their arms about in a state of, well, ecstasy – hearing things in the music that they couldn't hear before. A new low-rent crowd started mixing with the converted hairdressers and Factory obsessives of old. It was, at times, a volatile mix. But the drugs turned an often socially confused crowd into one sweaty nation, under the influence*

of a groove twisted out of a small silver box (the
Roland 303) invented by Japanese technicians to
provide a kind of karaoke backing for social-club
country-and-western singers.

## NEW DRUG ON THE BLOCK

LSD, the powering drug of rave's yellow smiley-faced
predecessor acid house, was hardly conducive to a evening's
social merriment, inducing as it does 12 hours of
hallucinations, distorted colours and occasional freak-outs
and attempts to fly out of upstairs windows.

Just as well ecstasy was diverted from its original purpose.
Ecstasy, real name '3,4-methylenedioxymethamphetamine'
(MDMA), was developed as a psychotherapeutic drug to
promote empathy and reduce hostility between estranged
spouses. It was a marriage-guidance drug and still is in
Switzerland (see Chapter 3 on the history of MDMA).

Ecstasy's discovery by pioneering boppers was
accidental, but once young folk used to freaking on acid
discovered its euphoric effect there was no stopping E as
a dance drug. MDMA is the ideal inspiration for the rave
culture because on the one sweaty hand it encourages
communal empathy with one's fellow humans and, on the
other sweaty paw, induces a blissful, isolated communion
between the dancer and the techno beat.

There's one problem, though. The shit that it's mixed
with does no such thing. Delightful substances found

cohabiting with an ecstasy tablet alongside the MDMA include fish-tank cleaners and dog-worming tablets – as well as other drugs like LSD, caffeine and antihistamine, and even the poison strychnine. There is an increasing incidence of adulterated E tablets appearing on the streets because of greater competition between drug traffickers (see Chapter 2). Shit, after all, is the drug dealer's bread and butter.

It is therefore paramount for kids investing their pocket money in a couple of yellow pills to scan them for shit before eating them. Paramount, maybe, but also well-nigh impossible without expert advice. (See Chapter 5 about proposed government moves to provide this.)

E tablets are like washing powder, and not only because they might contain washing soda alongside the MDMA. Ecstasy inspires brand loyalty; and accordingly new brands of essentially the same stuff are increasingly cluttering up the black marketplace, with low-level dealers attempting to push the individual benefits of their own product.

Ecstasy comes in small tablets the size of a headache tablet, or else in capsule form, and consists of MDMA combined with other substances to make up the weight. (There is also some inherent adulteration in ecstasy pills because of the binding agents used to press the pills.) Sometimes, the MDMA part of the tablet is, in fact, an analogue substance like the parent drug MDA that induces a more intense experience.

Though all basically the same thing, the tablets come in a massive variety of colours, with a massive variety of motifs embossed on them and a massive range of brand names to reflect the 'reversion to childhood/innocence reborn' ethos. There is consequently a three-times-massive marketplace of competitive E brands.

**A BRIEF GUIDE TO E**
Here's a look at some current E brands, including their names, their design and the particular childhood memories they attempt to tap into. Given the ever-increasing enormity of brands on offer, this is by necessity just the thin end of the wedge. Ecstasy brands fall into different categories that purport to fulfil different purposes.

PURITY OF DRUG
These supposedly let on what's inside the pill to reassure nervous consumers that they're getting what they've paid for. Don't believe a word of it. Look at the following examples:

- **Triple X** – MDMA and its two analogues, MDA and MDEA.
- **Madman** – Pure MDMA (assonant with 'adam', an older name for MDMA).
- **Madwoman** – Pure MDEA.
- **Adam And Eve** – MDMA and MDEA.
- **Eva** – Tablets with letters 'E' embossed on one side and 'A' on the other; contains amphetamine plus MDMA.

- **K Capsules** – Contain MDMA plus ketamine.
- **China White** – May contain 3-methylfentanyl a very potent heroin substitute known under the same street name as the ecstasy pill.
- **Coke Biscuit** – Implication that pill contains cocaine – unlikely, because there couldn't be enough included to vivify a gnat.

STRENGTH OF DRUG
- **E 130** – Capsule with 'E 130' printed on the side; 10mg stronger than typical MDMA dose of 120mg.
- **Pink 125** – Pink tablet; 5mg stronger than typical dose of 120mg.
- **Phase 4** – MDMA plus sufficient amphetamine to keep you manic for four hours.
- **Phase 8** – As phase 4 but twice as speedy.

SHAPE
- **Snowballs** – Rough-edged, almost spherical pill; don't eat the yellow ones.
- **Disco Burgers** – Like most tablets, shaped like a hamburger, but coloured brown in order to add the Big Mac look.
- **Coke Burger** – As above, but imagine there's an oversized beaker containing mostly ice with it (rumours, as with 'coke biscuit' above, that the pills contain cocaine are unlikely to be true).

- **New Yorker** - Recalls yet another brand of hamburger - one that hasn't yet crossed the big pond eastwards.
- **Biscuits** - Big, flat and granular. None to date include a cream filling.

COLOUR CONNOTATION
- **M25** - Pink with a blue stripe across the middle and vice versa. (If this is how ecstasy users view motorways, then maybe there is a further case for long-term brain damage than is described in Chapter 4.)
- **Manchester United** - Red and black to (wrongly) match the colours of the soccer team supported by everyone worldwide except the people of Manchester (who support City).
- **Dennis The Menace** - Red and black to match the colours of the Beano comic-strip rapscallion; possibly the same pill as Manchester United, marketed toward the die-hard inhabitants of the 'regression to childhood' set.

SECONDS OF PUDDING/FIRST IN LINE AT THE TUCK SHOP
- **Rhubarb And Custard** - Red and yellow pills that recall the most repulsive dessert ever devised by man (one source suggests that the 'barb' part of the name indicates that the pill contains barbiturate).
- **Love Hearts** - Variably coloured pills with a heart embossed in the centre; memories of passing a sherbety sweet to the girl in ponytails and mouth braces come

flooding back (these allegedly contain the tranquillizer methaqualone alongside the MDMA).

- **Banana Splits** - Yellow and white pills to remind you of the syrupy reward for eating all your greens at restaurants; older ravers may also recall the goofy animal characters Fleegle, Snorky, Bingo and Drooper, or at least The Dickies' cover of their theme song.
- **Strawberries And Cream** - Pink and white pills that relive lazy summer afternoons watching Becker versus Lendl in the Wimbledon men's tennis finals.
- **Strawberries** - Straight pink versions of the above pills for lactose-intolerants.
- **Parma Violets** - Purple tablets that evoke small chalky sweets with indeterminate flavour that were occasionally bought out of curiosity and vomited out of necessity.

CARTOON CHARACTERS

This is the other ultimate reversion-to-childhood motif, harking back to the days when Saturday mornings were spent not in bed but downstairs watching television.

- **Super Mario** - Plumb the depths of euphoria.
- **Superman** - Is it a bird? Is it a plane? No, it's an angular letter 'S' embossed on a pill.
- **Pink Panther** - Did you ever see a tablet ever so pink?
- **Batman** - *Powww! Thuddd! Thwaappp!*

- **Bart Simpson** - Eat my shorts.
- **Mickey Mouse** - Join the club.
- **Donald Duck** - Send you quackers.

EMBOSSED

Embossed shapes, designs or logos afford ecstasy tablets a supposed quality trademark, like the 'By royal appointment' stamps on jars of marmalade. They are also harder to fake.

- **P And T** - Pete Tongs (after a UK disc jockey ), Partick Thistle (Scottish football team), 'party timers' or 'peeping toms'.
- **Shamrocks** - So Irish you can taste the poteen.
- **Love Doves** - the definitive PLUR drug; comes in several varieties to reflect the bird's comportment, including 'both wings up', 'both wings down', 'one wing up and one wing down', 'double doves' (which are embossed both sides) and the transmogrifying 'white robin'.
- **Euro** - € sign embossed on the pill.
- **Smiley** - White with acid-house face.
- **VW** - Yellow or grey with Volkswagen logo.

**DOSE OF CRAP**

The typical E dose to sustain a night's bopping is a single tablet containing 75-150mg of what may or may not be MDMA. This should take around 40 minutes before initiating a euphoric rush that resides to an empathic happiness. Ecstasy is not really a hallucinogen, though some of the aforementioned shit it's mixed with might be.

For some users the oral ingestion of ecstasy has become decidedly passé. They yearn to offer their other orifices a bit of the action. To them the mouth is so 1997.

Snorting, smoking and injecting are the most popular alternatives. All are of varying dangerousness and predictability; and the first one, which involves crushing up E tablets with a razor blade, leaves users blowing a cocktail of snot and shards into their handkerchief for days.

The most extreme and apparently quite sensational non-oral method of ecstasy ingestion is that of 'plugging': to follow the example of the suppository and take the instruction 'Stick it up your arse' a tad too literally. This is a logistical nightmare (though presumably the baggy pants help); but those bold adventurers in the realm of ecstatic anal application report a 30 per cent slower release time and an accordant extension of the initial euphoric rush.

Not everyone regards this as the ideal way of taking E. 'It would have to be a pretty damn good time to convince me to stick a pill up my ass,' says one US raver. 'Plus if it falls back out you can't exactly change your mind and decide to eat it. If it is that great, what's the procedure anyway, do you just sort of stick it up there and try not to take a shit for a couple of hours?'

## THE NEW WAVE OF RAVE AND ECSTASY

The last few years have seen some unprecedented violence at street level, including seizure of weapons, shootouts with police in NYC and Detroit, and even internecine murder between dealers.

Rave is still inexorably an ecstasy culture, but the reverse is no longer the case. Ecstasy is increasingly available in schools and private homes; it is no longer just a club drug. This has led to a wider user base and age range. People over 40 now regularly drop E, especially former cocaine users who reckon that ecstasy carries similar euphoric qualities, lasts longer and is safer. This has raised the interest of crack and heroin dealers – an altogether more insalubrious lot than the chumps who formerly palmed some E for their mates – and is currently dragging the E trade into the same gangland shit as its opium-based siblings.

To appreciate the process that has brought about this situation, we need to look at the world of ecstasy.

**TWIN DILEMMA**

With a terrible beauty, the twin towers of New York's World Trade Center collapsed like dominoes, interring 3,000 innocent souls in a mass grave. Some took their death in their own hands and jumped from high windows to save being crushed under the rubble. Firefighters earned a crust that never came as they perished alongside their white-collar compatriots.

Soon the tributes arrived: enemies from both sides of the Middle-East conflict united to express their disgust; Royal Guardsmen played the 'Star Spangled Banner' while American tourists wept behind the railings; nations grieved; and planes were grounded. The trafficking of ecstasy into the US stopped completely.

Three weeks later, it started up again. These ravers can't wait for ever, you know.

The events of 11 September 2001 were a real downer for the ecstasy smugglers. The grounding of passenger planes effectively nullified their usual mode of operation, leaving a lot of very unhappy punters worldwide. Even when planes were allowed to resume flight, the smugglers were reluctant to go back to work.

Ecstasy is usually smuggled via commercial flights. The smugglers' problem in the weeks after the New York attacks was the paucity of commercial flyers. People were still shell-shocked from the television images and also fearful to fly for threat of further terrorist attacks. Holiday makers suddenly lost their appetite for sun and fun, while commuters chose to travel overland rather than risk the air. Planes became decidedly empty, security became decidedly vigilant...and drugs couriers became decidedly conspicuous.

One of the major destinations for ecstasy smugglers is Newark Airport in New Jersey, mainly on account of its nine daily flights from The Netherlands (still the source of most MDMA manufacture). Thomas Manifase, a special agent in charge of its Customs Investigation Office, says: 'I think the smugglers sensed the intense inspections and shut down their operations.'

This enforced cessation of ecstasy smuggling led to the mother of all back orders in the US and UK. It dealt mid-level dealers a loss of income that would leave foot-and-mouth-disease-stricken farmers looking like Bill Gates in comparison. It also deprived the rave generation of the fuel to power its bopping and hugging.

When operations started up again, on around 20 October 2001, unstoppable quantities of E flooded into airports worldwide. Manifase says: 'Over half a million tablets were seized in seven to eight weeks... That's huge.' It's especially huge when added to the increase that's boarding the planes anyway. After all, a low-cost, high-profit industry like ecstasy trafficking was bound to take off in a big way.

## MALIGNANT GROWTH

The word 'exponential' could have been devised to describe recent years' growth in ecstasy trafficking.

- In 1999, 3.5 million E tablets were seized; in 2000, the number was 9.3 million.
- In the US fiscal year (beginning 1 October and) ending 30 September 2001, 851,000 E tablets were seized at Newark Airport, twice as many as during the previous year.
- During fiscal year 2001 until December 2001, the seizures of MDMA at Newark Airport were already 65 per cent of the entire previous year.
- During the eight months prior to December 2001, seizures of ecstasy numbered over 542,000 tablets smuggled from Europe – a record number and a great concern to law enforcers.

On 30 May 2000, George Cazenavette III, agent in charge of the New Orleans Field Division of the US Drug Enforcement Administration (DEA), released this statement to address his perception of increased ecstasy use in New Orleans:

*In an effort to diminish the flow of drugs into this area, the New Orleans Field Division has dedicated*

*six enforcement groups that actively investigate
drug trafficking organizations responsible for the
transportation and distribution of drugs throughout
the metropolitan area.*

This was not an unqualified success. There was a subsequent
arrest of ecstasy traffickers caught transporting MDMA
from Houston, Texas, to be distributed in New Orleans,
Miami and New York. The group had passed on thousands
of ecstasy tablets to local high-school and college students
mostly at New Orleans raves. One defendant admitted to
selling over 250,000 tablets during around 20 trips to New
Orleans, each pill going for $10–15 (£7–10). Other defendants
told of their smuggling techniques – they had hidden the
pills on their person and carried them into cities on
commercial airlines, then stashed them in secret storage
vaults before separate runners carried them on to raves.

On 26 July 2000, US federal agents intercepted 2.1
million ecstasy tablets, comprising nearly 500kg (1,100lb)
of MDMA, valued at $40 million (£28 million), at Los Angeles
International Airport. This was the biggest ecstasy bust to
date. The drugs were found in 15 boxes on a flight from
Paris, and comprised more than a quarter of the 8 million
ecstasy tablets seized in the US so far that year. By
comparison, only 400 tablets of MDMA were seized in the
United States during the whole of 1997. 'That's 2.1 million
tablets of ecstasy that won't go to our kids this year,' were

the words of Stephen Wiley, the FBI special agent in charge of the strategy. The group responsible had been linked to other large global seizures, which included 300kg (700lb) of MDMA seized by US Customs in December 1999.

## MEN IN WHITE

To understand why this growth is happening, we must first trace the ecstasy back to its source – a couple of geeks in a hidden laboratory.

In the flatlands of Holland and Belgium, an array of clandestine laboratories are to be found, producing MDMA on demand for an insatiable market. A typical lab is likely to comprise a sordid bedsit with an electric stove, a kettle, an ashtray...and a high-speed commercial pill press. Alternatively, it could be a converted caravan – a mobile laboratory to allow manufacturers of MDMA a nifty escape from Europol.

The natural advantages of setting up in Holland and Belgium include the following:

- Holland is a centre of the international chemical industry, so both personnel and certain precursor chemicals (a chemical that gives rise to another more important one) are readily available;
- Both countries have a state-of-the-art transport infrastructure and some of the world's busiest ocean ports.

Ecstasy users can at least take one crumb of narcotic comfort: the source MDMA inside their tablet was certainly synthesized by qualified chemists. Ecstasy traffickers demand the best from their manufacturers. Whether they deliver the best to their customers is another point entirely. MDMA manufacturers comprise graduate chemists, or at least experienced commercial-lab technicians, who have, for their own nefarious reasons, allied with the dark side.

This is not to say that occasional DIY fanatics won't attempt to knock up a batch of MDMA in their kitchen. Recipes for MDMA are available on the Internet for those who really want them, including this one:

> Take the petals off the MDMA flower. Grind them up and boil in dilute $H_2O$. Let sit overnight and beautiful MDMA crystals will form.

There are obviously logistical problems facing those who take the small-industry approach to MDMA manufacture. The majority of MDMA is therefore still made overseas in Holland and Belgium. Between the mid-1990s and 1999 these two countries accounted for 80 per cent of MDMA consumed worldwide, with little threat to their dominance, despite the concerted efforts of law enforcers. Now other countries and continents are trying to muscle in.

The greatest worry for US law enforcers is the opportunity for Mexican and Colombian traffickers to try and get in on the act. These countries have the same advantages that Belgium and The Netherlands have: availability of personnel and drugs; and (in this instance, overland) smuggling routes into the United States. Mexican Drug Trafficking Organizations (DTOs) even have an exemplar on which to base MDMA trafficking; the hombres have been shifting amphetamines into the States for years. Some Colombian and Mexican DTOs are certainly increasing their MDMA operations. For example, in 2000 a shipment of 60,000 ecstasy tablets was seized en route to the US.

Traffickers based in former Dutch colonies – the Dominican Republic, Dutch Antilles and Surinam – are also operating.

## CHEMISTRY DELICATESSEN

Chemists process MDMA using the constituent chemicals of safrole, piperonal and the snappily named 3,4-methylenedioxpenyl-2-propanone, which are illegally diverted from source countries including Germany, Poland, China and India. They synthesize MDMA in the form of a white powder, which is mixed with a binder like methyl cellulose (therefore E tablets are technically never pure MDMA), pressed into pills and packaged. Associate traffickers then sell them to mid-level wholesale distributors in quantities of at least 1,000, after which they are transported to distribution centres such as Houston, Jacksonville, Phoenix, Pittsburgh, Washington DC and London.

Although most distribution is to the US and UK, figures from the Vienna-based International Narcotics Control Board (INCB), which sent missions worldwide in 2001, found MDMA consumption and seizures increasing in continental Europe, east and Southeast Asia, Australia and New Zealand. The last two countries, in particular, suffered a steady increase in MDMA seizures due to a rising demand for the drug.

## SMUGGLING METHODS

These are the five methods of MDMA smuggling, in order of popularity.

### COURIER

Until recently the smuggling of ecstasy usually consisted of entrepreneurial independent individuals smuggling through small amounts of E. However, the trend over the last couple of years has ominously tended towards methods akin to the heroin smuggler. In other words, the big boys have taken over.

Here, in descending order of seriousness, are some of the methods used to sneak MDMA past Customs officials:

- Concealed in a false-bottomed suitcase;
- Fitted into the hollow heel of shoe;
- Hidden in hollowed-out furniture;
- Put in a baby carrier, and a baby put on top of it;
- Stitched into clothing;

- Taped to the torso or legs;
- Swallowed in a condom and then excreted in the host country.

Once the pills are sneaked through Customs and tipped out, unstitched or excreted, they are transported to distribution centres such as Houston, Jacksonville, Phoenix, Pittsburgh and Washington, DC.

Customs officials have targeted Dutch commercial flights for ecstasy surveillance, which is why trafficking organizations can divert couriers to one of three transit countries en route: Mexico, Canada and the Dominican Republic. Other roundabout routes include countries close to The Netherlands like Germany, Switzerland and France. The drugs are then transported to a hub city by plane. Hub cities include Atlanta, Los Angeles, Miami, New York and Newark.

The new and rising bands of Israeli and Russian DTOs have become particularly dab hands at smuggling MDMA via couriers. This is worrying to US drug enforcers, who are finding drugs from these sources increasingly harder to detect. There are a handful of cited reasons:

- These Israeli and Russian DTO operatives are borderline fanatics, and are unusually willing to follow their leaders' orders to the letter. They are therefore less likely to reveal sources if interrogated.

- The operatives are better trained and more proficient at smuggling than their European counterparts. Their smuggling profile is therefore greatly reduced.
- Recruitment of female couriers in preference to male ones deflects the attentions of the seemingly male chauvinist Customs officials.
- Drug-detection dogs are frequently not trained to sniff out the new-fangled MDMA. Israeli and Russian traffickers are well aware of this.

## EXPRESS MAIL

There is one small problem with courier smuggling: people get caught doing it. A preferable alternative method is to smuggle the contraband via much less suspicious sources, using people who don't know they're carrying it – postal delivery workers, for example. Send a stash of E via express mail and guarantee yourself overnight delivery courtesy of the Fed Ex company, and not to a stash site but directly to the mid- or low-level dealer. Again, it is Israeli and Russian groups that form the vanguard of this particular smuggling method and show those European slackers exactly how it should be done.

The apparently foolproof way of evading X-ray detection is to hide loose ecstasy tablets in amongst the pieces of a jigsaw puzzle.

Traffickers can track the shipment through each stage of the shipping process by making use of the various express mail services' Internet facilities. If they notice that the package is being unusually delayed at any stage of the process, they'll assume it's been opened and give it up as a lost cause.

According to a report by Lorraine Brown, special agent in charge of the Office of Investigations US Customs Service:

> *On 19 December 1999, inspectors at the Federal Express facility in Memphis, TN, intercepted approximately 100lb [45kg] of MDMA destined for the Riverside, CA area. The RAIC/Riverside office, in conjunction with the Inland Regional Narcotics Enforcement Team, conducted a controlled delivery of the seized MDMA, resulting in the identification of an MDMA smuggling and distribution organization spanning two continents and five countries. The ensuing investigation led to the execution of more than 12 search warrants, resulting in 13 arrests, the seizure of approximately 1.5 million tablets, $4,662,292 [£3,216,981] in US currency and $808,472 [£557,846] worth of merchandise and luxury automobiles. Information developed during the course of this investigation contributed to the development of a secondary investigation that resulted in the seizure of an additional approximately 2.1 million MDMA tablets at the Los Angeles International Airport on 22 July 2000.*

On the same day that Britney Chambers died (see Chapter 5), a 24-year-old Dutchman was charged with attempting to smuggle $70,000 (£50,000) worth of ecstasy into Miami. He had swallowed 3,500 pills, boarded a plane in Amsterdam and was apprehended by Customs officials at Miami International Airport.

DEEP BLUE E

There have been reports of maritime MDMA smuggling from Europe to Florida and the Caribbean, and also to New York via Montreal, and the trend will likely increase when traffickers realise the main advantage of maritime smuggling over mail smuggling – quantity. You can fit considerably more ecstasy tablets inside a small cargo hold than even the biggest and most intricate of jigsaw puzzles.

OVERLAND

This is a new method catering for the recent influx of Mexican ecstasy traffickers offering healthy competition to the Europeans and Israelis. MDMA is transported across the southwestern US border in private motor vehicles or even by motorcycle gangs.

**GOOD E TWO SHOES**

Ecstasy has a good reputation. That may seem a contradiction in the light of the Betts, Spinks, Kirkland and Chambers cases (see Chapter 5), but, relatively speaking, it is very much the case. Compared to cocaine and (especially) heroin, MDMA is a positively benevolent drug in the eyes of the traffickers, who have minor interest in the benignity of the drugs they shift but major interest in the consequences should they get caught doing so. They reckon that MDMA is safer to transport in two respects: Customs officials are less vigilant with it than they are with the genuinely addictive cocaine and heroin; and punishments will be less severe if their operatives are caught.

Consequently many criminal gangs with access to weapons and no compunction about hurting people have switched entirely to the domain of MDMA dealing, where they have little to fear from the occasional middle-class entrepreneur with PLUR ideals.

This increased competition has caused the breaking up of the original Holland/Belgium MDMA monopoly, with various Central American, eastern European and Middle Eastern DTOs getting in on this new and thriving market. A competitive global MDMA market has therefore opened, with the usual dramatic results:

- Dramatic increase in produce;
- Dramatic decrease in price;
- Dramatic fall-off in quality.

There is an increasing involvement of non-European MDMA DTOs that includes those from the Dominican

Republic, Asia, Colombia and (especially) Mexico, where MDMA is both produced and distributed for US consumption. In July 2001, the United States Customs Service (USCS) seized 55,000 MDMA pills smuggled into the US at Brownsville. This is the largest shipment ever seized along the US-Mexico border. In this instance, a private vehicle was being driven by Dominican nationals setting off from Mexico City.

MDMA has also been identified in Asia and Southeast Asia – in countries like Burma and Thailand. Also, two MDMA laboratories were recently seized in China, indicating that some DTOs operate there. Current evidence, however, suggests that this Chinese takeaway service is only a small-fry operation.

On top of this, some old-style DTOs have begun trading kilogrammes of cocaine for tablets of MDMA. In one instance the DEA observed one 1kg (2¼lb) of cocaine being traded in Spain for around 13,000 MDMA pills, and then smuggled back to the US.

## MIDDLE-EASTERN PROMISE
Israel is another boarder of the happy MDMA bandwagon.

- There are reports of Hell's Angels allying with Israelis to smuggle MDMA across the US-Canada border.
- In two recent cases Israelis were arrested in New York with 600,000 MDMA pills.

- US and Mexican groups have allied with Israeli and Russian criminal groups, who source their MDMA from Europe.
- Drugs from ethnic sources have been found as far apart as Chicago, Houston, Miami, New Orleans and San Francisco.

## THE EUROPEAN MARKET

Within Europe the MDMA trade is held firmly in the hot mitts of organized crime, and has been for some time. More recently, though, the aforementioned Israeli/Russian partnerships moved into a particularly significant patch of European territory. Former eastern bloc countries are celebrating their embracement of the free market with, for example, Polish gangs trafficking both the precursor chemicals and the finished drug both within the motherland and abroad. Spain and the Iberian Peninsula are surfacing as ideal shipment areas for MDMA leaving Europe. There have been some incidents indicating that Dutch and Colombian traffickers have bartered ecstasy for cocaine in Spain – in July 2000, four individuals (two Dutch and two Colombian) were arrested by Spanish authorities for possession of large amounts of ecstasy and cocaine.

Getting the ecstasy past Customs is just the beginning of it. Once the courier, the Fed Ex man or the salt has done their bit, the drugs are picked up by mid-level wholesale distributors to pass on to retail distribution groups or individual dealers. Quite what constitutes 'mid' is indeterminate, however. These mid-level wholesalers are supplied with anything from 1,000 to 500,000 pills at a time. Indeed, the trend is toward larger operations at mid-level. Other drugs – heroin and cocaine, in particular – usually pass through far more levels at retail distribution or individual levels, because at each level the drugs are further adulterated (or 'cut') to increase profit. With a drug like MDMA, where pills are pressed in the source labs, this is not an issue. MDMA smuggled in by methods other than express mail (where it is picked up direct by the dealers) is sent to stash sites in a hub city. US-based distributors are reasonably proficient at their job – they have worked out strategies, drawn up rosters and established an element of continuity and consistency to their distribution patterns. They tend to receive their tablets in relatively small doses of 1,000 to 2,000 pills, and stagger nightclubs to ply their narcotic wares at the same venues on specific nights.

The primary tactic employed by American law enforcers to counter the DTOs is to concentrate on the mid-level wholesale and retail levels. These seem to lack the guile of their heroin and cocaine counterparts and sell to unfamiliar and new customers in obvious places – like rave clubs and university campuses – leaving them vulnerable to the hoary old police tactic of sending in an undercover cop to score some gear. Information obtained from these 'buy-bust' operations can then be collated for use in bigger investigations.

It is more difficult to address the smuggling process itself because if US law enforcers manage temporarily to control one avenue, such as federal mail delivery, DTOs just shift the smuggling to another mode like maritime. As ever, the judiciary is stepping in to help, by proposing an increase of federal penalties for MDMA trafficking to bring them into line with those for methamphetamines – to remove, in other words, MDMA's good name.

## CONSUMPTION TRENDS

Ecstasy is no longer just a club drug. Increasingly it is being sold in more diverse places such as schools, private homes and on the streets. These trends have increased the MDMA user base no end. This is excellent news for the competing trafficking cartels.

## INFORMATION COLLATED FROM US SURVEY GROUPS
MONITORING THE FUTURE (MTM)

This survey was conducted in 2000 to discover drug-taking tendencies in US adolescents:

- From 1999 to 2000, MDMA use increased among the three grade levels measured in the study – eighth, tenth and twelfth. This is the second consecutive year MDMA use has increased.

- MDMA use increased among eighth graders from 1.7 per cent in 1999 to 3.1 per cent in 2000, from 4.4 per cent to 5.4 per cent among tenth graders, and from 5.6 per cent to 8.2 per cent among twelfth graders. Also among twelfth graders, the perceived availability of MDMA rose from 40.1 per cent in 1999 to 51.4 per cent in 2000.

- African-American students showed lesser rates of ecstasy use than white or Hispanic students.

## DEA AND THE US CUSTOMS SERVICE (USCS)

- During 2000, around 6.4 million people over 12 years old had tried MDMA at least once in their lifetime: an increase from 5.1 million the previous year.

- Arrests for MDMA violations increased from 681 in 1999 to 1,456 in 2000.

- The number of DEA cases initiated against MDMA traffickers jumped from 278 to 670 during the same period.

- MDMA seizures by the DEA and USCS have increased every year since 1988.

## COMMUNITY EPIDEMIOLOGY WORK GROUP (CEWG)

- MDMA is now being used in other social settings beyond raves and campuses.

- MDMA is the most prominent narcotic used in Chicago; sold in singles bars in Denver; used by a wide variety of people and in a wide variety of places in Atlanta; and is the middle-class drug of the moment in Washington DC.
- In 1999 there were eight MDMA-related deaths in Miami, and five in Minneapolis/St Paul.
- In Boston during January to September 2000, MDMA was the most frequent subject of calls to the Poison Control Center.
- Snorting of MDMA has been reported in Atlanta and Chicago, as has injecting in Atlanta, and rectal insertion in Chicago.
- Ecstasy frequently consists of substances entirely different from MDMA.
- MDMA is increasingly mixed with marijuana.
- Ecstasy tablets seized by the DEA increased from 13,342 in 1996 to 949,257 in 2000.

NATIONAL HOUSEHOLD SURVEY ON DRUG ABUSE (NHSDA)

Each year, NHSDA reports on the nature and extent of drug use among the American household population aged 12 and older. The 1998 survey is the latest for data relating to MDMA use.

- About 1.5 per cent (3.4 million) of Americans had used MDMA at least once during their lifetime.

- By age group, the heaviest use (5 per cent or 1.4 million people) was reported as those between 18 and 25 years of age.

## POPULARIT-E

There have been reports of massively increased referrals to US emergency rooms (casualty departments) during the last six years that has corresponded with an equivalent increase in MDMA seizure. This suggests that MDMA is still growing in popularity. Greatly increased emergency-room reports over the past six years, as well as a corresponding increase in MDMA pill seizures over the same period, strongly indicate that MDMA is still growing in popularity. If current trends are maintained, it is predicted that the US MDMA incidence will approach that of methamphetamine by 2003.

The United Kingdom mirrors the US in sterling fashion:

- Medium-level dealers can sell bags of 50 Es for less than £200 ($290).
- The street price of E has dropped from around £25 ($35) in the mid-1990s to as little as £2 ($3) in some northeastern towns.
- As in the US, E has moved from a drug exclusively associated with raves to one that has spread to bars, colleges, high schools and even junior high schools (junior schools).

**FOREIGN BODIES**

In accordance with the greater competition between rival MDMA traffickers, recent years have seen a change in the sociological make-up of the mid- and low-level ecstasy dealers. As mentioned earlier, the mid-level retail of E originally involved independent entrepreneurial Caucasians carrying out their work with a hint of genuine benevolence to complement their self-centred moneymaking schemes. Now they've got competition.

Over the past two years there has been a more widespread distribution involving more dealers from ethnic backgrounds, including Mexicans, Colombians, Dominicans, African-Americans, Arabs, Vietnamese, Chinese, Hungarians and Romanians.

It is, after all, a very profitable and expanding business and retail distributors need little incentive to sign up for it. Each MDMA pill sold at the retail level can earn the dealer £7-21 ($10-30) in profits. Individual distributors say that they can sell as many as 1,000 pills a night at clubs because many users buy several pills during one night.

The happy atmosphere in the field of ecstasy dealing has been comprehensively blown by this new intake of traffickers. Replacing the amiable people selling MDMA to their mates, partly for a small profit but mainly just for sheer generosity, are the worst elements of the criminal underground aggressively competing for profits. At street level the distribution of MDMA now involves established drugs gangs that formerly shifted heroin and cocaine – including Chinese, African-Americans, Arabs, Vietnamese, Canadians, Dominicans, Colombians, Hungarians, Mexicans and Romanian – all at each other's throats.

Consequently, something previously unheard of in the ecstasy culture is coming to carry the same significance as glowsticks – internecine gang warfare and violent crime. This has included:

- MDMA involved in the murder of rival gangs;
- Shoot-outs with police in New York City and Detroit;
- Weapons seized with MDMA at street level.

It was violence that marked the end of the UK 'Madchester' scene in the early 1990s. The lead singer with The Stone Roses, Ian Brown, who actually saw a gang leader get shot at a reggae concert, said at the time, '[There was] a feeling of community strength...coming out of a club at the end of the night feeling like you were going to change the world. Then guns come in, and heroin starts being put in ecstasy. It took a lot of the love-vibe out.'

## DOUBLE E-DGED SWORD
The Internet has become a haven for mail-order shopping, where the lack of the high-street stores' overheads allows retailers to be unprecedentedly competitive. The flip side of this is that drugs retailers can do exactly the same thing.

In March 2002, *Globalization And New Technologies*, a report from the International Narcotics Control Board (INCB), detailed the Internet 'recipe' sites and other increasingly technological methods used by DTOs to further their trade, such as touting through chat rooms and storing on computers encrypted details of law enforcers' bank details and even grid co-ordinates of landing strips. They use their great wealth to recruit bent hackers with enough expertise to keep the DTOs several steps ahead of the law. The report added that some Internet techniques only came to light after law enforcers interviewed 30 American and Colombian suspected drug smugglers. These included:

- DTO-run chat rooms protected by impenetrable firewalls;
- Hugely sophisticated encryption technology;
- Host computers situated on ships outside US jurisdiction;
- Personal information on DEA investigators collected by criminal computer hackers;
- Details of freight consignments altered through hacking into Customs databases;
- Diversionary websites, which are deliberately difficult to hack into and therefore serve to waste law enforcers' time;
- Laundering money quickly via global money markets, online casinos and Internet banking services.

The gist of *Globalization And New Technologies* is that too little co-ordinated attempt is being made to put a stop to this, especially from countries other than the US, UK and Japan, which are therefore becoming 'data havens' for DTOs' online operations.

The increasing number of global trafficking organizations, and the consequent profit motive taking over from the ravers' PLUR ideals, has heralded an accordant increase in the number of impure MDMA tablets in the guise of 'ecstasy'. It is important to emphasize that there are two categories of 'impure' ecstasy pill:

- Those that are deliberately adulterated with other substances, and are knowingly taken as such by druggies who like to mix and match. (See 'A Brief Guide To E'.)
- Those that are, without the consumers' knowledge, mixed with any old shit to make up the volume.

It is the second category that is relevant here. Recently, MDMA traffickers have begun to deal in Es that are of necessity adulterated in the source laboratories where the pills are pressed. This particularly takes place in the non-European labs – like those in Mexico and the Dominican Republic – and can take the form of tablets that forge 'reputable' ecstasy brands. Examples are the following, although this is really just skimming the chemical surface:

- Yin-yang pills containing only MDE (3,4-methylenedioxy-ethylamphetamine, a more hallucinogenic analogue of MDMA);
- Green-triangle pills containing only DXM (dextro-methorphan, a drug that can cause audio hallucinations);
- Wild-flower pills containing MDA only;
- Mitsubishi, containing caffeine only (in other words, glorified Pro-Plus pills).

Users who had taken these pills reported nausea, delirium, itchy skin, loss of motor control, and audio and visual hallucinations.

**TRAFFIC SCRAM**
The trafficking and distribution of MDMA is increasingly becoming like that of heroin and cocaine, with the worst elements of the criminal underground in fierce competition with each other. The consequence is gang violence and increasingly adulterated MDMA. This is a very worrying trend, and there is seemingly no end to it. This is very far from the original purpose of MDMA, and must cause those who pioneered it as a therapeutic aid to roll in their graves or shake their chemical-stained fists in anger (as applicable). To learn more of these people, we must look at the history of the drug MDMA.

# HISTORY

Ecstasy under its current streetname, when used as a dance drug, dates back no further than 20 years. Before that, under its real and decidedly less snappy name of '3,4-methylenedioxynmethylamphetamine' (MDMA), it appears for around 40 years either in the labs of experimental psychotherapists or else being fed to guinea pigs, usually the armed forces. During the 30 years following its patent, it just sat on its backside and put its feet up all day.

Around 90 years old, then – give or take an insignificant decade or two – which is frankly nothing when put alongside the millennium-spanning annals of recorded alcohol and cannabis use. The history of ecstasy is a mere cat's eye on the freeway of narcotic substances.

**BLAME THE PARENT**

MDA, the parent drug of the MDA group of drugs that includes MDMA, was synthesized by two German scientists in 1910. Quite what these men had in mind when they devised the drug is uncertain; it was certainly not the subject of human research. Possibly MDA was intended as a medium pharmaceutical for the preparation of other chemicals, rather than something specifically therapeutic or recreational.

MDMA itself was probably first synthesized by Merck Pharmaceuticals, a German company, which attempted to synthesize a medicine called hydrastinine and discovered MDMA as an unexpected by-product. This was duly patented in 1914.

There is a source, however, that steadfastly insists that MDMA was first synthesized by two Polish chemists, S Biniecki and E Krajewski, as late as 1960. Although this argument goes against such irrelevances as clear documentation to the contrary (the patent itself, MDMA's 1950s listing as 'Experimental Agent 1229' and so on), it is unfair to dismiss it as (to use a technical term) false without hearing it out.

The drug MDMA was not an initial success and lay in a pool of near oblivion for nearly 30 years. Around 1939, it was used as an experimental substance in studies of adrenaline. This was the first time lucky animals were the beneficiaries of MDMA's euphoric and life-affirming effects before having their brains cut open (see pp128–9). Seeing as the effect of adrenaline on the animal kingdom is generally irrelevant to humans, these tests were not continued for long, and MDMA disappeared for a couple more years.

In 1941, US pharmacists dropped plans to market MDMA as an appetite suppressant because of its unpalatable side effects. Also in 1941, doctors tested MDMA as a relief for Parkinson's disease but they soon rejected it when one trial subject experienced increased rigidity. A decade-long MDMA moratorium followed until 1953/1954, when the CIA and the army tested it on the US military – sometimes without the subjects' knowledge – as part of a series of drugs experiments looking into:

- chemical warfare;
- the extraction of information from prisoners;
- immobilization of enemy troops.

It proved to be useless for these purposes. Accordingly, MDMA was coded 'EA1299' by scientists at the ECWS. Everyone forgot about MDMA.

Any prospective drug needs its messiah to preach its Sermon on the Mount, though. In the case of MDMA, the messiah was (and still is) a remarkable chemist called Alexander Shulgin. But more on him later.

Shulgin's John the Baptist was a US researcher called Gordon Alles, who was to MDMA what Albert Hoffman was to LSD: he synthesized it, dropped it, then spread the good news far and wide. In 1957, Alles described MDMA's effects of heightened perception and visual imagery to a scientific meeting, thus setting off the chain of events that would bring the effects of MDMA to the attention of Alexander Shulgin some ten years later.

The earliest part of Shulgin's life that matters is his research work at the Dow Chemical Company during the 1950s. Chemistry was not only his job but also very much his hobby. In his free time, he would use company-owned agents and facilities to create all manner of mind-expanding substances, and in due course went one step too far: he committed the heinous crime of being caught at it. Once the Dow Chemical Company was discovered in possession of the formulae for several prohibited substances, and the miscellany was traced back to one of the laboratory staff, Shulgin was sacked.

He didn't care. As he said: 'I personally have chosen some drugs to be of sufficient value to be worth the risks; others, I deem not to be of sufficient value... I used to [smoke tobacco] quite heavily, then gave it up. It was not the health risk that swayed me, but rather the fact that I had become completely dependent on it.'

Shulgin believed that, with hallucinogens, the potential for learning far outweighed the risks inherent in the drug. He saw no moral distinction between prohibited drugs like pot and heroin, and everyday substances like caffeine. His take on heroin, for example, was that: 'I have tried heroin. This drug, of course, is one of the major concerns in our society, at the present time. In me, it produces a dreamy peacefulness, with no rough edges of worry, stress or concern. But there is also a loss of motivation, of alertness, and the urge to get things done. It is not any fear of addiction that causes me to decide against heroin; it is the fact that, under its influence, nothing seems to be particularly important to me.'

Shulgin used variously psychedelic drugs, most of which he synthesized himself, to 'change channels', to explore different facets of his unconscious mind.

## ANIMAL CRACKERS

Red squirrel monkeys and rats were safe from Shulgin (see Chapter 4 for accounts of MDMA experiments on animals). He had no use for animal research, not for any misguided 'animal rights' reason but because they were of no use to him. The lanes and alleys that twist around, say, cats' unconscious minds had no relevance to Shulgin's research because their brains are the size of walnuts and their vocabulary of miaows, hisses and purrs were not the ideal medium for an in-depth documentation of neurological experience.

Shulgin cited the shaman of Native American and other aboriginal groups as his exemplar. Like the shaman, Shulgin's policy was straightforward – he took the drugs and saw what happened...only somewhat more systematically.

Reckoning that two's a marriage but three's a drugs party, Shulgin invited a select group of scientists and psychologist friends to join him and his wife in an ongoing sequence of psychedelic sleepovers. Realising that the act of consuming virgin psychedelics is the very definition of 'unpredictable', a set of house rules were of necessity set up. These included the following:

- Any one of the group could have absolute veto over the drugs taken, and the conditions under which they were to be taken;
- People were not to have drug-induced sex with non-partners, however unprecedentedly and devastatingly attractive they suddenly found the hitherto unassuming person sitting opposite to be;
- If, however, they wished to make psychedelic whoopee with their usual spouse or partner, then the gist was 'Be our guest – the bedrooms are upstairs and we promise not to listen.'

At the time of publication of his autobiography, *PiHKAL: A Chemical Love Story* (Transform Press, 1991), Shulgin had settled on steady groups of 11 friends with whom to experiment.

### COMETH THE MDMA, COMETH THE MAN

Alexander Shulgin, of course, did not himself originally synthesize MDMA. That was the handiwork of the aforementioned Merck Pharmaceuticals.

Shulgin happened upon MDMA by chance in 1967, though it is fairly certain that he would eventually have found it in any case. He was working at the University of

California in San Francisco when a graduate student invited him to try the drug.

To say that Shulgin was impressed would be a gross understatement. He describes the psychological effect as 'like a window: not psychedelic in the visual or interpretive sense but the lightness and warmth of psychedelics was present and quite remarkable'. He further adds: 'I was suddenly one with myself, one with the world; I was a person who had no secrets from himself and one who could trust others to be as honest with him as he was with himself.'

Shulgin took to embarrassing people on trains by discarding the Martini from its glass and replacing it with his own cocktail of MDMA and quinine. He described the drug as 'penicillin for the soul' and maintained that it could be all things to all people. He claims that he cured one man of bad LSD flashbacks, and cured another man – a stutterer – so successfully that he went too far the other way and became a speech therapist.

By the late 1960s, knowledge of MDMA and its analogues was spreading via various sources.

It was, however, the parent drug MDA that first hit the streets of America's west coast in 1968. Here it was known as 'the love drug'.

The government eventually took umbrage to this and controlled MDA under US drug law in 1970. The hippies' response was immediate. In 1972, canny dope heads introduced a 'designer drug' to the streets of San Francisco.

A designer drug is a substance that carries similar effects to a listed illegal drug, but has been synthesized to evade the law. This 'new' drug, MDMA, soon became a students' recreational drug and, later in the Reagan years, the yuppies' substance of choice.

Simultaneously, US psychologists, who had discovered MDMA, were using the drug – which they now called 'adam' – in several different ways, most significantly as a marriage-guidance drug. Indeed, the ever-neutral Swiss still use it in this way.

These therapists continually worried that their wonder drug would (as did LSD) emerge as a popular street drug and become outlawed by the US government. They were damn right to worry.

On 27 July 1984, the Drug Enforcement Administration announced that it was adding MDMA to the list of Schedule I substances (the sort that carries the most stringent penalties for dealers or users). It claimed that MDMA had no legitimate medical use and was responsible for an undisclosed number of hospitalizations. This was one of the most counterproductive moves ever: it rocketed a hitherto minority drug to overnight stardom.

One MDMA practitioner, psychiatrist Dr George Greer, reckoned that if he synthesized the drug himself, and obtained his patients' informed consent, he could legally administer it to his patients. Aided by Shulgin, he manufactured a batch of MDMA and gave it to around 80 patients over five years. Over nine out of ten patients reported significant benefits, including the following:

- Improvement of communication and intimacy with spouses;
- General decrease in psychological problems;
- Improvements in interpersonal relationships, self-esteem and mood.

Some patients reported these as long-term (years, even) improvements, even after only one or two MDMA sessions.

Greer and 15 other medical professionals petitioned the DEA, explaining that in their own first-hand professional experiences MDMA had definite legitimate medical use. The DEA held nine days of hearings about its intention to schedule MDMA. Witnesses supporting Greer and his colleagues testified that in their opinion MDMA was an invaluable and safe psychotherapeutic drug. The DEA countered that there was no hard evidence to support this, only word of mouth.

Judge Young, who led the hearings, issued his findings on 22 May 1986. He found that MDMA did not meet any criteria necessary for scheduling. In his opinion:

- MDMA had a safe professional medical use;
- MDMA had no great potential for abuse;
- MDMA should be placed not in Schedule I but Schedule

III, which allows medics to use and prescribe a drug but not for the public to buy it over the counter.

## LAWN BLOWER

The Reagan-appointed DEA administrator John Lawn refused to accept the judge's recommendation. He announced that, from 13 November 1986, MDMA would be permanently placed in Schedule I.

Unsurprisingly, the medical community – in this instance fronted by Harvard professor Lester Grinspoon – retaliated with a lawsuit against the DEA. Surprisingly, it was successful and the federal court temporarily removed MDMA's Schedule I status pending reconsideration by the DEA. The DEA duly reconsidered – and duly threw MDMA back into Schedule I. It cited these reasons:

- Unapproved so-called therapeutic use of MDMA continued in many sections of the USA;
- An escalation of clandestine MDMA production, distribution and abuse was occurring nationwide;
- There was an open promotion of MDMA as a legal street drug in some areas;
- An estimated 30,000 dosage units of MDMA were distributed each month in one Texas city;
- Drug-abuse ventures reported MDMA-related incidents among patients (MDMA had neurotoxic effects on rats and monkeys – see Chapter 4).

The lawsuit had one unintended consequence: it gave MDMA the sort of free mass publicity for which advertising agents would willingly sell their grandmothers.

Suddenly an awful lot of people learned about a substance called MDMA that encouraged empathy and inhibited hostility. US MDMA use increased from a reported 10,000 instances during the whole of 1976 to 30,000 doses in a single month in 1985. The DEA went further – it reported that it was those sturdy Texans alone who were taking these 30,000 monthly doses. A 1987 survey showed that 40 per cent of students at Stanford University in California had used MDMA.

Gradually the younger and wilder new users – those outside the USA as well as within it – realised that this might be the exact substance to enhance their particular hobby: wearing kids' clothes and dancing in warehouses. All it needed was a snappier name...

## DISCORD OF THE DANCE

MDMA was never intended as a recreational drug, let alone a 'dance' one. It was not particularly devised with any purpose in mind, but eventually found its ideal use as a psychotherapeutic drug under the guidance of Alexander Shulgin. As such, it would today carry no greater stigma than prescription drugs like Valium or Prozac.

The fact that young people diverted MDMA into a dance drug was of invaluable benefit to the stagnating club scenes of Europe and the US, but an accordingly massive loss to the world of psychotherapy. Even if MDMA was to be legalized as a therapeutic prescription drug, it could never be exploited for commercial purposes because of its 1914 patent. Before marketing MDMA, a drug company would need to hold exclusive rights to sell the drug, in order to recoup the expensive costs of the trials that would necessarily take place. Ecstasy looks likely to remain a dance drug indefinitely.

Shulgin did not really bother himself over the physical effects of MDMA so long as the mental ones were sufficiently beneficial. To discover both the mental and physical effects of taking MDMA - and therefore who was right in the therapists vs DEA litigation described earlier - we will need to look in depth at the health qualities of ecstasy.

# 04 HEALTH

Ecstasy does not kill. The most upsetting aspect of seeing snaps of teenagers' corpses alongside those of their earlier smiling selves in tabloid newspapers is its counterproductivity. It's very useful for voyeurs, but not at all helpful for reasoned debate. The parents of Leah Betts and Lorna Spinks in the UK were indeed courageous to allow their dead or dying children's images to be displayed for the ostensible greater good. They were also misguided; ecstasy does not kill.

For sure, things associated with ecstasy can and occasionally do kill, but the constituent drug MDMA decidedly does not. Leah Betts died of water intoxication having taken a single unadulterated ecstasy tablet. Her best friend took the exact same brand and dosage, and lived to rave again.

Ecstasy affects people differently. This is true both physically and psychologically. You cannot overdose on MDMA, but you can, and will, respond differently from other people to its effects. People who have died because of taking ecstasy were the wrong people to take it or (to reverse the cliché) in the wrong place at the wrong time. Either that or what they took wasn't just MDMA. Pure MDMA does not kill. Here is what it does.

## CHEMICAL EFFECTS OF MDMA ON THE THOUGHT PROCESSES

Once MDMA is ingested (as opposed to injected, smoked or snorted), it dissolves, enters the bloodstream and is carried to the brain neurons. This is where the fun starts.

In reality, the brain is not a control room but a control blob occupied by neurons. There are 100 billion of these connected by tendril-like nerve fibres (axons) and shorter ones (dendrites). Unfortunately, the tendrils can't quite reach each other, and consequently there is a gap (synapse) between them. To cross the gap, the brain uses chemicals, known as neurotransmitters.

The two relevant neurotransmitters to MDMA are called serotonin and dopamine. Serotonin heavily influences emotional state (depression, love and so on), while dopamine controls alertness, arousal and energy levels. Anti-depression drugs like Prozac or 5-hydroxytryptophan (5-htp, which is the chemical your body makes serotonin from) increase serotonin levels in the synapse to elevate mood, while amphetamines like Ritalin increase dopamine levels to produce greater focus and energy.

While the signal is traversing the synapse, we are talking chemistry, and drugs such as MDMA are chemicals. It is in this synapse stage that thought becomes a chemical process and the application of external chemicals makes its impact. MDMA initially increases serotonin levels in the brain, causing the feelings of empathy and security typical of the ecstasy experience. It then depletes serotonin and energy reserves, letting dopamine get into the serotonin neurons and leaving them too weak to defend themselves against the damage. Energy depletion is very closely linked to hyperthermia, making avoiding overheating even more important. (Important note: while the body creates glucose for temporary energy storage, any of the common sugars can be used to provide energy to the cells. You don't see many fizzy drinks with glucose in them, but sucrose will work just as well for replenishing energy.)

Ecstasy brings the phrase 'all things to all people' into a whole new, hot and sweaty arena of meaning. Even by narcotic standards, its effects are rarely the same twice, are rarely the same for different people and, indeed, you can't quantify them. The only evidence is the testimony of users. The general consensus is that:

- there are initial feelings of nausea, which soon go away;
- there is a mild euphoric rush, at about 20 to 40 minutes;
- the rush rescinds and is followed by feelings of serenity, calmness and dissipation of hostility and anger;
- those pioneers who admit to taking the drug anally report a smoother 'coming up' and a 30 per cent more effective chemical release;
- a gradual comedown can involve tiredness and mood swings (this is hard for parents to detect, because teenagers behave like this anyway);

- there follows a hangover, due to lack of sleep, that lasts for three days or so - far longer than an alcohol hangover;
- MDMA is not an aphrodisiac as such, but the feelings of empathy it causes can inspire couples to have casual sex, which they may regret - even by casual-sex standards - when they awake the following morning (or more likely afternoon);
- MDMA can lessen the predatory sexual natures of men - cattle markets are rare in raves;
- intercourse on E is especially sensual, because of the heightened perceptions induced by the drug, but orgasms are often inhibited and men can suffer the same sexual dysfunction that beer drinkers call 'brewer's droop';
- there is a heightened perception of surroundings and audio signals, without the hallucinations associated with LSD; MDMA is therefore to some extent a 'mind-expanding' drug (there are indications that a small part of the MDMA can be converted into the more hallucinogenic parent drug MDA in the body, which might cause hallucinations with large doses).

## DOWNERS

Bad ecstasy experiences are usually due to higher doses. Like LSD, the experience (for good or ill) depends on the mood and expectations of the user and the amenability of the surroundings. Bad experiences can include the following:

- visual and auditory hallucinations;
- anxiety attacks;
- confusion;
- panic;
- insomnia;
- psychosis;
- LSD-type flashbacks if the drug is used continually;
- traumatic events or negative emotions brought to the surface in those who have tried to use the drug as a self-psychotherapeutic drug without professional guidance.

An E guru provides this sound advice:

> It takes anywhere from one to two weeks for your serotonin to rebuild. Doing ecstasy many days in a row, or a lot of pills in a night, doesn't really get you 'higher' on MDMA. Once your serotonin is depleted, you're not getting high off of the MDMA in the pill anymore, you're just getting high off of the fillers (crystal, caffeine, ketamin, whatever is in it), and as your sleep deprivation gets greater and greater you will feel higher but it's only because of the sleep deprivation.

Again, there are multitudes of testimonies to back this up. This one comes from a druggie of a previous generation checking out this newfangled ecstasy lark:

*Well, after dropping my first E, I can say I don't think I will be doing it again. I dropped half a tab and waited for an hour before dropping the rest. Within half an hour of dropping the second half I thought to myself I hope this don't get any more intense. It was on the whole an uncomfortable experience (very chemical, I thought, and some sweating also. The tabs had been chemically tested I learnt and did contain MDMA). It was changeable though, and there were pleasant times but I was glad when it all ended. I have not taken stimulants for over eight years so that might have something to do with it. It was not like speed or acid, but it did feel a lot like mushrooms, I thought, but without the hallucinations. I did some yoga and that was good, the way in which my body moved and flowed with ease and without pain or discomfort, and music sounded brilliant. I couldn't sleep for over 36 hours after taking it, and felt slightly disoriented the next day and also had a headache. I took some codeine to chill out later the next day and it wasn't until after I eventually slept did I feel normal again. It was an interesting experience, but I doubt if I will repeat it. It is definitely a young people and party drug. I could imagine if I was out in the countryside with nature and a group of people around a campfire, the experience would have been more rewarding. Being an "old fart" I suppose my metabolism can't handle it the way it used to, or I have been spoilt by all the years of good pharmaceuticals and other drugs now obsolete, that resulted from pharmacy break-ins and other sources in the '60s and '70s. I will stick with the opiates, I think.*

## STARK RAVING MAD

An anonymous correspondent to the UK *Guardian* newspaper of 1 January 2002 wrote this missive of New Year's cheer:

*After taking [ecstasy], our son experienced a deep depression and progressed to becoming very psychotic, inhabiting in his mind a terrifying world unrelated to reality. He was admitted as an emergency to a psychiatric ward. There were periods of lucidity and, with lots of love, he recovered. It took six months. He suffered a lot and so did we. The MDMA content of ecstasy tablets can vary by 70-fold and they can contain a variety of other substances – you haven't a clue what you're getting. In addition ecstasy (and, I understand, cannabis) can trigger longer-term mental problems in some susceptible people. Yes, the casualty departments on New Year's Eve will*

> *no doubt be full of alcohol-related cases. Sadly,*
> *I'm sure the psychiatric wards will also be coping*
> *with people with drug-induced psychosis – who*
> *had no idea that ecstasy could have these effects.*

'Susceptible people' is, of course, the key phrase here. The drug consumed by the son had seemingly triggered a latent psychiatric disorder. The correspondent is indeed right that ecstasy and cannabis can trigger such effects – but then so can alcohol, chocolate and spaghetti bolognese made with too much garlic. It isn't the drug itself, but the person who takes it, who's at fault in these instances.

## A FUNGI TO BE WITH

E does not only extract its narcotic toll. There is also a physical toll to pay in a currency that includes scabs, rashes, fungi and body odour.

Professional typists complain of repetitive strain injury; joggers, themselves on a high from the body's very own amphetamine endorphins, can take on more exercise than their bodies can cope with and end up injuring themselves. Typists, though, only move their fingers; joggers only exercise for maybe an hour. Ravers are more committed than that; they can move their entire bodies intensely and vigorously for the whole night. No wonder they collect unsavoury skin conditions like trainspotters collect numbers. Blemishes to be found on many ravers' persons include these beauties:

- damaged joints and backs due to dancing on a concrete floor;
- fungal and viral infections of the foot;
- unsightly and itchy yeast infections in the groin area;
- friction burns on the arse cheeks, known as 'raver's rash';
- damaged foot joints, known as 'techno toe';
- chunks of flesh gouged out due to tightening and convulsions of the jaw (those babies' dummies are not only a fashion accessory, but a very practical gumshield).

Casual, unprotected sex carries the usual cachet of possible pregnancy, sexually transmitted diseases and feelings of guilt/disgust when you wake up with someone you would not usually touch with a barge pole.

In its favour, though, E is likely to inspire mutual, considerate intercourse. Considering the list of unpleasant complaints listed above, that is probably just as well.

### THAT'S JUST TAKING THE PISS

Actress Sarah Miles, of *Ryan's Daughter* fame, has admitted to drinking urine (her own, thankfully) to keep her skin clear and body healthy. It is no new practice – indeed, canny medieval quacks used to piss in a bottle and sell it as a mouthwash – but there is no evidence whatsoever to back up pee's purported panacean propensities.

Ravers, however, have a very good reason to consume their own piss: 60 per cent of MDMA enters the urine unchanged. MDMA is therefore recyclable. Drink two glasses and you effectively have another ecstasy tablet free.

To date, there have been around 90 E-related fatalities in the UK and around 40 in the United States. The US has far fewer fatalities because of its typically more spacious venues and lesser booze culture (see Chapter 1). Statistics of fatalities relate to the number of times MDMA is used, which is unknowable (the oft-quoted figure of a million users each weekend could be wildly exaggerated, according to private questionnaires), and the number of times someone dies afterwards, which is extremely difficult to assess. On top of this confusion, regular users must increase the dose to maintain the same effect, which leaves us with the old cliché: 'Which came first, the chicken or the Marengo sauce?'

However, ecstasy-related fatalities almost certainly represent a tiny minority of ecstasy consumed. One estimate, by the Council Biostatics Unit (CBU), using 1996 figures to attempt to calculate the death rate in 15- to 24-year-olds, came up with a rate of between one in 100,000 and one in 200,000. This makes taking ecstasy technically safer than both rugby and horse riding.

The varying effects of ecstasy on different people, coupled with a seeming non-correlation between toxicity and blood levels, makes the likelihood of fatalities very hard to estimate. Some users with high levels of MDMA in their blood survive, while a normal 100-150mg dose causes death in others. In the UK, deaths have involved a range of doses from one to five tablets in a single session.

To re-re-reiterate, ecstasy itself does not kill; it's the associated causes that do. There are three main causes of death.

## HEATSTROKE

- MDMA speeds up the heart and blocks signals to the brain that tell the body to slow down.
- The body temperature rises above its danger limit of 40°C (104°F).
- Convulsions, dilated pupils, very low blood pressure and accelerated heart rate follow.
- Blood coagulates where it shouldn't (like the lungs) and air can't get through.
- There follows paralysis or coma and sometimes death.
- Alternatively, blood doesn't coagulate where it should, resulting in haemorrhaging occurring from internal lesions.
- Symptoms of heatstroke include grossly inflated cardiac rhythm, hyperthermia, convulsions, acute renal failure, widespread coagulation of the blood and the rupturing of tiny vessels.

## WATER TOXICITY

For most ills, drinking a lot of fluid is the right thing to do. Under MDMA, however, it can have fatal consequences.

Young women are most at risk of this because of their hormonal balance.

- High levels of oestrogen can prevent their bodies from coping with water retention. On top of this the MDMA is broken down and stimulates the release of vasopressin, a hormone that encourages water retention and prevents urination.
- The break-up of MDMA also releases a chemical called HMMA that causes the woman to drink fluids.
- The concentration of sodium in the bloodstream falls dangerously low (young women require much more sodium in their bloodstream than post-menopausal women or men).
- Water is retained in sponge-like brain neurons, and the pressure shuts down primary bodily functions like breathing and heart rate.
- There follows dizziness, disorientation and possible collapse and death.
- It is far better to sip a pint of water over the space of an hour than to down several pints of it at once. It is also wise to eat in order to replace sodium lost while sweating.

HEART FAILURE
- MDMA causes a significant rise in blood pressure and heart rate.

- People with formerly undiagnosed heart conditions can suddenly get an *ad hoc* practical diagnosis at an inconvenient moment.

An encouraging sign for the future is that proprietors of UK nightclubs (where the vast majority of E-related collapses happen) are being told in no uncertain terms to clean up their act. At the announcement of a March 2002 campaign called 'Safer Clubbing', Home Office Drugs Minister Bob Ainsworth said:

> *Although drug use has stabilized nationally, unfortunately for many young club-goers illegal drug use has become an integral part of their night out. Of particular concern are those clubbers who use a cocktail of drugs and alcohol that is likely to greatly increase the risks to their health and safety.*
>
> *Club owners and dance promoters have a duty to make sure that they have done everything possible to reduce the risks faced by the young people who are their paying customers. The Safer Clubbing guide will help them, and those that license them, to adopt best health and safety practice.*
>
> *It is important that we begin to change the culture and attitudes to drug taking that have become a lifestyle choice for so many young people enjoying the club scene. But, we have to recognize that some*

> *clubbers will continue to ignore the risks and carry on taking dangerous drugs. If we cannot stop them from taking drugs then we must be prepared to take steps to reduce the harm that they may cause themselves.*

This is encouraging because it suggests the UK Home Office is adopting a more realistic approach to drugs than its former 'just say no' one. It issued these guidelines to help club owners comply with licensing laws:

- provide adequate supplies of drinking water;
- prevent overcrowding;
- ensure proper air conditioning and ventilation;
- take steps to prevent overheating;
- ensure the venues comply with health and safety legislation.

Specific recommendations were:

- that clubs should hire police-approved staff to prevent the hire of criminals as door supervisors;
- that door supervisors should be trained to carry out searches;
- that security should regularly patrol all areas of the venue;
- that club staff should be trained in first aid so they can

recognize and assist people who are intoxicated through drugs, alcohol or a mix of both;

- that club owners should provide a chill-out room, with a calm, cool atmosphere.

Encouragingly, most commentators – including spokesmen for the police and the parents of Lorna Spinks (see Chapter 5) – have been supportive of the measures. Deputy Assistant Commissioner Michael Fuller, head of the Metropolitan Police Drugs Directorate, said:

*We are delighted to have contributed to the 'Safer Clubbing' guide and welcome the launch of this multi-agency initiative. Tackling drug misuse in London is one of the Metropolitan Police Service's priorities and this initiative highlights the important role club owners and event organizers can play in reducing the risk of violence and disorder in clubs across the capital.*

Dr John Ramsey, head of the toxicology unit at St George's Hospital, London, agreed:

*'Safer Clubbing' draws together components required to minimize the harm caused by drugs. It clearly sets out the responsibilities of all participants including clubbers themselves. It recognizes the*

*importance that environmental factors play in safeguarding the health of clubbers and minimising the toxicity of MDMA (ecstasy), and encourages all agencies and groups to work together.*

Alan and Liz Spinks also concurred:

*We hope that the principles and advice contained in the 'Safer Clubbing' guide are adopted by all those involved in the clubbing environment. The recommendations in the document are practical and pragmatic. They target the safety of clubbers and we fully endorse them. They will help to reduce the likelihood of a crisis occurring, help with its early detection and improve reaction in the critical period immediately afterwards.*

LONG-TERM EFFECTS

We've established that ecstasy does not kill. Nor does it have the addictive attributes of opiates nor induce the craving connected with cocaine. The perfect drug, then? Not necessarily. There is another, more disturbing, question to consider. Does E do your head in in the long term? Happily, there is a definite answer to this one: no one knows.

One user certainly thinks it's happened to her. The fact that she appears to like the idea seems, ironically, to back up her assertion: 'E abuse has left me with permanent brain "damage", but it's not all bad! I now find myself with amazing psychic abilities, I can see in the dark, I have a photographic memory, I can take as many pills as I want without getting comedowns, I don't get hangovers from alcohol any more, I don't need to eat, I can smell and taste stuff (I always had very poor sense of smell and taste before, oh, and I'm tripping 24/7/365!!! so it's not all bad!!!!!'

The following report from *ABC News* agrees with her assessment, but not her opinion as to its worth:

## UNKNOWN RISKS ACROSS THE BOARD

Ecstasy, a synthetic drug manufactured mostly in Europe, is a hallucinogenic stimulant that gives its users a feeling of euphoria. The popular drug has spread beyond rave parties to college campuses and even into middle-class, professional America. Its growing pervasiveness is troublesome because the prevailing belief is that it's perfectly safe – in part because some scientists think it might have therapeutic effects. Also, it does not produce extreme behaviors as some other illegal drugs do. It just seems to make you feel good.

'My experience has been very safe with it, and everyone around me has been safe,' says one 29-year-old professional who runs her own business and chooses not to use her name. 'I don't know anyone who's addicted to it or has problems with it.'

But a number of users do report a depression they call 'Suicide Tuesdays'. Dozens of people are reported to have died after ecstasy raised their body temperature to extreme levels. And scientists who study how ecstasy works in the brain say there is a great deal of evidence that should make us worry.

## LADY MUCK

Like alcohol and the police force, ecstasy makes life harder for its female participants than its male ones. Beyond the aforementioned short-term problem of sodium depletion, there is also the apparent long-term possibility of limb abnormalities in babies, as detailed by this report from *The Daily Telegraph* of 22 October 1999:

> *Heart and limb abnormalities in babies are linked for the first time to young women using the drug ecstasy during their pregnancies.*
>
> *A study funded by the Department of Health found that heart defects were up to five times higher than expected and limb abnormalities were 38 times higher. Overall, the congenital defect rate was 15.4 per cent, when 2 to 3 per cent was normal. That represents 'a significantly increased risk', the researchers say today.*
>
> *Dr Patricia McElhatton, head of the National Teratology Information Service, which investigates birth defects and advises doctors on drugs in pregnancy, said the results were a cause for concern.*

She said: 'Numbers in the study were very small and it has been quite difficult to tease the information out but we think there should now be more research into this.'

The group undertook the investigation after receiving 302 inquiries between 1989 and 1998 about taking ecstasy in pregnancy. It traced 136 women, aged between 16 and 36, who had taken ecstasy alone (74) or ecstasy and other illegal drugs and/or alcohol in pregnancy. Other drugs included cocaine, amphetamines, LSD and cannabis, heroin and methadone.

A total of 78 babies were born. The rest of the pregnancies were terminated or ended in miscarriage. The miscarriage rate was not unusual but terminations at 35 per cent were higher than average.

The report in The Lancet says 12 babies were born with abnormalities to drug-taking mothers. One baby who had no obvious abnormalities died. This baby's mother had taken ecstasy, cocaine, heroin and methadone during the pregnancy.

Three babies had a club foot, a rate of 38 per 1,000 live births, when the national rate was 1 per 1,000. One baby had a toe malformation and another a skull abnormality. Heart defects in babies among mothers taking ecstasy and/or other drugs were 26

*per 1,000, when 5 to 10 for every 1,000 live births*
*was expected.*

*A spokesman for the Health Education Authority*
*said that 1 in 10 16- to 29-year-olds said they had*
*used ecstasy at least once. He said: 'People should*
*be aware of the adverse effects of taking drugs. At*
*present ecstasy has been linked only with brain*
*injury in later life after long-term use.'*

## BRAIN DRAIN

'Repeated ecstasy exposure has been shown to lead to
clear brain damage and that brain damage is correlated
with behavioural deficits in learning and memory
processes,' says Alan Leshner, the director of the National
Institute on Drug Abuse, which is a part of the US National
Institute of Health. 'This is not a benign fun drug.'

Normally, your brain controls mood partly by passing
the chemical serotonin – in small amounts – from one brain
cell to another. But ecstasy forces lots of serotonin across
the gap. Some new research suggests it leaves brain cells
weakened and may cause irreversible brain loss.

'We know from primates, non-human primates, that
the damage lasts for years,' says Una McCann, a
neuroscientist at Johns Hopkins University.

Some scientists, on the other hand, report ecstasy
may have benefits in strictly limited cases.

'One group we're interested in studying are individuals

with end-stage cancer who have severe depression and anxiety and physical pain, which have not responded to conventional measures,' says Charles Grob, a psychiatrist at Harbor UCLA Medical Center.

If medical use is ever allowed, it is far off. For now, government agents are battling the spread, and the myths, of a pill called ecstasy, which for them, at least, is anything but.

Red squirrel monkeys are shy, good-natured and egalitarian simians that occupy the Pacific wet lowlands of Costa Rica and Panama. They are currently in decline because their habitats are fragmented by such concerns as deforestation, tourism, agriculture, insecticide spraying and electrocution from power lines.

It's just as well that American scientists dole out plenty of ecstasy to cheer them up. At St John's University in New York, scientists exposed red squirrel monkeys to 5mg of MDMA twice daily for four consecutive days, while a control group was administered salt water for the same duration. (These MDMA doses were much higher and more frequent than typical human ones.) The MDMA caused neurological damage that persisted six to seven years later – nerve fibres had died and damaged neurons grew back abnormally – while the salt-water monkeys were unharmed (this is a definition of 'unharmed' that involves slicing monkeys' brains in half).The MDMA monkeys had a greater serotonin depletion in some parts of the brain than in others.

Supporters of MDMA question whether animal experiments are of relevance to humans. Perhaps worryingly for ecstasy users, the May 2000 edition of UK medical periodical *The Lancet* suggests in an article that they may indeed be. In particular, *The Lancet* points out that these MDMA apologists are ignoring the central research principle of 'inter-species dosage scaling', which allows for the differences in body size, based on body weight and surface area.

Correlations have been established between laboratory animal species and human patients undergoing treatment. For example, the toxicity of anti-cancer drugs in laboratory animals has correlated with the toxicity observed in humans when the species doses were scaled to body surface area. This is documented with reams of evidence that pro-drugs campaigners cannot – if they're doing their job thoroughly – simply dismiss as irrelevant.

The very limited human research that has taken place is indefinite. Recent legal measures have allowed for limited MDMA research in the UK. Accordingly, researchers made a comparative study between the effects upon humans of MDMA and alcohol (presumably, unlike with the monkeys, there was no shortage of volunteers in either category).

The test subjects were required to count backwards in sevens from a three-figure number. The MDMA subjects made twice as many mistakes as the alcohol ones. Further tests at the time (1997) seemed to confirm that ecstasy may well have long-term mental health consequences, as reported in *The Daily Telegraph*:

> *Fears that use of ecstasy can cause long-term brain damage leading to depression and memory loss later in life are heightened today in a new report.*
>
> *Scans of heavy users of the drug found distinct alterations in their brains, even among those who had given up several years beforehand. The imbalance they discovered related to serotonin, a chemical that helps control depression, anxiety, memory disturbance and other psychiatric disorders.*
>
> *The authors of the study conclude today that people who use ecstasy, the drug that has epitomized the '90s club scene, are 'unwittingly putting themselves at risk of developing brain injury'.*
>
> *Their message was echoed yesterday by Prof David Smith, pharmacologist at Oxford University, who said: 'It is something that a lot of us are worried about with ecstasy, but young people don't want to know about long-term brain damage.'*
>
> *The experiment was carried out on 14 people who had formerly taken the drug on average 200 times over four to five years. They had stopped taking it between three weeks and several years previously. Fifteen people who had never used ecstasy were also scanned. The researchers*

*suspected that the damage might occur to parts of brain cells known as axons, which transmit signals to neighbouring cells.*

*The scientists, led by Una McCann of the National Institute of Mental Health in Bethesda, Maryland, injected each person with a radioactive substance that seeks out a marker chemical found in axons.*

*The scans, which revealed how much radioactive substance there was in each brain, showed there was a clear difference, with much less of the marker chemical in the drug takers. The scientists have concluded that these people have fewer brain cells capable of producing serotonin. Dr George Ricaurte, one of the authors, said: 'These losses are significant and, along with our early studies in animals, suggest that nerve cells are damaged.'*

*The researchers, writing in* The Lancet, *said there were no signs of recovery in the people who had gone for longest without taking ecstasy. The other question was how much damage was required to cause psychological effects. Professor Smith said: 'It could be that the effects are subtle, leading to depression later on in life.'*

In April 2002, contrary evidence came to light, suggesting that the case for long-term brain damage was far from proven and, moreover, that, for logistical reasons, politicians have allegedly covered up inherent flaws in the tests that have been carried out. Again, the report is from *The Daily Telegraph* (19 April):

> Much of the scientific evidence showing that ecstasy damages the brain is fundamentally flawed and has been mistakenly used by politicians to warn the public of the dangers of the drug, a report said yesterday.
>
> The inquiry by [UK science periodical] New Scientist found that many of the findings on ecstasy published in respected journals could not be trusted. It said it was an 'open secret' that some researchers who failed to find impairment in ecstasy users had trouble getting their findings published.
>
> 'Our investigation suggests the experiments are so irretrievably flawed that the scientific community risks haemorrhaging credibility if it continues to let them inform public policy,' the report said.
>
> It found there were serious flaws in brain scans which allegedly show that ecstasy destroys nerve cells involved in the production and transport of serotonin, a vital brain chemical involved in a range of functions including memory, sleep, sex, appetite and mood.
>
> In 1998, George Ricaurte and Una McCann at Johns Hopkins University in Baltimore published a paper in

The Lancet *that seemed to provide the first evidence that ecstasy use led to lasting brain damage.*

*The research involved brain scans with a radioactively tagged chemical probe that latched on to the serotonin transporter proteins that ecstasy targets. The thinking was that brains damaged by ecstasy would give off less radioactive 'glow' than those where the serotonin cells were intact.*

*The scans, which showed the brains of ecstasy users did on average glow less, were used in public-information campaigns. In America they strongly influenced harsher penalties for ecstasy offences.*

*But two independent experts told* New Scientist *there was a key flaw. They said the way brains reacted to this kind of scan varied enormously with or without ecstasy.*

*Some healthy brains glowed up to 40 times brighter than others and even a number of ecstasy users' brains outshone ecstasy-free brains by factors of 10 or more. Another study by Dutch scientists led by Liesbeth Reneman and Gerard den Heeten at the Academic Medical Centre in Amsterdam was similarly flawed.*

New Scientist *said it found that 'despite the poster depiction of "your brain on ecstasy" there never was – and never has been – a typical scan showing the typical brain of a long-term ecstasy user'.*

*Stephen Kish, a neuro-pathologist at the Center for Addiction and Health in Toronto, said: 'There are no holes in the brains of ecstasy users. And if anyone wants a straightforward answer to whether ecstasy causes any brain damage, it's impossible to get one from these papers.'*

*Marc Laruelle, an expert on brain scanning at Columbia University, New York City, said: 'All the papers have very significant scientific limitations that make me uneasy.'*

*Similar uncertainty surrounds evidence that ecstasy impairs mental performance. In the majority of tests of mental agility, ecstasy users performed as well as non-users.*

*Andrew Parrott, a psychologist at the University of East London, found that ecstasy users outperformed non-users in tests requiring them to rotate complex shapes in their mind's eye.*

So at present, the answer to the question 'Does ecstasy use cause long-term brain damage?' remains as definite as ever: no one knows. The same applies to the contrary question, which admittedly comes from left side, 'Is ecstasy good for you?'

The Erowid website – a standard reference centre not only for druggies but also New Agers and others who follow 'alternative' lifestyles – thinks it might be: '[A] researcher at Harbor-UCLA Medical Center says there could be an upside to ecstasy... Charles Grob, a psychiatrist, has secured first-ever FDA approval for human trials of the drug. The experiments are designed to lead to tests of ecstasy as a possible painkiller for the terminally ill and for use in psychotherapy. "Hundreds of thousands of young people have taken it," Grob said. "But we know very little about it. There's lots of talk about potential dangers, but we want to explore it extensively." Few in the scientific community are enthusiastic about MDMA's potential benefits. Many likened advocates of its therapeutic attributes to 1960s boosters of LSD. "When LSD was first discovered, that same view of therapeutic use was popular but it turned out to be completely wrong," said Dr. Stephen Stahl, an LSD expert in the UCSD School of Medicine's Psychiatry Department.

**MERRY MAN**

If one thing is clear, it's that the health ramifications of ecstasy use are anything but. According to one seasoned ecstasy user: 'If I had to give a flashcard-sized piece of advice to users it would be take 5-htp, don't take more than one dose of MDMA a week (preferably less) and get something to eat/drink before, during and after. Given this sort of care, I can find no credible evidence or argument that the user will suffer neurotoxic effects. As the person who drinks a beer a day will not damage his liver, the MDMA user that takes a modest dose once a month is extremely unlikely to damage their brain. I suppose the real test is, "would I use MDMA?" And the answer is that I would, I have, and may very well do so again in the future. Whether I understand the risks I'm taking, I leave to the judgment of the reader.'

# POLITICS

## BRASS ATTACKS

Minor celebrities and politicians will spout any old crap to boost their egos. In 1997, UK satirist Christopher Morris took brilliant advantage of this by duping self-righteous 'personalities' to promote entirely fabricated public causes, and incorporating these promotions into his spoof-documentary series *Brass Eye* (UK Channel 4, original air dates 25 January to 9 March 1997). These 'good causes' were not only entirely fabricated, they were patently so. The scenarios were so ludicrous as to make it obvious that these 'celebrities' had no idea of what they spoke, and no authority to say it.

Morris's masterpiece was the *Brass Eye* show about drugs. This included such excruciating gems as agony aunt Claire Rayner's disgust at the apparent Japanese practice of smoking cannabis through a dog, and a spoof report about a man who had to sell drugs in order to keep his blind wife in talking books and his disabled teenage daughter in dildos, but the *pièce de résistance* was the fabrication of a new designer drug called 'cake' and the apparent efforts of two supposed pressure groups to combat it. These groups were called Free the United Kingdom from Drugs (FUKD) and British Opposition to Metabolically Bisturbile Drugs (BOMBD). Several television 'personalities' were persuaded to assist FUKD and BOMBD make a promotional film. The result was a prank that showed up both the suspicious motives of personalities prepared to put their public names to 'good causes' and, more generally, the sheer inanity of opinion that forms around emotive subjects like ecstasy and the designer drugs based on it.

This edition of *Brass Eye* is undervalued. It should be shown regularly to expose the ignorant hysteria that emotive subjects unfailingly draw towards themselves. It's this programme that schools should show to impressionable kids if they want to help them decide their future – not 'harrowing' images of dead or dying girls, because they don't work.

**DEAD-END KIDS**

The images of Leah Betts' and Lorna Spinks' near-dead and dead bodies respectively, attached to respirators in hospital beds and with blood flowing from every facial orifice, certainly shocked contemporary youth into considering and sometimes stopping their ecstasy habits. Temporarily, at least.

Daniel Lennox, who was the Student Union officer at APU in Cambridge at the time of Lorna Spinks' death, said: 'That put a lot of people off trying [ecstasy] at all... People that had been doing it stopped for quite a long time afterwards because of the shock tactics in the papers.'

A lot of people started up again, though. Shock tactics work in the short term, but people soon repress the shock as a survival mechanism. Moreover, the tactics may well work, but towards the wrong end. Neither Betts nor Spinks was killed outright by MDMA itself (see Chapter 4), but by what they did when they'd taken it.

Leah Betts was the eldest daughter of Paul and Janet Betts and was studying A levels at Basildon College in Essex. She bought the ecstasy tablet that didn't kill her on Saturday 14 October 1995 for £10, after she finished her day job at Alder's department store in Basildon. She consumed it at around 8:30pm that evening whilst celebrating her 18th birthday at a club in Latchindon. Later she told her mother she felt unwell; and collapsed early the following day. Leah's stepmother, Janet Betts, a nurse and a drugs adviser, administered mouth-to-mouth to no avail and Leah fell into a coma. She was taken to Broomfield Hospital in Chelmsford but was never revived. Janet Betts said subsequently, 'She looked stunning that night. She had just blown the candles out and cut the cake. What a waste.'

Leah's father, Paul Betts, added, 'Just before 1:30am on Sunday she rushed to the bathroom. When she collapsed she screamed for Janet to help her. We could see from her dilated pupils that something was wrong. Jan screamed

Paul and Janet Betts allowed photographs of Leah's comatose body be published, as a deterrent to other teenagers against ecstasy. They were very brave to do this: they underwent an experience that is the greatest dread of any parent, whose magnitude non-parents can't even begin to contemplate, and throughout their grief thought of others first. They are still vocal supporters of the anti-drugs movement and they wish to help others learn from their own dreadful experiences. This is the very epitome of unselfishness.

If only they were qualified to do this, it might have just worked. Unfortunately, they aren't – not even Janet Betts – and she's a drugs adviser. There seems to be a public consensus that parents who have faced the tragic death of their children – usually because of murder or else a drugs-related fatality – automatically hold an authoritative voice about how to address the subject.

Some senior policemen agree. Detective Chief Inspector Brian Story of Chelsmsford Police, who handled the Betts inquest, said in a press conference: 'Mr and Mrs Betts are very brave. They are speaking out, and what they are doing will help young people not just locally but across the country.' Many think him wrong.

One of Paul Betts' considered recommendations was that the supplier of his daughter's tablet should to be hanged. That's not going to happen unless they take their trade to Thailand. This was grief speaking, not authority. Some argue that people distracted by grief and unable to make a rational decision are really a distraction from reasoned argument, and that emotion should be kept well out of it.

While Leah Betts was still comatose, Paul Betts wrote this open letter to UK parents: 'I feel love for my daughter, anger and hatred for the bastards who supplied her. I thought I knew my own daughter, but does any parent really know where their children are all the time and what they are doing? Children will always be tempted to try something new. In our time it was cigarettes. Today that new experience is drugs. Wherever children are there may be scum like [the suppliers of] these rogue tablets which have probably destroyed my daughter's life. These people prey on our children like vultures and they don't care what their evil trade is doing. Our children must become more aware of the dangers. Drugs are like sex education – a subject to be brushed under the carpet. This can't be right.'

Paul Betts' last point is spot on. Drugs must indeed be addressed in schools and escape the same taboo that has prohibited frank sex-education lessons and consigned many couples to unwanted pregnancies.

It's the only one of his points that is spot on, though – the rest of his letter is phenomenally wide of the mark.

- The 'bastards', or bastard in the singular, who supplied Leah Betts was not some mobster. It was more likely one of Betts' close college friends, who would be only

137

marginally less distraught than Paul Betts himself at the tragic consequence of their action.

- Children still try cigarettes now. Nicotine is a drug. Leah Betts' life wasn't destroyed by a rogue tablet; what she took was uncontaminated MDMA. It was water toxicity that comatized and later killed her.

- When the letter was written, ecstasy dealers did not 'prey on children like vultures'. MDMA is not an addictive substance and criminal dealers cannot force a habit. Low-level dealers were likely to be entrepreneurial middle-class men, or else young people passing on tablets to their friends.

Six years later it happened again. Lorna Spinks, a 19-year-old, first-year Sociology student at APU in Cambridge, was supplied with the ecstasy tablets, which helped to kill her, before she arrived at Cambridge nightclub the Junction. She took two ecstasy tablets and later collapsed because of overheating: her body temperature increased to 43°C (109°F), three degrees above the safe level, and every organ in her body failed. She died 36 hours later in the Intensive Care Unit of Cambridge's Addenbrookes Hospital.

Lorna Spinks' parents, Alan and Liz, who lived in Cessy, France, had to drive 1,100km (700 miles) through the night to be at their daughter's bedside. Liz Spinks said: 'I knew that things were very bad because the doctors were liaising with us during the journey and asking how long we would be. We realised then that she was critical. They took us to see her and it just wasn't our Lorna.'

If anything, Spinks' parents went even further than those of Betts with their well-meaning shock tactics: they actually conducted interviews in the presence of their daughter's corpse and allowed pictures of it to be published. They wanted every teenager and parent in Britain to look at it. Mrs Spinks explained why they did this: 'I would say to any parent to think about what this family is going through. To see their child look like Lorna, she was so...so pretty, and when she was dying she looked like a monster. It looked like she had been run over by a truck. All her organs had been affected. She was bleeding everywhere. They couldn't do anything else and eventually her heart stopped. She's a lovely girl. Her granny called her the Golden Girl, the Lovely Lorna. She was very, very popular and had lots of friends.'

She added that they were unaware that their daughter had taken ecstasy in the past, but had since learned from her brother Adrian that she had taken it on occasion.

The pills that helped to kill Lorna Spinks were, in a sense, rogue tablets. They weren't adulterated; rather they were exceptionally strong – an MDMA bumper pack containing twice the usual dosage. This is why the tablets did help to kill her, unlike that taken by Leah Betts, which decidedly did not do so. Spinks, in effect, took four usual doses of MDMA, which when combined with fast dancing amongst heaving bodies packed on a dance floor, would have caused her body to overheat.

Music student Aaron Strange, aged 19, was found guilty of supplying the ecstasy tablets that helped to kill Spinks and was given 18 months in a young offenders' institution (two concurrent nine-month sentences after two other attempts to deal ecstasy came to light). Strange was unlucky: he was just in the wrong place at the tragically wrong time, and the people who bought the pills from him were just as guilty as he was. His defence lawyer said that his client was devastated by Lorna's death, and the consequences of what he did would stay with him for the rest of his life. Moreover, Strange didn't sell the tablets to Spinks herself: he handed them to someone else in her social group. Whoever did pass them on to Spinks was technically a dealer as well.

Alan Spinks was more conciliatory than Paul Betts in his demands for retribution, but he was nevertheless nonplussed by what he perceived as the leniency of Strange's punishment. He said: 'He sold some pills for monetary gain which killed someone, and that shouldn't happen. The sentence seems very light. He will probably spend just nine months in a young offenders' institution, which is meant to be a lenient place. I don't feel any great vengeance towards Aaron Strange. He is a very small wheel in a much bigger and more sinister system. However, I do think the powers-that-be have missed an opportunity to show that they are prepared to be strong on drugs. I don't think his life should have been ruined forever but I do think he should have received a lesson and been made an example of.'

Speaking more generally at the original corpse-side interview, Alan Spinks said: 'We would discuss drugs quite openly with Lorna, and she said that she wasn't taking anything other than cigarettes and alcohol. I always believed that. So the message is for the parents to be absolutely sure that adolescents come across this stuff.'

Cigarettes and alcohol, of course, are far bigger killers than ecstasy.

## CLOSED MINDS

If this easier-going approach mirrored the overall feelings of people connected with the incident – the feelings of Aaron Strange were at least taken into account – the difference between this and the opprobrium of Paul Betts was one of severity, not reasoned opinion. The words were more conciliatory, but the opinions seemed as prejudiced as ever.

APU's communications director, Roy Newson, said: 'Our thoughts must be with the family. What they are going through is beyond imagination and the university will support their efforts to prevent anything of this type happening to any other youngster. At APU, we deplore the illegal use of drugs and our policy is that their use is completely unacceptable.'

Deplore it he may, but accept it he must. Students take drugs – it's practically part of their syllabus. Some university health units refuse to treat anyone who suffers accidents following drink or drug use, so it's no wonder students sometimes snuff it. Offering informed medical or therapeutic assistance to students who have suffered ill drug effects would be far more productive.

Paul Bogen, the director of the nightclub where Lorna Spinks collapsed, was more clued up. He said staff at the Junction had acted swiftly after Lorna collapsed and added: 'The Junction has worked over many years with the police to establish effective procedures for the health and safety of its users. Inevitably, a tragedy like this requires us to review procedures. We do not condone the use of prohibited drugs on or off our premises and will continue to work with the police and relevant agencies to discourage their use.'

That's pretty much spot on. The nature of 'effective procedures' that can help with ecstasy incidents needs to be clarified, though. They necessitate ample water (with clear instructions that it is to be sipped), access to chill-out rooms, and one other factor which the Junction, in common with every other UK nightclub, won't have – a drugs professional located inside the club who can check ecstasy for rogue tablets.

## AMERICAN VICTIMS
Ecstasy fatalities do happen in the USA. They're relatively uncommon, but they do happen.

## JILLIAN KIRKLAND
Jillian Kirkland died in August 1998 after taking ecstasy at a rave in the State Palace Theater in New Orleans. After 16 days in intensive care at Charity Hospital, Jillian died at the age of 17. Her mother apparently still makes a four-hour trip every day to visit her daughter's grave. When interviewed, she chokes and recalls Jillian as 'only 17, a beautiful 17'.

## BRITNEY CHAMBERS
Britney Chambers of Denver, Colorado, collapsed on her 16th birthday on 27 January 2001. She was given the clover-leaf-embossed pill that didn't kill her by friends at Monarch High School in Louisville and took it at her mother's house later that day. Misinformation killed Britney Chambers: she knew that ecstasy had dehydrating effects but hadn't heard of water toxicity, so she drank 13.5 litres (24 pints) of water within 45 minutes and fell into a coma when her brain cells swelled up. When she had been brain dead for several days her family gave permission for doctors to take her off life support.

## TRAVIS SCHUEGER
Police arrested 20-year-old Travis Schueger, along with his 18-year-old girlfriend, Rebecca Sheffield, on suspicion of distributing the pill, and bail was set for $7,500 (£5,200) and $2,500 (£1,700) respectively. They arrested four juvenile girls in the same case, who faced felony charges of distribution of a controlled substance.

## HYST-E-RIA

When a topic like ecstasy – a drug whose true qualities are relatively unknown to scientists, let alone the tabloid-buying public – hits the news, the resulting hysteria can produce consequences that are both ill considered and borderline dangerous. Governments are pressurized to introduce rushed legislation that singularly fails to address the real issues, while the drug users themselves rebel against this authoritarianism and therefore miss out on potentially life-saving advice.

But Brits don't have the monopoly on drugs hysteria. The American public is pretty darn good at it too. They have to be, otherwise President Clinton wouldn't have appointed Gen Barry McCaffrey as drugs tsar.

Maybe only public hysteria could have induced Clinton to appoint a militaristic public hero as drugs tsar. McCaffrey was probably well meaning in his actions, but his simplistic and dogmatic approach to the job was only matched by his manipulative sentimentality. Notoriously he used to flaunt a bracelet during television interviews; when he was invited to explain why he was wearing a female adornment, his eyes would well up as he explained how it was passed on to him by the parents of a 12-year-girl whose young life was cut short by heroin.

McCaffrey didn't believe there was a national drugs problem in the US so much as a series of community epidemics, which each locality must tackle separately. In other words he bred parochialism, and drafted in all levels of government (federal, state and local), non-governmental organizations, the private sector and individual citizens to propagate distrust.

His anti-ecstasy campaign was typical of his approach:

- Anti-ecstasy radio ads placed in radio stations in 106 markets across the country;
- Internet banner advertisements about ecstasy added to websites popular with young people;
- The key words 'ecstasy', 'MDMA', 'club drugs' and others bought by the campaign to monopolize Internet search engines (in other words, when people did an Internet search on 'ecstasy' – irrespective of whether they were chemists looking for an MDMA recipe or students researching 'the sublime in romantic English verse' – they would get one of Barry McCaffrey's banners);
- The pop-up banners directed readers to one of two websites, intended for youth and parents respectively.

McCaffrey's adult site www.theantidrug.com tells parents how to bring up their kids in a manner that accords the word 'patronizing' a whole new vista of meaning. The site is offered, in true imperialist fashion, in Spanish, Cambodian, Chinese, Korean and Vietnamese translations. The tone of the site is unrelentingly dogmatic. For example, parents teaching their kids about marijuana are advised to adopt the following approach: 'Some parents who saw marijuana being widely used in their youth still wonder, "Is marijuana really so bad for my child?" The answer is an emphatic "Yes!"'

Objective research tended to show that the campaign had made not a jot of difference, even though McCaffrey reckoned that it had worked a treat. President Clinton agreed with him, too, as indeed he had to in order to save whatever of his face still remained. 'If you're a teenager or parent it is nearly impossible to avoid seeing or hearing our anti-drug messages on television or radio several times a week,' the president smugly proclaimed.

In 1998 Clinton and McCaffrey duly expanded the media campaign for another five years on a national basis, upping the cost to a massive $1 billion (£700,000,000). The idea – inspired of all things by the blanket coverage of the *Star Wars* films – was to swamp America's youth into anti-drugs submission. The target was for 90 per cent of US teens to see four anti-drug messages a week.

Again, McCaffrey reckoned he'd come up trumps. He said: 'The percentage of youth who said they were scared of taking drugs increased during the evaluation period. Teens said that the four ads targeted to their age group made them less likely to try or use drugs.'

According to Clinton and McCaffrey:

- The paid placement of anti-drug advertisements brought significant increases in awareness of Campaign ads and messages among all age groups and key ethnic groups;

- The ads proved highly effective. The number of youth who agreed that the ads made them 'stay away from drugs' increased a substantial eight percentage points between baseline study and follow-up;
- The number of youths who agreed that the ads told them something they didn't know about drugs increased 8.2 per cent.

On 13 September 1999, McCaffrey joined second-man-on-the-moon Buzz Aldrin to address students from Stuart-Hobson Middle School to introduce a youth drug-prevention area on NASA's website.

The idea was to develop an extensive information network involving hundreds of websites and chat rooms across the Internet, targeting youth, parents and other significant adults. NASA was the first US government agency to place irrelevant anti-drug links on its websites as part of this National Youth Anti-Drug Media Campaign.

Aldrin said, 'For young people who want to follow in my footsteps, on the moon, you have to be drug-free. Explore space, not drugs.'

McCaffrey proved a dab hand at making 'spaced out'/'literally in space' comparisons himself: 'If your dream is to reach the stars, you can't get there by getting high. Through participation in the website initiative, NASA is serving as a leader in the campaign to keep America's youth drug-free. It is critical that all of us in the government and private sectors do everything possible to send this strong message to kids. An important part of this campaign's strategy is to surround youth with drug-free messaging, wherever they spend their time, especially in locations where it might not be expected.'

The drug-prevention area of the NASA website takes 'patronizing' to the highest possible standpoint. It includes:

- clean-living quotes from astronauts;
- electronic postcards with anti-drug messages;
- information about the negative effects of specific drugs;
- games;
- entertaining links – in NASA's own words, 'to keep kids coming back'.

Its intention was 'to emphasize that illicit drug use harms the mental, physical and social skills [of kids] needed to become an astronaut or work for NASA'.

NASA was the first of 19 government agencies to sully their websites in this way – either with the all-out 'drugs and games' separate section, or just including one of Barry's banners.

McCaffrey and Clinton claimed that data from teen questionnaires revealed that the advertisements were very successful at the national level:

*There was a dramatic 59.3 per cent increase in the number of teens who 'agree a lot' that the 'Frying Pan' ad [a US public-information film portraying a skillet-wielding girl smashing an egg and her whole kitchen then being used as a supposed metaphor for heroin use] made them less likely to try or use drugs (rising from 23 to 36 per cent). The survey results also indicated that parent audiences found the advertising informative. Parents stated that the ads gave them a better understanding of the problems of drug use in young people.*

Others disagreed. 'How about a campaign that encourages stupid, apathetic morons not to fuck until they feel like actually raising a kid?' is the ironic comment of US journalist Jason Roth. He doesn't take a pro-drugs stance, but rather insists that the slant of drugs education should be toward people taking responsibility for their lives, and that drugs merely allow them to escape this responsibility. In his opinion, an effective drugs campaign must comprise, to paraphrase his words:

- a campaign that emphasizes the importance of self-esteem and individual responsibility;
- a campaign that reinforces the importance of reality, the need to be conscious of it and the fact that drugs prevent you from being so;

- a campaign that talks about the importance of using your own mind to identify reality and make some attempt to deal with it;
- a campaign that says maybe it's all right if kids are eccentric or individualist, just as long as they understand the importance of setting goals, thinking for themselves and making their own decisions.

Roth asserts that the McCaffreyite media campaign is grossly counterproductive, in effect encouraging kids to increase their drug taking as an act of revolt against McCaffrey, and destroying their confidence by labelling them as 'losers'; it is therefore likely to make kids take up drugs as an escape from reality. He maintains that the media campaigns of McCaffrey and others have 'spouted their pseudo-moralistic bullshit' in a way that:

- wastes millions of taxpayers' dollars;
- allays the guilt of capitalist advertisers and consumers by showing advertising agents seemingly acting selflessly for the good of all;
- gives counterproductive messages about drug use;
- talks down to people in the most self-righteous tone possible.

### THE TOUCHABLES
Some detractors of McCaffrey reckoned that the anti-drugs measures had the opposite effect to that intended – that

what, is in effect, 'prohibition' of drugs conversely gives kids more access to drugs. This is likened to the prohibition of alcohol during the 1920s in the United States, which federal government ostensibly brought about to protect children from the misuse of alcohol, but eventually had to repeal for exactly the same reason.

A 1998 survey of US high-school children suggested that what McCaffrey termed a 'drugs war' conversely made drugs easier to obtain. Kids like to play soldiers, after all. Students reckoned that banned narcotic substances were easier to obtain (for those under the US age limit of 21) than banned alcoholic ones. The poll revealed that, in the kids' experience:

- marijuana was 'fairly easy' to obtain;
- cocaine was 'easily' available;
- ecstasy was 'easily' available;
- LSD was 'easily'' available.

The obvious conclusion, say pro-legalization groups, is that all drugs should be legalized and therefore placed under government control. This, of course, should be beneficial to federal and local government, because they could levy taxes on the drugs while keeping the prices high as a deterrent to people starting a drugs habit or an incentive for them to give one up – thus killing two birds with one stone.

Conversely, in a black-market drugs are becoming ever

more available and ever less expensive as market forces come into play. McCaffrey turned his coke-free nose up at that: 'American parents clearly don't want children to use a fake ID at the corner store to buy heroin.'

The pro-legalizers' comeback to that pearl of wisdom was that black-market drugs dealers tend not to require any ID, fake or otherwise.

Kevin Zeese, president of Common Sense for Drug Policy (CSDP), said that McCaffrey's advertising campaigns were profoundly counterproductive:

> *General McCaffrey clearly preferred funding TV commercials to investing in America's youth. We are spending nearly twice as much on the ad campaign, the glittering jewel in his drug-war crown, than the federal government spends on after-school programs for kids, even though research shows alternative activity programs to be the most effective way to prevent adolescent drug abuse... Barry McCaffrey says that we are turning the corner in our fight against drugs. If that's true, then American parents ought to be very concerned about what horrors are lurking around that corner.*

McCaffrey seemed to be especially one-sided in his treatment of ecstasy. None of the following statement of his is proven:

> *[Ecstasy] is not a safe drug. This is a powerful and destructive substance that can wreck mind and body. Ecstasy destroys serotonin-producing neurons and reduces serotonin, a neurotransmitter involved in controlling mood, sleep, pain, sexual activity, and violent behavior... MDMA causes long-lasting damage to areas of the brain critical for thought and memory... People who take MDMA even just a few times will likely have long-term, perhaps permanent, problems with learning and memory.*

At least *that* statement of his is only unproven. This one's plain inaccurate:

> *In my judgment, ecstasy is the fastest growing drug problem among teens. I don't think we've reached the end of the curve yet. I think we're still on an uphill climb as to the level of damage it's going to do in our society. One of the reasons for that is there is so much misleading information about this drug.*
>
> *I had the opportunity to go to Denver, Colorado, to announce the arrest and prosecution of about 30 individuals in an ecstasy distribution ring. The case started out on the 16th birthday of Britney Chambers. On her birthday, one of her friends gave*

> *her an ecstasy pill that killed her. Local law*
> *enforcement arrested the perpetrator that*
> *distributed that pill. But the DEA was able to get*
> *back to the organization that brought those pills*
> *into the country, and even back to the original*
> *source in the Netherlands. What was troubling to*
> *me was that after Britney Chambers died, headlines*
> *in the newspapers read 'Tainted Ecstasy Kills Teen'.*
> *The news story made it seem that ecstasy alone*
> *wasn't enough to kill, only if it was tainted. The fact*
> *is, in Britney's case, it wasn't tainted. It was pure*
> *ecstasy. This is the kind of knowledge gap we're up*
> *against – the belief that ecstasy is somehow safe.*

It may have been pure ecstasy, but it didn't kill her. Water toxicity did.

## DESPERATE DISPLEASURES

Unsurprisingly, McCaffrey's measures to combat ecstasy were draconian at best, and grossly counterproductive at worst.

This is illustrated by consequences following the death of Jillian Kirkland. Contemporary reports wrongly attributed her collapse to 'a lethal dosage of MDMA' and panic measures ensued, spurred on by alarmist newspaper reports and editorials like this one from *The Times-Picayune* of 30 August 2000:

*Devotees of raves talk about the sound of loud electronic music that's irresistible to young dancers. They talk about the lights, from the elaborate laser displays to the glow sticks that they swing around the dance floor. They talk about the ethos: peace, love, unity.*

*What they are less eager to talk about is the drugs.*

*But drug use is part of the phenomenon. And while not every young person whose social life revolves around the all-age, all-night dance parties uses them, designer drugs are inextricably linked to the rave scene. [Actually, ecstasy hasn't been a designer drug since it became illegal.]*

*Just ask emergency room personnel. They know when a big party is on in New Orleans, because they see the casualties: 23 brought into the Charity Hospital emergency room for drug-related problems after a rave at the State Palace Theater last month and another five last weekend. It's typical to see an ambulance posted outside rave venues, too.*

*The toll from last weekend's rave included a minor who is in guarded condition at Charity after suffering seizures, kidney failure and a 106°F [41°C] temperature. Although doctors expect him to survive, his case is frighteningly reminiscent of 17-year-old Jillian Kirkland, an Alabama girl who died here in*

*1998 from drug overdose complications. She was in convulsions for more than an hour on the dance floor of the State Palace Theater before she was taken to the hospital, where she died several weeks later... Getting rid of the drug sellers and users is paramount, but police should make a concerted effort to weed out underage participants, too...*

*An all-night party that ends up in the emergency room or the morgue is hardly a fun, harmless social phenomenon. It's a travesty that can't be tolerated.*

The cited nightclub, the State Palace Theater, became the subject of a joint federal/New Orleans Police Department (NOPD) operation, whose prejudice and ineptitude would be laughable had it not threatened three men who didn't supply drugs with 20 years in jail.

There were no clued-up operatives to investigate the matter, nor appropriate laws to follow it up, so a clueless operative (DEA agent Michael Templeton) and an inappropriate law (the 1986 Title 21, USC Section 856 a.k.a. 'The Crackhouse Law') were used by a grand jury to indict brothers Robert and Brian Brunet, who managed the State Palace Theater where Kirkland collapsed, and also Donnie Estopinal, who promoted its raves.

This law prohibited maintaining a property 'for the purpose of distributing or using a controlled substance'. It was never intended to apply to owners of nightclubs, but to private landlords allowing crack-cocaine dealers to use their property.

The law found no evidence to link Brunet, Brunet and Estopinal to drug possession, distribution or manufacturing. Desperation ensued: police cited the common rave fashion accessories as tacit acceptance of ecstasy use within the premises: glowsticks apparently brought about the E euphoria and the babies' dummies guarded against jaw convulsions. If dance promoters for some depraved reason allowed dancing, especially that sort where degenerates touch each other's bodies, they were turning a blind eye to the tactile E culture. (Apparently, in New Orleans people never touch each other unless they've taken ecstasy.) If they went one further and actually distributed water to allay dehydration, they were giving implicit permission to high-level narcotics dealers to ply their trade.

The defendants, unsurprisingly, would have none of it. Having developed the State Palace Theater from a dilapidated cinema into a prime rave venue that drew upwards of 4,000 dancers and booked $25,000- (£17,000) a-time DJs like Paul Oakenfold, the Brunet brothers took umbrage at being likened to sink-estate crack dealers. They reckoned that their venue was friendly, non-violent, welcoming and inclusive, attracting punters who would drive for hours to attend raves.

They maintained that, while realising that subcultures do usually involve a motivational drug, they personally tried their damnedest to prevent banned substances being passed on their premises, to the extent of hiring off-duty NOPD cops to help out their own bouncers.

However, after Jillian Kirkland's collapse, media pressure forced the NOPD to pull its cops from the premises – a stupendously counterproductive move. Allegedly, after that the NOPD would not even come to arrest dealers bagged by the club's own security guards.

## COUNTRY MANNERS

This seeming misunderstanding of the rave scene by federal agents could well have been compounded by the naivety of the undercover operative Michael Templeton. Formerly a rural police officer, Templeton was dropped in at the deep-end-replete-with-rave-machine of club events involving rollerskating transvestites, fire eaters and trapeze artists. To call it culture shock would suggest something too blasé.

Templeton wanted to find the big fish of the ecstasy world. Unfortunately, all the boys inside the State Palace Theater were veritable minnows – the big fish were overseas in Holland. The minnows would have to suffice.

Although Templeton apprehended several ecstasy dealers over a three-year stint, he didn't arrest any, because of the perceived trivial punishments handed to low-level dealers.

On 9 March 2001, prosecuting lawyers withdrew the charges, apparently because they had offered a deal offering token prison sentences (one or two years as opposed to 20) in return for a guilty plea.

However, the American Civil Liberties Union (ACLU) urged the defendants to fight their case. Graham Boyd, head of the ACLU Drug Policy Litigation Project, said: 'Go after the people who deal the drugs, but you can't go after the people who provide the music; and you especially can't go after only the ones who provide a certain kind.'

The Brunet brothers, in fear of much expensive legal battle, and possibly deterred by the possibility of 20 years in jail if they were to fight the charges and lose, reached (on 17 May 2001) a plea agreement whereby in return for having criminal charges against them dropped they would raise the minimum age of entry to the State Palace Theater to 18. On top of this they would ban overt 'drugs paraphernalia' like glowsticks, pacifiers and masks. Oh, and chill-out rooms were out, too. Those places that save lives...no need for them.

Donnie Estopinal, the rave promoter, refused to have anything to do with this and is no longer employed at the State Palace Theater.

**FIGHT FOR THE RIGHT TO PARTY**

The Electronic Music Defense and Education Fund (EM:DEF), a charity set up, in its own words, 'To raise and provide funds for legal assistance to innocent professionals in the electronic dance music business who are targeted by law enforcement in the expanding campaign against "club drugs"', thought that this set a bad precedent and was determined to fight it:

> EM:DEF is committed to raising money to challenge the provisions of the settlement. The plea agreement led both Time magazine and The Times-Picayune to call the case in New Orleans a failure. After seeking prison time for Robert, Brian, and Donnie, the DEA has settled for a $100,000 [£70,000] fine against a corporation – a fine that was inconsequential compared to the cost of fighting the trial.
>
> The case in New Orleans had been on hold for several weeks while prosecutors determined what to do after a refusal to accept a plea by Robert, Brian, and Donnie. The plea and our proposed challenge to the plea will not eliminate the precedent that was set; however, it will prevent law enforcement from banning glowsticks and other items at electronic music events. Private businesses may still ban the items, but public venues will not be allowed to if we win. Furthermore, it will undermine the entire substance of the plead conviction. What will remain painfully clear to anyone evaluating the DEA and their investigation is that they failed to find any wrongdoing on the part of the promoter and management for the club, but bullied

*a plea agreement anyway to try and save face. There is simply no other interpretation that fits.*

*The case has since been re-opened with the separate charge against each defendant for each and every rave hosted at the State Palace Theater. This could bring an effective punishment of life imprisonment for each man.*

The single-minded measures of McCaffrey may well have led to the incarceration of innocent men like the Brunet brothers, banged up for dogmatic reasons, while the real problem (adulterated MDMA) still walks the streets. McCaffrey, of course, had other ideas.

McCaffrey has apparently on occasion been caught being economical – if not downright spartan – with the truth. The Multidisciplinary Association for Psychedelic Studies (MAPS) – a non-profit drugs research organization – claimed that McCaffrey gave misleading information about what Dr David Smith told him. Smith gathers research on adverse MDMA-related events at the Haight-Ashbury clinic in LA. McCaffrey attributed to him the statement that hundreds of people a month were coming to the clinic seeking treatment for E-related psychosis and severe depression. What Smith in fact said was that there might be hundreds of MDMA-related reports a month submitted to the clinic but, even if there were, the numbers of reports of psychosis and severe depression were a very small minority.

On resigning his post on 6 January 2002, McCaffrey said: 'I'm enormously proud of what we've done. We had exploding rates of adolescent drug use, and we've reduced it.'

Many disagree. They reckon that this is a definition of 'reduced' that involves an increase of illegal drug use by junior-high students of 300 per cent, greater accessibility of drugs, drugs prices at an all-time low and increasing instances of adulterated drugs.

## BRITISH BULLSHIT

McCaffrey's reluctant British counterpart, the UK's very own drugs tsar, was Keith Hellawell. His deputy was Michael Trace, former director of the Rehabilitation for Addicted Prisoners' Trust. Hellawell was only reluctant in as much as he hated the tag 'drugs tsar': it sounded too despotic for his approach, and suggested that the problem would be tackled through force alone. In other words, it suited McCaffrey but it didn't suit Hellawell.

The approach of copying the Americans and appointing a 'tsar' was typical of Tony Blair's new 'New Labour' government of 1997. It needed to communicate major policy initiatives, and few things do this better than bold headlines announcing that a pseudo-Russian emperor will tackle an area of concern. 'Drugs' was just such an area: the number of new addicts aged under 21 had risen by a third during preceding years, as accordingly had drug-related fatalities. Blair was determined to appoint the right person to address the problem. Nothing but a tsar would do.

Because Hellawell was a hard-nosed Yorkshireman with a difficult childhood and working-class background, he knew first-hand of the link between social deprivation and crime. Even admitting that such a link exists put Hellawell at immediate loggerheads with the type of rightist politician who reckons that ten-hour shifts in a sweat shop at subsistence wages count as gainful employment. Hellawell said: 'I always thought if the root cause of criminal activity was in social deprivation; I wanted to spend money on tackling that, rather than dealing with the consequences. Ten or 15 years ago I was criticized because it was unfashionable; I was set in the role of a radical, having strange ideas. Now it's the way things are going to be done.'

He didn't shirk political blame either: 'Successive Conservative governments stated that the solution to the drug problem lay with the criminal justice system.'

When Hellawell was appointed drugs tsar in 1998, the populist media gleefully lambasted his liberal approach before its Middle-England readership. Readers of the *Daily Express*, the *Daily Mail* and *The Daily Telegraph* had wanted a British McCaffrey, someone who would kick serious druggie butt. Instead they got a seeming 'loony lefty' who symbolically shat on the values their parents fought Hitler for. Hellawell's 'do-gooder' policies included:

- launching one of the first dedicated drugs squads since the 1960s;
- cautioning cannabis users rather than throwing them in jail to develop a smack habit;
- advocating special drugs courts, which sentenced offenders to addiction clinics rather than jail;
- taking degrees in social policy and law;
- reforming 'outdated' attitudes like the notion that black people are responsible for most crime;
- shutting police-station bars so officers couldn't get pissed after work before being released onto the street;
- speaking out against assaults by prison officers on inmates;
- advocating reform of the law on prostitution and the legalization of brothels;
- sending a Christmas card to 'Yorkshire Ripper' Peter Sutcliffe.

Middle England's denizens feared for their future. They didn't need to, for Tony Blair's New Labour government would eventually see them good. Hellawell was a most unusual type of tsar: he had no real power. For a start he was told that nothing in the 1971 Misuse of Drugs Act was up for negotiation. The most expensive pair of handcuffs couldn't have tied his hands behind his back better than that.

In one respect, and one only, this suited him fine. Strangely for a liberal, Hellawell didn't embrace that emblem of leftist free-thinkers and rightist libertarians alike – legalization of drugs. While Hellawell believed that jail was unsuitable for those convicted of possession of soft drugs, he maintained that no listed drug – not even cannabis – should be legalized or decriminalized. He said: 'The debate on decriminalization has gone on for some time. I'm happy for the debate to go on, but it needs to be informed... All that I have seen over the years about that debate has led me to believe that decriminalization or legalization would not help.' In a way this is hardly surprising – he was an ex-copper, after all.

Hellawell was really just a Blair-constructed straw man to be burned down at a later date. For a start, initially he had no budget of his own. He personally was paid £103,000 ($149,000) per year, but he had no money allotted to institute reform. He could draw up a strategy, but he couldn't pay for its implementation.

Michael Trace later explained that, despite the lack of budget, the initial six months were a success, because at that stage Hellawell and he were carrying on an open-minded consultation period with experts in the field, looking at preventative and educational measures rather than law enforcement. Meanwhile, his (and Tony Blair's) press secretary Alastair Campbell were emphasizing New Labour's 'hard on drugs' public stance, backed up by cabinet ministers giving major speeches to that effect. Behind the scenes, though, they were happy to let Hellawell and Trace continue with their 'softly softly' approach.

Ann Taylor, chair of the Cabinet subcommittee on drugs, outlined three key objectives for this strategy on the cheap: to reduce...

- drug supply;
- health risks;
- demand among young people.

The basis for this grand plan in tackling drugs was to make educators, social workers, police forces, law enforcers, magistrates, medics and rehabilitators work together. In this respect, Hellawell was like McCaffrey – he favoured a regional approach, with local media campaigns aimed at young people, including leaflets, posters and interactive websites.

Hellawell instigated a revised school curriculum with new guidelines on teaching drug education, where community police officers would support teachers.

He also began towing a 'drugs are bad' party line and also borrowing mannerisms from McCaffrey and adapting them to the British sensibility – his equivalent of McCaffrey's 'bracelet' interviews being homilies to halcyon days when girls played hopscotch in the street and boys' boredom threshold wasn't lowered by crack cocaine and computer gaming.

At this time Mo Mowlam – probably the only member of Blair's cabinet that the British public in any way liked – was appointed the new minister in charge of the Cabinet

Office's drug co-ordination unit. Her approach was far more liberal than those of her colleagues and she favoured 'radical' measures such as the legalization of cannabis for medical use. This put her at immediate loggerheads with Home Secretary Jack Straw and the then Health Secretary Alan Milburn.

When a Police Foundation report on drugs-law reform called for less restrictive cannabis and ecstasy laws, Straw – knowing that Mowlam would be sympathetic to its recommendations, and with the backing of Tony Blair – pulled rank and rebutted the report without allowing her a say in the matter.

Mowlam got her unit to respond to the report by drawing up a fully costed breakdown of drugs laws and tax called 'Nuclear Option'. Again, Straw overruled her and bucked the issue by getting civil servants to draw up a paper exploring slightly laxer policing of cannabis (this has since come into force).

**RIGHTI-NO**
David Floyd, writing in the socialist *Chartist* magazine, gave his opinion that rightist opinion was all too influential upon this ostensibly centrist government:

> *Sadly, though, the Tories are a factor in the current state of the debate on drug policy. This involves a quaint coalition of Liberal Democrats and columnists*

*from the* Independent On Sunday *[UK newspaper with no political allegiance] delivering sensible arguments against prohibition, pitched against tabloid front pages screaming 'ecstasy killed my daughter', while [Home Secretary] Jack Straw cowers under the table in his office with his hands over his ears. It's not much of a contest.*

The catchphrases adopted by the new campaign were the atrocious 'People Power' and the kneecap-threatening 'Rat On A Rat', which encouraged citizens to grass up drug dealers for the greater good of all.

Although the ten-year plan to tackle drug abuse had targets to cut consumption of heroin, cocaine and other drugs, no baseline figures were published, which made it impossible to judge if the targets were being met. In other words: it was useless.

The ten-year 'strategy' included:

- a minimum sentence of seven years' imprisonment for those convicted of a third offence of supplying Class A drugs like ecstasy;
- an extension of drug testing to identify offenders committing crime to buy drugs;
- piloting of Drug Treatment and Testing Orders forcing offenders to take detoxification treatment;
- a £20 million ($29 million) joint initiative with the police

to accelerate the development of arrest referral schemes;

- rigorous enforcement of community sentences for people convicted of crimes such as shoplifting that fed their drug habit.

## LEFT-WINGER NOT KNOWING WHAT THE RIGHT-WINGER IS DOING

This report by Jay Rayner, from the *Guardian* newspaper, indicates the in-house turmoil within which Hellawell was finding some semblance of sanity in early 2000:

> It was meant to be a good news day, a way for Britain's drug tsar to reclaim the political agenda from what he has come to call, with increasing disdain, 'the spin machine'. Sadly for Keith Hellawell, the spin machine had not yet finished its cycle.
>
> Before an audience of 100 teachers and drug workers in a motel on the outskirts of Gloucester last week, the former Chief Constable of West Yorkshire announced the recruitment of 680 new drug workers. '£500,000 [$700,000] of government money has been put aside for the recruitment drive,' Hellawell said. 'And training will be given. I can't say yet what form the training will take, but it will be paid for out of the seized asset fund.'
>
> He said the same announcement was being made simultaneously by Cabinet Minister Mo Mowlam, to

*whom he reports. At that moment Mowlam was appearing on BBC Radio 4's* Woman's Hour, *but she seemed to have other things on her mind. While passing reference to the recruitment drive was made, she used the broadcast instead for something more pungent: an attack on elements in Whitehall which, she said, 'were trying to put the knife in' by briefing journalists that her brain tumour illness had left her unable to do her job.*

*Mowlam's assault on her detractors was widely reported the next day. The announcement about the recruitment of new drug workers was ignored.*

*Once again Hellawell had seen significant progress in his war on drugs obscured by fallout from the Whitehall spin machine. Mowlam is well known to be less than fond of Hellawell, whom she is said to regard as being 'too Chief Constable'. She has more time for his deputy, Mike Trace, who comes from the world of field work with addicts. But Hellawell is more likely to see it simply as part of a growing problem he has in getting his message across. He has been derided for allegedly suggesting that the government should consider buying Afghanistan's entire opium crop to stop it getting on to the streets as heroin.*

*He has been lambasted for apparently suggesting the Internet is encouraging drug use among young* people and criticized for failings in pilot drug treatment schemes he has introduced.

He will also know that the support he has expressed in today's Observer for the 'depenalization' of the possession of cannabis - a recommendation of a forthcoming report by the Police Foundation - will prove controversial.

He is irritated by the way he is portrayed in the media. 'I do get cross when I read about what I have or haven't done, said or haven't said,' he said. 'The spin machine looks like it's trying to pin a tail on the donkey with its eyes shut. They've found me and decided I'm going to be the target of derision.'

Yet he still does not feel he can afford to ignore the hacks. In Gloucester he spent 20 minutes talking to the drug workers who had travelled from all over the country for a conference on drug use among young people with special needs. But he gave the smattering of journalists present almost two hours.

'We're actually doing everything we said we would do and doing it on time,' he told them. 'People from other countries have seen what we're doing in Britain and they say they don't understand the stick I'm getting. At the United Nations congress on drug use in 1998 I was given a full session to present our programme to 190 nations. Even General Barry McCaffrey, who's heading up the American drug programme, was surprised at the speed with which we've got everything going.'

He launches into a list of successes: the reduction in criminality among offenders who have been part of referral schemes for treatment, the introduction of drug-free wings in some prisons, the small reductions that have been seen in the numbers of people saying they have ever tried drugs. But mostly he wants to talk about the turnaround in official attitudes to the problem of drugs.

'Successive Conservative governments stated that the solution to the drug problem lay with the criminal justice system,' he said. 'Now funds are being shifted into treatment and education.' Hence the need for 680 new drug workers: the agencies implementing drug treatment and education policy have the money to do the job, he said, they just don't have the bodies to do it. Now that problem would be solved.

He has, he says, managed to get more than £250 million [$360 million] of new money out of the Treasury to fight his war. His list of achievements is indeed impressive, but there are still problems. More than 50 per cent of offenders issued with Drug Treatment and Testing Orders, one of Hellawell's pet projects, piloted in three areas so far, have returned to using drugs.

'Yes,' he says, 'but the general level of criminality and drug spending among them has dropped.'

There are also increases in the use of cocaine. This, he admits, is a cause for grave concern. 'In the last British Crime Survey covering 1996-8 we saw an increase of cocaine use from 1 per cent to 3 per cent among the 15-29 age group, mostly around the club scene in London, Liverpool and Nottingham. This is a threefold increase.

'In the next two years we are going to see a further increase. It's becoming cheaper and more socially acceptable. Clearly this is bad news for someone like me in this job.' But, he insists, the important issue is to look at drug policy as a whole.

'What I have done is lift the stone on the hidden truth about drugs in Britain, which is that we need to discriminate between different drugs and the relative harm caused and then talk openly about the difference we can make. The focus is going to be on the drugs that cause the major harm.'

This means accepting that cannabis use - and even the recreational use of ecstasy and amphetamines - is a low priority and that resources should instead be concentrated on narcotics such as heroin and cocaine.

The problem is that to talk of such things is seen by Labour to be politically dangerous, hence the *ridiculing of Clare Short when she said it might be worth considering decriminalising marijuana and the backlash Mowlam experienced when she admitted having inhaled... Sources have suggested former Cabinet Minster Jack Cunningham was responsible for most of it.*

*Sometimes Hellawell says it is simply the media misrepresenting him. He says the story about buying the Afghan crop of opium is a case in point. 'The issue did arise. I simply asked whether there is any logic to the fact that the opium crop in some countries is licensed and legal, because it is used to produce diamorphine for medicinal purposes, and illegal in others. I just said we might look at this question.'*

*Hellawell loves talking about studies and reports, to prove how well he is doing. The journalists in Gloucester who had come to report his visit were less than interested.*

*They wanted to know whether he was going to recommend giving more powers to local police so they could lock up the dealers crowding the city's streets. These are the questions the public ask. Near the city centre, where the Starbucks coffee shops and the cosy bookshops give way to the clutter of inner-city decay, is the Vauxhall Inn in Barton Street. Two months ago the brewery put in a new landlord because drug dealing was rife in and about the pub.*

*The windows are now obscured by signs promising immediate police action against anybody found dealing or taking drugs on the premises. The pub itself has improved remarkably, but the problem itself still exists.*

*Around the corner are modern public lavatories which Joe Lynch, the new landlord, says should never have been built. 'It's a constant menace,' he says. 'That is the biggest place for taking and receiving.'*

*Inside, is a yellow plastic box fixed on the wall by the council for used needles. A general election is expected within 18 months. New Labour will then seek a second term in government based on its record.*

*On the doorsteps of Barton Street the small print of Hellawell's successes is unlikely to be as attractive to the electorate as the headlines politicians like to use. And the drug tsar knows it.*

The Blair government finally applied the torches to straw man Keith Hellawell, and with it the position of 'drugs tsar', in August 2001. In truth, the kindling had been laid for some time.

After Hellawell's departure, the new Home Secretary David Blunkett took over responsibility for co-ordinating national policy, and the position of 'drugs tsar' became redundant. He said: 'I have not had an opportunity to discuss with [Hellawell] what role he might play in the future. I want to look at that as part of what we do in the whole area of drugs policy. I have got to talk to him and mark out what the best way forward will be.'

His future role turned out to be that of token part-time adviser, with sod-all responsibility.

Mike Trace summed up Hellawell's emperorship as that of a man who began with a genuine commitment to action, but was gradually seduced by the spin-doctoring influence of his employers. He said: 'In the first year [Hellawell] worked like a dog and was committed to what he was trying to achieve; I think that was a great time for him. As time passed, I think he became disengaged from the hard slog of implementation, concentrating on appearances only. It is a shame because there is more to him than that. In the last year he attracted a lot of criticism. The drug strategy we developed contained some crucial programmes that need to be followed through. It would be disappointing if this work – reducing drug-related crime, health problems and social exclusion – loses momentum under the new arrangements.'

## THE PRO-E STANCE

*As one of the 200,000 'feared' to be taking illegal drugs, ie ecstasy, this New Year's Eve, and having done so every year for many years now, may I ask*

*what it is the government is fearful of? Ecstasy is
not a dangerous drug and there will be many people
proving this on New Year's Eve. The casualty wards
meanwhile will be full of alcohol-related cases.*
 – Anonymous correspondent to the *Guardian*
newspaper, 28 December 2001

The problem with hysteria is that it uses the 'common-sense' argument, wielded by those deficient in reasoning skills, to pummel the feeblest of contrary opinion into pinko commie mush. For example, when in April 1996 Mary Hartnoll (a senior social worker working in Glasgow) had the temerity to point out that scaremongering about ecstasy was contrary to youngsters' experience, and that ecstasy was a 'relatively safe drug', the usual suspects lined up to offer their worthless opinions:

- Paul Betts: 'To come from such a prominent person, it's absolutely stupid. She should get her facts right. American research has found that ecstasy causes permanent and irreversible brain damage. If she wants to promote that, she's a silly woman.'
- Tory MP Nigel Evans: 'There must be many youngsters living a hell of an existence who would like to meet Mary Hartnoll so that she can see what impact this so-called relatively safe drug means to those who do not instantly die.'

- Councillor James Coleman, chairman of Glasgow's licensing board: 'I don't know where Miss Hartnoll gets this information. We believe that the majority of young people don't take drugs and her type of message sends out the wrong signal.'
- A Scottish Office (of the then Tory government) spokesman: 'There is no such thing as a risk-free drug. The misuse of any drug can cause serious harm or lasting damage and even death. It would be quite wrong to send a false message to society, especially the young, that drugs are not harmful.'

That is just the fate awaiting those who only suggest ecstasy 'isn't as dangerous as it's made out to be'. Those who go one further and actually promote the cause of ecstasy have a particularly hard time of it.

In January 1997, Brian Harvey, lead singer of UK teen band East 17, gave a notorious interview. Any pearls of musical wisdom gleaned from this *tête-à-tête* are long since forgotten, but the peripheral matter of ecstasy use decidedly isn't. Harvey...

- said that ecstasy can make you a better person.
- boasted that he had taken 12 Es at once with no ill effects.
- further boasted that he had driven a car on E and remained totally in control of the vehicle.

This was music to the ears of the then-Prime Minister John Major, who would have to call a general election within the year, and whose Conservative Party's popularity was currently crawling around at seabed level. Not only did he mention it in Parliament, but he incited Tory MPs to demand Harvey's arrest on the charge of incitement to break the law.

Harvey was duly sacked from East 17, though too late, because the combo's records were already banned by 17 UK radio stations. Furthermore, five pages of the *Daily Mirror* – a populist UK tabloid – were devoted to recycling old news about the dangers of E. These were bordered by pictures of young angels apparently 'killed' by the drug.

Had Harvey stuck with the 'ecstasy is good for you' line without moving onto his multiple-pill-popping and car-driving bravado, he may have raised a contentious but valid debating point. As it was, he wasted his opportunity by breeding hysteria. On 19 April 2002, the *Daily Mirror* reported that Harvey had never rebuilt his career after that interview and was now filing for bankruptcy. It concluded:

> The R&B artist [Brian Harvey] has been jinxed since being sacked from East 17 for taking the drug ecstasy. Last year he was severely attacked by machete-wielding thugs outside a nightclub in Nottingham. And to make matters worse, his new singing career has bombed despite costly marketing campaigns.

*A source said, 'Brian is very depressed. His luck has run out. He's penniless and, ironically, is living in Walthamstow E17. He really wants people to stand up and listen to his new music but no one is interested in him anymore. Filing for bankruptcy is the final straw for him.'*

Other supporters of MDMA are more considered in their approach, though decidedly less prominent.

'Jason', a mid-20s graduate from northeast England, is nearly always stoned on E. He believes that E-taking is rife among professionals and a good thing too. Quoted in the *Newcastle Journal*, he said: 'It is extremely common – people just do not realize. The whole thing about drugs has been demonized unfairly. Those who have first-hand experience know they are not half as dangerous as they are meant to be.'

### SENSIBLE LIMITS

Students for Sensible Drug Policy (SSDP) is a student organization that, in its opinion, aims to deliver the true facts about drugs legislation. A publicity document reads: 'We are the generation the drug laws were supposed to protect. It's up to us to stand up and say, this isn't working.'

Beyond the above arguments, SSDP argues that in practice drugs prohibition is discriminatory, with the rules being more stringently applied against poorer communities, with wealthier people being able to afford better lawyers (this is true throughout the legal system), and ethnic peoples.

## WASTE OF PRISON RESOURCES

Many argue that prison is best reserved for violent criminals who are a genuine threat to society, and yet almost a quarter of the two million Americans in jail are there for non-violent drug offences, many of them parents.

Nora Callahan, director of the November Coalition, a pressure group fighting the cause of 'so-called' drug-war prisoners, cites that there are over a million 'drug-war orphans' in America and asserts that they are more than five times as likely as other kids to end up behind bars themselves. She writes: 'Our relentless and punitive prosecution of the drug war against adults, and the subsequent explosion in our prison population, has had dire consequences for children as well.'

Supporters of MDMA believe that media coverage of fatalities and long-term brain damage is wildly exaggerated. They argue that animal experiments have no relevance to humans and, indeed, condemn the butchering of monkeys for information that is, in their opinion, of no proven use. They claim that the problem of serotonin depletion has been known for years and can be remedied by taking an antidepressant like Prozac or – for those of an herbalist bent – St John's Wort.

**THE ALEXANDER TECHNIQUE**

When scientists still can't agree whether cannabis – a drug that has been around for several millennia – is carcinogenic, it is no surprise that the mere 90-year-old MDMA is a near-total enigma to them. Spokespeople on ecstasy tend to preach a version of the curate's egg: they are right in parts. It is up to the prospective ecstasy user, or the concerned parent, to decide for themselves which particular parts are right and act accordingly.

Let us end with the advice of ecstasy guru Alexander Shulgin. He's the most knowledgeable bloke around.

BE INFORMED

- Ecstasy does not kill, although attendant circumstances sometimes do.
- Excessive non-stop dancing turns you into an odorous, scabrous parody of humanity.

BE UNINFORMED

- Ecstasy may or may not cause long-term brain damage in humans – no one knows.

Now choose...

## ADDITIONAL INFO

**FURTHER READING**

IN PRINT

- Shulgin, Alexander and Shulgin, Ann: *PiHKAL: A Chemical Love Story* (Transform Press, 1991)
- Holland, Julie (editor): *Ecstasy - The Complete Guide: A Comprehensive Look At The Risks And Benefits Of MDMA* (Park Street Press, 2001)

ONLINE

- **www.drugscope.co.uk** - website of the UK's foremost drugs charity. Objective, bang up to date and essential
- **www.ecstasy.org** - open-minded ecstasy resource, though it does border on pro-E propaganda; comprehensive and informative nonetheless
- **www.theantidrug.com** - the 'Anti Drug' was the brand name for General Barry McCaffrey's 'Yeah paranoia, nay pills' campaign. This is its self-explanatory website
- **www.freevibe.com** - www.theantidrug.com's sister site, intended for 'yoof' paranoiacs, is a teen magazine slanted toward drugs

- **www.clubbed.com** – the rave must-have. Provides all manner of facilities from searching for local parties to checking on current instances of adulterated drugs
- **alt.drugs.ecstasy** – the main rollers' Internet newsgroup. Lurk here to catch the rave dialect diamond in the rough, or even abandon that Caps Lock key and have some crack with the ravers